TWENTIETH-CENTURY WARS

GENERAL EDITOR: JEREMY BLACK

'Maley's book is arguably the key text both for students and researchers on Afghanistan's recent history. Underpinned by extensive scholarship and judicious argumentation, [it] is also of great relevance to any appraisal of a vital element of US and Western efforts in the "war on terror".' – Gregory Kent, *Roehampton University.*

A whole generation has grown up in Afghanistan knowing little but the ravages of war. The dramatic overthrow of the Taliban regime in 2001 was simply one event in a series of interrelated struggles which have blighted ordinary people's lives over the last three decades, and which continue to interfere with reconciliation and reconstruction.

This new edition of *The Afghanistan Wars* provides a meticulously-documented history of these successive waves of conflict. It explores in detail:

- the roots of Afghanistan's slide into disorder in the late 1970s
- how the Soviet Union came to the rescue of unworthy clients and was then sucked into a quagmire
- the frightening consequences of state breakdown and self-interested meddling by Afghanistan's neighbours in the period after communist rule collapsed
- the rise and fall of the Taliban regime.

Thoroughly revised in the light of the latest research, the second edition also features a new final chapter which examines post-Taliban Afghanistan, bringing the story up to the present day and mounting a strong case for continuing support for this troubled country.

William Maley is Professor and Director of the Asia-Pacific College of Diplomacy at The Australian National University. He is the author of *Rescuing Afghanistan* (2006), editor of *Fundamentalism Reborn? Afghanistan and the Taliban* (1998), and co-author of *Regime Change in Afghanistan* (1991).

TWENTIETH-CENTURY WARS

General Editor: Jeremy Black

Published titles

Gerard DeGroot	*The First World War*
Francisco J. Romero Salvadó	*The Spanish Civil War*
Spencer C. Tucker	*The Second World War*
Peter Lowe	*The Korean War*
David L. Anderson	*The Vietnam War*
D. George Boyce	*The Falklands War*
William Maley	*The Afghanistan Wars* (2nd ed)
Robert Johnson	*The Iran-Iraq War*

Forthcoming

William Allison	*The Gulf War of 1991*

Twentieth-Century Wars
Series Standing Order ISBN 0–333–77101–X

You can receive future titles in this series as they are published. To place a standing order please contact your bookseller or, in the case of difficulty, write to us at the address below with your name and address, the title of the series and the ISBN quoted above.

Customer Services Department, Macmillan Distribution Ltd
Houndmills, Basingstoke, Hampshire RG21 6XS, England

THE AFGHANISTAN WARS

Second Edition

William Maley

© William Maley 2002, 2009

All rights reserved. No reproduction, copy or transmission of this
publication may be made without written permission.

No portion of this publication may be reproduced, copied or transmitted
save with written permission or in accordance with the provisions of the
Copyright, Designs and Patents Act 1988, or under the terms of any licence
permitting limited copying issued by the Copyright Licensing Agency,
Saffron House, 6-10 Kirby Street, London EC1N 8TS.

Any person who does any unauthorized act in relation to this publication
may be liable to criminal prosecution and civil claims for damages.

The author has asserted his right to be identified as the author of this work in
accordance with the Copyright, Designs and Patents Act 1988.

First edition published 2002
Second edition published 2009 by
PALGRAVE MACMILLAN

Palgrave Macmillan in the UK is an imprint of Macmillan Publishers Limited,
registered in England, company number 785998, of Houndmills, Basingstoke,
Hampshire RG21 6XS.

Palgrave Macmillan in the US is a division of St Martin's Press LLC,
175 Fifth Avenue, New York, NY 10010.

Palgrave Macmillan is the global academic imprint of the above companies
and has companies and representatives throughout the world.

Palgrave® and Macmillan® are registered trademarks in the United States,
the United Kingdom, Europe and other countries.

ISBN-13: 978–0–230–21313–5 hardback
ISBN-10: 0–230–21313–8 hardback
ISBN-13: 978–0–230–21314–2 paperback
ISBN-10: 0–230–21314–6 paperback

This book is printed on paper suitable for recycling and made from fully
managed and sustained forest sources. Logging, pulping and manufacturing
processes are expected to conform to the environmental regulations of the
country of origin.

A catalogue record for this book is available from the British Library.

A catalog record for this book is available from the Library of Congress.

10   9   8   7   6   5   4   3
18 17 16 15 14 13 12 11

Printed and bound in The United States of America

For my mother, Jean Maley, and in Memory of my father,
Raymond Maley, CVO

Contents

Acknowledgements

Afghanistan is a remarkable country, almost as remarkable as its peoples. Over the course of the journey of many years that led to the writing of the first and second editions of this book, countless Afghans have helped me in one way or another. Yet just as remarkable is the large community of scholars and aid workers that has coalesced around Afghanistan. Many years ago, the late Louis Dupree warned me that once Afghanistan got into your blood, you could never be rid of it. In this, as in so many other things, he was right.

It might therefore seem invidious to identify individuals for particular gratitude, but to omit the following names would be more than churlish, given the extent to which my own thinking has been shaped by the insights of those with whom I have come into contact. Here, I can only list them with my thanks: Nasiba Akram, A. Rasul Amin, Sayed Aqa, Anthony and Ruth Arnold, Reginald Austin, David Avery, Paul Bonard, Pippa Bradford, Henry S. Bradsher, Lakhdar Brahimi, Rob Breen, Alan Brimelow, Geoff Brooks, Ian Bullpitt, Grahame Carroll, Pierre Centlivres, Micheline Centlivres-Demont, Roy Clogstoun, Pamela Collett, Rupert Colville, Wolfgang Danspeckgruber, Umer Daudzai, Anthony Davis, Tahsin Disbudak, Gilles Dorronsoro, Nancy Hatch Dupree, Mohammed Eshaq, Abbas Faiz, A. G. Ravan Farhadi, Robert P. Finn, Patricia Garcia, Bernt Glatzer, Frédéric Grare, Tom Gregg, Thomas Gurtner, Brett Hackett, Ejaz Haider, Habib Hala, Ingrid Hayden, Dumisani Hanyani, Nick Hordern, David C. Isby, Chris Johnson, Kiyotaka Kawabata, Masood Khalili, Bruce Koepke, Christopher Kremmer, Najibullah Lafraie, Geoff Leach, Marion Le, Jonathan Lee, Conny Lenneberg, Jolyon Leslie, Jens Lüneburg, Citha Maass, Richard Mackenzie, Spozhmai Maiwandi, Ian and Margaret Mansfield, Nabi Misdaq, Hossein Moghaddam, Saad Mohseni, Yassin Mohseni, Sayed Askar Mousavi, Ali Mullaie, Kabir Osman, Sayed Padshah, Mervyn Patterson, Sue Pennell, John Renninger, Engineer Abdul Rahim, Fahim Rahimyar, Samantha Reynolds, Haider Reza,

Hilary Riggs, Olivier Roy, Abdul Rahman Sahak, Fazel Haq Saikal, Kassem Saikal, Mahmoud Saikal, Maliha Saikal, Nadir Saikal, Nouria Salehi, Eckart Schiewek, Susanne Schmeidl, Ralph Seccombe, Nazif Shahrani, Abdulkader H. Sinno, Scott Smith, Soliman Stanekzai, Barbara Stapleton, Barry Stride, Astri Suhrke, Hiroshi Takahashi, Koichiro Tanaka, Fiona Terry, Andrew Tesoriere, Ramesh Thakur, J. Alexander Thier, Darka Topali, Rosemary Trott, Julian Type, Bill Van Ree, Francesc Vendrell, Patrick Vial, Ali Wardak, Farouk Wardak, Marvin G. Weinbaum, Egon Westendorf, Andrew Wilder, Steven Wolfson, Daoud Yaqub, and Samina Yasmeen.

There are four more specialists on Afghanistan to whom my debt is very large indeed. Ashraf Ghani, Ahmed Rashid, Barnett R. Rubin, and I have been sharing thoughts about Afghanistan for a considerable period. Through the good offices of Lakhdar Brahimi and Francesc Vendrell, we were able to meet as a group at different times in New York, Oslo, and Berlin, and it has been a pleasure as well as a privilege to share their company. And Amin Saikal, a dear friend of many years' standing, has been a constant source of support, information, and critical comment, almost on a daily basis. I simply don't know how to thank him, but I'm sure he will tell me!

William Maley
Canberra, May 2009

Note on References

References in this book follow the Harvard system, in which a reference to the surname of an author or authors and the date of a work's publication direct the reader to a fuller bibliographic record in the 'References' list that immediately precedes the index. The final number or numbers in the in-text reference refer the reader to particular pages in the work cited. The names of authors cited in this way are not included in the index.

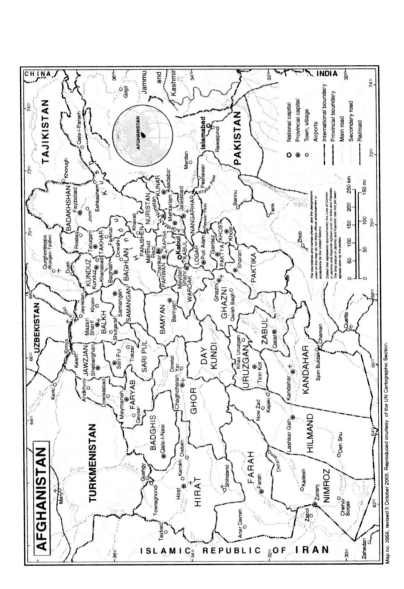

Map no. 3958, revised 5 October 2005. Reproduced courtesy of the UN Cartographic Section.

Introduction

Afghanistan is a land of extremes. For nearly fifty years of the twentieth century – from 1929 until 1978 – it was one of the most *peaceful* countries in Asia. It maintained its neutrality during the Second World War, avoided war with its neighbours, and was internally free of mass killings and mayhem. All this fell apart with a Marxist coup in 1978. From that point, it saw out the century in an ocean of blood. Afghanistan's wars have come in three waves. First, from 1979 to 1989, following the USSR's December 1979 invasion of the country, an embattled communist regime and its Soviet backers were battered by popular resistance groups, known as *Mujahideen*, some of whom received significant external support. The Soviet–Afghan war was one of the seminal events of the late twentieth century, a struggle which cast into sharp relief the defects of the Soviet model of mono-organizational socialism, and contributed to the mood swing which ultimately led to the end of the Cold War and the disintegration of the Soviet Union itself. But more than this, it confirmed Clausewitz's depiction of war as a continuation of politics with the admixture of other means. Military force proved unable to provide a legitimate foundation for communist rule: no matter how impressive the military performance of elements of the Soviet armed forces, they were unable to deliver the *political* outcomes by which success was defined. Big Nations do indeed lose Small Wars (Mack, 1983).

Popular resistance continued following the completion of the Soviet withdrawal from Afghanistan in February 1989, and in April 1992 the communist regime collapsed. A new wave of war then engulfed the country, of a transnational variety. Not content to allow the Afghans to choose their own political course, Afghanistan's neighbours, especially Pakistan, ruthlessly interfered in its internal affairs, prompting a struggle for control of the capital, Kabul, which left its southern suburbs devastated and any semblance of a working state in ruin. The short-term beneficiary was the so-called 'Taliban movement', a Pakistan-backed force of anti-modernist religious extremists from the Pushtun ethnic group which seized Kabul in September 1996 and sought to 'stabilize'

1

the country through a policy of ferocious repression. Unfortunately, the Taliban also provided hospitality to religious zealots from other parts of the world, a policy which boomeranged in September 2001 when followers of one of the most notorious of them, the Saudi extremist Osama Bin Laden, not only assassinated the military leader of Afghanistan's anti-Taliban forces, Ahmad Shah Massoud, but flew hijacked aircraft into the World Trade Center in New York, and the Pentagon in Washington DC, causing huge damage and vast casualties in the heartland of American power. The third wave of war then struck Afghanistan. The United States deployed air power on a scale beyond the Taliban's imagination and within two months the Taliban *regime* had been ground into dust. However, the Taliban *movement* managed to survive this onslaught, finding sanctuary in Pakistan for both its core leadership and some of its fighters; and with world attention shifting to Iraq following the US invasion of that country in 2003, the new Afghan government and its NATO backers have been confronted with a vicious insurgency that shows no sign of coming to an end.

Until its slide into war, Afghanistan was popularly regarded in Western circles as an obscure, if somewhat exotic, land in which tourists could enjoy warm hospitality and peer at a 'traditional' society in relative safety. The reality of Afghanistan was vastly more complicated than this, but its complexities were rarely captured outside the pages of scholarly works such as Louis Dupree's masterly book *Afghanistan* (Dupree, 1973). The Soviet invasion of Afghanistan in December 1979 led to a burst of serious writing about the country, and this was sustained over the following two decades (see Maley, 1987b; Maley, 1997b). As a result, there is now an extensive body of literature dealing with Afghan politics and society, and about the travails through which the peoples of Afghanistan have passed (see, in particular, Roy, 1990; Gromov, 1994; Kakar, 1995; Rubin, 1995a; Rubin, 1995b; Akram, 1996; Bradsher 1999; Haqshenas, 1999; Rashid, 2000; Goodson, 2001; Ewens, 2002; Liakhovskii, 2004; Misra, 2004; Saikal, 2004; Coll, 2005; Dorronsoro, 2005; Ewens, 2005; Husssain, 2005; Westad, 2005; Jones, 2006; Giustozzi, 2007; Crews and Tarzi, 2008; Gutman; 2008; Johnson and Leslie, 2008; Rais, 2008; Rashid, 2008; Sinno, 2008a). In addition, since the overthrow of the Taliban regime, the Afghanistan Research and Evaluation Unit (AREU) in Kabul has produced a remarkable corpus of scholarly work on Afghanistan's politics, economy, and society. In this book, I set out to build on these works in two ways. First, each wave of war in modern Afghanistan is examined in detail, for only by examining all three waves can one properly grasp the context within which efforts to reconstruct

Afghanistan – politically, economically, and socially – are occurring. Second, the course of conflict in Afghanistan has depended upon decisions made in a range of venues, and it is important to shed as much light as possible on all, rather than concentrate on one at the expense of others. Until recently, this would have been an almost insurmountable problem, but the release of declassified Soviet documents dealing both with the invasion and with the eventual withdrawal of Soviet forces has shed light on a number of processes which had long remained obscure, as has the unravelling of the Taliban regime.

In tracing the course of Afghanistan's wars, I am guided by two broad considerations. First, Afghanistan is an extremely complex country, and the challenge for researchers is to find ways of conveying the complexities of Afghan culture, society, and politics in ways which readers nevertheless find accessible and easy to understand. Second, armed conflict in Afghanistan takes place in a sociopolitical context, and any history of war in modern Afghanistan needs to provide a rich account of that context if the successes and failures of military operations and strategies are to be properly appreciated. My account of the conflict falls into three parts. The first deals in detail with the Soviet–Afghan War. Chapter 1 plots the road to war, and Chapter 2 discusses Soviet strategy, tactics, and dilemmas. Chapter 3 traces the development of Afghan resistance. At this point, I move to a more detailed discussion of the course of the Soviet–Afghan War: Chapter 4 deals with the period in which Babrak Karmal headed the Communist regime in Kabul (1979–1986), while Chapter 5 deals with the 'Najibullah–Gorbachev' period (1986–1989), marked by personnel and policy changes in both Kabul and Moscow. The analysis of this wave of war concludes with an examination in Chapter 6 of the road to Soviet withdrawal, and in Chapter 7 of the consequences of the Soviet–Afghan War. The second part of the book deals with the Afghan transnational war. I first discuss the struggle of old forces. Chapter 8 explores the Najibullah interregnum (1989–1992) and the factors which led to the collapse of the communist regime, while Chapter 9 deals with the rise and fall of the Rabbani Government (1992–1996). I then turn to the rise of new forces, and in Chapter 10 supply an analysis of the rise and rule of the Taliban movement. The third part of the book deals with Afghanistan in the context of the Bush Administration's War on Terrorism: Chapter 11 offers a detailed account of the overthrow of the Taliban, and Chapter 12 examines the roots of ongoing strife in Post-Taliban Afghanistan. 'Every War Must End', Fred C. Iklé once wrote (Iklé, 1991), but some wars end more easily than others.

The consequences of the wars of modern Afghanistan will continue to be felt, not only through the fractured regional politics of Southwest and Central Asia, but also through their wider historical ramifications. In tracing these ramifications, it is important to avoid the sin of reductionism, which tempts one to attribute complex historical processes and developments to a single causal factor. But equally, it is important that the contribution of conflicts such as those in Afghanistan to wider global political changes be properly recognized. That is what I aim to do in this volume.

Drawing lessons from complex historical processes is always a perilous undertaking: the philosopher Karl Popper used to say that history has no meaning but that we can give it a meaning (Popper, 1977: Vol. II: 278). With that cautionary observation in mind, there are three significant lessons which can be derived from the wars of modern Afghanistan, and which Afghans would do well to ponder, although very many will have absorbed them already.

The first relates to the relationship between religion and politics. The two can be uneasy partners. The great religions, Islam included, have been powerful sources of moral inspiration for individuals, but as roadmaps for politics they have been much less useful. 'The fundamentalist goal of transforming society into a simpler one based on religious ideals', writes Jonathan Fox, 'is difficult, if not impossible, to reconcile with some of the basic ideals of western democracies, including religious freedom and individual liberty' (Fox, 1998: 59). Indeed, the concept of state sovereignty which crystallized in the Peace of Westphalia of 1648 was in part an attempt to put an end to the struggles over religious authority which had torn Europe apart during the Thirty Years' War. There has never been any credible evidence of mass popular demand for fundamentalist rule in Afghanistan. On the other hand, there is compelling evidence that the *individual* Muslims who make up the overwhelming majority of the Afghan population want to be able to practise their religion in their own ways, free of interference from atheists, or Arab extremists, or others with a barrow to push.

The second is that revolution is a dangerous process. The perils of the revolutionary-utopian impulse have been made clear in Afghanistan by 'revolutionary' actors that brought untold sorrow to the lives of ordinary people. The true revolutionary mindset is conducive to the practice of terror: to save a revolution from its enemies, to give effect to the dictates of an ideology, or to satisfy the perverse psychology of the revolutionary leader (Mayer, 2000: 96–7). It sees no place for caution, for scepticism, for incremental change. For their own good, societies are to be reshaped, whether they like it or not. Revolutionaries, and those who support them, tend to sow the wind and reap the whirlwind. If there is a word that deserves to be banished from all of the languages of Afghanistan, it is revolution.

The third relates to the character of the state. A state which turns on its own people is a terrible thing. Yet on the other hand, the complete disintegration of the state can work massively to the detriment of ordinary people, exposing civil society to the predations of forces which are deeply destructive of order and justice. Civil society flourishes when the state is invested with the capacity to discharge the functions which are appropriate to it, but constrained from interfering in the lives of individuals and communities in any other ways.

Here, the peoples of the wider world, who have witnessed agonizing waves of war sweep over the people of Afghanistan, bear a special responsibility. An old Kabul proverb – *Kuh har qadar boland bashad, baz ham sar-e khud rah darad* – states that there is a path to the top of even the highest mountain. With characteristic determination, the Afghans are now striving to reach that summit. They should not be left to climb alone.

1

The Road to War

The road to war in Afghanistan was not a straight one. There is by now a vast and sophisticated modern literature on the causes of war (see, e.g., Waltz, 1959; Aron, 1966; Blainey, 1973; Holsti, 1996; Doyle, 1997; Black, 1998), building on the insights of such classical theorists as Thucydides, Hobbes, Rousseau, and Kant, which points to the potential roles of individuals, state structures, and anarchical interstate orders in contributing to the outbreak of war. There is also a very useful body of work on the role of perception and misperception in the shaping of policy (Jervis, 1976; Vertzberger, 1990). Making proper use of this material is always a challenge. On the one hand, it is perilous to become fixated with any single factor which the literature identifies. As the late Bernard Brodie once shrewdly observed, 'any theory of the causes of war in general or of any war in particular that is not inherently eclectic and comprehensive, that is, which does not take into account at the outset the relevance of all sorts of diverse factors, is bound for that very reason to be wrong' (Brodie, 1973: 339). At the same time, to explore all the insights which these writings can offer to those interested in the causes of the Afghanistan War would rapidly exhaust the patience of the reader. My hope is rather that echoes from these magisterial analyses will be audible at many different points in the pages which follow.

Interstate wars rarely occur without warning, and even when they are preceded by only a short crisis, as was the case with the Franco–Prussian War (Richardson, 1994: 161), they are typically between either known adversaries, or parties with sharply divergent interests. While the Soviet–Afghan War was not strictly an interstate war, it shared several of these characteristics. With hindsight, many signs in the 1970s pointed to looming trouble in Afghanistan and its neighbourhood. However, Afghanistan had for nearly half a century been one of the most stable countries in Asia – something often overlooked – and perhaps as a result, the warning bells were overlooked as well.

The aim of this chapter is modest: to set the scene for the discussion which makes up the core of the book. First, I offer a brief overview of Afghan society and politics. Second, I examine the evolution of Soviet–Afghan relations over the quarter of a century before the April 1978 Afghan coup. Third, I trace the sequence of events which led from the coup to the Soviet invasion. The Soviet–Afghan War was in no sense inevitable: it came about as a result of gross misunderstandings of Afghan society on the part both of Afghan communists and their Soviet backers, political structures which subjected neither of these groups to checks and balances, and a configuration of international relations which provided few incentives for caution on Moscow's part.

The Afghan context

Afghanistan as a territorial unit

Afghanistan is a landlocked country in Southwest Asia. A vast mountain range, the Hindu Kush, runs from the north-east to the south-west, but fertile valleys between and adjacent to mountain peaks provide some relief from the austerity of the mountains, the surfaces of which lie largely above the tree line. The staggering physical beauty of even its more inhospitable spaces has long fascinated visitors, and spawned a rich body of travel literature. Through the writings of travellers such as Freya Stark and Ella Maillart, Afghanistan became a metaphor for exotic isolation, and for detachment from the pressures of the wider world, which had largely passed it by.

Afghanistan crystallized as a territorial unit in the nineteenth century. Some of the lands which make it up had long carried the label 'Afghanistan' (Gille, 1997), but the label did not identify a recognized state, but rather a realm in which people known as 'Afghans' (whom contemporary Western scholars call 'Pushtuns') lived. The origin of the name 'Afghan' is itself a matter of speculation (Vogelsang, 2002: 17–18), with some scholars tracing it to a Persian word meaning 'lamentation' (see Dupree, 1973: xvii), while another ingeniously derives it from the Greek *epigoni*, the term used to refer to youths recruited by Alexander the Great from towns on the territory of modern Afghanistan (Marigo, 1988).

Afghanistan as a political unit emerged as a buffer-state between British India and the expanding Russian empire. The great cities of Afghanistan – especially Herat and Balkh – had long been widely known, not merely as neighbours of the great Silk Road between Europe and China, but as targets of pillage by the conquest empires such as the

Chinggisid and the Timurid. Yet the conquest empires were notoriously prone to fragment in the face of succession struggles (Barfield, 1989), and by the eighteenth century winds of change were blowing in Central Asia, winds powered by the development and expansion of the modern bureaucratic state. Afghanistan did not feel these directly. It was never subject to European colonial occupation, and only on rare occasions, and with considerable cost, did European states seek to pursue military campaigns upon its soil. Nonetheless, its history was to be shaped by interaction with London and Saint Petersburg. The degree of consent given by powerholders within Afghanistan to the processes by which Afghanistan's boundaries were fixed is highly debatable. The borders between Russia and Afghanistan were largely demarcated through Anglo–Russian negotiations in 1873 and 1887 (Fitzhardinge, 1968), and the legitimacy of the Durand Line' – drawn in 1893 between India and Afghanistan – was to be a major source of friction after the partition of the Indian subcontinent in 1947 (Qassem, 2007). Nonetheless, by the 1950s, the reality of Afghanistan as a component of the international system was widely accepted.

The peoples of Afghanistan

While 'Afghanistan' can be translated as 'Land of the Afghans', to read this as 'Land of the *Pushtuns*' would risk detracting from its social and cultural diversity. It was to recognize this diversity that the 1964 Constitution explicitly stated in Article 1 that 'The Afghan Nation is composed of all those individuals who possess the citizenship of the State of Afghanistan in accordance with the provisions of the law. The word Afghan shall apply to each such individual.' It is in this sense that the word 'Afghan' is used in this book, that is, with no ethnic connotations. In a recent monograph, Mousavi has argued that the term 'Afghanistani' should be used for these purposes, since the word 'Afghan' connotes 'Pushtun' (Mousavi, 1997: 5–10). While this was certainly the sense in which the word 'Afghan' was used in major nineteenth-century works (and continues to be used in parts of Afghanistan), such usage has now almost completely died out in English-language sources.

The population of Afghanistan has never been counted in a complete census, but the results of a partial census in 1979, adjusted to take account of other relevant data, suggested a population of approximately 13.05 million, including around 800,000 nomads (Eighmy, 1990: 10). This population was in no sense homogeneous, and indeed it is something of a misnomer to talk of 'Afghan society', for the term suggests a degree of coherent structure which was never really present. Rather, Afghanistan has encompassed a kaleidoscopic collection of 'micro-societies' (often identified by the label *qawm*, or 'network'), with porous and flexible boundaries. One scholar even went so far as to dub Afghanistan a 'Nation of Minorities' (Jawad, 1992). Ethnicity, religion, occupation, and gender have historically offered to Afghans a range of bases upon which they may seek to identify with their fellows, and while some of these are effectively ascriptive – that is, unchangeable, or changeable only at enormous social cost – the *relative* emphasis given to one over another is frequently a matter of strategic choice. The following observations should be read with this qualification in mind.

Afghanistan is first of all a *multiethnic* country (Schetter, 2003). Anthony Smith, in one of the most detailed studies of the dimensions of ethnic group formation, has pointed to a collective name, a common myth of descent, a shared history, a distinctive shared culture, association with a particular territory, and a sense of solidarity, as the salient markers of ethnic distinction (Smith, 1986: 22–31). A detailed study of ethnic groups in Afghanistan (Orywal, 1986) identifies no fewer than 55, although exact numbers are debatable, since how people are seen by others need not coincide with how they see themselves. This also stands in the way of any serious attempts to determine the proportions of different ethnic groups in the overall population, although scholars tend to agree that Pushtuns comprise the largest single ethnic group, followed by Tajiks, Uzbeks, and Hazaras (see Glatzer, 1998: 169). In some of these ethnic groups, most notably the Pushtuns, one finds distinctively *tribal* forms of social organization, marked by a belief in the existence of common ancestors and by the prevalence of norms of reciprocity and solidarity which give rise to social and (on occasion) political obligations.

Afghanistan is overwhelmingly a Muslim country, albeit with small Hindu, Sikh, and even Jewish minorities. However, while the bulk of Afghanistan's Muslims are adherents of the orthodox 'Sunni' school, the heterodox 'Shiite' school has a significant number of followers, especially among the Hazaras. While the differences between Sunni and Shiite Islam are grounded in the history of political succession in the early Muslim community (see Momen, 1985; Lapidus, 1988), they have at times given rise to fierce intergroup antagonisms, with variations in doctrine and ritual being seen as heresies. Afghanistan has not been insulated from such tensions (see Roy, 1990; Olesen, 1995). Afghanistan also has had strongly developed 'Sufi' brotherhoods, which on occasion have been drawn into the political life of the country, albeit in subtle ways. Islam in Afghanistan, like any religion in any country, functions as a social force only through these agents, the absorption into 'religion' of values and traditions which originate from the sphere of secular culture and can claim no spiritual sanctity; or the influence of schools of religious thought – modernist, radical, or ultraconservative – which have flourished elsewhere in the Muslim world. The Islam of the intelligentsia was and is different from the Islam of the village prayer-leader or mullah, and this is central to an understanding of the dynamics of the Afghanistan conflict.

The Afghan economy has always been dominated by agricultural and pastoral activity, in which the bulk of the population is engaged. While only 12 per cent of the land is arable, that land is intensively exploited, and subject to complex patterns of ownership (Wily, 2003: 3–4) In the relatively small number of cities – Kabul, Kandahar, Herat, Jalalabad, and Mazar-e Sharif – one found a certain amount of secondary industry, but little in the way of heavy industry (see Nägler, 1971; Fry, 1974). In contrast to the situation in neighbouring Pakistan, rural 'society' was not in any meaningful sense 'feudal', for rural notables – tribal *khans*, village *maleks* and the like – were not 'lords' with 'subjects', as in European feudal orders (Pipes, 1999: 105–7), but rather participants in complex local politics in which collective institutions of consensus-building (known variously as *jirgahs* or *shuras*) played key roles. A social order which is structured in this way is likely to prove resilient in the face of external assaults, for it derives its cohesion from self-sustaining institutions of governance rather than from the leadership of individuals who can be eliminated in a decapitating strike.

Politics of this type was an exclusively male preserve: in Afghanistan, most women have performed strictly circumscribed social roles based on the economy of the household. While Afghan popular tradition has venerated particular women as moral leaders (notably Malalai, who challenged the British, and more recently Nihad, a Kabul schoolgirl killed while demonstrating against the Soviet invasion), it was only in urban areas, and then only from 1959, that women had much opportunity to move beyond the realm of the household and occupy a corner of the public sphere (see Dupree, 1984; Rahimi, 1986; Tapper, 1991; Dupree, 1992; Centlivres-Demont, 1994; Maley, 1996; Dupree, 1998). However, this does not mean that a crudely patriarchal interpretation of gender relations in Afghanistan is illuminating. On the contrary, Afghan women have historically shown considerable skill and creativity in asserting their interests within networks of kinship. A failure properly to appreciate these complexities was one reason why Afghanistan's Marxist rulers erred so catastrophically when they attempted to restructure gender relations with the blunt instrument of state power.

The Afghan state

The instrumentalities of the Afghan state – using the term not to describe a territorial unit, but 'a complex set of institutional arrangements for rule' which 'reserves to itself the business of rule over a territorially bounded society' (Poggi, 1978: 1) – developed in somewhat different stages. The whole process of 'state formation' is very complex, for states can vary in the ways in which they are structured, in the mix of tasks which they perform, and in the means by which they seek to secure compliance with their dictates. Furthermore, the contours of the state at any one time are unlikely to reflect the application of design principles to some raw material of state building, but rather the outcomes of discrete decisions by different people at different times and places.

For this reason, even though a monarchical system existed from 1747 until 1973, dating the birth of Afghan state instrumentalities is contentious. Some would point to 1747, when the Ahmad Shah Abdali, a Durrani Pushtun of the Sadozai clan, assembled a tribal confederation independent of both the Safavid dynasty in Persia, and the Mughals in India. However, his dynasty, while it ruled until 1818, was in a state of almost continuous tension with powerful tribal khans, and its domestic institutions were weak (Ghani, 1985). In 1826, Dost Muhammad of the Muhammadzai clan established his ascendancy, and with only two brief intervals – the installation of the hapless Sadozai puppet of the British, Shah Shuja, during the First Anglo–Afghan War from 1839 to 1842 and the rule of the Tajik Habibullah Kalakani in 1929 – Muhammadzais occupied the apex of the political system until April 1978. Dost Muhammad set up a system of tax farming in which his sons played a central role, and expanded the territories under his control (Noelle, 1998), but the system faced a crisis upon his death, and while his son Amir Sher Ali put in place some further embryonic state institutions during his reign from 1868 to 1879 (Kakar, 2006: 15–22), they were not sufficiently robust to survive the Second Anglo–Afghan War, from 1879 to 1880, in reasonable shape.

Many would date the foundation of the modern Afghan state from the reign of Amir Abdul Rahman Khan (1880–1901). First, he established a *bureaucratic* state of a type for which there was no precedent in Afghanistan, even though he remained dependent on tax farming to raise internal revenue, which came largely from land taxes (Kakar, 1979: 73–91). Second, through an extremely bloody process of internal conquest, he subordinated numerous internal power holders to a dominant central authority, and in the process resettled large numbers of Pushtuns amidst non-Pushtun populations (Tapper, 1983). The human costs of this process of conquest were enormous (Edwards, 1996: 123; Lee, 1996: xxii), something which should be borne in mind by anyone inclined to see Abdul Rahman Khan as a role model for an Afghan ruler in the twenty-first century. This was also a problem for his immediate successors, his son Habibullah (1901–1919) and his grandson Amanullah (1919–1929), neither of whom was disposed to use terror on anything like the scale which Abdul Rahman Khan had been contented to accept; and in the case of the latter, it led to a crisis. His ambitious plans for the modernization of Afghanistan, stimulated by his father-in-law and mentor, the journalist and intellectual Mahmoud Tarzi, presumed state capacities, and a degree of legitimacy of state action, which simply were not present (Poullada, 1973). His nemesis, Habibullah Kalakani, a controversial figure in the history of Afghanistan (Khalii, 1984; McChesney, 1999) himself enjoyed only a brief and turbulent interval on the throne, which came to an end when he was overthrown, and executed in violation of a pledge of safe conduct sworn on the Holy Qur'an by his captors – a precedent not forgotten by modern Tajik opponents of Pushtun domination. The lesson of the crisis was one which his replacement Nadir Shah, king from 1929 to 1933, and Nadir's son Zahir, who succeeded his father upon Nadir's assassination in November 1933, learned well: power in Afghanistan was substantially diffused, and this diffusion of power constrained what the state could attempt.

State and society

The pattern of relations between state and society contributed greatly to the slide towards disorder – at first almost imperceptible, but over time increasingly troubling – which marked the later years of Muhammadzai power. Fundamentally, this arose for two reasons. The first was that the state was not accountable for its policies in any meaningful sense to a responsive community, and enjoyed relatively low reservoirs of legitimacy. The second, which is considered in more detail in the next section, was that in the 15 years before the communist coup, the national political elite was rent by increasingly severe divisions, in a period in which expectations of state performance were rising.

When we speak of state–society relations, we are fundamentally concerned to map patterns of domination and subordination, and to identify the bases upon which domination is established and maintained. To do so, we need to identify the key capabilities of the state. Migdal has identified these as including 'the capacities to *penetrate* society, *regulate* social relationships, *extract* resources, and *appropriate* or use resources in determined ways' (Migdal, 1988: 4). We must also note the diverse character of state institutions. Migdal has usefully distinguished four different types. First are the *trenches*, consisting of 'the officials who must execute state directives directly in the face of possibly strong societal resistance'. Second are *the dispersed field offices*, that is, the 'regional and local bodies that rework and organize state policies and directives for local consumption, or even formulate and implement wholly local policies'. Third are the *agency's central offices*, the 'nerve centers where national policies are formulated and enacted and where resources for implementation are marshaled'. Fourth are the *commanding heights*, the 'pinnacle of the state' where the 'top executive leadership' is to be found (Migdal, 1994: 16).

As the great German sociologist Max Weber argued, domination can be exercised on both normative and prudential bases. Domination which is normatively based, that is, based on voluntary acceptance by the ruled, is often called 'legitimate'. Legitimate domination can be exercised on a number of different grounds: Weber pointed to the importance of *legal-rational, traditional* and *charismatic* authority. However, he also took pains to emphasize the importance of certain types of elite cohesion, noting that 'organized domination requires control of the personal executive staff and the material implements of administration' (Weber, 1948: 80).

When Zahir Shah ascended the throne in 1933, the Afghan regime obtained the bulk of its revenue through taxes on land. For the next two decades, the state was under the effective control of two of the king's paternal uncles: first, Muhammad Hashem Khan (who served as prime minister until 1946) and Shah Mahmoud Khan (prime minister from 1946 until 1953). During their rule, the fiscal basis of the state changed significantly. By 1953, taxes on land and livestock represented only 14 per cent of government domestic revenue; by contrast, 39 per cent came from taxes on foreign trade, and a further 10 per cent from asset sales (Rubin, 1995a: 60). The following decade, during which Zahir Shah's cousin Muhammad Daoud served as prime minister, saw an even more dramatic shift, largely as a result of Daoud's courting of external backers which I shall discuss in more detail shortly. In 1953, only 7 per cent of state expenditure was funded by foreign aid, with 93 per cent funded from domestic revenue. By 1963, foreign aid funded fully 49 per cent of state expenditure, with domestic revenue covering just 38 per cent, the balance coming from domestic borrowing (Rubin, 1995a: 296). The implications of this shift in the fiscal basis of the state were considerable. A prescient aphorism of the Sasanian period, recorded first by Ibn Balkhi, runs as follows: 'There is no kingdom without an army, no army without wealth, no wealth without material prosperity, and no material prosperity without justice' (cited in Springborg, 1992: 264). Unfortunately, the need to deliver justice can be short-circuited by foreign support, which injects wealth for the state's direct use. The removal of Daoud in 1963 and the inauguration of the so-called 'New Democracy' period was not a reaction against this approach to running the state, but rather against other elements of Daoud's policies. The regime on the eve of New Democracy was *partially legitimate*, largely because the instrumentalities of the state, although ubiquitous, did not seek to exploit its penetrative, regulatory, extractive and appropriative capacities. But its foundations were becoming shakier.

The decline of state legitimacy: 1964–1978

The 'New Democracy' experiment began with the drafting of a new Afghan constitution, which provided for institutions with a strongly democratic flavour. An elected lower house (*Wolesi Jirgah*) lay at the heart of its attempt to install a new system of government, but equally important was its attempt to exclude the royal family from the political executive. From 1963 to 1973, a series of commoners occupied the position of prime minister, and relatively free elections were held in 1965 and 1969. The jurists responsible for the drafting of the constitution took pride in its undoubtedly progressive dimensions (Reshtia, 1997), and there is no doubt that those interested in politics enjoyed more freedom than ever before. However, the new order failed to secure legitimacy on legal-rational grounds. Politics in the absence of formalized parties proved disorderly and inefficient. Plato's description of democracy as an agreeable form of anarchy proved all too precise. More seriously, the Afghan bureaucracy proved extraordinarily dysfunctional. Writing at the time of the communist coup, Kakar observed that 'Afghan civil servants are probably among the lowest paid in the world. It is impossible for them to live decently on their salaries unless they are supplemented by other sources of income. Corruption and embezzlement are accepted facts of Afghan bureaucratic life and are objected to only when excesses are committed' (Kakar, 1978: 200). Similar problems existed at the levels of the trenches and the dispersed field offices where 'the government was faced with indigenous political structures and where its own agents were not well respected' (Barfield, 1984: 175). Problems of financial corruption were compounded by widespread *nepotism*, which saw patron–client relations overwhelm competence and dedication as routes to advancement. In the military, this had deadly consequences, as young non-elite Pushtuns in the officer corps 'found their road to promotion and choice assignments blocked by the old inner circle of Pushtuns with close connections to the royal family' (Magnus, 1986: 335).

These weaknesses came to a head in 1972. Afghanistan was struck by famine, and the state's response was pitiful. The very appearance of famine testified to the regime's inadequacies: as Sen has recently argued, 'no famine has ever taken place in the history of the world in a functioning democracy' (Sen, 1999: 16). Michael Barry records that one official of the Ministry of Agriculture in Kabul remarked: 'If the peasants eat grass, it's hardly grave. They're beasts. They're used to it' (Barry, 1974: 182). Such barbaric indifference to suffering spoke volumes for the failure of New Democracy to generate genuine accountability of rulers to ruled, and it was no surprise when Zahir Shah's divided regime was overthrown in a palace coup by former prime minister Daoud in July 1973.

Daoud's republican regime lasted for nearly five years, but faced significant problems from its outset. Daoud was a man of great energy, in sharp contrast to the quiescent if manipulative Zahir Shah. However, his coup had compromised the legitimacy of the state to a greater extent than was initially apparent. To ordinary Afghans, for whom the governments of the later phase of 'New Democracy' had been discredited by their lamentable performance, the change in regime may not have seemed all that striking; after all, Daoud was a member of the royal family and had a long history of political activity. However, his advent marked the disappearance not just of a king, but of a monarchical system more generally, which offered at least the semblance of a rule for peaceful succession to political authority. Bureaucracy under Daoud was no more efficient than under the king; the regime's claims to traditional authority were slender. One thus saw three tactics predominating as Daoud sought to secure his position in urban areas and at the commanding heights of the state. The first was increased use of coercion. Under Daoud, the Afghan government built the largest prison in Asia, at Pul-e Charkhi on the outskirts of Kabul. Opponents of his regime, most notably former prime minister Muhammad Hashem Maiwandwal, lost their lives in regime custody (Arnold, 1985: 60). The second was the attempt to clothe Daoud's seizure of power in the garb of 'revolution' (*inqilab*). This was a very dangerous rhetoric to inject into Afghan political discourse, not only because it opened the door to reflection on the need for a bigger and better 'revolution' than Daoud was attempting, but also because the gulf between the rhetoric of 'revolutionary' change and the reality of business as usual under a nepotistic Pushtun elite exposed the regime's claims as mere propaganda – of which a *legitimate* regime has no need (Ferrero, 1942: 200). The third tactic Daoud used was to work in coalition with other political forces, notably the communist *Parcham* group. In the short run, this assisted him in overthrowing the monarchy. In the long run, it contributed materially to his own overthrow and death in April 1978. 'After me the deluge' could have been his motto.

The Soviet context

The Soviet system

Afghanistan had the misfortune to be located on the doorstep of a restive autocracy, the Union of Soviet Socialist Republics (also known as the USSR or the Soviet Union). The Soviet political system continues to be the focus of scholarly attention, and many aspects of Soviet political history remain hotly debated. This is not the place to explore in any detail the contours of those debates, but a brief overview may assist the reader. The USSR was a classic 'Communist' political system (White, 1983), marked by the dominance of a single party, a formal commitment to Marxism-Leninism, a command economy, and special relations with other communist parties. In the mature Soviet system on the eve of the Soviet invasion of Afghanistan, the Soviet Government, organizationally based on the Council of Ministers and the ministries and state committees which its members headed, pursued policies broadly determined by the leadership of the Communist Party of the Soviet Union, which under Article 6 of the 1977 Constitution of the USSR was formally accorded the role of 'guiding and directing force' of Soviet society. The party, with nearly 17 million members, had ceased to be a 'vanguard' party; but party membership remained the key point of entry for those who aspired to become part of the elite. While primary party organizations existed at workplace level, and a theatrical 'Congress' was held roughly every five years, real power was located in the party's professional bureaucracy, the Secretariat (with its own departments); in the party Central Committee, which met several times a year (Mawdsley and White, 2000); and in the 'Politburo' (Political Bureau) of the Central Committee, which brought together the top dozen or so Soviet leaders, and came as close to being a real Cabinet as did any Soviet organ. Known from 1952 to 1966 as the 'Presidium', it comprised both voting and non-voting (or 'candidate') members. The formal Head of State was the Chairman of the Presidium of the Supreme Soviet, a largely rubber-stamp bicameral 'Parliament'; but the key leader was the principal party secretary, known from 1952 to 1966 as the 'First Secretary', and then from 1966 as the 'General Secretary'. The power of a General Secretary tended to grow during his term of office compared to what it was at the outset, as the tools of patronage at his disposal permitted him to promote those whom he believed to be supporters, but after 1953 this power was never absolute, and, arguably, the power of successive General Secretaries was increasingly circumscribed by a range of normative and prudential constraints. The party's tentacles penetrated all corners of society, prompting T. H. Rigby to describe the Soviet system as 'mono-organisational' (Rigby, 1976; Rigby, 1990), and recruitment into the elite was carefully controlled by the party via the *nomenklatura* or 'list' system (Harasymiw, 1969). Competing parties did not exist, and dissident voices were subject to severe repression by organs of the state, entailing on occasion imprisonment in labour camps, internal exile, or even incarceration on spurious 'psychiatric' grounds.

Soviet relations with Afghanistan

The international relations of Russia following the Bolshevik revolution of 1917 followed a somewhat tortuous path. The Bolsheviks' early hope that their revolution would be replicated in the capitalist states of Western Europe went unrealized, although Hungary was briefly ruled by the Communist Béla Kun, and Germany witnessed short-lived outbreaks of localized revolutionary extremism. As Joseph Stalin consolidated his position within the Soviet leadership following the death of V. I. Lenin in 1924, he positioned himself to declare a commitment to 'socialism in one country', which soon became official Soviet policy. This did not mean, however, that the leadership of the new 'Union of Soviet Socialist Republics' was without a foreign policy. On the contrary, it retained an interest in what was occurring in its immediate neighbours, and one of these, of course, was Afghanistan. This was, in part, because Central Asia remained an area in which Bolshevik power was contested, albeit on a diminishing scale as the 1920s drew to a close, by the so-called 'Basmachi movement' (Maley, 1991a: 181). However, it was also because some saw Afghanistan as a vital interest of the British, whose intervention against Bolshevik rule in 1918–1920 was bitterly resented. The 'road to Paris and London', L. D. Trotsky had remarked, 'might lead through Kabul, Calcutta and Bombay' (Deutscher, 1954: 457). During Stalin's lifetime, Soviet–Afghan relations remained low-key. The Soviet leadership was increasingly alarmed during the late 1930s by the threat posed by Nazi Germany, and almost wholly preoccupied from June 1941 with the prosecution of the war against the Nazi invaders – a war in which Afghanistan remained neutral. Thereafter, Moscow's interests focused on theatres of more direct competition with the Western powers, notably Europe, East Asia, and – to the extent that the Middle East attracted Soviet interests – Iran, which during the Second World War had been divided into Soviet and British spheres of influence.

In 1953, however, two momentous events occurred. First, Stalin died, leaving no designated successor. Within a few days of Stalin's death, Nikita S. Khrushchev secured the position of First Secretary of the Central Committee of the Communist Party of the Soviet Union, and set out to consolidate his position by adopting new policy positions, a process which culminated in his denunciation of Stalin's 'cult of personality' at the twentieth Party Congress in February 1956 (Taubman, 2004: 270–89). Second, in Afghanistan, Muhammad Daoud was appointed prime minister. Committed to a programme of state building, he recognized the need for externally supplied resources to fund his plans. And with the change of leadership in Moscow, the Soviet Union loomed as a potential supplier.

Khrushchev was to develop a foreign policy approach which displayed some sensitivity to the changing configurations of world politics. In 1955, a conference at Bandung in Indonesia, attended on Afghanistan's behalf by the diplomat Said Qassem Reshtia, marked the birth of what came to be known as the Non-Aligned Movement. Alert to the opportunities which this offered, Khrushchev advanced a new theory of international relations, which, as well as positing the possibility of 'peaceful coexistence' between socialist and capitalist countries, located socialist and *developing* countries together in a 'Zone of Peace' (Kubálková and Cruickshank, 1980: 161–3). This theoretical innovation opened the door to direct engagement between the USSR and the developing world. More concretely, in December 1955, he and the Chairman of the Soviet Council of Ministers, Nikolai Bulganin, paid an official visit to Kabul, the first ever by a Soviet leader (Novichkova, 1956). In the context of substantial US indifference to Afghanistan – Washington having shown little interest in cultivating Daoud as long as he prosecuted a border dispute with America's ally Pakistan (Poullada, 1981) – this set the scene for Soviet penetration of Afghanistan in two vital respects. The first was military. Following an arms shipment in 1955 from Moscow's Warsaw Pact satellite Czechoslovakia, the USSR in July 1956 agreed to a loan of $32.4 million to Afghanistan for military purposes (Bradsher, 1985: 28). By 1979, according to CIA estimates cited by Bradsher, Soviet military aid to Afghanistan had totalled $1.25 billion. Further, 3,725 Afghan personnel had received military training in the USSR, Russian was the technical language of the Afghan armed forces, and Afghanistan was heavily dependent upon Soviet sources for spare parts (Bradsher, 1999: 2). The second sphere of penetration was economic. Afghanistan came to occupy a position behind only India and Egypt as a recipient of Soviet economic aid, which by 1979 cumulatively totalled approximately $1.265 billion. In the year of the communist coup, some 2,000 Soviet technical and economic experts were at work in Afghanistan (Noorzoy, 1985: 159–60). The net effect was to promote those industries which would most readily market their output in the USSR, such as fruits and natural gas. In this way, the Afghan economy became increasingly dependent upon the Soviet.

The Soviet cultivation of Afghan communists

The question of whether the communist movement which was to affect Afghanistan in such a devastating fashion from 1978 was largely home-grown or merely a piece in a larger jigsaw remains difficult to answer. The role of the Soviet Union in promoting communist movements elsewhere had long been clear; indeed, the Communist International or Comintern, which functioned from 1919 to 1943, provided institutional foundations for the exercise of such influence. However, the inspiration provided by communism did not derive simply from Soviet-backed organizations. For those who dwelt in impoverished societies such as Afghanistan, the appeal of a simplistic Marxist rhetoric could be profound, notwith-standing the deep flaws in logic and analysis on which it rested (see Kolakowski, 1978; Walicki, 1995). The vulgarized precepts of Marxism-Leninism were a heady brew for circles of Afghanistan's urban youth, and their leaders. Even without Soviet inspiration, a Marxist movement of sorts would surely have taken shape in Afghanistan. But at key points, the history of the movement which did develop was critically influenced by Soviet pressures, facilitated by the scale of the Soviet presence in Afghanistan following the Khrushchev-Bulganin visit. Of course, to speak of a 'movement' risks imputing too much coherence to what was for much of the time a field of battle between different antagonistic sects or networks divided on lines of ethnicity, socioeconomic status, or ideol-ogy. These divisions, indeed, were critical in explaining the chaos which was to befall Afghanistan once the Daoud regime was overthrown.

The Soviet-aligned Afghan communists fell into two broad factions, which took the names of newssheets which they managed to publish for a very brief period in the early days of 'New Democracy'. One was the

Khalq ('Masses') faction, prominently led by Nur Muhammad Taraki (1917–1979) and Hafizullah Amin (1929–1979), both Ghilzai Pushtuns. This faction was Pushtun-dominated, with few Kabulis at the top. Taraki had been recruited as a Soviet agent in 1951 (Andrew and Mitrokhin, 2005: 386). The other was the *Parcham* ('Banner') faction, led by Babrak Karmal (1929–1996), a Persian-speaking Kabuli of Durrani Pushtun background. Karmal was also recruited as a Soviet agent in the 1950s, with the code name MARID (Andrew and Mitrokhin, 2005: 387). While Pushtuns made up the largest single bloc within the *Parcham* faction's leadership, they remained a minority, and Kabulis played a prominent role (Rubin, 1995a: 91–2). From 1965 to 1967, these factions united to form the *Hezb-e Demokratik-e Khalq-e Afghanistan* ('People's Democratic Party of Afghanistan', or PDPA). Because of leadership tensions, the alliance proved short-lived. Indeed, an observer of radical politics in the late 1960s would more likely have been struck by the vigour of another group, the Maoist *Shula-i Javid* ('Eternal Flame'), founded by Dr Abdul Rahman Mahmudi, which drew support from long-marginalized Hazaras, and a degree of inspiration from the revolutionary rhetoric emanating from China during the Cultural Revolution, notably Lin Piao's 'Long Live the Victory of People's War'. However, in 1977 the two pro-Soviet factions reunited, almost certainly at Moscow's instigation. *Parcham*, having been purged by Daoud in 1975, was in an ugly mood, and the new alliance with *Khalq* heightened the threat which Daoud faced, to a greater extent than he realized.

Daoud, while prepared to use *Parcham* for his own purposes, was first and foremost a nationalist. This lay at the heart of a spectacular clash which he had with Soviet General Secretary Brezhnev on 12 April 1977, during a state visit to the USSR. As recounted by an eyewitness, Brezhnev demanded the removal from northern Afghanistan of experts from NATO countries. An angry Daoud described Brezhnev's remark as a flagrant interference in the internal affairs of Afghanistan, and continued 'we will never allow you to dictate to us how to run our country and whom to employ in Afghanistan. How and where we employ the foreign experts will remain the exclusive prerogative of the Afghan state. Afghanistan shall remain poor, if necessary, but free in its acts and decisions' (Ghaus, 1988: 179). How prominent a role might this clash have played in the overthrow of Daoud barely a year later? Unfortunately, this is impossible to determine with any certainty. To say that by responding in this way Daoud signed his own death warrant involves imputing to the Soviet leadership both a central role in the initiation of the April 1978 coup, and a motivation to play such a role derived from a loss of faith in

Daoud resulting from the clash a year earlier. As we shall shortly see, evidence of either of these is scanty. However, it is possible to defend a more cautious conclusion, namely that the growing disenchantment with Daoud may have disinclined the Soviet leadership to take active steps to block his overthrow by the Afghan communists once they were so inclined.

The sclerotic Soviet elite

In responding to these events, however, the Soviet regime was hampered by its own sclerosis. By the late 1970s, the ageing of the Soviet elite was beginning to affect Soviet politics and policies in subtle but increasingly damaging ways. The origins of this problem were quite remote in time: during the 1930s, a large group of activists, known as the *vydvizhentsy* ('those moved forward'), rose rapidly as a result of the elimination of large numbers of so-called 'Old Bolsheviks' during the Great Purge. A very large number of *vydvizhentsy* survived the Stalin period to dominate the three decades after his death. This became even more pronounced following the removal of Khrushchev as First Secretary of the Central Committee in October 1964: his successor, Leonid I. Brezhnev, born in 1906, adopted what was known as the 'stability of cadres' policy, in order to allay the concerns of those party officials whose positions had been destabilized by radical reorganizations under Khrushchev. The effects of this policy on the Soviet elite were dramatic. By 1980, the average age of full members of the Politburo of the Communist Party was 70.1, compared with 55.4 in 1952; the average age of Central Committee Secretaries was 67.0, compared with 52.0 in 1952 (Bialer, 1980: 83).

At the upper echelons of the party elite in particular, the bulk of important positions were held by individuals whose formative experiences were anything but liberal. Brezhnev's key associates in the foreign policy sphere were very much of this ilk. The Soviet Foreign Minister, Andrei A. Gromyko, born in 1909, had held the position since 1957, but had earlier come to prominence as Stalin's Ambassador to the USA from 1943. The Soviet Defence Minister, Dmitri F. Ustinov, born in 1908, had served as Stalin's Minister for Armaments during the Second World War, although the bulk of his career, before his appointment as Defence Minister in 1976, had been as a party official. The Head of the International Department of the Secretariat of the Party Central Committee, Boris N. Ponomarev, was born in 1905, and had been a Comintern activist in his youth. The Chairman of the Committee of State Security (KGB), Iurii V. Andropov, was a little younger than the others, having been born in 1914, but as Soviet Ambassador to Hungary in 1956 had played a major role during the Soviet crushing of the Hungarian revolution against communist rule (Meray, 1959: 189).

In addition, the Soviet *system* was singularly free of mechanisms of accountability to ensure that policy failures would be punished. To Juvenal's famous question *quis custodiet ipsos custodes?* – 'Who will guard the guardians themselves?' – the Soviet model had no answer. Here lay one of its greatest contrasts with even a poorly functioning democracy. One observer accurately described the Soviet leadership as a 'self-stabilizing oligarchy' (Rigby, 1970), and this lay at the heart of its weakness. Promotion within the system owed a great deal to the ability of a bright achiever to find an appropriate patron, and to rise on the tide of that individual's patronage (Willerton, 1992). But to profit from a patron in this sense involves a willingness to function as a loyal client, and this in turn could involve turning a blind eye to much that was going wrong. As a result of this and other factors, the system was increasingly riddled with corruption. 'Official corruption', wrote Clark, 'diverted the energies of relatively competent bureaucrats from the administration of state policies to the orchestration of self-aggrandizement' (Clark, 1993: 219; see also Holmes, 1993: 214). As economic performance declined, the Soviet system faced a range of pressing problems (see Dibb, 1986; Malia, 1994: 351–401; Keep, 1995: 165–328) but the Brezhnev leadership's handling of Afghanistan was to be treated during the later Gorbachev period as one of the key symptoms of the deeper malaise of 'stagnation' (*zastoi*).

From coup to invasion

The April 1978 coup

Terrible events can be triggered unexpectedly by an assassin's bullet. On 17 April 1978, a prominent Parcham ideologue variously described as being of Ghilzai Pushtun or of Qizilbash origin, Mir Akbar Khyber, was assassinated in Kabul. The identity of his assassins remains a mystery to this day. Some have attributed the slaying to Daoud's Interior Minister, Abdul Qadir Nuristani (Harrison, 1979: C5), while others have pointed to the *Khalq*'s Hafizullah Amin as the likely instigator (Rubin, 1995a: 317; Dorronsoro, 2005: 85). But whoever was responsible, the reverberations from their shots can still be felt. They led directly to the overthrow of Daoud ten days later. A large crowd turned out for Khyber's funeral, and Daoud, panicked by the size of the crowd, launched a crackdown against

PDPA elements, which in turn led directly to the 27 April coup. The coup leaders dubbed their seizure of power the 'Saur Revolution' (*Inqilab-e Saur*), taking its name from the month Saur ('Taurus' in Afghanistan's traditional zodiac calendar) in which the coup had occurred. Since the seizure of power was not in any sense a product of mass revolution, this rhetoric was in some ways as hollow as that which Daoud had deployed to justify his own takeover. The difference was that while Daoud was in no sense a revolutionary, those who overthrew him stood ready to launch a revolution from above, of a type which Afghanistan had never experienced, and for which – as it turned out – they were strikingly ill prepared both intellectually and organizationally.

The coup was launched around 10–11 a.m. on Thursday 27 April 1978 by communist officers who doubtless feared exposure by civilian associates who had been arrested about 34 hours earlier. The four key figures were Abdul Qadir, Aslam Watanjar, Sayid Muhammad Gulabzoi, and Muhammad Rafi. Qadir and Rafi were from the *Parcham* faction; Watanjar and Gulabzoi were *Khalqis*. Tanks under Watanjar's command moved against the Presidential Palace (*Arg*), and were supported by MiG-21 ('Fishbed') fighters and Su-7 fighter-bombers flown from the Bagram air base north of the capital. Daoud and his immediate associates were overrun at around 4–5 a.m. on 28 April, and massacred (Dupree, 1979: 14–15). For the coup leaders, there was to be no turning back. A widespread wave of arrests followed, which shattered the worlds of many middle-class Kabul families: decades on, the anguish of these days continues to haunt those who were caught up in them (see Gauhari, 1996). Former prime ministers Nur Ahmad Etemadi and Muhammad Musa Shafiq were subsequently murdered; activists of *Shula-i Javid* and the nationalist *Afghan Millat* party were also targeted.

In Afghan circles, the conviction that the USSR orchestrated the coup remains widely held (Haqshenas, 1999: Vol. I: 5). Yet while a range of circumstantial factors – for example the accuracy with which targets in Kabul were bombed – prompted speculation (noted by Harrison, 1979: C5) that the Soviet Union organized the coup, no credible direct evidence has surfaced to support this claim (Allan and Kläy, 1999). The accuracy of bombing proves very little: after all, the British before Pearl Harbor had scorned the capacity of the Japanese air force (Weinberg, 1994: 261). A subsequent decision to reward Soviet personnel for 'military actions' in Afghanistan from 22 April 1978 ('Dlia tekh, kto voeval', *Krasnaia zvezda*, 12 October 1989: 2) hints at some low-level cooperation between Soviet and Afghan communists *before* the coup, and eyewitness testimony shows that Soviet personnel threw their weight behind the coup once it began (Ghaus, 1988: 197–8). According to Vasili Mitrokhin, the KGB residency in the Soviet Embassy in Kabul received 'advance warning of the coup' from Gulabzoi and Rafi, whom Mitrokhin described as Soviet agents, but officials at KGB headquarters were unenthusiastic about the idea (Andrew and Mitrokhin, 2005: 386). The Soviet Ambassador to Afghanistan, Aleksandr M. Puzanov, was caught unawares, but this is hardly decisive: while Puzanov had been sufficiently prominent in the early 1950s to catch Stalin's eye, and even served briefly as a candidate member of the Party Presidium, by 1978 his career was in its twilight – he was born in 1906 – and he could easily have been bypassed. More telling is the point noted by Garthoff that for the three days after the coup, the Soviet official newsagency TASS referred to the events in Kabul as a *coup*, rather than a popular revolution (Garthoff, 1994: 988). Coming from a controlled, official medium in a state which attached great significance to fine ideological distinctions, this was a notable pointer to Moscow's limited role in the events in Kabul.

Communist factionalism and policy failures

After a few days of rule by the coup leaders, a new regime was announced which drew on the key civilian figures of the PDPA. Taraki was named president and prime minister; Hafizullah Amin became Foreign Minister; Qadir was Defence Minister; and Babrak Karmal was appointed Deputy Prime Minister. However, this mixing of *Parcham* and *Khalq* activists did nothing to overcome the smouldering antagonism between the two groups, and within a matter of months it had resurfaced with a vengeance (Arnold, 1983: 64–73). Declassified Soviet documents provide direct evidence of the depth of the rift (Westad, 1994; Westad, 2005). In a meeting with President Taraki and Ambassador Puzanov on 18 June 1978, Karmal warned that for the sake of 'unity' in Amin's sense of the term, 'thousands of honest communists in Afghanistan will be subject to terror, persecutions, their names will be slandered'. This was too much for Taraki, who ordered Karmal out (Hershberg, 1996–1997: 134). Within three weeks Karmal was posted as Afghan Ambassador to Czechoslovakia, with his *Parcham* associates Anahita Ratebzad, Nur Ahmad Nur, Abdul Wakil, and Dr Najibullah also receiving diplomatic postings – from which they wisely disappeared later in the year when summoned home as the purge of *Parchamis* intensified. The purge swept up the coup leaders Qadir and Rafi, whose known connections with the Soviets probably saved their lives. Thousands of other Afghans were not so fortunate. A climate of profound fear pervaded Kabul, as Taraki's secret police AGSA (in Pushto *Da Afghanistan da Gato da Satalo Edara,* or 'Afghan Interests Protection Service'), headed by Asadullah Sarwari, used torture and killing as means of regime consolidation. The American anthropologist Louis Dupree, held for some days before being expelled from Afghanistan in November 1978, has left a chilling portrait of Sarwari and his methods (Dupree, 1980a; Dupree 1980b). In Pul-e Charkhi prison, large numbers of prisoners were executed without any semblance of a trial. Sayid Abdullah, the prison commandant, stated that 'a million Afghans are all that should remain alive. We need a million *Khalqis.* The others we don't need, we will get rid of them' (Barry, 1980: 183). This approach was sanctioned from the top. In November 1978, Amin attributed to Taraki the remark that 'those who plot against us in the dark will vanish in the dark' ('Our Revolution is Secure', *Asiaweek,* 17 November 1978: 40). It was certainly a sentiment that Amin himself shared, as subsequent events were to show.

A central cause of the rift between *Khalq* and *Parcham,* apart from the well-known personal differences between Amin and Karmal, was the fact that the leaders of the PDPA were not remotely ready to rule a country, much less implement the ambitious plans contained in their platform. For this they would have needed a cohesive and legitimate state bureaucracy, as well as a groundswell of support for their ideas. They lacked both. Their regime began as a coercive one, and by the eve of the Soviet invasion had been substantially repudiated. The shortage of skilled cadres meant that the party's ambitious plans had no prospect of being comprehensively implemented, and for this reason the *Parcham* activists preferred a more gradualist approach. This cut no ice with the *Khalqis,* who constituted not so much a vanguard party of the Leninist variety as a 'movement of rage'. For them, smashing the old order was an end in itself. The 'backwardness of past centuries', proclaimed the party platform published in the *Khalq* newspaper in April 1966, was to be eliminated 'within the lifespan of one generation' (cited in Arnold, 1983: 140).

The *Khalq* approach to politics had two dimensions: a promulgation of radical policies, and an assault on those who found the policies offensive or unpalatable. Ruling by decree, the regime sought to implement wide-ranging land reforms, and a reordering of gender relations. The land reform package was totally unrealistic in that it ignored both the needs of nomads and the importance of water and seed supplies; while the decree relating to women was seen as atheistic meddling in key Islamic rituals. None of these areas was immune to *well-designed* and *carefully implemented* reforms: it was above all the 'Big Bang' approach of the *Khalqis* that raised a storm, combined with the underlying reality, emphasized by Rubin, that 'the choice the peasants were given was not between domination and exploitation on the one hand and freedom and equality on the other. Their choice was between leaders whom they knew, with whom they shared much, and leaders whom they did not know, who believed in an alien ideology and who showed by their actions that they could not be trusted' (Rubin, 1995a: 119). The regime was utterly ruthless in its use of force: in the village of Kerala in the eastern province of Kunar, on 20 April 1979, government forces massacred all the male inhabitants in cold blood. In a grim foretaste of coming years, Soviet advisers were reportedly present during the slaughter (Girardet, 1985: 107–10). However, this coercion did not fragment opposition to the regime. Rather, in the context of strong pre-existing norms of social solidarity, it simply led to an intensification of resistance to the regime (Maley, 1991b).

The Soviet view of Afghan developments

The first truly acute crisis of the regime came with the Herat uprising in March 1979, and this caused the Soviet leadership to begin to focus more carefully on the events occurring on its doorstep. The Soviet reaction to events in Afghanistan at this time was one of growing alarm, initially muted by a well-grounded caution.

The mass uprising began in Herat with a mutiny in the 17th Division of the Afghan Army on 15 March, in response to the brutality of the *Khalq* activists. One of the leaders was Major Ismail Khan, whose name figures prominently in the subsequent history of the Afghanistan war. *Khalqis* and Soviet advisers were attacked, and the city rocked with the sound of residents chanting *Allahu Akbar* ('God is Great') from the roofs of their houses. While soldiers brought from Kandahar ultimately restored the regime's control, a request from Taraki for Soviet troops to put down the uprising triggered a major discussion in the Politburo of the Afghanistan situation. The record of this discussion is of very considerable historical interest. Memoirs from Soviet politicians and generals must be treated with due caution: Count Ciano's famous comment that victory finds a hundred fathers, but defeat is an orphan (Muggeridge, 1947: 502) highlights the kind of bias of which it is necessary to be wary. By contrast, to the Soviet leadership in 1979, it would have seemed almost inconceivable that records of their discussions would ever be published, and while their observations must still be construed in the light of their individual purposes and strategies, they offer a much less distorted image of their thinking at the time than memoirs do.

On 17 March, Foreign Minister Gromyko presented a grim picture of the situation, stating that the number of insurgents was 'thousands, literally thousands', and asserting as a 'fundamental proposition' that 'under no circumstances may we lose Afghanistan' (Hershberg, 1996–1997: 137). Aleksei Kosygin, Chairman of the Council of Ministers, bluntly asserted that 'Amin and Taraki alike are concealing from us the true state of affairs' (ibid.: 138), and noted that 'they have continued to execute people who do not agree with them' (ibid.: 139). Interestingly, he numbered Soviet advisers in Afghanistan at this time at 550 (ibid.: 139), and these appeared to be the sources of the information that was put before the Politburo members. In a telephone conversation with Kosygin on 17 or 18 March, Taraki adopted an almost hysterical tone: 'Why can't the Soviet Union send Uzbeks, Tajiks, and Turkmens in civilian clothing? No one will recognize them' (ibid.: 146). Kosygin, an extremely shrewd man, was not so easily caught, and in a meeting with Taraki in Moscow on 20 March set out a position which the Soviet leadership was to pay a heavy price for abandoning within nine months:

> The deployment of our forces in the territory of Afghanistan would immediately arouse the international community and would invite sharply unfavourable multipronged consequence ... I would again like to underline that the question of deploying our forces has been examined by us from every direction; we carefully studied all aspects of this action and came to the conclusion that if our troops were introduced, the situation in your country would not only not improve, but would worsen. One cannot deny that our troops would have to fight not only with foreign aggressors, but also with a certain number of your people. And people do not forgive such things. (Hershberg, 1996–1997: 147)

The Amin period

In September 1979, there occurred a series of events which fundamentally shifted the Soviet approach to Afghanistan, and displaced Moscow's careful approach with one grounded in considerations of pride and emotion. In a messy sequence of strike and counterstrike, Amin, who had manoeuvred his way into the office of the prime minister in March 1979, succeeded in removing Taraki, who was subsequently murdered

Westad, 1994: 61–2). Taraki's associates Watanjar, Gulabzoi, and Sarwari sought and obtained Soviet protection, and were later smuggled to Soviet territory (Saikal and Maley, 1991: 42–3; Andrew and Mitrokhin, 2005: 395–6). Given that Taraki had met with Brezhnev on his way home from a meeting in Havana of the Non-Aligned Movement earlier in the month, the murder of Taraki was a considerable affront to the Soviet leadership, and to Brezhnev in particular (Bradsher, 1999: 84; Halliday, 1999: 679). The relationship between Amin and the Soviets deteriorated sharply. Amin had no doubt that Ambassador Puzanov had been plotting with Taraki to secure Amin's removal: indeed, his Foreign Minister, Dr Shah Wali, said as much at a meeting on 6 October (Garthoff, 1994: 1006), and Puzanov was shortly thereafter removed and replaced by Fikrat A. Tabeev. From this point onwards, the slide towards a Soviet invasion of Afghanistan began to gather pace.

The brief period of Amin's ascendency is widely recognized by Afghans to have been one of the worst in Afghanistan's modern history. Amin was a quite remarkably sinister figure. He had no strategy for domestic consolidation beyond the application of terror, and this he pursued with a pathological single-mindedness. On the one hand, as recorded by the French Dominican scholar Serge de Beaurecueil, for many years a resident of Kabul, Amin attempted to blame Taraki for the killings of the *Khalq* regime, by posting a list of 12,000 names of persons who had lost their lives (Gille and Heslot, 1989: 54–8). Yet on the other, his secret police pursued perceived enemies with fanatical ferocity. By late 1979, he had left himself with little strategy but the further use of terror, but even that had ceased to work. Faced with Soviet anger, he had no real scope to build bridges to other powers such as the United States: the US Ambassador to Kabul had been killed in a shootout following his seizure by unidentified kidnappers in February 1979 – a bloody outcome for which Washington apparently blamed Amin. The wider world showed no interest in saving Amin's skin.

In late 1979, the attention of key foreign ministries was focused elsewhere. The United States was massively preoccupied with the occupation of its Tehran Embassy by radical Iranian students on 4 November 1979 (Farber, 2005). The Iranian revolution had not simply humiliated the Carter Administration; it had corrupted the whole security architecture derived from the 1969 enunciation by President Nixon of the Guam Doctrine, which posited a special role for pro-American regional powers in guaranteeing regional security. The major Western European powers, in alliance with the USA, were also locked in competition with the Soviet Union in Europe, where the Soviet move to deploy SS-20

Intermediate Range Ballistic Missiles prompted NATO on 12 December 1979 to decide to respond by deploying both Pershing II and Ground Launched Cruise Missiles. However, this decision was important more as a symptom of the freeze in East–West relations, rather than as a factor which might have led the Soviets to feel that they had little to lose by invading Afghanistan. For ironically, it was on the very day that NATO reached its decision that the Soviet leadership crossed its own Rubicon as far as the Afghan situation was concerned.

The Soviet invasion

On 12 December 1979, a meeting of the Soviet Politburo, chaired by Foreign Minister Gromyko, reportedly accepted the recommendation of four key Soviet leaders and Politburo members – Communist Party General Secretary Brezhnev, KGB Chairman Andropov, Defence Minister Ustinov, and Gromyko himself – that Afghanistan was to be invaded. The Politburo decision record, no. P 176/125, was discreetly headed *K polozheniiu v 'A'* ('On the situation in "A" '), and recorded in the handwriting of Party Secretary Konstantin Chernenko, a long-time Brezhnev associate. It was countersigned by all full members of the Politburo except Chairman of the Council of Ministers Kosygin, who was seriously ill at the time and died the following year; according to one source, this record was actually 'antedated' (*zadnim chislom*) rather than signed by all members when the decision was actually taken (Kornienko, 1993: 110). However, Soviet troop movements suggest that a possible invasion was in prospect from at least 7 October, when a regiment of the Soviet 105th Airborne Division, based in Ferghana in the Turkestan Military District, was unexpectedly instructed to begin training with newly mobilized motorized divisions (Bradsher, 1999: 89–90).

The Soviet 105th Airborne Division provided the spearhead for the invasion. Directed from Termez in Uzbekistan by Soviet Marshal Sergei L. Sokolov, its troops began to fly to the Bagram Airbase, north of Kabul, from 29 November. Two weeks later it had been joined by a substantial armoured unit. From 11 p.m. on 24 December, more of the 105th Airborne began to arrive at Khwaja Rawash airport in Kabul, with Soviet Airborne troops also flying to Bagram, to the Shindand base near Herat, and to Kandahar. Troops of the 360th Motorized Infantry Division crossed the Afghan border near Termez, and headed for Kabul. The crunch came in Kabul on 27 December. While some accounts (e.g., Dobbs, 1996: 18–19) paint Amin as craving Soviet assistance, his relocation from the Arg to the Tajbeg Palace in southern Kabul – almost as far from Kabul airport as one can go without actually leaving the city – suggests otherwise. It was there that he met his end. The elimination of Amin ('Operation AGAT') was the responsibility of Department 8 of Directorate S of the First Chief Directorate of the KGB. The Head of Department 8, Vladimir Krasovskii, and of Directorate S, Vadim V. Kirpichenko, flew to Kabul to supervise the operation, which was under the direct control of Krasovskii's deputy, A. I. Lazarenko. According to Kirpichenko, Ambassador Tabeev was not informed in advance of the operation to eliminate Amin. The assault group which stormed the Tajbeg Palace was led by Colonel Grigorii Boiarinov, who was killed by forces loyal to Amin (Andrew and Mitrokhin, 1999: 389–91), but it succeeded in killing Amin and a number of his relatives who were with him at the time. At about the time that this was happening, an explosion knocked out the Kabul telephone system, and at 8.45 p.m., a radio station in the USSR, transmitting on the same frequency as Radio Kabul, overpowered its signal and broadcast a recording in which Babrak Karmal announced the overthrow of Amin. In this there was a rich irony, for during his March negotiations with Kosygin, Taraki had requested 'a large radio station, which would allow us to broadcast propaganda throughout the world' (Hershberg, 1996–1997: 149). At a Politburo session two days later, Leonid Zamiatin, Head of the International Information Department of the Party Secretariat, had tabled proposals 'to redirect a booster transmitter with a strength of 1000 kilowatts which is located close to Dushanbe near the border with Afghanistan' (Hershberg, 1996–1997: 151). One doubts whether Taraki foresaw all the possible uses of such a transmitter.

The disastrous plunge into the Afghan quagmire was driven by a number of different factors, which reinforced each other. First, the decision-making process lacked the checks and balances necessary to avert looming catastrophe. Experts were not properly consulted (Bogomolov, 1988), and the Soviet professional military, even if they were wary of involvement as many now maintain, were not prepared to risk charges of Bonapartism by challenging the party leadership (Bradsher, 1999: 83–4). The distaste that the leadership felt for Amin after the murder of Taraki overwhelmed the wisdom which Kosygin had reflected during the March negotiations, and Kosygin was himself too ill by late 1979 to offer a steadying hand. Second, the leadership carried a heavy burden of historical memory. Andropov was described as having a 'Hungarian complex' which disinclined him to accept the overthrow of a socialist regime. Following the Soviet invasion of Czechoslovakia in August 1968, the Brezhnev Doctrine had asserted the common responsibility of the socialist states to counter threats to socialism in any one state of the socialist community, a term which the USSR had applied to Afghanistan in May 1979 (Arnold, 1983: 84–5; see also Jones, 1990). For figures such as Gromyko, Ponomarev, and party ideologist Mikhail A. Suslov, such considerations may have tipped the balance of calculations otherwise based on interest. Third, the Soviet Union was much more concerned with developments in the so-called 'Third World' than is often now remembered. The Khrushchevian model of the world which co-located socialist and developing countries had triggered extensive theoretical debate (see Papp, 1985; Hough, 1986; Allison, 1988), and prompted figures such as Ponomarev's right-hand man for the Third World, R. A. Ul'ianovskii, to assert that there was 'no country that would not be ripe for socialism' (Kornienko, 1993: 108). But fourth, the Soviet leadership had little understanding of the likely Afghan reaction. Hungary and Czechoslovakia were poor precedents, since their social and political structures differed radically from those in Afghanistan. By the time the Soviets invaded Afghanistan, the peoples of Afghanistan were on the verge of being thoroughly aroused, and it was this challenge with which Soviet strategy and tactics were to prove inadequate to cope.

2

Soviet Strategy, Tactics, and Dilemmas

Having opted to inject its armed forces into a somewhat unpromising theatre of operations, the Soviet leadership was immediately confronted with a number of choices relating to the strategy to be pursued in Afghanistan, and to the military tactics which would best further that strategy. Many of the most important of these decisions were left to the Soviet military to take. In Chapters 4 and 5, I will discuss in more detail the most important specific operations in which the Soviets engaged, setting these in the context of the politics of the times. The aim of this chapter is to introduce the reader to the Soviet armed forces, and to examine in some detail the general types of strategic objectives and tactical approaches which the Soviets pursued. First, I give a brief sketch of the Soviet military. Second, I examine key dimensions of Soviet military strategy, both at a theoretical level, and in terms of the broad objectives of the Afghanistan commitment. Third, I outline briefly the different tactical approaches which the Soviet military adopted in Afghanistan. Finally, I set out four major challenges which the Soviets confronted in Afghanistan, and which they ultimately found it either difficult or impossible to meet.

The Soviet armed forces

Some history

In one sense, the Soviet armed forces (*Vooruzhennye sily SSSR*) could trace their history back to the detachments of Red Guards which helped seize the Winter Palace in Saint Petersburg during the 1917 October Revolution, but for practical purposes their origins were much more recent. The 1921 uprising of sailors of the Kronstadt garrison killed off the Party's enthusiasm for revolutionary sentiment within the military, and the charge of 'Bonapartism' – seeking to rise to political heights through military achievements – was a potent means of discrediting opponents. The Great Purges of the 1930s wiped out vital components of the officer corps, notably the distinguished revolutionary soldier Marshal Tukhachevskii, and set the scene for the emergence of those commanders who were to serve with such prowess from the German invasion of the USSR in June 1941 to the Soviet occupation of Berlin in April 1945, most famously Marshal Georgii Zhukov. However, as Zhukov was himself to discover in October 1957, when he was unceremoniously retired as Defence Minister to make way for Khrushchev's associate Marshal Rodion Malinovskii (see Colton, 1979: 175–95), it did not pay for a soldier to become too powerful. At the time of the invasion of Afghanistan, the Defence Minister came from a *party* background; and the Chief of the General Staff was Marshal Nikolai Ogarkov, who had held the position since January 1977, and according to a careful observer was 'an outstanding military intellectual and theorist' (Herspring, 1990: 126). Notably, however, he did *not* have a career path which had led him through the 'line branches' of the Soviet military, and as a result, there was little risk that he could draw on networks of patronage of a kind that could permit him to challenge the political leadership in a crisis. As far as Afghanistan was concerned, Ogarkov proved no obstacle to the execution of the invasion decision, even though there is some evidence that he was personally opposed to it (Odom, 1998: 460–1).

Within the USSR, the instruments of state propaganda were extensively used to promote the image and reputation of the armed forces. To some, this was a significant dimension of Soviet 'militarism' (Pipes, 1980), but it can be argued that the objective of such propaganda was actually somewhat more subtle than such terminology would suggest. Undoubtedly, the projection of an image of the armed forces as fulfilling a 'sacred duty' (*sviashennyi dolg*) could help to legitimate particular steps which the leadership took using the military as tool. However, powerful and respected armed forces helped both at home and abroad to consolidate the image of the USSR as a powerful and respected state. In this sense, the performance of the Soviet military significantly impacted upon the way in which the Soviet system would be viewed. Military failure could have important wider ramifications, even if the theatre of operations in which failure occurred was not fundamentally important in terms of the USSR's basic interests.

The structure and functioning of the Soviet armed forces

The Soviet armed forces consisted of a number of different elements, varying significantly in scale. At the time of the Soviet invasion of Afghanistan, it was almost two decades since the size of the armed forces had been officially disclosed, but according to the International Institute for Strategic Studies in its publication *The Military Balance 1979–1980,* the armed forces totalled 3,658,000 persons, with the Army accounting for 1,850,000 and the Air Force 475,000. The personnel of the Army were organized into 47 tank divisions, 118 motorized rifle divisions, and 8 airborne divisions. Of these 173 divisions, 31 were deployed in Eastern Europe, 66 in the European part of the USSR, 6 in the central part of the USSR, 24 in the southern part of the USSR, and 46 broadly on the Sino–Soviet border (IISS, 1979: 9–10). Not all divisions were necessarily manned to the same degree of strength, or equally well equipped. These figures should be regarded as somewhat conservative: different methodologies of estimation delivered higher numbers (see Miller, 1988). The USSR itself was divided into 16 'Military Districts', of which that adjacent to Afghanistan was the Turkestan Military District.

The Soviet armed forces were heavily dependent upon conscription in order to provide troops at lower levels. Conscripts made up 70 per cent to 75 per cent of the forces' manpower, with conscripts serving two years in the Army from the age of 18. The commissioned and senior non-commissioned officers of the Army were drawn from the ranks of career and re-enlisted soldiers. While all modern militaries are hierarchical in structure, the Soviet military was particularly so. Where this surfaced most painfully was in the phenomenon of *dedovshchina,* or savage abuse of first-year recruits by second-year recruits (see Holloway, 1989–1990: 14–15; Brown, 1992; Odom, 1998: 286–9), which may have been a contributing factor in the 800-odd suicides each year among servicemen (cited in Solnick, 1998: 185). Yet paradoxically, this also corrupted the authority of officers, since many officers were reluctant to confront the practice lest they be held to account for an unusually large number of disciplinary offences among their subordinates. This was a deep structural sickness which a conflict such as the Afghan could only aggravate, and helps explain the abominable behaviour and routine violation of the laws of armed conflict on the part of the Soviet occupation force. If the conscripts represented the lowest order of the Soviet military, the military elite came in two forms. On the one hand was the High Command, which derived its elite status from hierarchical location. On the other were the Special Purpose Forces (*Voiska spetsial'nogo naznacheniia*) or

Spetsnaz, which derived their status from the nature of their tasks, and their connection with the Soviet military intelligence service (*Glavnoe razvedyvatel'noe upravlenie* or GRU). They were to play a number of significant roles in Afghanistan (Gromov, 1994: 198–205).

Ethnicity was to prove the source of a different array of tensions. Given the multiethnic character of the Soviet Union itself, it was inevitable that the Soviet armed forces would also be ethnically diverse. The 'high technology' services were dominated by Slavs, with non-Slavic groups concentrated in the ground forces, many of them in construction battalions (Wimbush, 1985: 232–3). In the ground forces, problems could arise because of language: non-Russian conscripts might speak Russian only poorly, if at all. This certainly fuelled anti-minority sentiment from members of the Slavic majority; Slav soldiers commonly used racist epithets to describe their Central Asian colleagues, and in Afghanistan, these tensions became acute (Daugherty, 1995). Furthermore, the relatively high birth rate among Central Asian Muslims was argued by some to confront the Soviet armed forces with two interconnected problems: 'the language problem and the patriotism problem' (Rakowska-Harmstone, 1990: 79). There is anecdotal evidence pointing to fraternization between the Afghan population and Soviet soldiers of Central Asian background during the early months of 1980 (Wimbush, 1985: 242; Sarin and Dvoretsky, 1993: 88); however, whether the subsequent replacement of some of these Central Asians with Slavs was a conscious move to maintain the political cohesion of the force, or simply a routine replacement of reservists after their 90-day period of active duty came to an end (Jones, 1985: 208), remains in doubt.

Political control of the military had always been a matter of concern to the party elite, and the device for ensuring it was the Main Political Directorate of the armed forces. At the time of the invasion of Afghanistan, it was headed by General Aleksei A. Epishev, who had been its head since May 1962. Epishev, despite his military title, was not a line professional. He had served as Deputy Minister of State Security under Stalin, and then served in turn as First Secretary of the Odessa Party Committee, Soviet Ambassador to Roumania, and Soviet Ambassador to Yugoslavia. The Main Political Directorate, which was responsible to the party Central Committee, comprised a hierarchy of staff honeycombed through the military, in much the same way as the Party existed at workplace level in civilian enterprises. Political officers were tasked with maintaining morale and ideological commitment, through indoctrination, criticism and self-criticism, and maintaining an atmosphere of activity and flux to keep the military on their toes (Kolkowicz, 1967: 84–98). The context of all this activity, of course, was a formal commitment to the ideology of Marxism-Leninism. Any erosion in this was likely to fuel a crisis of faith at different levels of the military.

Soviet strategy

Strategy, according to Colin S. Gray, is 'the use that is made of force and the threat of force for the ends of policy' (Gray, 1999: 17). Strategy in this sense obviously requires that there be a policy-making process which is capable of generating meaningful ends and objectives. However, the precise dimensions of such a process will vary from state to state and actor to actor. In particular, the strategy pursued by the Soviet Union in Afghanistan was in part a product of long-term ideology, culture, and interests, but more a product of improvisation. The Soviet Union was well equipped with doctrine to govern its behaviour in the event of a thermonuclear or a large conventional interstate war, and Odom has argued that 'only the official ideology provided an adequate rationale for the whole of the Soviet force structure' (Odom, 1998: 14). MccGwire, in a controversial study, has argued that a careful analysis of Soviet doctrine pointed to a shift in the mid-1960s and a further shift in the mid-1970s, with the avoidance of the nuclear devastation of Russia acquiring key importance (MccGwire, 1987: 44). What is most striking from these studies, however, is that the USSR's counter-insurgency doctrine was strangely impoverished (McMichael, 1991: 38–44; Van Dyke, 1996). In no small part this was because classical Marxism found it difficult to come to terms with identities other than those grounded in class. Apart from the civil war of 1918–1920, and the Basmachi rebellion of the 1920s to 1930s, the experiences of the Soviet military and civilian leaders had largely been of conventional interstate war or planning for it, and the Soviet Union in the late 1970s was simply too vast a state to be threatened in any meaningful sense by an insurgency on its territory; it is striking that the post-Soviet crises in Chechnya (see Lieven, 1998) did not create an existential threat to the USSR's Russian successor. As a result, counter-insurgency activity received very little attention at the Voroshilov General Staff Academy (Wardak, 1989), and field commanders were likely to pursue inappropriate courses of action, with inappropriately organized forces. It was only in 1983 that the Soviet forces of the 40th Army developed a properly integrated counter-insurgency force with decentralized command and 'non-linear' tactics based on 'independent operations conducted at the brigade and battalion level' (Van Dyke, 1996: 693).

Strategic objectives

The Soviet invasion force consisted of a mixture of Airborne and Motorized Infantry personnel, totalling approximately 85,000 troops, and was labelled the '40th Army'. Official sources referred to it as a 'limited contingent' (*ogranichennyi kontingent*). The force was not one specially crafted to fit the situation in Afghanistan. Rather, it reflected what could rapidly be mustered for the purpose of the invasion, and for the immediate objectives of securing the capital, key military bases, and main roads. These objectives – largely *short term* in nature – in turn became the policy objectives around which Soviet strategy was built. The defeatist nature of such an approach is almost immediately obvious. Instead of fostering an expansion of the territorial control of a threatened regime, it emphasized hanging on grimly to a few core assets. However, this was not how it appeared to the Soviet leadership at the time, or to the Afghan: indeed, according to Sultan Ali Keshtmand, who became Chairman of the Council of Ministers of the Democratic Republic of Afghanistan in June 1981, Karmal stated shortly after the invasion that he expected Soviet forces to remain in Afghanistan for only six months (Halliday, 1999: 680).

If the Soviet leadership had one overriding policy objective in sending forces into Afghanistan, it was to revitalize a failing regime of Marxist orientation. Measures directed at advancing this end figured prominently in the discussions which KGB Chief Andropov had with Karmal and his associates in Afghanistan in early 1980. On 7 February 1980, he reported to the Politburo that he 'particularly stressed the necessity of establishing genuine party unity, heightening of the military readiness of the army, strengthening relations of the party and government with the masses, instituting normal economic life in the country and activizing the foreign policy activities of Afghanistan in accordance with the demands of the situation' (Hershberg, 1996–1997: 165–6). The role of Soviet troops was clearly set out in a 7 April 1980 report to the Politburo from Gromyko, Andropov, Ustinov, and party official Vadim Zagladin. The report defined their tasks as 'defending the revolutionary regime in the DRA [Democratic Republic of Afghanistan], defending the country from external threats, including sealing off the borders of the country together with the Afghan forces, ensuring the safety of the major centers and communications, and also building up and strengthening the combat readiness of the Afghan armed forces'. The report continued: 'Only when the situation in Afghanistan stabilizes, and the situation around the country improves, and only upon a request of the DRA leadership, may we consider the question of the eventual withdrawal of our troops from the DRA' (Hershberg, 1996–1997: 171).

Securing centres of political importance was an obvious objective from the moment of the invasion. Of greatest importance was Kabul. Capital cities are not necessarily of fundamental military or economic importance, but their significance as a matter of political symbolism is profound. The fall of Berlin in 1945, the fall of Peking in 1949, and the fall of Saigon in 1975 all brought major conflicts to a close. Thus, the securing of Kabul was of indisputable importance. However, other urban centres were also vital to control: Herat, which had already been the source of much heartache, along with Kandahar, Jalalabad, and Mazar-e Sharif. Despite the existence of airports in all these cities, the main-tenance of control over them effectively required the control of the roads connecting them as well. By the 1970s, Afghanistan had 1,553 miles of paved road, and a further 10,750 miles of 'other motorable roads' (Ispahani, 1989: 127). A vast, if incomplete, 'ring road' linked Herat, Kandahar, Kabul, and Mazar-e Sharif, with the Salang Tunnel cutting through the Hindu Kush to the north of Kabul between Charikar and Pul-e Khumri. Important side-roads linked Kabul to the Khyber Pass and Pakistan via Jalalabad, Kandahar to the Chaman Pass and Pakistan via Spin Baldak, and Mazar-e Sharif to the Soviet Union via Hairatan (see Cordesman and Wagner, 1990: 106–7). To protect these roads, and the traffic moving along them, was a large and complex task, but one of enormous importance.

Turning the Afghan Army into a fighting force on behalf of the regime was an equally large and complex task. The armed forces were certainly supplied with a great deal of equipment (much of it inappropriate, as things turned out, to the needs of counter-insurgency), but their problems of personnel and morale proved intractable. In highly institutionalized political systems, a framework of rules exists to ensure the obedience of those conscripted for military service. In a fluid situation such as that in Afghanistan after the Soviet invasion, mechanisms of rule-application tend to break down, and evasion of conscription becomes a realistic option. Where a nation stands united behind a cause, this is less of a problem: volunteers can be trusted to replenish the Army's manpower. However, where a regime's reservoirs of legitimacy are low, the result is likely to be a crisis of military efficiency. Halliday and Tanin rightly conclude that the Soviet invasion 'greatly weakened the armed forces' (Halliday and Tanin, 1998: 1364). Giustozzi's analysis suggests a reason for this: 'to the ordinary Afghan it was difficult to imagine why he should fight for a Revolution which had only meant trouble for him and his fam-ily' (Giustozzi, 2000: 108). As is commonly the case where regimes are unpopular and mechanisms of control are feeble, 'ghost pay-rolling' reportedly occurred (Giustozzi, 2000: 93), casting doubt on the veracity of official figures as to troop strength. Beyond this, the Afghan armed forces continued to be plagued by *Khalq-Parcham* rivalry, and while Karmal was a *Parchami*, a purge of the *Khalq* members was not a realistic option, since it would have left too large a hole in the officer corps. All in all, the task of putting in place a viable regime, so deceptively straightforward on paper, proved in practice to be a nightmare.

Andropov's concern for 'strengthening relations of the party and government with the masses' was ostensibly well judged, and in other circumstances would have described a fruitful path for the Soviets and the Karmal regime to follow. However, there was a deep tension between, on the one hand, the pursuit of such an approach by the regime, and on the other, the regime's dependence upon Soviet military support. The Soviet military was trained to be a *coercive* force, and used coercion to entrench Karmal's position. Yet the more it did so, the more it compromised Karmal's ability to exercise legitimate domination, since what it won for him was merely prudentially based compliance. This was a poor substitute for genuine popular support. As the events of 1989 were to reveal, the ruling regimes in the Warsaw Pact states of Eastern Europe survived because local populations feared Soviet military power, and once the threat of its use eroded to the point that it was no longer credible, the regimes fell rapidly in the face of genuine popular revulsion (Kuran, 1995: 261–88). At heart, Andropov had no real understanding of the bases of genuine normative support. No Soviet politician until the advent as General Secretary of Mikhail Gorbachev in 1985 was willing to face the challenge of public opinion, and Andropov, as Head of the KGB, was specifically charged with thwarting any outbursts of spontaneous political judgement on the part of the masses.

Soviet tactics

If Soviet strategy suffered from the intractable nature of the political situation in Afghanistan, so too did Soviet combat tactics, for 'success' in terms of immediate tactical objectives contributed to 'failure' in the wider political sense. This reflected the inability of Soviet field commanders to use their resources in a nuanced fashion. If the USA found it difficult to mount a 'hearts and minds' campaign in Vietnam, the Soviets failed in their attempts to do so in rural Afghanistan, largely because the nature of their field operations besmirched them in the eyes of ordinary Afghans. The following remarks are not intended to be comprehensive, but rather to highlight key elements of the Soviets' tactical approaches.

Infantry

Infantry – the classic formation of ground troops armed with 5.44 mm AK-74 rifles or similar firearms – formed the backbone of the Soviet contingent in Afghanistan, but initially suffered from three problems. The first was a lack of combat training: many young conscripts were expected to learn 'on the job' how to take part in military operations (Cordesman and Wagner, 1990: 135). The second was that illness frequently left infantry groups undermanned, to the point where their military effectiveness was severely compromised. The third, and most serious, was that their tactics, as Grau has neatly put it, were geared to 'a theater war against a modern enemy who would obligingly occupy defensive positions stretching across the northern European plain' (Grau, 1998: 201). In the early years of the war, major infantry sweeps were conducted, as we shall shortly see, but they did not deliver 'control' of the countryside in a meaningful sense: on the contrary, 'control' tended to revert to anti-regime forces with alarming speed once the Soviet infantry moved to a new destination. In 1983, significant changes were effected in the organization of counter-insurgency operations: 'Rather than drive the *mujahedin* from the countryside, the Soviets elected to drive off the population' (McMichael, 1991: 51). However, this was the diametric opposite of a 'hearts and minds' approach, and thus constituted a dead-end from a political perspective. Furthermore, infantry operations are vulnerable if not reinforced by appropriate armoured and aerial support. In Afghanistan, this was by no means always available, and as a result, the Soviet force suffered many avoidable casualties. It is not surprising that as the war went on, infantry became heavily involved in the defence of outposts and communications lines, which involved 35 per cent of the Soviet forces (Sarin and Dvoretsky, 1993: 92), and in the exercise of control in urban areas. Each was a thankless task.

Armour

Visiting Afghanistan even years after the Soviet withdrawal reminds one of the role which armour played during the war. Wrecked tanks and armoured personnel carriers litter the countryside, providing scrap metal for enterprising Afghans. The mainstays of Soviet armour in Afghanistan were the T-55, T-62, and T-72 tanks; the BMP-2 (*Boevaia mashina pekhoty*), a tracked vehicle; and the BTR-70 and BTR-80 (*Bronetransporter*), a wheeled vehicle. BMPs were highly vulnerable to rocket-propelled grenades because they were so packed with fuel and ammunition. Afghanistan's stark terrain militated against the use of massed tanks, and armour was instead used for convoy escort purposes, and to spearhead combined operations (Isby, 1989: 68–9). In what came to be known as the '*bronegruppa* concept', it proved feasible 'to use the firepower of the personnel carriers in an independent reserve once the motorized rifle soldiers had dismounted' (Grau, 1998: 203). This was probably the most notable Soviet innovation in the area of armour. Vehicles were also used to move troops, but the desire to keep troops and their transport together initially hampered *infantry* operations, given the obstacles to vehicle mobility posed by the terrain. Here, there was a need for a greater volume of air assets to complement infantry operations. However, air assets in sufficient supply were not forthcoming.

Tactical airpower

Air assets, both fixed-wing aircraft and helicopters, were used by Soviet forces to lethal effect in Afghanistan, although rarely in such a way as to advance the USSR's political objectives. While aircraft were used extensively for resupply purposes in Afghanistan, and for bombardments to depopulate important rural areas, their main use was in support of ground operations. The main helicopters used were Mi-24 ('Hinds'), which carried four anti-tank missiles, had a maximum speed of 275 km/h, and a 300 km range. With a crew of two, they could carry 8–10 troops. Fixed-wing aircraft came in different forms; while Tu-16 and Su-24 bombers operated from bases in the USSR itself, MiG-23/27 ('Flogger') and Su-25 ('Frogfoot') aircraft were deployed in Afghanistan from 1980. As McMichael puts it: 'Attack aircraft were used most often for planned strikes against clearly identified targets, while helicopters performed the majority of on-call strikes' (McMichael, 1991: 83). Directed against the civilian population, these assets proved lethally effective; they were somewhat less effective against smaller resistance groups. The main problem was shortage of assets. Grau concludes that 'the Soviet Army never brought in enough helicopters and air assault forces to perform all the necessary missions', and that 'airborne and air assault forces were usually understrength' (Grau, 1998: 203–4). Furthermore, from late 1986, the supply of Stinger missiles to the Afghan resistance forced Soviet aircraft to take evasive actions which to a degree compromised their military effectiveness.

Spetsnaz forces and sabotage

The expanded use of Spetsnaz forces in Afghanistan marked an important turning point. With the increased use of Spetsnaz forces, the

USSR moved towards overcoming one of its greatest weaknesses, namely the limited autonomy granted to relatively small groups of troops in a theatre of operations in which flexibility and local initiative were vital (Urban, 1990: 65). They formed the core of a more specialized counter-insurgency force, which, comprising not only Spetsnaz but also airborne, air assault, and designated reconnaissance troops, came to total between 15 per cent and 20 per cent of the force. Two brigades, with eight distinct Spetsnaz battalions, were deployed in Afghanistan, and each battalion had its own zone of responsibility. In Spring 1985, Spetsnaz forces were deployed along the Afghanistan–Pakistan border with a view to attempting to close it; more than 60 per cent of Afghanistan's borders with Pakistan fell under Spetsnaz control (Gromov, 1994: 199). The Spetsnaz forces were better equipped and trained than their regular counterparts. However, they also suffered their losses, and Gromov recalled three occasions on which Spetsnaz groups were completely wiped out by resistance groups (Gromov, 1994: 203), usually because of isolation from armour or air cover. On occasion, too, the benefits of surprise were lost, with Spetsnaz forces inserted only after a period of bombing and reconnaissance. This may have minimized casualties on the Soviet side, but it also allowed the most accomplished resistance forces to make good their escape (Grau, 1998: 59). In addition, Spetsnaz operations were on occasion complicated by acute tensions between Spetsnaz soldiers and regular infantry officers (Schofield, 1993: 99–104).

Scorched earth

When Soviet forces opted 'to drive off the population', they set about doing it in some of the most barbarous ways one could imagine (Maley, 1991b). A British journalist, visiting the ravished countryside, remarked that it was as if someone had dropped a bomb in the Garden of Eden (Bell, 1987). Mud-brick buildings, of the kind which predominate in Afghan villages, were no match for aerial bombardment, rockets, and artillery. In addition, abundant testimony emerged as to the atrocities committed by the occupation force (Laber and Rubin, 1988). It is worth noting here that these tactics involved major violations of international humanitarian law; and arguably genocide (Fein, 1993). In an argument which has not been seriously contested, Reisman and Silk (1988) maintained that the Afghanistan conflict was covered by the entirety of the First, Third, and Fourth Geneva Conventions of 1949, which Afghanistan had ratified on 26 September 1956, and not simply by the more limited 'Common Article 3' which applies to armed conflict 'not of an international character'. However, it is equally clear that even the provisions of Common Article 3 were routinely violated by Soviet forces. As one of countless examples, one might note the experience of a woman from the vicinity of Mazar-e Sharif who reported an encounter with a Soviet search party in August 1985: 'They asked me if I knew where the *mojahedin* were hiding. I had my little boy in my arms. I said I didn't know. So they took a *kalashnikov* and just shot my little boy in front of me' (Barry, Lagerfelt, and Terrenoire, 1986: 95). Such tactics advanced the short-term objective of clearing territory, but did nothing to establish an independently sustainable basis for regime authority. After the Soviet withdrawal, a courageous Soviet journalist called upon Soviet authorities to 'punish the guilty to clear ourselves of the filth' (Batkin, 1989). Instead, the USSR Supreme Soviet issued an amnesty for crimes committed in Afghanistan (USSR Supreme Soviet, 1989).

Mine warfare

Mines played a significant role in the Soviet Union's military tactics, as Afghanistan's grim legacy of minefields bears witness. A mine is a munition placed under, on, or near the ground or other surface area which is designed to be exploded by the presence, proximity, or contact of a person or vehicle. 'Blast' mines cause damage through the expansion of heated gases, while 'fragmentation' mines injure through the dispersal of shrapnel. Anti-tank mines were used extensively in Europe and North Africa during the Second World War, with anti-personnel mines serving to prevent the ready removal of anti-tank mines by sappers. More generally, Banerjee (1997) has pointed to six different types of minefield: defensive ('to prevent an easy breakthrough by enemy armour'); tactical ('to channel and direct the move of enemy's attacking armour'); border ('to prevent infiltration by hostile groups'); dummy ('to provide a sense of deterrence'); nuisance ('during a withdrawal'); and protective ('to provide immediate close protection to a defensive position'). Soviet forces mined remote areas to prevent their being used as secondary routes of movement by the resistance; they also mined the verges of major roads, and lands in the vicinity of significant outposts, as well as near major headquarters such as the Tajbeg Palace, captured during the operation to eliminate Hafizullah Amin in 1979. Of the Soviet mines used in Afghanistan, the remote-delivered PFM-1 and PFM-1s ('Butterfly') mines won particular notoriety, because they were frequently mistaken for toys by children who then suffered the consequences. The PMD-6, PMN, and PMN-2 blast mines were also used; as were the OZM-3, OZM-4, and OZM-72 bounding fragmentation mines; the POMZ-2, POMZ-2m, and POM-2s fragmentation mines; and a range of anti-tank blast mines. There is no reliable estimate of the total number of mines in Afghanistan, as mine action agencies are interested in clearing mine *fields*, which can disrupt community life irre-spective of the total number of mines which they contain (Maley, 1998a). The 1993 *National Survey of Mines Situation in Afghanistan* identified 2,353 minefields, occupying 388.75 square kilometres (MCPA, 1993), but further research has identified even more.

Intelligence and communications

Intelligence lies at the heart of effective military operations, although it cannot compensate for low morale or poor tactical execution. Information to facilitate military operations was gathered in a number of different ways. Helicopters were of course used for reconnaissance purposes (McMichael, 1991: 84). However, once it became necessary to collect more detailed 'human intelligence' (HUMINT), the Soviet force ran into difficulties, largely because of its dependence on instrumentalities of the Afghan regime, although these improved over time as the regime's secret police, KhAD, became more effectively consolidated with KGB sup-port. The USSR also established four 'signals intelligence' (SIGINT) in Afghanistan: near Kabul, in Herat, at Garmushki near the Iranian border, and in Qasideh in the Wakhan corridor (Ball, 1989: 30). However, the two latter stations were focused on Iranian, Chinese, and Pakistani military signals (Richelson, 1986: 101), and the resistance in Afghanistan tended to use human messengers and made limited use of radios (Cordesman and Wagner, 1990: 123) which denied to the sophisticated Soviet SIGINT capability a signal to trace. The USSR's own radio communications in Afghanistan left much to be desired. Radio sets issued to troops in the field tended to have limited ranges, and coped poorly with mountain-ous terrain. However, procedures were also cumbersome and inefficient, prompting an observer to issue the following scathing assessment: 'One cannot help but conclude that the widespread deficiencies in tactical com-munications are fully reflective of endemic Soviet inflexibility, lack of imagination, compartmentalisation of even basic technical skills to spe-cialists, and reluctance to depart from rote, textbook procedures, even when they don't work' (McMichael, 1991: 103).

Operational relations with the Afghan Army

Finally, if the USSR hoped to engage in an 'Afghanization' programme, its objectives were thwarted by the weaknesses of its Afghan allies in both political and military spheres. I have already noted the scale of the problems involved in turning the Afghan Army into a fighting force. Here, I would simply add that this had direct implications at the operational level as well. The Afghan Army was 'riddled with inform-ers' (McMichael, 1991: 107), and Soviet soldiers often spoke scornfully of their Afghan counterparts as *obez'iany* or 'monkeys' (Schofield, 1993: 88). However, for political reasons it was deemed necessary to incorporate Afghan Army personnel in all major operations. This cre-ated understandable tensions: 'If all or part of a unit planned to defect, the first action normally taken was to shoot the Soviet adviser, if one was present' (McMichael, 1991: 46). Over time, the capacities of the Army improved, but never to the point where it was an equal partner with the Soviet force: the relationship was inevitably one of superior and subordinate.

Soviet dilemmas

The Soviet Union faced four major dilemmas as a result of its commit-ment in Afghanistan. These dilemmas combined to create a situation which at best required dextrous political management, of a kind for which the regime was not noted in the later Brezhnev era, and at worst had the potential to corrode the legitimacy of the regime, if not at the mass level then at least in the eyes of up-and-coming cadres.

The first dilemma arose from the domestic unpopularity of the war in the USSR. This factor has often been overlooked. The effectiveness of the KGB at the time of the invasion made 'public opinion' seem an irrelevant constraint, and critics of the invasion such as the physicist Andrei Sakharov were silenced, either by internal exile (in Sakharov's case to the 'closed' city of Gorkii) or more brutal means. Furthermore, at the relevant times, gauging mass attitudes was a far from straightfor-ward task. However, even in highly autocratic systems, significant public disaffection can either constrain, or come to constrain, the options which political leaders can exercise. Attitudes towards the war in Afghanistan served to prompt both wider political changes, and then a reconsideration of the wisdom of the commitment itself. In 1984, human rights activists in Moscow conducted a 'poll', reported in the emigré journal *Strana i mir*, which concluded that 62 per cent of respondents did not support the war, and 41 per cent of Communist Party members in the sample did not either (US State Department, 1985). A June 1985 report from Radio Free Europe/Radio Liberty suggested that only one quarter of the Soviet adult urban population approved of Soviet policy or expressed 'confidence in the eventual success of official policy' (RFE/RL, 1985: 1). And the advent of candour in the Soviet media from 1986, combined with the withdrawal of Soviet troops from Afghanistan by February 1989, permitted much sharper expressions of opinion, although doubtless shaped in part by criticisms of the policy emanating from the political elite, and by the benefit of hindsight. Thus in a March 1991 survey conducted by the All-Union Centre for the Study of Social Opinion (*Vsesoiuznyi tsentr izucheniia obshchestvennogo mneniia*, or VTsIOM), 89 per cent of respondents stated it was 'not necessary' to have sent Soviet forces to Afghanistan in December 1979, while 71 per cent agreed with those who described the despatch of Soviet forces to Afghanistan as a 'state crime' (VTsIOM, 1991: 25–6). These figures can do no more than give a taste of what opinion was at the time, but they strongly suggest that there was simply not the mood to support a prolonged war, a mood of the kind which, for example, sustained Britain during the darkest days of the struggle against Hitler. In this context, it is notable that the Soviet media in the early years of the war, far from using Afghanistan as a platform for the promotion of patriotic fervour, said as little about it as they could (Broxup, 1988).

Managing the human and material costs of the war for the USSR constituted Moscow's second dilemma. Figures supplied to Gorbachev in January 1988 by the Chairman of the Soviet Council of Ministers pointed to mounting average daily expenditure: 4.3 million roubles in 1984, 7.2 million in 1985, 10.0 million in 1986, and 14.7 million in 1987 (Ostermann, 2003–2004: 256). Foreign Minister Shevardnadze in a speech to the 27th Party Congress in July 1990 stated the costs of the war as 60 billion roubles, excluding 'human casualties and other suffering' (BBC *Summary of World Broadcasts* SU/0808/C1/15, 5 July 1990). But even material costs of the war defy ready calculation. The mysteries of the Soviet military budget, together with the difficulty of converting into Western currencies sums expressed in Soviet roubles, and the problem of deciding what costs should be attributed to the war *itself*, make it positively misleading to attempt to sum up the war's costs in a simple figure. But as to human costs, three points deserve to be made. First, statistics published after the withdrawal of Soviet forces point to significant mortality. According to one set of figures, between 25 December 1979 and 15 February 1989, 13,833 Soviet soldiers were killed or died of wounds or illness. Of these, 1979 were officers. Of the 49,985 wounded, 7,132 were officers. Some 6,669 became invalids (Liakhovskii and Zabrodin, 1991: 213). These losses were not evenly spread through Soviet society: as

Odom observes, those families 'with more income and better social positions were better able to keep their sons from being sent to Afghanistan' (Odom, 1998: 247). To these figures should be added the remarkable total of those who fell ill in Afghanistan: 404,414 (Odom, 1998: 249). Second, the dead tended to be very young: 8,655 of the Soviet war dead, or 62.6 per cent, were under 20 years old (Liakhovskii and Zabrodin, 1991: 215). They came to be known as *tsinkovye mal'chiki*, or 'Zinky Boys', from the zinc lining of the coffins in which their remains were returned to the USSR. Svetlana Alexievich has provided a moving and poignant account of the grief which these deaths caused to the families of the dead, and a useful reminder of what a tragedy the war was to be for large numbers of ordinary families north of Afghanistan's border (Alexievich, 1992). Third, the USSR was left with a burden of embittered and disgruntled war veterans (*afgantsy*), whom one author described as 'disempowered plebeians of the Soviet social order' (Galeotti, 1995: 45). The social costs of dealing with the problems of the veterans continues to emburden the states which emerged following the disintegration of the Soviet Union in late 1991.

The third and fourth dilemmas I have already noted, and simply reiterate for the sake of completeness: the narrow support base of the Karmal regime posed a fundamental political challenge to the Soviet leadership from the moment of the invasion, while the propensity of resistance to intensify as a result of the regime's dependence upon Soviet backing limited the USSR's options in meeting the challenge. These problems, firmly in Kosygin's mind in March 1979, were forgotten by his colleagues who took the decision to intervene in Afghanistan, and the consequences were to prove devastating. However, neither would have had this effect had there not been networks of Afghans determined to oppose the Soviet presence. It is to the nature of these networks, and to the support which they received from the wider world, that it is necessary now to turn.

3

The Development of Afghan Resistance

If there was one thing predictable following the Soviet invasion, it was that Soviet forces would encounter significant popular resistance. What was unclear was just how significant that resistance would be, how well-organized, how sustainable, how determined. However, there were grounds at the outset for the Soviet leadership to be pessimistic. In his great treatise *On War*, published posthumously in 1832, Carl von Clausewitz had analysed the circumstances under which what he called 'a general uprising' could be effective, and identified five preconditions: that the war 'must be fought in the interior of the country'; that it 'must not be decided by a single stroke'; that the 'theatre of operations must be fairly large'; that the 'national character must be suited to that type of war'; and that the 'country must be rough and inaccessible, because of mountains, or forests, marches, or the local methods of cultivation' (Clausewitz, 1984: 480; see also Smith, 2005: 31–4). The parallels with the situation in Afghanistan in 1980 are almost perfect.

This chapter explores the nature of the Afghan resistance in more detail. It is divided into three sections. The first deals with the character of resistance forces in Afghanistan, and the circumstances which sustained resistance activities. The second section deals with the role played by Pakistan as a pivotal neighbouring state in providing operating bases for some resistance groups, and hospitality for millions of Afghan refugees. The third deals with the wider support which the struggle of the Afghans received from an increasingly engaged world. The Afghan resistance was a complex phenomenon, and its complexity was accentuated by the diverse interests of its different elements, of military circles in Pakistan, and of political leaderships in the Western world, the Middle East, and China. A tragic result of these divergences of interest was that when the Afghan communist regime finally collapsed in 1992, there was

48

no unified group or party capable of exercising legitimate rule throughout Afghanistan's territory. The consequences in terms of Afghan political order remain all too palpable.

Popular mobilization in Afghanistan

Islam as a basis of resistance

Popular resistance to an occupying force is by no means inevitable, and in many cases of foreign occupation, significant elements of the population of the occupied country have opted either to collaborate – as did many French following the fall of France and the establishment of the Vichy regime – or to remain passive, either because of a lack of interest in politics, or from a desire to move with the currents of prevailing winds. In Afghanistan's case, determined resistance emerged, particularly in rural areas where the writ of the state was weak. Resistance was motivated by a range of factors, including calculations of interest, but the power of Islam as a basis of resistance proved of fundamental importance. Religions can provide a basis for resistance in at least two different ways. On the one hand, religious doctrines and practices may endow certain individuals with *authority*, which they can then use to lead others in a political struggle. On the other hand, religion can serve as an *ideology of resistance*, by providing direct legitimacy to resistance in certain circumstances, even in the absence of authoritative figures to exercise a leadership role. On the whole, the role of 'authoritative religious leaders' was somewhat limited in Afghanistan: Sunni Islam lacks a 'clergy', or indeed a hierarchical leadership, and authoritative figures were thus more to be found in Afghanistan's Shiite minority, and in spiritual Sufi brotherhoods. But as an ideology of resistance, Islam was to prove extraordinarily important.

This ideology was shaped in the crucible of the early Muslim community in the Arabian peninsula, where unbelievers represented a serious threat to the survival of the Prophet and his followers. The term which emerged to describe resistance to such attacks was *jihad*, which can be translated as 'struggle', 'striving', or 'effort' (Lewis, 1988: 72: see also Cook, 2005; Bonner, 2006; Kelsay, 2007). It was this term which Afghan opponents of communist rule routinely used to describe their struggle (in contrast to the Arabic *harb* or the Persian *jang*, both of which literally mean 'war'). From the same Arabic root as jihad were then derived the words *mujahid*, and its plural *mujahideen*, which identify practitioners of jihad. The word 'mujahideen' came to be used as a generic term for the Afghan resistance and its various components. The significance of these designations derives from their moral implications. As Lewis puts it: 'According to Muslim teaching, *jihad* is one of the basic commandments of the faith, an obligation imposed on all Muslims by God, through revelation. In an offensive war, it is an obligation of the Muslim community as a whole (*fard kafiya*); in a defensive war, it becomes a personal obligation of every adult male Muslim (*fard 'ayn*)' (Lewis, 1988: 73). It finds justification in the Holy Qur'an, a verse of which enjoins believers to 'Fight for the sake of Allah those that fight against you, but do not attack them first' (2: 190).

This is not to suggest that Islam's potency as an ideology of resistance leads mechanistically to a community of martially minded believers. Doctrine is flexible and subject to constant reinterpretation, and in any case is only one of a number of sources of individual motivation (Eickelman and Piscatori, 2004). However, the legitimation of action by reference to divine sanction can prove a powerful source of energy and commitment. Stalin's famous question to Churchill during the Second World War – 'How many divisions has the Pope?' – displayed a blindness to the significance of religious commitment which was to cost his successors dearly in Afghanistan. He might better have followed the warning, based on experience, of his colleague Emilian Iaroslavskii, Head of the League of Militant Atheists: 'Religion is like a nail. The more you hit it, the deeper it goes.'

Grassroots resistance and tribal warfare

The Afghan resistance at its outset was basically a grassroots movement. This is frequently overlooked, especially by those whose focus of interest is skewed towards radical groups supported indirectly by the United States which have returned to haunt America in the post-communist era. But the bulk of Afghan Muslims who initially took up arms against the USSR and its clients were not Muslim intellectuals, but practitioners of what one might call 'village Islam', which scorned atheism and defined apostasy as departure from ritual. The Soviets were widely known to be atheists, and this damned them and their associates in the eyes of many Afghan villagers. This distaste for atheism tended to be reinforced by a concern for both the independence of Afghanistan as a political unit, and a desire for personal autonomy which the assertion of state power would compromise, but it was the Soviets' avowed atheism which created a *moral* basis for opposition. It helped turn what were pockets of resistance, albeit substantial ones, into a more full-fledged insurgency, albeit one with its own distinctive rhythm.

Warfare as conducted by these groups took a pre-modern form. Olivier Roy has developed a model of 'traditional warfare' in contradistinction to *jihad*. Traditional warfare involves the personal vendetta writ large; military encounters 'affect everyday life only slightly'; and the objective 'is not to destroy the adversary, but to improve one's relative standing *vis-à-vis* other *qawms* and to establish new social equilibrium'. Traditional warfare 'is a domestic competition between equals'; tribal war 'is neither ideological nor political' (Roy, 1995: 63–5; see also Centlivres, 1997). Elements of such warfare were apparent through the life of the Afghan resistance. As Louis Dupree pointed out, combat had a seasonal character ('Can't farm and fight'): it was necessary for combatants to take time off to plant crops and then to harvest them (Dupree, 1989: 30–1). War was prosecuted by loose networks, often based on norms of reciprocity in a tribal context, rather than trained, organized, professional militaries. This is not to say that one did not find persons with military skills participating in such combat; on the contrary, former Afghan Army conscripts who had returned to their villages after compulsory military service often had some skills which were useful in confronting the Soviet challenge, and managed to achieve some local prominence because of the 'slaughter of the tribal aristocracy' under the Taraki and Amin regimes (Lemercier-Quelquejay and Bennigsen, 1984: 209). In other areas, such as Logar, war brought the local *mulla* (prayer leader) to prominence, often as precursor to the establishment of a repressive local regime (Kakar, 1995: 141–4), of a kind which the Taliban were later to emulate on a nationwide scale.

In contrast to a 'pure' model of traditional warfare, however, the grassroots of the Afghan resistance tended to pursue localized objectives, but on the basis of a deeper and *politicized* value system. This made the resistance difficult to decapitate or coopt. As Jalali and Grau have argued: 'The Mujahideen structure would be difficult to fit into a line-and-block chart and there was never a central leadership that was critical to the cause. Yet this inefficient disunity may have been a strength of the Mujahideen. No matter which commanders or leaders were killed, the Mujahideen effort would continue and the Soviets would never be short of enemies' (Jalali and Grau, n.d.: 401). This difficulty for the Soviets was compounded by their scorched-earth tactics, which helped create a generation of Afghans with nothing left to do but fight, as their property had been destroyed, and their families killed or scattered.

Beyond this, it is perilous to generalize about the grassroots resistance. From the outset of the revolts in summer 1978, significant variations in the behaviour of elements of the resistance could be detected (Shahrani and Canfield, 1984). Groups differed in scale and capacity, in passion and degree of engagement, in the pre-existing solidarity networks on which they built, in terms of the issues which provoked them into action, and even in specific values. While some of these groups had reasonable weaponry – mostly captured in operations against the communists or handed over by defectors – others had little more to use than 'ten-rupee jezails' of the type immortalized by Kipling in his apposite verse 'Arithmetic of the Frontier'. However, as time passed, the shape of the resistance changed as the need for a regular flow of weapons and ammunition drew the grassroots increasingly into contact with other, externally based, resistance groups. This set the scene for future tensions, for while few grassroots groups had a state-building agenda, this was exactly what dominated the thinking of some of the more important external groups with which they were increasingly obliged to align themselves. The military activities of the resistance were also diverse. 'Hit-and-run' operations figured prominently in their tactics: for the most part they wisely eschewed attempts to hold territory, although before 'running' from fixed targets they tended to help themselves to whatever military equipment might have been stored at the outpost or facility under attack. Jalali and Grau (n.d.) divided the resistance's main form of offensive operation into 'ambushes', 'raids', 'shelling attacks', 'mine warfare', and 'blocking enemy lines of communication'. While these activities were not necessarily driven by an overarching strategic vision, their overall purpose was obvious: to make the Soviet presence in Afghanistan costly.

Resistance political parties

Within the Afghan resistance there emerged a number of significant 'parties', based for the most part in Pakistan. Not remotely like modern parties in competitive democracies, some were little more than personalized networks built around religious notables, while others were rigidly hierarchical organizations of Leninist stripe, organizationally if not ideologically, which gave them a certain robustness. Some came into existence as a result of the war. Others were outgrowths of an Islamic political movement which had been developing within circles of the intelligentsia since the time of Zahir Shah. The history of these groups has been well documented (see Roy, 1990: *passim*; Kakar,

1995: 79–95; Olesen, 1995: 274–97; Rubin, 1995a: 196–225; Dorronsoro, 2005: 137–72; Sinno, 2008); here I can only identify those which were for one reason or another to prove politically important. It is important to distinguish between different Sunni Muslim parties, and between Sunni and Shiite parties.

Sunni Mujahideen parties were conventionally divided by commentators between 'moderate' and 'fundamentalist', but the distinction was an unfortunate one (Saikal and Maley, 1991: 62). In the former category were placed three parties broadly sympathetic to the monarchical regime of Zahir Shah, and led by Pushtuns: the *Mahaz-e Milli-i Islami Afghanistan*, led by Sayid Ahmad Gailani, a notable Sufi who had been pir (master or spiritual leader) of the Qadiriyya Sufi brotherhood in Kabul since 1947; *the Jabha-i Milli-i Nijat-e Afghanistan*, led by Sebghatullah Mojadiddi, a well-known member of the Naqshbandiyya Sufi brotherhood who had been imprisoned by Prime Minister Daoud for allegedly plotting to assassinate Nikita Khrushchev; and the *Harakat-e Inqilab-e Islami Afghanistan*, led by Mawlawi Muhammad Nabi Muhammadi, who had been a colourful member of the Wolesi Jirgah during the New Democracy period. Muhammadi's large but loosely structured party attracted many traditional religious figures who were subsequently to support the Taliban (as did Muhammadi himself); this in itself serves as a warning against the too-ready use of expressions such as 'moderate'.

Four parties were classified as fundamentalist. Somewhat confusingly, two went by the name *Hezb-e Islami*, or 'Party of Islam'; one was led by Mawlawi Muhammad Younus Khalis, and the other by Gulbuddin Hekmatyar, the former a Khogiani Pushtun, and the latter a Pushtun from Kunduz. Khalis attracted some powerful field commanders; Hekmatyar attracted support from the Pakistani military, but suspicion from Afghan circles, largely because of his ruthless and uncompromising character (Ahmad, 2004). A small party, the *Ittehad-e Islami Afghanistan*, led by Abdul Rab al-Rasoul Sayyaf, was notable for the financial support it received from Saudi Arabia. Finally, the *Jamiat-e Islami*, led by Burhanuddin Rabbani, a Badakhshi Tajik who had taught in the Faculty of Theology at Kabul University, was a modernist Islamic party, and notably more open than Hekmatyar's party, in which the dictates of the leader were relentlessly enforced.

Among the Shia of Afghanistan, parties tended to be dominated by religious dignitaries, given the greater salience of religious hierarchy among Shiites, and included the *Shura-i Ettefaq* of Ayatullah Beheshti, the *Sazman-e Nasr* of Abdul Ali Mazari, Muhammad Akbari's *Sepah-i Pasdaran*, and the *Harakat-e Islami* of Asif Mohseni. The Shura took shape as a governing body of notables in the period after the communist coup, as the inaccessible Hazarajat region was neglected by forces focusing on the exercise of control over urban areas. It fell victim not so much to internal Afghan developments as to the vicissitudes of politics in neighbouring Iran, always something of an inspiration for some Shia in the Hazarajat. The acute tensions between different Shiite groups in Iran in the aftermath of the 1979 revolution which overthrew the Shah were to some degree reflected in groups which took shape in the Hazarajat, and the result was severe civil strife from 1982. In 1990, the bulk of the parties, under Iranian pressure, combined to form the *Hezb-e Wahdat* or 'Party of Unity'. However, Mohseni's party, which had drawn on Qizilbash as well as Hazara Shia, and had been engaged militarily against the Soviets on a number of occasions, retained its own identity. I will discuss the complications of resistance in the Hazarajat in more detail later.

Regional commanders

Within this context, there emerged a number of important regional commanders whose power was more institutionalized, although often the commanders were also charismatic individuals. Those who developed such regional power bases tended to be the most enduring and salient figures in the internally based resistance. For some this reflected the pulling power of military prowess; for others it reflected agendas in which regional organization was designed to put in place a proto-state as precursor to a wider state-building agenda. Among ethnic Pushtuns, the most accomplished regional commander was Mawlawi Jalaluddin Haqqani, a Jadran Pushtun associated with Khalis's *Hezb* who came to play a role in the short-lived 'National Commanders Shura' following the Soviet withdrawal, and who subsequently joined the Taliban. Otherwise, the two most notable regional commanders were Ismail Khan, of mixed Pushtun and Tajik ancestry, who came to prominence in Herat in March 1979; and Ahmad Shah Massoud, a Tajik born in the Panjsher Valley in the summer of 1952, who mobilized forces in that valley and other areas in the northeast of Afghanistan, and came to world attention through the testimony of foreign visitors. Yet there were significant differences between these two also. Massoud was a former engineering student who had read widely on guerrilla war, and most who met him found him highly charismatic (Barry, 2002). Ismail was formerly an Afghan Army officer, and opinions differed on his charisma; instead, he worked with a solid deputy, former Army officer

Alauddin Khan, who was assassinated in June 1996. Massoud came closest to capturing the 'mix of millenarian zeal, revolutionary ideology and organization, and guerrilla warfare' which mark insurgency in its pure form (Desai and Eckstein, 1990: 463). This is not, however, to say that he was an extremist: he rather reflected a modernism immanent in many Islamist movements, and a desire for 'Islamic revolution', but without the Fanonist overtones that corrupted the *Khalq* or the Leninist approach that suffused Hekmatyar's *Hezb*.

Urban resistance activities

The Afghan resistance was not a purely rural phenomenon. The emphasis of the Soviet occupying forces on securing cities and communications routes meant that urban resistants were confronted by a more concentrated force, which, while offering targets for attack, was also better positioned to gather information about its opponents and strike effectively against them. While Kabul was under nightly curfew throughout the Soviet occupation of Afghanistan, the size and increasing effectiveness of KhAD also limited what its urban enemies could achieve. Nonetheless, on occasion the regime was confronted with examples of determined opposition. In January 1980, there were major displays of resistance in Kandahar and Herat. In Kabul, there was a notable popular uprising on 22 February 1980, fuelled by the distribution of so-called 'night letters' (*shabnamaha*). Troops shot at the protesters with live ammunition, and rockets were fired at them from helicopter gunships. Kakar estimates that 800 Afghans were killed (Kakar, 1995: 117). While sheer force put down this uprising, it did not break the spirit of the regime's opponents. In April 1980, a student procession in the grounds of Kabul University again ended in a hail of bullets. One of the victims was Nihad, a girl from the penultimate year of the Rabia Balkhi High School, whose death was to become a defining event for anti-communist students (Gille, 1980: 10). The student resistance was ultimately crushed: fear and in some cases poverty led to the denunciation to KhAD of some of the most determined student leaders. However, it was a source of mortification for the *Parchamis*, who were seen to be dependent upon the USSR to control unarmed Afghans. One other form of urban resistance also needs to be noted. In 1983, the regime struck at some of Afghanistan's most notable intellectuals, who had formed a human rights group at Kabul University: these included the Western-educated Hasan Kakar, Professor of History, and Habib Hala, Professor of Journalism. Imprisoned after a farcical show trial, these professors were adopted as 'Prisoners of Conscience' by Amnesty International in London (Amnesty International, 1984: 3). The costs to the regime of this act of repression, publicized the world over, greatly exceeded any conceivable benefit it could have delivered.

The role of Pakistan

Pakistan played a major role in supporting certain Afghan resistance figures almost from the moment of the Soviet invasion, and more generally in helping to sustain resistance, which is more vulnerable when it lacks safe havens in one or more neighbouring countries (Miller, 2000: 76). However, it was a role driven not by altruism, but by calculations of Pakistan's interests at a number of different levels, and at different times by different leaderships. In order to make sense of Pakistan's positions, it is important to outline some of the peculiarities of Pakistan's geopolitical context, both with respect to Afghanistan and in the wider politics of the Indian subcontinent.

Pakistan emerged as a state from 15 August 1947 as a result of the partition of British India by the *Indian Independence Act*. Its birth pangs were extraordinarily traumatic, and go a long way to explaining the existential insecurity which has dogged Pakistan since its emergence, leading one analyst to dub it an 'insecurity state' (Thornton, 1999: 187). In contrast to independent India, which has been formally a democratic state for almost the entire period since its creation, Pakistan has endured prolonged periods of military rule – from 1958 to 1962, 1969 to 1972, 1977 to 1988, and most recently from the October 1999 coup. Even when military rule has not been exercised directly, the fear of military intervention has impacted on the practice of politics, supplying members of the civilian elite with incentives to use political office as a positional good for the purpose of personal enrichment while they can. In this, the modern Pakistani elite has moved far from the ethos of the founders of Pakistan, most notably Mohammed Ali Jinnah (Ahmed, 1997).

Longer-term Pakistani interests

Pakistan has been confronted by problems of national integration and identity since its creation. Perilously, it emerged as a territorially bifurcated state, with India separating 'East Pakistan' from 'West Pakistan'. Relations between the two wings were strained almost from the moment of partition, as the new Pakistani leadership asserted the primacy of Urdu as the national language, in the process affronting the overwhelming majority of East Pakistanis, who were Bengali speakers (Ahmed, 1996: 220–1). This fuelled Bengali nationalism, and in 1971, following the victory of Sheikh Mujibur Rahman's Awami League in the December 1970 elections, East Pakistan broke away with Indian support to form the state of Bangladesh (Choudhary, 1974; Cloughley, 1999: 144–238), having endured a genocide at the hands of elements of the Pakistan Army. This trauma was by no means the only one to wrack the body politic of Pakistan. Its sense of identity suffered in two other spheres. One related to the position of Kashmir, a Muslim-majority state adjoining Pakistan whose Hindu ruler opted for integration with India in October 1947 (Ganguly, 1997). The Kashmir situation led to war between India and Pakistan in 1948 and 1965, and to serious clashes in the so-called Kargil conflict in 1999 (Ganguly, 2001; Bose, 2003). The Kashmir dispute has poisoned Indo–Pakistan relations, and con-tributed to a high degree of paranoia in Pakistani military circles. It is also part of the context of relations between Pakistan and Afghanistan. For while each of these states has an overwhelmingly Muslim popula-tion, Afghanistan before 1978 was far closer to *India* than Pakistan, hav-ing even voted against the admission of Pakistan to the United Nations. The reason for this was another poisonous territorial dispute, this time between Afghanistan and Pakistan, and known as the 'Pushtunistan dispute'.

Avoiding any revival of the Pushtunistan dispute was a core Pakistani interest as Islamabad contemplated its future relations with the Afghan resistance. Pakistan's support for groups such as Hekmatyar's *Hezb*, and the Taliban, makes far more sense when one takes into account Pakistan's hostility to the *ancien régime* in Kabul as a result of this dispute. The conflict dated from the demarcation in 1893 of a boundary between Afghanistan and British India by Sir Mortimer Durand – the so-called 'Durand Line' (Dupree, 1961; Haroon, 2007: 13–21). The effect of this exercise in boundary-drawing was to split the Pushtun ethnic group, with some in Afghanistan but others in the North-West Frontier region of India. The long-term consequences proved momentous (Johnson and Mason, 2008). For a decade before partition, Jinnah and the Muslim League had been opposed by the Pushtun separatist leader Khan Abdul Ghaffar Khan ('The Frontier Gandhi') and his followers, who were close to Mohandas K. Gandhi and the Indian Congress. The cause of Pushtun separatism, reflected in the demand for an independent 'Pushtunistan', was supported by a string of Afghan rulers, most strikingly Daoud during his period as prime minis-ter (Dupree, 1973: 538–58; Ganguly, 1998: 162–92); an intersection in downtown Kabul was named 'Pushtunistan Square', and a 'Pushtunistan Day' was celebrated annually in Afghanistan. From September 1961 to May 1963, diplomatic relations between Afghanistan and Pakistan were suspended. While Afghanistan pursued the issue of an independent Pushtunistan with less vigour in the 'New Democracy' period than it had during Daoud's premiership, the memory of the dispute was seared into the consciousness of a generation of Pakistani civilian and military leaders, who feared an insecure rear in the event of major hostilities with India. This points to the second core Pakistani interest in Afghanistan, namely to promote forces in Afghanistan which would be anathema to New Delhi. Following the Soviet invasion of Afghanistan, India, after some sharp bureaucratic conflicts, adopted a position which essentially accommodated the Soviet invasion, at least in a public sense (Saikal, 1989). The effect of this posture, far from protecting India from the rise of 'an Afghanistan dominated by Islamic extremist forces' (Dixit, 2000: 23), was to provide Pakistan's military leader Zia ul-Haq with one more reason to back such forces. By cutting itself off from channels of influence with the Afghan resistance, New Delhi gave a free hand to those who wished to support the most extreme and radical groups.

The position of General Zia

General Zia ul-Haq, Pakistan's Army Chief, had seized power in Pakistan on 5 July 1977, after months of crisis following a bitterly contested general election. Zia took the title of 'Chief Martial Law Administrator'. Prime Minister Zulfiqar Ali Bhutto was detained, released, and then rearrested; after a controversial trial for allegedly plotting the elimination of a political opponent, he was hanged on 4 April 1979. The effect of this execution was to make General Zia an international pariah, and his standing internationally was not helped by his obvious religious zeal, for which there was little taste in major Western countries given the fears triggered by the overthrow of the Shah of Iran. As one commentator has observed, 'He developed a "saviour" or "messiah" complex and ruled the country with the aura of a God-ordained mission to transform Pakistani society on Islamic lines' (Rizvi, 2000: 166).

General Zia's stance towards Afghanistan was driven by a combination of international and domestic factors. The international factors were relatively straightforward and understandable. The Soviet invasion brought the Soviet armed forces directly to Pakistan's borders, and for Pakistan this could not but be seen as a threat, given not only the USSR's longstanding warm relations with India, but also Moscow's support for the fragmentation of Pakistan barely a decade earlier. However, the Soviet invasion did not simply confront Pakistan with threats; it also provided it with opportunities. Pakistan was manifestly *the* state from which any international opposition to the Soviet presence in Afghanistan would need to be mounted. No one grasped this more swiftly than Zia: as Jalal put it, 'the Soviet invasion of Afghanistan gave him just what was needed to establish his regime's non-existent international stock without which the domestic agenda of repression seemed destined to end in tears' (Jalal, 1995: 103). The upshot was the eventual approval by the US Congress of a package of economic and military assistance to Zia's regime worth $3.2 billion over a six-year period, assembled after Zia had scorned an initial offer of $400 million (Weinbaum, 1994: 18). The significance was primarily symbolic: Zia had come in from the cold. However, he was also able to exploit the Soviet presence in Afghanistan in more overtly domestic ways as well: he managed to find common cause, over Afghanistan, with Pakistani religious parties such as the *Jamaat-i Islami* which thitherto had been wary of what they saw as the luke-warm character of his Islamization programme. This was initially not a very important consideration, but over time, Pakistan's religious parties increasingly built their own ties to Afghan parties and groups which they found congenial, and the long-run consequences of this were to prove disturbing. In conditions of exile and social disloca-tion, the severe attitudes of the more extreme Pakistani religious cir-cles exercised a considerable influence on young Afghans who had never known normal family lives in Afghanistan and were discon-nected from the channels of socialization through which the moderate dimensions of Afghan life were replicated.

Pakistan as host of Afghan refugees

There was one further reason why Pakistan could not ignore the Afghan imbroglio even had its leaders been minded to do so. The porous border between Afghanistan and Pakistan made Afghanistan's eastward neigh-bour a natural destination for Afghan refugees (Maley, 1989a; Schmeidl and Maley, 2008), who quit Afghanistan in their millions. Muslims who abandon territory under atheist control are typically labelled *muhajireen*, since they emulate the emigration (*hijra*) of the Prophet Muhammad from Mecca to Medina in 622 AD, and there is no dishon-our associated with such movement. Measuring the scale of the exodus was never an exact science, since some refugees went unregistered while others registered more than once (see Dupree, 1987; Dupree, 1988a). Nonetheless, according to the data of the Office of the United Nations High Commissioner for Refugees (UNHCR), by the end of 1979, 600,000 refugees were already outside Afghanistan, about two-thirds in Pakistan and the remainder in Iran. By the end of 1980, the figure had risen to 1.9 million, and the total was estimated on 1 January 1990 at a staggering 6.2 million, of whom an estimated 3,272,000 were in Pakistan (Colville, 1997). Subsequent analysis has suggested that the numbers in Pakistan may have been greater, and perhaps far greater, than even this enormous figure (Kronenfeld, 2008).

The refugees in Pakistan were for the most part 'acute' rather than 'anticipatory' refugees, since they were driven to flight by 'great political changes' and 'movements of armies' (Kunz, 1973: 132). However, their flight was the product of a myriad of individual decisions, rather than a shift *en masse* (Connor, 1987: 183–4). The overwhelming majority of the refugees were Pushtuns (Sliwinski, 1989a: 46), and their ethnic affinity with the majority in the province of Pakistan to which they most readily fled – the North-West Frontier Province – also aided their re-establishment in exile, although this process was of course not without significant trauma (Saikal and Maley, 1986: 13–17). Although Pakistan was not a party to the 1951 *Convention Relating to the Status of Refugees*, it had initially sought the help of UNHCR in April 1979 to deal with the refugee outflow, and it established a 'Chief Commissionerate of Afghan Refugees' to manage the so-called 'Refugee Tented Villages' in which the bulk of the refugees were located. While many Afghan refugees were to experience harassment at the hands of corrupt Pakistani officials, overall Pakistan performed remarkably well in sheltering and feeding as many refugees as it did, although in the vital area of education (where Pakistan was understandably dependent upon outside assistance), the achievements were extremely limited, and the long-term consequences of this neglect quite lamentable (see generally Schmeidl, 2002). The 'Refugee Tented Villages' were not simply politically neutral residential areas for the indigent; they developed their own internal political organizations, in which Afghan *maleks* (officials), resistance parties, and committees of public order vied for influence (Centlivres and Centlivres-Demont, 1988a). These internal political structures were linked to the wider mechanisms of Afghan resistance, in a Cold War context (see Schöch, 2008). Refugee camps very often become important resources for those engaged in struggle against oppression (Terry, 2002; Lischer, 2005), and the Pakistan-based camps for Afghan refugees were to prove no exception.

Pakistan as a conduit of external aid: the role of ISI

The Pakistan Army became the prime channel through which outside military assistance was directed to Afghan resistance groups, and the process was the easier to manage because Pakistan was effectively under military rule for most of the period of the Soviet–Afghan War (although a civilian prime minister, Mohammad Khan Junejo, took office on 23 March 1985, also the day on which Zia ul-Haq was sworn in as 'elected' president). The Pakistan Army was numerically substantial, totalling 400,000 at the time of the Soviet invasion of Afghanistan, with 16 infantry divisions. At the time of independence, the officer corps was Punjabi-dominated (Cohen, 1985: 42), and the pattern has persisted to the present: figures cited by Rizvi suggest that the Punjab provides 65 per cent of the officer corps (Rizvi, 2000: 240). Zia ul-Haq was himself a Punjabi. However, some key figures closer to the implementation of the Army's Afghanistan policy were Pushtuns, notably Lieutenant-General Akhtar Abdul Rahman, the Director-General of the Inter-Services Intelligence (ISI): according to one of his closest associates, he 'was intensely proud of the Afghan blood he had inherited' (Yousaf and Adkin, 1992: 23). In addition to ethnic affinity, religious sentiment was increasingly emphasized after Zia seized power: the superficially secular traits of the Army, inherited from the British military tradition, were blended with Islamic justifications for policy positions, and religious groups such as the *Jamaat-i Islami* began to make their presence felt within the ranks of the Army. For all these reasons, as well as from calculations of interest, the Pakistan Army threw itself into the process of backing the Afghan Mujahideen with considerable gusto.

At the heart of the Pakistan Army's Afghanistan policy was the Afghan Bureau of the ISI. The ISI itself was remarkably unencumbered by checks and balances, even in comparison to other intelligence agencies. Its Director-General reported directly to General Zia, and the head of its Afghan Bureau directly to the ISI Director-General. However, its Afghanistan operations were dependent on total secrecy, partly because of Pakistan's desire to avoid Soviet reprisals for military activities against the Afghan communist regime orchestrated from Pakistani soil, but also because the USA put great store on 'plausible deniability' as an element of covert operations in Afghanistan. Former US Secretary of State George Shultz recorded in his memoirs a conversation which President Ronald Reagan had with Zia in 1988 after the signing of the Geneva Accords on Afghanistan: 'I heard the president ask Zia how he would handle the fact that they would be violating their agreement. Zia replied that they would "just lie about it. We've been denying our activities there for eight years"' (Shultz, 1993: 1091; see also Nawaz, 2008: 390). Over time, Pakistan's role as conveyor of arms to the Afghan resistance, as well as trainer and logistical supporter of Afghan combatants, became an extremely substantial one. However, it was anything but neutral, and Pakistan's urge to play favourites distorted the Afghans' struggle, with disturbing longer-term consequences.

Pakistani manipulation and the Afghan resistance

That Pakistan would seek to play favourites was in one sense not the least bit surprising. Pakistan had been closely tied to various Afghan groups since before the April 1978 communist coup. When Daoud renewed his Pushtunist rhetoric following the July 1973 coup in Kabul, Zulfiqar Ali Bhutto had responded by building ties with Afghan groups hostile to Daoud. He and his adviser on Afghan affairs, Naseerullah Babar, toyed briefly with the idea of seeking to restore Zahir Shah, but ultimately settled on the strategy of supporting anti-Daoud Islamic groups. It was in this way that the young radical Gulbuddin Hekmatyar first received Pakistani backing, which he was to enjoy for over two decades. In 1975, the Pakistan Army had backed Afghan Islamist groups who mounted an uprising against Daoud in July. Daoud crushed his opponents with relative ease, and Hekmatyar in Paktia failed altogether to win popular support (Roy, 1990: 75). However, in a sign of what was to come, Hekmatyar's failure did not lead Pakistan to abandon him as worthless. And through the 1980s, Hekmatyar and his *Hezb-e Islami* were well-provisioned by ISI despite a dearth of evidence that they were militarily effective against the Soviets or the Kabul regime. As Weinbaum put it: 'ISI officials seemed to be more impressed with the frequent ruthlessness of Hekmatyar's leaders than with the scope of their fighting or accomplishments against Soviet and Kabul government troops' (Weinbaum, 1994: 34).

Yet at the same time, General Zia, who had witnessed the September 1970 crisis in Jordan in which King Hussein's Hashemite monarchy had turned on Palestinian groups, was determined that no Afghan group was to become sufficiently powerful or organized as to pose any kind of threat to its host. This concern militated against exclusive reliance on Hekmatyar. However, it did not mean that those parties which Pakistan was prepared to tolerate were representative of Afghan anti-communist forces in general. The seven Sunni parties which I mentioned earlier were especially privileged by Pakistan, and in principle (although not altogether in practice), refugees were 'required to be affiliated to one of the parties in order to obtain assistance from the Pakistan refugee program' (Human Rights Watch, 1991: 106). Zahir Shah and his immediate Rome-based family were refused permission to visit Pakistan, and the nationalist party *Afghan Millat* was frozen out as well. While personality clashes and ethnic divisions would have made cooperation between the Afghan parties difficult to elicit even in the best of circumstances, Pakistan's role as dispenser of largesse significantly accentuated the tensions between the different groups. Hekmatyar's *Hezb*, in particular, knew that its continued receipt of arms was not dependent upon its military performance, and it therefore showed a marked tendency to invest in public relations in Pakistan, stockpile arms for future use against other resistance groups, and freeload on the courage and commitment of ordinary Mujahideen in Afghanistan.

With hindsight, the United States gave the ISI far too free a hand in distributing US-funded weaponry. 'The ISI', Weinbaum presciently observed, 'was assumed in Washington to have a good understanding of the Afghans and invaluable contacts among the resistance parties. As a result, the United States was misinformed about the popularity of former king Zahir Shah among the refugees as well as about rank-and-file support for some of the hard-line Islamic resistance groups' (Weinbaum, 1994: 32). Pakistan's approach was not remotely concerned with Afghanistan's post-communist future. As Rubin notes, a 'commander's success in mobilizing a large coalition, in setting up a civil administration to replace the state in a region of the country, or in attracting support and defectors from Kabul city or the regime army were all considered irrelevant'. Rather, Pakistan's criteria for effectiveness were 'a high level of outside funding, weak links to the local society, educated commanders, and ideological proximity to the ISI' (Rubin, 1995a: 201). It is perhaps understandable that Pakistan developed such criteria. But given the patent anti-Americanism of figures such as Hekmatyar, it boggles the mind that key American policymakers were prepared to go along with them (see Coll, 2005; Gutman, 2008).

International support for the Afghan resistance

Beyond Pakistan's involvement, the Afghan resistance also received support through a range of international channels. The forms which this assistance took varied from the strictly moral to humanitarian and material, but each was important in its own way, and served to keep the Afghanistan issue alive.

The UN response to the Soviet invasion

The United Nations (UN) was the first international organization in which opposition to the Soviet invasion was articulated, and also the most important, although its scope for concrete action was limited. Under Article 24 of the 1945 Charter of the United Nations, the Security Council is given 'primary responsibility for the maintenance of international peace and security'. In 1980, its 15 members included the USA, USSR, Britain, France, and China as 'permanent' members, which under Article 27.3 enjoyed a right of 'veto' of all non-procedural matters. For this reason, there was no prospect that the Security Council would adopt any resolution condemning the Soviet invasion, and it did not: the USSR on 7 January 1980 vetoed a draft resolution on the situation in Afghanistan put forward by a group of non-aligned members led by Bangladesh. However, this was not the end of the matter. In 1950, the UN General Assembly had adopted Resolution 377 (v), known at the time as the 'Acheson Resolution' but subsequently better known as the 'Uniting for Peace Resolution', which provided for the convoking of an Emergency Special Session of the General Assembly in the event that the Security Council was unable to act in response to a threat to, or breach of, the peace. On 9 January 1980, the Security Council adopted Resolution 462 by which – without explicitly mentioned the Uniting for Peace Resolution – it decided to call an Emergency Special Session of the General Assembly. Since this resolution was procedural, the Soviet dissenting vote did not amount to a veto, and the Emergency Special Session thus went ahead, from 10 to 14 January. Since there had been no Emergency Special Session since the 1967 Six-Day War, the mere convoking of the session was a notable event, and an embarrassment for the Soviet Union. However, the Session also adopted (104 to 18, with 18 abstentions) Resolution ES-6/2 of 14 January 1980, which called for 'the immediate, unconditional and total withdrawal of the foreign troops from Afghanistan'. While not binding in a legal sense, this signalled extreme disapproval of Soviet actions, and became the model for a resolution adopted at regular sessions of the General Assembly from 1980 until the signing of the Geneva Accords in 1988 which reiterated the demand for a troop withdrawal. On the last occasion on which such a resolution was put, in 1987, it passed by 123 votes to 19, with 11 abstentions. The ongoing strength of support for the resolution contrasted sharply with dwindling support for General Assembly resolutions dealing with Indonesia's 1975 invasion of East Timor; after 1982, Portugal had ceased to put forward such resolutions, for fear that they would not secure sufficient support (Maley, 2000b: 65).

However, while this clear condemnation of the invasion of Afghanistan provided valuable legitimation for popular resistance, in another respect the UN's response to the invasion was remarkably clumsy. The UN is an organization of states, of which the state of Afghanistan had been a member since 1946. In most cases, the question of who should represent a state is uncontroversial, but where a 'government' has been installed by invasion, there is a strong case for not accepting the credentials of its representatives. Unfortunately, this issue was overlooked at the time of the January 1980 Emergency Special Session: one 'reason for lack of attention given to the credentials issue', according to the Pakistani diplomat Riaz M. Khan, 'was the fast pace of developments, especially during the short interval between the Security Council meeting and the convening of the UNGA Emergency Special Session' (Khan, 1991: 15). The unintended, but significant, consequence of this was to accord the regime installed by the USSR a status which it hardly merited, and to skew subsequent UN involvement with the Afghanistan issue away from the crucial question of internal political order and towards the purely external dimensions of the situation, by giving the Kabul regime an effective veto over the engagement of the resistance in serious negotiations over Afghanistan's future. Even as late as 1988, UN Secretary-General Pérez de Cuéllar was to remark that it would be 'against our philosophy to be in touch with the enemies of governments' (Franck and Nolte, 1993: 150; see also Rubin, 1995b: 43).

Western reactions to the invasion

The Carter Administration was deeply affronted by the Soviet invasion of Afghanistan, which had not been anticipated by the US Central Intelligence Agency (Weiner, 2007: 365–7). However, its involvement in Afghanistan had begun to deepen even before the invasion took place. In a 1998 interview with the French weekly *Le Nouvel Observateur*, Dr Zbigniew Brzezinski stated that US support for the Mujahideen had begun six months before the Soviet invasion (Brzezinski, 1998). According to Brzezinski's account, President Carter signed a directive on 3 July 1979 approving aid to the opponents of the Afghan communist regime, and Brzezinski himself offered to Carter the opinion that this would result in a Soviet military intervention. This action he characterized as knowingly increasing the probability that the USSR would invade Afghanistan. Even allowing for the possibility of hyperbole on Brzezinski's part – a reasonable assumption given that the July 1979 directive provided only for non-lethal medical and propaganda assistance

(Cogan, 1993: 76) – it is hardly surprising that the US Administration should have been willing to support the overthrow of the regime of Taraki and Amin given the assassination of Ambassador Dubs in February 1979. It is notable, however, that the likely effects on ordinary Afghans of turning their country into Moscow's Vietnam seems to have weighed all too lightly on policy circles in Washington (Maley, 2000a: 6).

Once the invasion occurred, President Carter, under Brzezinski's influence, offered a relentlessly geopolitical interpretation of the Soviet invasion as positioning the USSR to threaten the free flow of oil from the Persian Gulf, and constituting 'the most serious threat to world peace since the Second World War' (Grasselli, 1996: 121). In the light of evidence which has since become available, this apocalyptic view cannot be sustained. However, it was far from clear in January 1980 that it was unsustainable, and as a result there was widespread support in Congress and internationally – especially from British Prime Minister Margaret Thatcher and Australian Prime Minister Malcolm Fraser – for some of the measures which the Administration proposed to use to signal its dismay. While the prospects of Senate ratification of the new Strategic Arms Limitation Treaty (SALT II) had always been poor, the invasion of Afghanistan doomed them altogether. Carter also proposed two major positive measures in response to the invasion. One was a partial grain embargo, reflecting US awareness of the Soviet Union's need to import grains from time to time in significant quantities. The other was a US boycott of the Olympic Games, which in 1980 were to be held in Moscow. The Olympic boycott sent a powerful message. The grain embargo was much less effective, since it was rapidly mired in domestic political controversy, and other states could not be compelled to cooperate to make it effective. Sanctions are a tricky tool to employ, and this certainly proved to be the case in respect of Afghanistan (Nossal, 1989).

Given that US support for the Afghan Mujahideen had commenced even before the invasion, it is unsurprising that the invasion itself led to the development of a robust programme of military assistance. A conservative estimate of the total value of covert US aid to the resistance by the year of the Soviet withdrawal is nearly US$2 billion (Cogan, 1993: 77). Immediately after the invasion, Carter signed a new directive providing for the supply of lethal weapons to the Mujahideen, and a shipment of .303 Enfield rifles arrived by 10 January 1980 (Cogan, 1993: 76). As time passed, a sophisticated weapons pipeline developed, with equipment delivered by ship to Karachi or by plane to Islamabad (from China or Dhahran in Saudi Arabia). Weapons were then moved to Rawalpindi and Quetta by the ISI, and thence distributed by truck to the resistance parties (Yousaf and Adkin, 1992: 99). The weapons for which the US paid were predominantly from China and Egypt, and included Soviet RPG-7 anti-tank grenade launchers, which the resistance used to great effect, as well as DShK 12.7 mm heavy machine guns, mortars of various sizes, AK-47 rifles, and Egyptian Saqr-20 107 mm multiple rocket launchers with an 8 kilometre range (McMichael, 1991: 31).

The nature and scale of US assistance was not constant. The inauguration of President Reagan in 1981 brought to office a leader who was instinctively sympathetic to the Afghan Mujahideen, and in this he was supported by CIA Director William J. Casey, and even by members of Congress who otherwise were wary of the so-called 'Reagan Doctrine' which favoured assistance to anti-communist insurgents (Scott, 1996: 31). However, others in the Administration were wary of fuelling resistance to the point that a major Soviet escalation would result, perhaps engulfing Pakistan as well. Nonetheless, in 1985, National Security Decision Directive 166, entitled *Expanded US Aid to Afghan Guerrillas*, approved the use of 'all means available' to remove Soviet forces from Afghanistan. This led to a significant increase in the quantity and quality of military assistance. Finally, on 25 September 1986, the resistance commenced use of Stinger anti-aircraft missiles, designed to overcome one of the Mujahideen's greatest weaknesses, namely vulnerability to air attack. The supply of Stingers came only after ferocious interagency battles in Washington (Kuperman, 1999; Lundberg, 1999), and to this day there is debate over how significant a role the Stinger missile played in prompting the Soviet withdrawal from Afghanistan. Nonetheless, as a marker of continuing US commitment, the arrival of the Stinger missile was unquestionably of great significance.

The USA was the principal backer of the resistance in financial terms. However, other states provided support in diverse ways. The Thatcher Government was firmly opposed to the Soviet invasion, and British Special Air Service (SAS) personnel not only trained resistance fighters, but entered Afghanistan for operations. A range of countries – including Austria, Belgium, Canada, Denmark, Egypt, West Germany, France, Greece, Ireland, Italy, Japan, Norway, Singapore, Sweden, Switzerland, the United States, and the United Kingdom – provided medical treatment for Afghans with complex neurological or orthopaedic injuries under an 'Afghan Medical Programme' run with US backing by the Intergovernmental Committee for Migration (ICM). Furthermore, many governments put the Afghanistan issue on their agendas for bilateral discussions with the USSR: China even identified the Soviet presence in Afghanistan as one of the key factors which would have to be addressed if the Sino–Soviet dispute were to be resolved (Holmes, 1989). All these measures helped reassure the Mujahideen that they were not fighting alone.

Arab reactions to the invasion

The resistance also received significant support from a number of Arab governments. President Anwar al-Sadat of Egypt was a close ally of the United States, and in addition had access to stocks of Soviet-made weaponry dating from the period of close Soviet–Egyptian relations prior to 1972. Sadat's Egypt became a major link in the weapons supply chain. But even more important a role was played by oil-rich Saudi Arabia. The Saudi General Intelligence Service, headed by Prince Turki al-Faisal Saud, provided funds to support the resistance, although it is almost impossible to work out the volumes involved. According to one source, Arab monies roughly matched US funding (Yousaf and Adkin, 1992: 77), but these Arab monies included direct gifts from private Arab sources to resistance parties – and some party leaders (notably Sayyaf, who spoke excellent Arabic) were adept at tapping such sources. The motivation for this support was more complex than one might at first glance have thought. One consideration was undoubtedly the need to support Muslims under attack by atheistic communists. Another was the need to shore up the Sunni Muslim resistance forces at a time when the possible spread of Iranian influence was greatly feared. However, the Sunni Islam of the Saudis, shaped by the doctrines of Muhammad Ibn Abdul Wahhab, differed in significant ways from the practices of the Afghan Sunnis. In the nineteenth century, Amir Abdul Rahman Khan had campaigned against 'Wahhabism' (Noelle, 1995) and attempts by radical Arabs to 'educate' their Afghan brethren on such matters as the proper form of prayer caused great offence during the Soviet–Afghan War (Gall, 1988: 48–51). As Dupree put it: 'The Saudis have spent megabucks among the refugees and resistance fighters in attempts to gain converts for their ultra-conservative, reformist brand of Islam, but with little success' (Dupree, 1989: 44).

Apart from direct involvement of Arab governments, Arab influence was felt in two other ways. First, a large number of religious-minded Arabs found the Afghan theatre an appropriate one in which to give voice to their pan-Islamist ideas: notable among these were the Palestinian Dr Abdullah Azzam, killed in a car bombing in Peshawar in November 1989 (Rubin, 1997a: 189–90); and the Saudi Osama Bin Laden, whose militance had taken him to a number of different countries (Davis, 1993b:

329; Dekmejian, 1994: 641; Randal, 2004: 68–81). It would be a considerable exaggeration to paint the Arabs who served in Afghanistan as constituting a coherent bloc: as the late Anthony Hyman observed, 'There is no Arab or Islamic "International", along the lines of a Comintern, for example' (Hyman, 1994: 86; see also Brown, 2008). However, they tended to be extreme in their views, and the majority ended up attached either to Hekmatyar's *Hezb*, or Sayyaf's party: a number of massacres were credibly blamed on such Arab volunteers. Afghans tended to refer to these volunteers either as Wahhabis or as 'Ikhwani', after the radical Muslim Brotherhood (*Al-Ikhwan al-Muslimun*). Second, 'private' Arab organizations became involved in providing humanitarian relief both inside Afghanistan and to refugees in Pakistan, often in ways which blurred what boundary there is between humanitarian assistance and more overt political and military support. The World Muslim League (*Rabitat al-Alam al-Islami*) was one of the most active of such organizations, but not far behind were charities such as the Saudi Red Crescent.

Western non-governmental organizations (NGOs)

The outrage which met the Soviet invasion led to actions not only by states, but by concerned individuals and non-governmental organizations (Lorentz, 1987; Dupree, 1988b). For much of the Soviet–Afghan War, the UN, constrained by the acceptance of the communist regime's credentials, was unable to undertake humanitarian actions in areas of the country beyond Kabul's control. Non-governmental organizations were not bound by similar constraints. As a result, NGOs penetrated the Afghan countryside in large numbers, not only providing services to the Afghan population, but in some cases also bearing witness as to what the Afghan population had to endure at Soviet hands.

Particularly important in this respect were medical NGOs, such as the French organizations Médecins Sans Frontières, Aide Médicale Internationale, and Médecins du Monde. Building on the work of earlier development programmes, they took up the task of providing medical care in areas which otherwise would have had no access to such services (O'Connor, 1994). Their work was by no means free of risk, and in 1983 attracted widespread attention when the Kabul regime managed to capture and put on trial a young French doctor, Philippe Augoyard, who was working for Aide Médicale Internationale. As in the case of the trial of the Kabul University professors, the appalling image of the regime which this projected to the wider world outweighed any possible benefits from disrupting the medical relief programme, and faced with an international outcry, the regime was ultimately obliged to release Augoyard, who then wrote a damning memoir of his experiences (Augoyard, 1985).

As well as those agencies specifically concerned with medical aid, a range of bodies became involved in supplying assistance both to refugees in Pakistan, and communities in Afghanistan itself. Initial efforts were of varying quality: in one spectacular case of cultural insensitivity, refugees were supplied with a consignment of 'aid' which consisted of sardines, briefcases, weight-reducing powder, brassières, and high-heeled shoes (*The New York Times*, 26 October 1980: 8). Fortunately, high standards were set as more proficient agencies began their work. Some were established relief agencies, such as the International Rescue Committee. Others arose in response to the Afghan crisis, notably the Swedish Committee for Afghanistan. These NGOs often received significant funding from Western governments. One commentator concluded that most NGOs engaged in cross-border operations were 'conscious agents of political interests' (Baitenmann, 1990: 82), but it is difficult to see how they could have been anything but political, given that they had to violate the dictates of the communist regime in order to do their work. In 1988, a coordinating body for NGOs (ACBAR, or 'Agency Coordinating Body for Afghan Relief') was finally established, with its headquarters in Peshawar.

Finally, the International Committee of the Red Cross (although not strictly an NGO, given its specific responsibilities under the 1949 Geneva Conventions) was to become heavily involved in Afghanistan, not just in the sphere of medical and material assistance, but also in its 'classical' activities of representations, protection of prisoners of war, and tracing (Maurice and de Courten, 1991; Forsythe, 2005). While its seven principles (humanity, impartiality, neutrality, independence, voluntary service, unity, and universality) prevented it from taking any public stand as far as the war was concerned, its first-aid posts on the Afghanistan–Pakistan border and its surgical hospital in Peshawar saved the lives of many wounded Mujahideen. Respect for the Red Cross is one of the few happy legacies of the Soviet–Afghan War.

4

The Karmal Period, 1979–1986

The Soviet–Afghan War fell into a number of distinct phases. In the most detailed study of the rhythm of the Afghan War, Goodson divides it into eight stages. This chapter is specifically concerned with the second and third stages which Goodson identifies, namely those which he calls 'National resistance and Soviet entrenchment (1980–1983)' and 'Air war, interdiction, and destabilization (1983–1986)'. The first of these he classifies as a period of medium but increasing intensity, and the second as a period of high and increasing intensity (Goodson, 1998: 486). What unites these stages, however, was the occupancy by Babrak Karmal of the position of head of the PDPA; indeed, Goodson argues that it was the replacement of Karmal as party leader that brought the third stage of the war to a close. While Soviet military tactics certainly shifted in 1983, because of new approaches to counter-insurgency activity and associated improvements in the use of airpower, the USSR's political dilemma remained the same: that Karmal's reputation was irretrievably contaminated by the way in which he had come to office. This justifies treating the Karmal period in its entirety. In 1942, Winston Churchill described the allied victory in Egypt as marking 'perhaps the end of the beginning'. The fall of Karmal played a similar role in the Afghanistan war. But history rarely falls into neat categories, and one can also argue that as far as Afghan communism was concerned, the rise of Mikhail Gorbachev marked the beginning of the end. It certainly did for Karmal, even though Gorbachev's rise initially led to a major escalation rather than reduction of Soviet military activities.

The chapter is divided into four sections. The first surveys military activities in five key regions: eastern and southern Afghanistan; northern Afghanistan; western Afghanistan; the Panjsher Valley; and the Hazarajat. The second examines the structure of the communist regime and the role of the PDPA during this period. The third traces the development of the communist secret police, and the specific roles it played in detecting and crushing opposition. The fourth looks at the way in which political change in the Soviet Union set the scene for the abandonment of Karmal by a new Soviet leadership, and the re-examination of the way in which Afghanistan should be approached. Underlying all this discussion, however, is a pervasive political reality: that the Soviet–Afghan War was not constituted by a string of decisive events – an Austerlitz, a Waterloo, a Stalingrad, a D-Day, or a Hiroshima – but rather by a hard grind of medium-intensity engagements, none capable of offering decisive strategic victory to either side, but which had a massive cumulative effect, most importantly in the minds of a changing Soviet leadership cohort.

Patterns of war

Eastern and southern Afghanistan

The war in the east of Afghanistan was perhaps more ferocious than in any other part of the country, although no complete survey of war damage has been carried out that would permit systematic conclusions to be drawn. The flow of refugees and internally displaced persons from this area attested to the intensity of fighting (Sliwinski, 1989b). The military rationale from the Soviet point of view was obvious: this area adjoined Pakistan, from which external aid to the Afghan resistance would come if it came at all. Sliwinski actually argues that the maximum exodus from eastern provinces occurred even *before* the Soviet invasion, as a result of aerial bombardments, but the two years following the invasion also witnessed substantial military operations because of the policy of 'establishing a cordon sanitaire along the Pakistan border' (Sliwinski, 1989b: 75).

A number of operations were notable either for their scale or for their impact on the course of battle in particular localities. In March 1980, a major operation was launched in Kunar, with an estimated 1,000 casualties among regime opponents and civilians (Cordesman and Wagner, 1990: 36). In June 1980, a Soviet motorised battalion was devastated in an ambush on the Khost–Gardez road to the south of Kabul. In July 1981, a major regime operation was successfully mounted near Sarobi to secure the Kabul–Jalalabad road, but in April 1982, the regime suffered a serious setback when intruders in Bagram airbase destroyed 23 aircraft. In 1983, as was noted in Chapter 2, Soviet tactics shifted towards clearing the population rather than simply attacking the resistance. However, major offensives directed at concentrations of resistance forces continued. In August 1984, the Soviets launched a coordinated operation to break the siege of the Jaji garrison in Paktia, following up with major strikes from January 1985 at other resistance targets, aimed at facilitating the establishment of more regime bases along the border with Pakistan (Urban, 1990: 163). And in April 1986, a force in which (for once) the Afghan Army was numerically more significant than its Soviet allies succeeded in seizing the Mujahideen's 'showcase' eastern base of Zhawar. From a wider perspective, however, these operations delivered somewhat less than one might have thought. The withdrawal of regime forces to the points from which they had initially been deployed typically created a vacuum to which resistance forces rapidly returned. The Soviets and their regime allies simply lacked the manpower and *matériel* to occupy on a permanent basis the territories from which they could occasionally eject their opponents (Akhromeev and Kornienko, 1992: 169).

In southern Afghanistan, the regime had severe difficulties even in asserting control over the whole of the city of Kandahar. The Kandahar area was the centre of activity of one of the most notable Durrani Pushtun commanders, namely Haji Abdul Latif; it was also in this area that a number of 'tribal' fronts developed, notably those associated with the Karzai family. Much of the fighting in this area took the form of skirmishes, especially with the militia of Esmatullah 'Muslim', formerly a soldier in the pre-communist Afghan Army, who, after working with the resistance, defected to the regime. This disordered situation in the early to mid-1980s carried through to the collapse of the communist regime in 1992, with disastrous long-term consequences.

Northern Afghanistan

In the north of Afghanistan, an odd duality came to characterise the conflict. On the one hand, the main city in the north, Mazar-e Sharif, was under regime control throughout the first phase of the Soviet–Afghan War. This was of considerable significance for the regime, since Mazar was the Afghan city closest to the Soviet border. The terrain in the immediate vicinity of the city is almost completely flat and treeless, and therefore does not lend itself to easy exploitation by guerrilla fighters. On the other hand, a vigorous young *Jamiat-e Islami* commander, a former schoolteacher named Abdul Qader who employed the name of Zabiullah as a *nom de guerre*, spearheaded active resistance in the surrounding areas, notably Baghlan to the south-east, Kunduz to the east, and Balkh to the west. He reportedly had 20,000 combatants under his command (Urban, 1990: 143), and mounted some spectacular operations, notably the destruction of the control tower at Mazar's civilian airport in May 1983 (Chevalerias, 1985: 6). However, he was hampered by tense relations with local combatants affiliated to Muhammadi's *Harakat-e Inqilab-e Islami Afghanistan*, drawn from Pushtun populations in the Balkh and Kunduz areas. Zabiullah was killed on 14 December 1984, aged only 30, when the vehicle in which he was travelling struck a mine. It has never been established whether his death was an accident or an assassination. The vacuum following Zabiullah's death took a long time to fill.

Western Afghanistan

Given how remote the Sunni Mujahideen in Herat were from supplies channelled through Pakistan, and how unpromising the terrain, it is remarkable that conflict in the west was as heavy as it proved to be. Shindand airbase to the south of Herat offered an alluring target, and Herat itself had the recent experience of major mobilisation during the March 1979 uprising. Major clashes between the Mujahideen and the regime took place in October 1981, and December 1981–January 1982. Throughout 1984, as Soviet tactics shifted, bombing occurred in the Herat area directed at depopulating areas sympathetic to the resistance (Jossinet, 1986: 9). On 12 June 1985, a series of explosions rocked the Shindand base, destroying up to 20 aircraft (Cordesman and Wagner, 1990: 55), and fighting three weeks later in Herat was so heavy that the regime governor withdrew (Urban, 1990: 180). A regime attack on Zendejan in January 1986 caused significant casualties, but produced no decisive military gain.

The Panjsher Valley

The Panjsher Valley, to the north of Kabul, is strategically important because it abuts the north–south road which connects Kabul to Mazar-e Sharif via the Salang Tunnel and Pul-e Khumri. During the Soviet–Afghan War it was the key base of Ahmad Shah Massoud, and forces of the USSR and the Afghan regime made major attempts to occupy it on a number of occasions. None was successful, but on occasions Massoud was driven into tactical retreat. The first major Soviet push into the Panjsher was in September 1980; it was followed by further assaults in November 1980, January–February 1981, August 1981, May 1982, August–September 1982, March–May 1984, September 1984, and July 1985. Of these nine operations, two were particularly notable: that of August–September 1982, on account of its scale and intensity; and that of March–May 1984, on account of the new counter-insurgency tactics which the Soviets tested. The former led to one of the most controversial developments of the war, namely the negotiation of a ceasefire between Massoud and the regime, which lasted from December 1982 to April 1984 (Gromov, 1994: 192). Critics of the ceasefire argued that it simply liberated Soviet forces to attack hard-pressed Mujahideen elsewhere. Defenders of Massoud argued that it was dictated by the dire humanitarian circumstances in Panjsher after the August–September 1982 attacks and the very hard winter which followed (Dupaigne, 1983), and ultimately allowed Massoud and his forces not only to fight another day, but to commence more coordinated operations in the north – in other words, to 'break out' (Roy, 1990: 199). According to one report, during the ceasefire he deployed forces to attack Soviet positions in the Shomali Valley to the north of Kabul, and in the vicinity of Balkh (Urban, 1990: 144). From this perspective, Massoud's approach simply applied an old strategic principle: *reculer pour mieux sauter.*

Massoud's successes derived from a number of factors. One was undoubtedly his personal charisma, to which many of his interlocutors have testified. Another was a genuine understanding of the nature of guerrilla warfare, on which subject he was much more widely read than most other resistance commanders. But equally important was his promotion of a more highly developed organisational basis for military action. His approach was more institutional than patrimonial (Dorronsoro, 2005: 133); and while maintaining the autonomy of his military force, he consulted extensively with both religious and civic notables through a system of councils (Rubin, 1995a: 234–7). This gave him the capacity to protect the civilian population by moving to evacuate threatened villagers to side-valleys when the main part of the Panjsher was under attack, and this in turn helped consolidate the loyalty of the residents to him.

The Hazarajat

The Hazarajat represents a special case, not only because of its geographic isolation, but also because of the dominant position of the Shia, which shaped the character of political and military organisation. Within the Hazarajat, there were a number of competitors for leadership: Harpviken identifies them as the *mir*, the *sayyid*, the *sheikh*, and the Radical Islamist (Harpviken, 1996: 28). The mir was a traditional leader, of a type more commonly known elsewhere as khan, malik or arbab, depending upon the particular roles played; the sayyid was a member of the Prophet's family; the sheikh was a traditional religious dignitary; and the Radical Islamist had typically been energised by the Iranian revolution. The *Shura-i Ettefaq* came to be dominated by sayyids, although many were also sheikhs. However, the internal politics of the Hazarajat were to be complicated by the reluctance of the Kabul regime or the USSR to commit scarce resources to a remote and isolated region of limited importance to their overall strategy. Kabul seemed as far away as ever, and this deprived the locals of an external enemy against which they needed to unite. This freed them to confront each other, which they did with a vengeance from 1982.

The structure of the regime and the role of the party

The limited autonomy of the Karmal regime

In examining the form of regime which the Soviets sought to defend by military means, it is important first of all to appreciate that its autonomy was limited. In this respect it followed a model which had come to apply in a number of the states of Eastern Europe in which Communist regimes had been installed in the aftermath of the Second World War, namely Poland, East Germany, Hungary, Czechoslovakia, and Bulgaria. These states were members of the Warsaw Treaty Organisation (commonly known as the Warsaw Pact) which provided for integrated military command; they were members of the Council for Mutual Economic Assistance (commonly known as COMECON) which provided for a degree of economic integration; and most importantly, they were exposed to the threat of Soviet invasion should their internal politics spin out of control from the Soviet point of view: such invasions occurred in Hungary in 1956 and Czechoslovakia in 1968. The local regimes secured at best 'quasi-legitimacy' (Pakulski, 1986), since they ultimately depended upon external military protection for their survival. However, the autonomy of even these regimes was not entirely illusory: the fact that the point could twice be reached where a Soviet invasion was *necessary* to restore a situation acceptable to the Soviet leadership highlights the scope for complex internal politics even within such ostensibly subordinated polities.

The position of the Karmal regime was that of an oddity within the Soviet sphere of influence. After the December 1979 invasion, official Soviet sources classified Afghanistan as one of the 'developing countries' (*razvivaiushchiesia strany*) rather than as one of the 'socialist countries' (*sotsialisticheskie strany*). However, on a number of occasions, the Soviets publicly treated Kabul's 'sovereignty' with a cavalier disregard, for example on 25 October 1985 when Boris Ponomarev announced that the sentence on the French journalist Jacques Abouchar, captured in Afghanistan on 17 September 1984, was to be commuted (Maley, 1985: 160). But that said, while the regime was very significantly limited by its shortages of both legitimacy and tax revenues – fully 61 per cent of reported state expenditure in 1980 was funded by rentier income (Rubin, 1995a: 113) – and was heavily dependent on Soviet advisers (Bradsher, 1999: 122–4), elements within it retained some capacity to resist unpalatable Soviet pressures through foot-dragging, because the Soviets during this phase did not see it as acceptable simply to abandon the Afghan regime to its fate. The Soviets understandably found their Afghan colleagues difficult to manage.

Factionalism within the Karmal regime and the weakness of the Party

Factionalism was something which the Soviet model had long deplored. At the Tenth Congress of the Russian Communist Party (Bolshevik) in March 1921 – that at which the famous theoretician Bukharin observed that 'the revolution is hanging by a thread' – V. I. Lenin had forced the adoption of a resolution entitled 'On the Unity of the Party' (*O edinstve partii*), which was designed to outflank the so-called 'Workers' Opposition' and secure the dominance of the position which Lenin wished to see adopted. The resolution was deployed in 1957 by Khrushchev against his opponents in the 'Anti-Party' group, and hung heavily in the air if ever fundamental policy divergences threatened to surface within the Soviet leadership. Of course, it was essentially a tool in the hands of whichever group in a divided Politburo could muster enough support in the Central Committee to come out on top. Sir John Harington's famous epigram on treason – *Treason doth never prosper, what's the reason? For if it prosper, none dare call it treason* – applied perfectly to the rule which the resolution on party unity formulated. However, it also helped fuel distaste for open factions, as inimical to the interests of effective party functioning.

The PDPA was faced by a severe problem of factionalism throughout the Karmal period. As noted in Chapter 2, the *Khalqis* were simply too important a component of the Afghan Army officer corps for a 'clean' purge of the faction to be successfully accomplished. However, too much blood had been shed for the different factions to coexist comfortably at the elite level, and Arnold's reference to 'Afghanistan's Two-Party Communism' was more than apposite (Arnold, 1983). Episodes of factional strife were many and varied: the flavour of what was involved can be brought out by reference to the career of just one figure, Abdul Qadir, the non-Pushtun *Parchami* whose crucial role in the April 1978 coup was noted earlier. Qadir had been appointed Defence Minister in the aftermath of the coup, but was purged with other *Parchamis*, and given a death sentence, commuted to 15 years' imprisonment in October 1979, doubtless as a result of Soviet pressure on Amin. Released following the Soviet invasion, he was wounded by a *Khalqi* gunman on 4 June 1980, but survived to be reappointed Defence Minister in 1982. However, he was assaulted in May 1983 by the former Commander of the Kabul City Garrison, Major-General Khalilullah, and had to be hospitalised. In July 1984, he reportedly shot and wounded his *Khalqi* colleague Aslam Watanjar (*Les Nouvelles d'Afghanistan*, nos 19–20, October–December 1984: 3), and on 3 December 1984, it was announced that he had been replaced as Defence Minister by the Pushtun *Khalqi* Nazar Muhammad (BBC *Summary of World Broadcasts* FE/78 18/C/1, 5 December 1984). Qadir survived to become Ambassador to Poland from October 1986, but was finally expelled from the party in June 1988; he wisely defected to Bulgaria (Bradsher, 1999: 322). Obviously not all senior party figures had as spectacular a career as Qadir, but the interfactional antagonisms were serious enough for the Soviet commentator Aleksandr Bovin – in the course of a discussion of Afghanistan in a Soviet television programme on 15 February 1987 – to refer to the 'negative role' of the 'dissensions, feuds and bloody clashes within the ruling party itself' (BBC *Summary of World Broadcasts* SU/8494/A3/3, 17 February 1987).

This weakness of the party at the top undermined any significant benefit from expanding its membership base. In his famous essay *Chto delat'?* ('What is to be done?'), Lenin had argued a case for a vanguard party of committed revolutionaries to overcome the problem of insipid proletarian consciousness. Following the establishment of the Bolshevik regime, the membership of the Soviet Communist Party had expanded vastly beyond that which could justify the label 'vanguard'; rather, the party discharged a number of clearly understood functions in a highly institutionalised system. In Afghanistan, with no institutionalised system, expanding mass party membership made sense only as part of a strategy of long-term political education and socialisation. Figures cited by Giustozzi claimed a party membership of 50,599 full and candidate members in 1980, rising steadily to 154,853 by March 1986 (Giustozzi, 2000: 253). However, given the scope for inflation of such figures, and the opportunistic motivations of many of those who did join, there is much to be said for Giustozzi's conclusion that 'the PDPA found it overwhelmingly difficult to expand beyond its traditional, restricted areas of influence' (Giustozzi, 2000: 40).

Relations between different bureaucratic agencies

In the Soviet model, the Communist Party played an overarching role, and while bureaucratic politics certainly existed, both within and between agencies of the state, the penetration of state hierarchies by the party – overseeing but not actually undertaking state activities – served to keep conflicts under control. The factionalism in the Afghan party meant that it could not discharge this important function effectively, and as a result, the agencies of the state tended to become factional bailiwicks and cooperated poorly if at all. The most important and troubling of these relationships was that between KhAD and the Interior Ministry (*Sarandoy*). KhAD, which is discussed in more detail in the next part of this chapter, was headed by Dr Najibullah, a *Parchami*; the *Sarandoy*, on the other hand, was headed by Sayid Muhammad Gulabzoi, a *Khalqi*. (Gulabzoi, one of Afghanistan's great survivors, managed to re-emerge as a post-Taliban politician and was elected to the lower house of the Afghan Parliament in September 2005.) KhAD managed to establish a presence in both the military and *Sarandoy* (Halliday and Tanin, 1998: 18), but tensions between KhAD and *Sarandoy* persisted. This problem was aggravated by the increasing tension between different Soviet agencies (Rubin, 1995a: 125–6), especially following the death of Leonid Brezhnev in November 1982 and the accession to the General Secretaryship of former KGB Chief Iurii Andropov, who moved rapidly to settle scores with a number of his old enemies, notably Brezhnev's long-time Interior Minister and associate Nikolai Shchelokov, who was dismissed from office in 1983 and committed suicide in December 1984. In the Afghan case, it appeared to be the responsibility of the 'Revolutionary Council' to ease interagency tensions, but in practice it lacked the authority to do so.

The failed legitimation strategies of the Karmal regime

The Karmal phase of the Soviet–Afghan War was marked by a number of attempts by the regime to explore new means by which it might seek to legitimate its rule (Maley, 1987a). Building a 'communist' society was not part of this rhetorical strategy; the *Fundamental Principles of the Democratic Republic of Afghanistan*, issued in Kabul in April 1980 by the Publication Department of the Ministry of Information and Culture, contained no mention at all of socialism or communism. However, Article 4 of the Fundamental Principles did identify the PDPA as 'the guiding and mobilising force of society and state, reflecting the will and interests of workers, peasants, the intelligentsia, all the toilers and national democratic forces, and a steadfast advocate of real interests of the entire peoples living in our indivisible homeland, Afghanistan', and one might therefore argue that a key element of the Soviet model was built into the principles, albeit without mentioning communism by name. Few Afghans seem to have been fooled by the ruse. Instead, the regime attempted to link itself to respected traditional symbols, and to pursue a local variant of the classic 'United Front' strategy.

Symbolically, the regime attempted to depict itself as the defender of the Islamic faith, of which the *Fundamental Principles* spoke in glowing terms. A Ministry of Islamic Affairs and Religious Endowments was established in March 1995, and systematic attempts were made to coopt prayer leaders to support the regime (Lobato, 1985; Giustozzi, 2000: 57–64). However, these efforts were largely fruitless: memories of the atheistic follies of the regime after the April 1978 coup were too recent, the atheism of the Soviets was notorious, and religious symbolism had been effectively expropriated by the Mujahideen for the purposes of resistance. The regime also sought to link itself to tribal tradition by convoking a 'Loya Jirgah' in Kabul in April 1985. This bore little resemblance to a 'genuine' Loya Jirgah, since the participants were kept isolated in two guest houses, prevented from mixing with locals, and reportedly were paid to attend (Maley, 1987a: 718). However, it did provide a platform for Karmal to revive another legitimating rhetoric, that of the Pushtunistan dispute, with the claim that everyone 'should know that we can never remain indifferent regarding the destiny of the free tribes and our Pushtun and Baluch brothers who exist under the ruthless boot of oppression and the cruelty of the militarist reactionaries of Pakistan' (BBC *Summary of World Broadcasts* FE/7940/C/11, 2 May 1985). This coincided with a concentrated effort to suborn Afridi tribesmen in Pakistan, but with at best patchy success.

Dealing with tribes was a major challenge for the regime, especially after August 1980 when its Minister for Tribal Affairs, Faiz Muhammad, who had occupied the same ministerial position from 1975 under President Daoud, was murdered while negotiating with Jadran tribesmen during a jirgah. A structure which was used to assist the cooptation of tribes was the 'National Fatherland Front' (*Jabhe-i Melli-i Padarwatan*), set up on 15 June 1981 under the leadership of Dr Saleh Muhammad Zeray, a Kandahari Pushtun and *Khalqi* who headed it until he was replaced by Abdul Rahim Hatif in March 1985. The Front was of very limited value, since it was transparently no more than a mask for the PDPA (Bradsher, 1999: 134; Giustozzi, 2000: 143). Other mass organisations were established for youth (the Democratic Organisation of the Youth of Afghanistan, based on the Soviet Komsomol) and women (the Democratic Organisation of Afghan Women, based on the Union of Soviet Women). The youth organisation claimed 20,000 members in July 1980, and 200,000 by September 1986 (Giustozzi, 2000: 252), while the women's organisation claimed 8,300 members in 1981–1982, and 108,931 in 1987 (Giustozzi, 2000: 47). Neither proved of much value in winning the wider population over to the regime, although activists of the Democratic Organisation of Afghan Women, notably Dr Anahita Ratebzad, Masuma Esmaty-Wardak, and Jamila Palwashah, were made available to the odd visiting feminist to preach the regime's virtues. But the organisations of youth and women had no influence at all on Soviet military strategy, which caused enormous suffering for rural women and children (Maley, 1996).

The Afghan secret police

The organisation of KhAD

The struggle against 'enemies within' was one of the key dimensions of the Soviet–Afghan War, and the body charged with pursuing it was the 'State Information Service' (*Khedamat-e Ettalaat-e Dawlati*, or KhAD). Established on 11 January 1980 as a department within the Prime Minister's Office, it was headed until 21 November 1985 by Dr Najibullah. He was succeeded by his deputy Ghulam Faruq Yaqubi, who headed the secret police until the communist regime collapsed in 1992. On 11 January 1986, KhAD was reconstituted as the Ministry of State Security (*Wizarat-e Amniat-e Dawlati* or WAD). In contrast to bodies such as the Army and the Interior Ministry, KhAD became a *Parcham* faction stronghold.

The model for KhAD was explicitly the Soviet KGB, which played a significant role in exercising domestic political control. According to Rubin, Najibullah reported directly to the KGB (Rubin, 1995a: 133), and like the KGB, KhAD was divided into a number of departments, dealing *inter alia* with counter-intelligence, surveillance of foreigners, surveillance of party and government members, surveillance of intellectuals, counter-insurgency, and operations across the border with Pakistan. All major towns under regime control had their own KhAD offices, and it was in these outposts that some of KhAD's worst atrocities were committed. KhAD was widely believed responsible for a campaign of bombings in the Pakistani city of Peshawar in 1985–1986, and was also involved in kidnappings such as that of the Australian aid worker Robert Williamson, who was seized with his wife near Quetta on 18 May 1985 (Maley, 1986: 20), and released only on 27 December 1985 after months of imprisonment in Kabul. KhAD was unquestionably the most effective instrumentality of the Karmal regime. This was partly because it was factionally homogeneous, and partly because it enjoyed the patronage of a well-developed and efficient Soviet 'parent'. However, it also had a competent leader, who was to mirror his Soviet counterpart, Andropov, by moving from his police position to a position as Party Secretary, and ultimately by obtaining the supreme leadership.

Najibullah as head of KhAD

Najibullah was born in 1947 in Kabul, but by descent was an Ahmadzai Pushtun from a family in the Gardez area. He was from a different generation than Taraki, Amin, or Karmal, and had cut his teeth politically as a student activist at Kabul University, from which he graduated with an MD degree in 1975. Despatched to Tehran in 1978 as Ambassador, he disappeared from his post as the purge of *Parchamis* accelerated, and resurfaced only with the Soviet invasion. As is widely known, Najibullah was ultimately to be murdered in grisly circumstances in September 1996 when the Taliban seized Kabul. This, together with revulsion at the damage to Kabul following his removal in April 1992, and the sense that at least he was a modernist, might incline the casual observer to regard him with some sympathy. It is thus all the more important to emphasise that his tenure as Head of KhAD was marked by barbarities of a high order, and that Najibullah played no small role in the spawning of the climate of lawlessness to which he was ultimately to fall victim.

As head of KhAD, he impressed a range of important Soviet interlocutors, and this accounted for his subsequent rise to overall leadership. He enjoyed the particular patronage of Vladimir Kriuchkov, who headed the KGB from 1988 to 1991. However, he was an utterly ruthless man. This is borne out not only by the range of KhAD brutalities over which he was prepared to preside, but also by testimony of those who knew him. One of the most interesting of these was his brother Siddiqullah Rahi, who defected to the resistance and subsequently published his memoirs: these depicted Najibullah as a violent man who even in his student days delighted in striking fear into his family, and whose private life departed sharply from Afghan moral codes (Akram, 1996: 210). A Soviet Military Intelligence assessment depicted him as a 'vicious politician, vain and ambitious', and went on: 'A Pushtun nationalist, he is one of the motivating spirits of the policy of "Pushtunization" of Afghan society. Within his closest circle he speaks only Pashto. He is inclined to select colleagues not for their professional qualities but for their personal devotion to him, predominantly relatives and fellow-villagers' (Ostermann, 2003–2004: 250). A man of great bulk, Najibullah was known colloquially as *Najib-Gaw* ('Najib the Bull'), and followed Machiavelli's advice that it is better for a prince to be feared than loved.

KhAD and urban repression

In rural areas, confronting the resistance was substantially the responsibility of the armed forces, although prisoners were likely to be handed over to KhAD for interrogation. But in urban areas, KhAD had a frontline role to play in confronting opposition. Here, the regime lived in fear not so much of violent overthrow by a popular uprising, but rather of the targeting of regime officials for assassination, and the bombing of public buildings. Regime figures killed in Kabul included Deputy Minister for Education Wali Yusufi in July 1980; the Deputy Head of KhAD, Brigadier Ghulam Sakhi Atal, in April 1981; the Commander of the Revolutionary Defence Militia, Sharafuddin Sharaf, in April 1981; the Head of the Central Army Corps, Abdul Wadood, in September 1982; the Head of Afghan Ariana Airlines, Captain Sayed Baba, in March 1983; and a Departmental Director in the Ministry of Education, Dost Muhammad, in May 1985.

   KhAD's response took two forms. One was a vigorous effort to penetrate urban resistance groups with a view to thwarting their anti-regime activities before they could be brought to fruition. The other was to deter people from becoming involved in anti-regime activities in the first place, through the use of high levels of coercive power against suspects. In practice, this amounted to the torture of prisoners, which was documented extensively by Amnesty International (Amnesty International, 1983; Amnesty International, 1984; Amnesty International, 1986); the United Nations Special Rapporteur on Human Rights in Afghanistan

(United Nations, 1985a; United Nations 1985b); and researchers under the auspices of Human Rights Watch (Laber and Rubin, 1988). Women were not spared, as the story of Fahima Nassery makes clear. Mrs Nassery, a mathematics teacher at the Aiasha-i Durrani High School in Kabul from 1969, was arrested in May 1981: 'I was taken to a room where I witnessed the most horrible sight of my detention. Cut fingers, noses, ears, legs, hands, breasts, and hair of women were piled there. In one corner, a decayed corpse was lying. The smell of blood and the decayed corpse were intolerable. I remained in that chamber of horrors until the following morning' (Rahimi, 1986: 108). There were female as well as male interrogators; some were her former students (Nassery, 1986: 11).

These policies were put into practice in the system of prisons which KhAD operated in Kabul. The largest and most notorious was that at Pul-e Charkhi, but equally frightening were those at the Prime Ministry (*Sedarat*), KhAD-e Shashdarak, KhAD-e Panj, KhAD-e Nizami, the 400-bed hospital, and military garrisons (Akram, 1996: 206). To staff these facilities, the organisation built up a staff which by 1987 numbered an estimated '15,000 to 30,000 professionals and about 100,000 paid informers' (Rubin, 1995a: 133). According to Bradsher, people joined not out of ideological commitment, but 'for exemption from military conscription, ten times as much pay as government clerical workers, and access to liquor, prostitutes, and extortion money' (Bradsher, 1999: 137–8).

KhAD and the creation of a deracinated 'janissary' class

One of the most intriguing of KhAD's roles related to orphans. On 5 September 1981, a new body was established called the 'Foster Home of the Fatherland' (*Parwareshgah-i Watan*), of which Najibullah was the first head; his successor, from November 1981 to August 1986 was Karmal's wife, Mahbouba. Its headquarters were in the Wazir Akbar Khan district of Kabul. Again, this body reflected Soviet practice from an earlier era; in January 1921, the Head of Lenin's secret police, Feliks Dzerzhinskii, had been appointed to head the Commission for the Amelioration of the Life of Children (*Komissiia po uluch-sheniiu zhizni detei*) which was set up to deal with the problem of waifs (*besprizornye or besprizorniki*) during the Russian civil war (Leggett, 1981: 246–7; Stolee, 1988: 68). Superficially, the protection of orphans of war is a commendable undertaking, but in this case there were more sinister overtones. In the Soviet Union, orphanages became major recruiting grounds for secret policemen (*chekisti*). And in Afghanistan, even before the 'Foster Home' was established, reports had begun to surface of schoolchildren being removed to the USSR ('Des lycéens afghanes déportées en U.R.S.S.', *Les Nouvelles d'Afghanistan,* no. 3, February–March 1981: 13). Subsequent more detailed research (Laber, 1986) suggested that the objective of this exercise was to create a 'janissary' class (named after the Christian guards whose role it was to protect the Muslim rulers of the Ottoman Empire) who would be detached from normal cultural influences and moulded to perform the functions required in a Soviet-type system of rule. 'During 1984–86', Rubin writes, 'this program created considerable resentment and fear in Kabul; many refugees said they had fled Kabul for fear that their children might be sent to the USSR' (Rubin, 1995a: 141–2).

Such strategies are for the long run only, and in the long run, the Afghan communist regime – to paraphrase Maynard Keynes – turned out to be dead. The sad legacy of this particular strategy is to be found in the large numbers of still relatively young Afghans scattered through the former Soviet Union and the former Eastern Bloc, often spurned by their erstwhile hosts but with nowhere left to go. They are readily visible to any Afghanistan specialist who travels in those parts of the world.

Soviet-KhAD relations and the roles of Soviet advisers

One point that is abundantly clear is that Soviet advisers played central roles in all of KhAD's diverse activities. They helped train its agents in the management of information, which is a key resource in the hands of a secret police force, as the opening of Stasi archives in the former East Germany made clear. Soviet advisers were so numerous that they had their own offices in the Darulaman district of Kabul (Rubin, 1995a: 133). However, the complexities of loyalties in Afghanistan meant that the relations between KGB advisers and KhAD agents were not straightforward. While a key aim of KhAD was to penetrate the resistance, some KhAD agents provided information to the resistance as well, and the knowledge that this could happen affected interpersonal trust between KGB staff and their Afghan counterparts. The scale on which this occurred should not be exaggerated, but in such circumstances, a little distrust goes a long way. KhAD was a proficient organisation, and was widely feared as a result, but it was not omnipotent.

The USSR and change in the Kabul regime

At the beginning of the 1980s, the Soviet Union appeared to be a permanent fixture on the global political scene. The chill which followed the invasion of Afghanistan provided an opportunity for the KGB to move against the USSR's dissident movement at a time when the marginal cost of doing so would be negligible, and it did so very effectively (see Alexeyeva, 1985; Karklins, 1987). Individual protests still occurred, as on 18 May 1983 when a broadcaster on Radio Moscow's English service, Vladimir Danchev, referred to tribes in eastern provinces 'joining the struggle against the Soviet invaders' ('L'annonceur moscovite', *Les Nouvelles d'Afghanistan*, no. 14, June–August 1983: 9). The most famous Soviet dissident, Academician Andrei Sakharov, also condemned the invasion, and was exiled with his wife Elena Bonner to the 'closed' city of Gorkii. However, such acts were isolated displays of moral courage, and appeared not to shake a monolithically powerful regime.

Problems of stagnation in the USSR

Nonetheless, this impression of stability was misleading. In a number of respects, the Soviet system was facing increased strain (Colton, 1986: 6–67; Miller, 1993: 21–37). First, the Soviet economy was teetering on the edge of a major slowdown. It was one of the most centralised in human history, and heavily bureaucratised. The basic planning mechanism was the State Planning Commission (*Gosplan*), originally established in 1921. Five-year plans set out targets for important economic aggregates such as investment, manufacturing production, agricultural output, and consumption. The planning organs, however, were more and more obviously unequal to the task of coordinating vast amounts of information, a task which markets accomplish in a decentralised fashion. While limited specific tasks could normally be performed by the swift mobilisation of resources that a command economy permitted, this was at the expense of wider levels of consumption and consumer satisfaction. By the last three years of Brezhnev's rule (1979–1982), it is likely that the USSR was already experiencing a decline in output (Harrison, 1993). Poverty was far more serious a problem than official statistics suggested (Matthews, 1986).

Second, a significant turnover in the Soviet elite was underway. In 1980, Chairman of the Council of Ministers Kosygin died; his replacement, Nikolai Tikhonov, was barely a year his junior. In January 1982, the conservative, incorruptible Party Secretary for ideology, Mikhail A.

Suslov, died at the age of 79; he had been a party secretary since 1949. His successor was Andropov, who left the KGB in order to become a party secretary and position himself for still higher office. Brezhnev himself died in November 1982, after some years in which his mental powers had been declining markedly (Brown, 1996: 53–4; Gorbachev, 1996: 108–39), and was succeeded by Andropov. This led to a period of some turmoil as Andropov, finally unleashed by Brezhnev's demise, moved against some of Brezhnev's corrupt long-term associates, including Interior Minister Schelokov, and the party First Secretary in Uzbekistan (and candidate Politburo member) Sharaf Rashidov. However, Andropov, 68 when he assumed the General Secretaryship, suffered failing health through much of 1983, and finally died of kidney disease in February 1984. In what ultimately paved the way for a new leadership generation, the Politburo opted for the increasingly feeble Konstantin Chernenko as General Secretary; his performance was so execrable that upon his death, a clear majority in the Politburo favoured a generational change, which came about with the elevation to the General Secretaryship of Mikhail Gorbachev. The tensions within the leadership during the 1982–1985 transition phase were considerable, and militated against decisive actions being taken, even when Andropov was inclined to act firmly.

Third, East–West relations were in a frigid condition. Some have gone as far as to label the period after the invasion of Afghanistan a 'Second Cold War'. Halliday argues that by the latter part of 1980, it was clear to the Soviet leadership that the 'international cost' of the invasion of Afghanistan, 'above all in relations with the US, was much higher than originally anticipated' (Halliday, 1999: 680). In the years which followed, Western pressure on the USSR, if anything, increased. The Anglo–American relationship survived the tensions of the Falklands War and, underpinned by the warm relationship between British Prime Minister Margaret Thatcher and US President Ronald Reagan, provided a firm basis for opposition to the Soviet system in general, epitomised in Reagan's famous description of the Soviet Union as an empire which was the 'focus of evil' in the world. Two other events contributed to the isolation of the USSR. One was the imposition of Martial Law in Poland in December 1981, directed at quashing the Solidarity free trade union. The other was the shooting-down of Korean Airlines flight KE007 on 1 September 1983, after the aircraft had strayed into Soviet airspace. Each led to the excoriation of the Soviet leadership by the USA. The *détente* of the 1970s, and whatever benefits it had brought the Soviet Union, was dead.

The rise of Gorbachev and the fall of Karmal

On 10 March 1985, Konstantin Chernenko died of emphysema. He was immediately succeeded as General Secretary by Mikhail Gorbachev. The new General Secretary, born in 1931, was the first occupant of the office to be born after the Bolshevik Revolution, although he had actually joined the Communist Party in Stalin's time. He had spent much of his career as a party official in Stavropol, and while he became a member of the Central Committee in 1971, it was only on 27 November 1978 that he came to Moscow as a Central Committee Secretary, and only in 1980 that he became a full member of the Politburo. Gorbachev was to trigger a revolution from above which swept away both mono-organisational socialism and the Soviet Union. But one of the first to feel the effects of the change was Babrak Karmal.

The two superficially had certain attributes in common. Karmal was only two years older than Gorbachev, and each had been communists for many years. But the differences between the two were more significant. Gorbachev, in the words of his adviser Andrei Grachev, was 'a genetic error of the system' (Brown, 1996: 88). Karmal was entirely orthodox, and incapable of responding to circumstances outside the framework of his stale ideological commitments. Gorbachev was a man of notable energy and drive, whereas Karmal was notable for his lethargy. And Gorbachev had a stable and happy personal life, while Karmal was a drunkard (Rubin, 1995a: 125, 320; Ostermann, 2003–2004: 251) whose long-term liaison with Dr Anahita Ratebzad was a matter of grotesque notoriety in Kabul. It is hardly surprising that Gorbachev found Karmal a substandard leader.

Gorbachev had not been part of the Kremlin leadership group which took the decision to invade Afghanistan, and once he became General Secretary, he had no particular personal reason to defend the decision. His approach to Afghanistan depended rather upon a calculation of the costs and benefits of the commitment in the mid-1980s, both for his own political programme, and for the state which he led. He did not take long to make up his mind. While he was prepared to give the military one more chance to deliver success on the ground (Bradsher, 1999: 275), in November 1985 he invited Karmal to 'forget socialism' (Chernyaev, 2000: 42), and at the 27th Congress of the Communist Party of the Soviet Union in February 1986, he pointedly referred to Afghanistan as a 'bleeding wound' (*krovotochashchaia rana*) (Communist Party of the Soviet Union, 1986: 69). Karmal was exceedingly reluctant to respond to these signals, for he clearly appreciated the oblivion that awaited an ex-leader of his stripe. In February 1986, he put on a bravado performance for a visiting Western journalist, whose report with hindsight seems somewhat surreal: 'Relaxed and looking well, the Afghan President laughed at Western diplomatic rumours that his health is failing. "I must have heard 10 times that I've been killed on various foreign radio broadcasts. I'm alive. I'm fighting. I'm working – with a cool head and a warm heart", he said, patting his chest' (Steele, 1986: 7).

But the writing was indelibly on the wall. Anatoly Dobrynin was witness to the final meeting between Gorbachev and Karmal: 'Gorbachev told Karmal point-blank that he should cede his position to Najibullah and take up residence in Moscow, where his family was already living. Karmal was dazed. He obsequiously begged Gorbachev to change his mind, promising to perform his duties in a more correct and active way. But Gorbachev was inexorable, because he did not believe any more that Karmal could find a way out of the deadlock which had in fact been created by the Soviet Union itself' (Dobrynin, 1995: 443). On 5 May 1986, Karmal was removed from the position of General Secretary of the PDPA Central Committee, ostensibly on health grounds. With this, the first phase of the Soviet–Afghan War came to an end.

5
The Najibullah–Gorbachev Period, 1986–1989

The fall of Babrak Karmal led to a period of what Goodson calls 'Resistance gains and Soviet withdrawals', marked by high and stable intensity (Goodson, 1998: 478). It concluded in February 1989 when the withdrawal of Soviet combat troops from Afghanistan was completed. While the next chapter examines in detail the specific processes by which the Soviet leadership decided to undertake the withdrawal, and the orchestration and conduct of the withdrawal, this chapter is concerned with the wider developments in both Afghanistan and the USSR which left the Soviet leadership with little taste for its Afghan commitment. A key theme which emerges is that while Afghanistan was more public a preoccupation in the Soviet Union during this period than it had been previously, the real interest of the Soviet leadership in its Afghan clients was declining sharply as it focused inward on domestic political reforms such as *glasnost'*, *perestroika*, and *demokratizatsiia*, the very changes which ultimately were to eat away the foundations of Soviet power. The reality of failure in Afghanistan was finally grasped in Moscow, and as the composition of the Soviet leadership changed, so did its commitment to adventures abroad.

The chapter is divided into three sections. The first examines the regime's increased use of militias, and then briefly looks at military activities between 1986 and 1989 in the regions that were discussed in Chapter 4. As in the Karmal period, there was a dearth of large, set-piece battles to tip the scale in either direction, but rather a large number of clashes which did not deliver a decisive victory to the resistance, but instead gnawed away at the regime's claims to legitimacy. The second examines the evolution during this period of the new leaderships in both the USSR and Afghanistan, and of their strategies for political consolidation. The third discusses the formal policy of 'national reconciliation' which was promoted by the USSR as a way of dealing with 'regional conflicts', and shows why it was unable in Afghanistan to deliver the kinds of outcomes for which the Soviet leadership had hoped. As an overview, it is important to note that 1986 was a year of particular ferocity in the war, with the Soviet force under General Mikhail Zaitsev embarking on a number of major new operations. This lends some credence to the view that before contemplating a withdrawal from Afghanistan, it was necessary for Gorbachev to give the Soviet military the chance to secure a desirable political outcome by military means. Its failure to do so arguably excluded it as a serious opponent of withdrawal, and silenced those members of the Soviet leadership who might otherwise have been inclined to argue that the USSR had not really tried to win the war.

Patterns of war

Militias

In a development that was ultimately to pave the way for his own downfall, Najibullah accorded an enhanced role to *militias*. In contrast to organised forces under hierarchically structured command and related formally to the state, militias were armed groups that served the state, but at a distance and in such a way as preserved the autonomy on which key militia leaders tended to insist. In their pioneering study of militias, Dorronsoro and Lobato identified a number of distinct types, of which the most important were the *Geruh az Defa-i Inqilab* ('Groups for the Defence of the Revolution'), *Ghund-e Qawmi* ('Tribal Regiments') which were under KhAD control, and the *Milishia-i Sahardi* ('Border Militia'). Some were based on *qawm* solidarity, while others were based on individual recruitment (Dorronsoro and Lobato, 1989: 100). A number of militia leaders were to achieve considerable notoriety, such as Rasul Pahlavan in the vicinity of Andkhoi, and the rambunctious Esmatullah 'Muslim' in Kandahar. Esmatullah in particular proved hard to handle: he noisily disrupted a 'Loya Jirgah' staged by Najibullah in Kabul in November 1987, and Najibullah the next day made his views of him quite clear: 'Unfortunately he is sick. He goes to extremes in using narcotics and alcohol, and it is these which caused his illness' (BBC *Summary of World Broadcasts* FE/0021/C/5, 9 December 1987). He finally died in a Soviet hospital in 1991 (Rubin, 1995a: 159). The militias were used to guard the peripheries of urban centres, as well as key roads (Dorronsoro, 2005: 183). The advantage of a militia system is that it can provide a 'halfway house' for those who wish to shift their allegiance, but not completely lose their autonomy. This is also the disadvantage of such a system: loyalty tends to be contingent rather than absolute. Giustozzi has argued that high salaries 'played a fundamental role in the rise of the regional and border militia' (Giustozzi, 2000: 209). As militias came to play a larger role in the regime's coercive capacity, maintaining the capacity to pay them on time became ever more important to the regime's survival. This was to come to a head in 1992.

Eastern and southern Afghanistan

Military activities in eastern and southern Afghanistan remained intense, although the focus of activities was no longer 'driving off' the population, as attempted from 1983, but rather ensuring that towns remained under the control of the Kabul regime. A number of operations attested to this. In August 1986, Soviet and regime troops undertook several major sweeps into Logar, and on 20 May 1987, they launched an operation with the apparent aim of relieving a besieged garrison in Jaji in Paktia. This they managed to do, but concerted resistance put paid to any idea of securing a firm foothold in the area, and on 13 June, they withdrew (Isby, 1989: 42; cf. Urban, 1990: 216–18). This inability to hold on to prizes was again apparent in the aftermath of the so-called 'Operation Magistral', in which the siege of Khost was broken. This has been described as 'the largest operation of the war' (Grau, 1998: 65), and involved 18,000 troops – 10,000 Soviet and 8000 regime (Urban, 1990: 230). It began on 28 November 1987, and on 29 December, the road to Khost from Gardez was finally opened to convoys. Yet by the end of January 1988, Soviet forces were obliged to abandon the positions which they had taken up on the Gardez–Khost road.

The south was a deeply troubled area. Kandahar remained an area of great difficulty for the regime; while it had a significant airport, it was markedly the most remote from Soviet territory of any major Afghan city, and very close to the border with Pakistan, although its relatively flat terrain did not lend itself readily to guerrilla operations. Missiles were also used by the resistance to powerful effect: on 27 July 1987, a missile shot down a plane carrying senior Soviet and Afghan personnel as it attempted to land at Kandahar airport. In Kandahar, the involvement of Esmatullah Muslim's militia in support of the regime gave an added bitterness to the conflict. The death on 3 June 1987 of Mohammad Eshaq ('Lala Malang'), a noted commander from Mawlawi Khalis's *Hezb-e Islami*, was a blow to the resistance, but Haji Abdul

Latif's forces continued to operate, and the Soviet withdrawal led to renewed heavy fighting in May–June 1988 near Kandahar, although without decisive shifts either for or against the regime. By contrast, on 17 June 1988, Qalat, the provincial capital of Zabul, was seized by the resistance, and although it was retaken four days later, it gave cause for alarm, since it was the first provincial capital to slide into opposition hands, and it also straddled the main road between Kabul and Kandahar. As Soviet forces withdrew, urban centres such as Qalat were also of *symbolic* importance: the fall of such a centre could easily trigger a cascade of defections from the regime. Hence the effort made to retake it.

Kabul, too, saw some spectacular Mujahideen strikes. For example, on 26 August 1986, a series of massive explosions occurred in an ammunition dump at Kargha after 107-mm and 122-mm rockets were fired into it. The regime blamed the blasts on 'technical problems', but the following day, Soviet television reported that the Mujahideen were responsible. Forces were despatched to secure the area and in nearby Paghman, historically a place of retreat for the Kabul elite from the bustle of the city, heavy fighting wrecked much of the town, including the *Arc de Triomphe de Paghman* which dated from King Amanullah's rule in the 1920s. On 9 October 1987, a car bomb in Kabul killed 27 people, and on 27 April 1988, the tenth anniversary of the communist coup, a truck bomb killed six and wounded many more. This period also witnessed rocket attacks on Kabul: an attack on 9 May 1988 killed at least 23 people, and from this point on, such attacks became more frequent. None of these pointed to the imminent loss of the city, but they highlighted the inability of the regime to develop a strategy to insulate the residents of the city from threats to life and limb.

Western Afghanistan

Herat remained an area of considerable tension, with heavy fighting in August 1986, and on 7 April 1987, serious clashes on the streets of the city killed more than 50 Soviet and regime personnel. However, Herat was not the venue for large-scale battles or operations such as Magistral. Rather, Ismail Khan concentrated on coordination, chairing a major meeting of commanders in Ghor in July 1987. Within the city itself, there was notable disaffection with the regime: on 22 May 1988, following the defection to the resistance of Major-General Fazal Ahmad Samadi, dissident soldiers blew up an ammunitions dump. However, the regime proved able to cope with these challenges: in Herat, neither side was fixated upon short-term gains.

Northern Afghanistan and the Panjsher Valley

The death of Zabiullah had a very bad effect on organisation in the north, and while major resistance operations continued, such as the 6 July 1986 attack on a huge Soviet convoy near Maimana, coordinated actions became more difficult to put together in the north-west. However, once the Soviet withdrawal from Afghanistan began, new opportunities presented themselves. One of the most dramatic events in northern Afghanistan was the brief fall of the town of Kunduz to resistance forces in August 1988, which led Najibullah subsequently to complain of 'the most disgraceful phenomena, that is flagrant treachery and shameful cowardice' (BBC *Summary of World Broadcasts,* FE/0292/C/1, 26 October 1988). Kunduz was a city of singular importance. It had a workable airfield, and straddled a major route from the USSR to Kabul; in the event that the road from Termez through Mazar-e Sharif to Pul-e Khumri was cut, the road from Sher Khan Bandar through Kunduz and Baghlan offered a workable alternative. These road routes were vital for the provisioning of Kabul, since an air bridge could not deliver sufficient *matériel* to sustain the capital if it were otherwise cut off. But in this case, the regime was lucky: some of the resistance groups which played a role in taking the city behaved badly and alienated the locals (Liakhovskii and Zabrodin, 1991: 131), allowing the regime to retake the town. The lessons here were better learned by the regime than by its opponents.

One of the most important developments in the entire war grew out of the Panjsher Valley: the establishment and the activation of the *Shura-i nazar-e Shomali*, or 'Supervisory Council of the North'. Massoud was the key instigator of this structure, which was part of his 'breakout' strategy following the conclusion of the 1982–1984 ceasefire. As his horizons grew beyond the Panjsher itself, he embarked upon a process of consultation with other commanders, and from 1986 the fruits of this cooperation were felt more widely. Strikes at Farkhar in August 1986 and Nahrin in November 1986 (Urban, 1990: 207) were symptomatic of the new level of coordination which Massoud had achieved. These were followed by Keran in October 1987 and Burqa in January 1988 (Roy, 1990: 210). However, while the formation of the Supervisory Council was a very important development, there remained forces outside its ambit. For example, Commander Najmuddin in Badakhshan was a significant commander, but Wahhabi forces, manipulated by both the Kabul regime and

Hekmatyar's *Hezb*, caused him considerable trouble at different times (Delpho, 1989: 49).

The Hazarajat

As noted earlier, from 1982 the Hazarajat experienced significant internal conflict, which saw the *Shura-i Ettefaq* in effect displaced by Islamist forces inspired by Iran. A consequence of this was that the Soviet Union and the regime made little effort to exercise direct control through military force: the Hazarajat was of no strategic significance. The token Soviet garrison in Bamiyan was evacuated in summer 1987 (Bradsher, 1999: 211) after coming under attack. But the most important development in the Hazarajat was not military but political: the crystal-lisation of a sense of Hazara political identity which would subsequently see a Hazara leadership bid for a slice of national power. How this played out, in a tragic way which obliged Hazaras to draw on all their stocks of resilience, we shall see in later chapters.

Political change in Moscow and Kabul

Elite turnover in the USSR

As noted in the preceding chapter, by the early 1980s, a significant turnover in the Soviet leadership was underway. The decrepit elite of the Brezhnev era was dying off in increasing numbers. Gorbachev, by exercising the patronage powers of the General Secretary, had consider-able say in the appointment of their replacements, and was able to craft a personal power base in the Central Committee more swiftly than many of his predecessors had been able to do. Brezhnev had been forced to accommodate his generational associates among the *vydvizhentsy*; by contrast, at the 1986 Party Congress, there was a 45 per cent turnover in Central Committee members, compared with a 22 per cent turnover at the last Brezhnev era Congress in 1981 (Mawdsley and White, 2000: 198). However, Gorbachev did face one notable limitation, which was to cause him great harm in the last year of his active political career, namely that his 'own network of trusted associates was, in comparative terms, small and weak' (Miller, 1987: 82).

One extremely significant event was the appointment of a new Foreign Minister. The death of Chernenko, as well as vacating the position of General Secretary of the Communist Party, also created a vacancy in the position of the USSR's nominal Head of State, that is, the Chairmanship of the Presidium of the Supreme Soviet. Rather than take it for himself (as his three predecessors had done), Gorbachev used it as a pretext to replace the 76-year-old Gromyko as Foreign Minister by moving him into an essentially honorific position. His replacement was completely unexpected: Eduard Shevardnadze, the First Secretary of the Georgian party organisation. Born in 1928, Shevardnadze had caught the attention of some in the leadership when, as head of the Georgian KGB, he had moved against the corrupt party First Secretary, Vasilii Mzhavanadze. He had known Gorbachev for many years, and by his own account had heterodox views on Afghanistan: in his memoirs he stated that in December 1979 he and Gorbachev 'learned from the newspapers that Soviet troops had invaded Afghanistan and hastened to meet to discuss it. We agreed that it was a fatal error that would cost the country dearly' (Shevardnadze, 1991: 26).

Gorbachev's consolidation of power: policy consequences

Gorbachev's selection as General Secretary of the Soviet Communist Party was an event of cataclysmic significance for a range of political forces within the Soviet Union and the wider world (see Hosking, 1990; Miller, 1993; Brown, 1996; Hough, 1997; Galeotti, 1997; Brown, 2007). It rapidly became clear that change was in the air. While Gorbachev's 'bleeding wound' comment at the 1986 Party Congress attracted some attention as a symptom of a new mood, it had less dramatic effect than the propagation of a policy of *glasnost'* ('candour') which began to acquire real bite after the explosion at the Chernobyl nuclear reactor on 26 April 1986. Together with Gorbachev's other main domestic policy positions – *perestroika* ('reconstruction') and *demokratizatsiia* ('democratisation') – this undermined the coherence of the system of mono-organisational socialism, and liberated forces which ultimately consumed the system (Karklins, 1994). For a reformer interested in bringing about major domestic change, an unpopular foreign commitment was an unnecessary burden. But from a classical Soviet perspective, Afghanistan could not be seen simply in these terms. An abandonment of the Afghanistan commitment could have undermined the notion that the gains of socialism were irreversible, and set a dangerous precedent for Eastern Europe. This problem was overcome through the articulation of a complementary theory of international relations which set the scene not only for the withdrawal of troops from Afghanistan, but for improved East–West relations and ultimately the disintegration of the Eastern Bloc.

The name given to this theory was *novoe myshlenie*, or 'New Thinking'. The term was not itself coined by Gorbachev: indeed, it had been used in a book published during Chernenko's tenure, and co-authored by the son of Foreign Minister Gromyko (Gromyko and Lomeiko, 1984). However, under the influence of Gorbachev, Shevardnadze, and Gorbachev's adviser Aleksandr Iakovlev, who had spent a decade from 1973 as Soviet Ambassador to Canada, it was given a distinctive twist, and in contrast to domestic policy, where innovations frequently require the cooperation of many different groups capable of dragging their feet, change in foreign policy was much more directly in the hands of the top leadership. *Novoe myshlenie* came to stand for a cluster of propositions (see Light, 1987: 294–315; Kubálková and Cruickshank, 1989: 6). These included the importance of interdependence and mutual security in the nuclear age and in the face of common problems such as ecological damage; the significance of peace as the highest human value, and the notion that security was indivisible; and the importance of comprehensive security based on a balance of interests rather than balance of power. Its key dimension, as Archie Brown put it, was a 'humanistic universalism' (Brown, 1996: 221). The radicalism of this approach should not be underestimated. It had across-the-board implications, shaping Moscow's approach to relations with the USA, to developing countries, to China, and to the Eastern Bloc. It had echoes of Khrushchev's 'peaceful coexistence', but without the latter's underlying sense of ongoing competition between capitalist and socialist systems. And in 1988, after the decision to withdraw from Afghanistan was announced, Gorbachev in two major speeches identified 'freedom of choice' as a universal principle (Brown, 1996: 225). Times had certainly changed.

Najibullah's consolidation of power

Najibullah's energy and dynamism may have made him seem an obvious choice in Moscow as Karmal's replacement, but in party circles in Kabul he was a controversial figure. He was despised by the *Khalq* faction, doubtless one reason why Soviet tanks surrounded Gulabzoi's Interior Ministry in Kabul during the Central Committee plenum at which Karmal was formally replaced. However, he was also regarded with profound suspicion by members of his own *Parcham* faction. His KhAD background was doubtless one factor at work here: secret police chiefs – Himmler and Beria being prime examples (Knight, 1993; Read, 2004) – are often viewed with a certain horror by their more squeamish colleagues. This created something of a vicious circle. With a weak base in the party, it was natural for Najibullah to continue to rely on KhAD, but since KhAD was an instrument of coercion and widely recognised as one, it was a poor base from which to try to secure any kind of legitimacy. In seeking to consolidate his position, Najibullah was confronted with challenges at two different levels. The first was that of the communist leadership in Afghanistan. Here, his position was, at a superficial reading, not so difficult. He enjoyed the full backing of the Soviet leadership, especially the KGB (Arnold, 1993: 150–2), and had indeed been recommended as Karmal's successor by the Soviet security organs (Dobrynin, 1995: 442). Except through assassination, he was in no danger of removal. However, unless he consolidated his power *vis-à-vis* his colleagues to the point that he could actually issue commands and not have them blocked through studied non-cooperation, his real power would be limited to what he could achieve directly through KhAD. The second level at which he faced challenges related to state–society relations more generally. Unless he could reconfigure the state into a legitimate agency which could mobilise and redistribute resources of its own, his regime would remain dependent upon externally supplied backing. In the former sphere, he was to achieve a measure of success. In the latter, he enjoyed very little success at all.

Karmal's removal as head of the party did not amount to his complete elimination from Afghan politics. Initially, Najibullah spoke as if a collective leadership of himself, Karmal, and Sultan Ali Keshtmand was to rule, but any such notion disappeared rapidly. Nonetheless, Karmal retained the position of Chairman of the Revolutionary Council until November 1986, when he was replaced (in an acting capacity) by a tribal nonentity, Haji Muhammad Chamkani, who in 1987 relinquished the position to Najibullah. Karmal's continued presence provided a certain cover for his associates to cause trouble for the new party leader. Najibullah responded ruthlessly, demoting a raft of Karmal supporters, and promoting persons loyal to him. His cleanout, over time, amounted to 'the systematic removal of all other significant people of influence within the PDPA' (Halliday and Tanin, 1998: 1368). At a plenum of the party Central Committee held on 10 July 1986, the Central Committee was enlarged, and three prominent figures were removed: the Herat party secretary, Abdul Ghaffar Azad; the secretary of the Revolutionary Council, Anwar Farzan; and the notorious former secret police chief from the Taraki period, Asadullah Sarwari (Gille, 1986: 4). On 4 December 1986, the *Parchami* Muhammad Rafi was appointed Defence Minister in place of the *Khalqi* Nazar Muhammad, and Abdul Wakil replaced

Shah Muhammad Dost as Foreign Minister; on 11 June 1987, Karmal's associate Dr Anahita Ratebzad, the only female Politburo member, was unceremoniously removed from her position; she and Karmal's half-brother, Mahmud Baryalay, were removed from the Central Committee on 17 October 1987. The biggest purge of all came in October 1988. Saleh Muhammad Zeray and Abdul Zuhur Razmjo were removed from the Politburo, and shortly after, Gulabzoi was abruptly despatched to Moscow as Afghan Ambassador. The nature of Najibullah's problem was set out very clearly in a speech he gave on 18 October 1987, which deserves to be quoted at some length:

> The enemies of party unity are ready to hoist the so-called revolutionary banners and accuse the PDPA Central Committee and its leadership of waiving the party's strategic policy in the interests of counter-revolutionaries. The enemies of party unity stubbornly resist the restructuring of party work. The enemies of party unity spread the spirit of defeat and disillusion, rumour and gossip, and they damage the authority and credibility of the PDPA leadership. The enemies of party unity prevent the expansion of the social bases of the revolution and the creation of coalition forms of administration and the multi-party system. The enemies of party unity create obstacles on the way of the party's policy for the eradication of mistakes and false calculations emanating from the wrong leap forwards to bring about social and economic transformation. The enemies of party unity openly assist in diminishing party authority and credibility among the people and in strengthening the positions of our ideological opponents. (BBC *Summary of World Broadcasts* FE/8707/C/18, 24 October 1987)

The vocabulary in this passage is so typical of Marxist-Leninist rhetoric that one wonders whether Soviet advisers penned it, but it undoubtedly reflected Najibullah's real views of his opponents.

Glasnost' and Afghanistan

One striking result of *glasnost'* was the appearance in the Soviet press and electronic media of more information about the situation in Afghanistan. The candour of this information also grew over time. The following items are merely samples from a wider body of material, but they do give some flavour of what began to appear. In July 1986, an article about life in Kabul spoke of the problem of 'securing peace and tranquillity in the city' (Shurygin, 1986: 6). In August 1987, *Pravda* reported that there were no fewer than 1.5 million Afghan refugees in Pakistan (Okulov, 1987: 6), and on 24 February 1988, a photograph of Afghan refugees in Pakistan appeared in *Literaturnaia gazeta*. In November 1988, Mikhail Leshchinskii, interviewed on Soviet television, observed that the ruling Afghan party had 'no support in the people', and was 'being torn by contradictions between factions and wings' (BBC *Summary of World Broadcasts* SU/0309/A3/1, 15 November 1988). A number of Soviet journalists, especially Artyom Borovik, were to play significant roles in exposing the realities of Afghanistan to Soviet audiences. Borovik, a son of the long-time head of the Soviet Peace Committee, went on to become a crusading investigative reporter in post-Communist Russia, and was eventually killed in a suspicious plane crash. Borovik's analysis of Afghanistan was set out in some detail in a book published in English (Borovik, 1990), but he won earlier fame with his field reporting, and in particular a sensational interview with Major-General Kim Tsagolov, Head of the Department of Marxism-Leninism at the M. V. Frunze Military Academy in Moscow (Borovik, 1988), about which I shall have more to say shortly.

The policy of 'national reconciliation'

The origins of 'national reconciliation'

Najibullah's specific policies were implemented under the overarching rubric of 'national reconciliation'. While Najibullah sought to give it Islamic roots (Rubin, 1995a: 165), the terminology was of Soviet origin – used in *Pravda* on 3 January 1986 (Bradsher, 1999: 146) – and was marketed as a way of resolving what the Soviet leadership described as 'regional problems', a code expression for the presence of Soviet troops in Afghanistan and Vietnamese forces in Cambodia (Maley, 1993a). Gorbachev in an important speech in Vladivostok on 28 July 1986 voiced 'support' for 'the line of the current Afghan leadership towards national reconciliation' (BBC *Summary of World Broadcasts* SU/8324/C/1–17, 30 July 1986), but as we now know from Chernyaev's memoirs quoted earlier, as well as from a range of other sources, Gorbachev had been pressing this line upon Karmal well before Najibullah became party leader. 'National reconciliation' was radically inconsistent with Marxism, since it emphasised nations rather than classes as appropriate bases for solidarity, and cooperation rather than struggle as an appropriate political strategy. In this sense, it was both an aspect of 'new thinking', and part of the process of ideological dismantling that the Gorbachev era had inaugurated. It also reflected the failure of military force to solve the regime's political problems. Najibullah stated this quite explicitly in July 1987: 'I want to emphasise particularly that during the nine years of the fratricidal war we have not been able to resolve even one of the issues which caused the war, not one. Now it has become clear that we cannot resolve these issues by military means' (BBC *Summary of World Broadcasts* FE/8622/C/1, 17 July 1987).

The content of 'national reconciliation'

National reconciliation consisted in practice of a mixture of symbolic and substantive measures. The former included steps such as the renaming of the 'National Fatherland Front' as 'National Front' on 15 January 1987, and of the 'Democratic Republic of Afghanistan' as the 'Republic of Afghanistan' (the name the country had carried from 1973 to 1978) on 13 July 1987. On 30 November 1987, a 'Loya Jirgah' adopted the *Constitution of the Republic of Afghanistan*, a document of 149 articles in 13 chapters, but in no sense did it perform the function of limiting power in any meaningful sense: rather, it reflected a conception of law simply as an instrument of policy. Its aim was to create the *image* of a constitutionalist order.

Substantively, the policy of 'national reconciliation' involved explicit obeisance to the importance of private sector activity in the economy, and of the 'sacred' religion of Islam as the religion of Afghanistan. 'Our revolution', Najibullah stated in October 1987, 'is not a proletarian or a socialist revolution' (BBC *Summary of World Broadcasts* FE/8707/C/1, 24 October 1987). These paralleled developments in the USSR under *perestroika*, where experiments with 'cooperatives' were underway, and systematic religious persecution by the KGB had largely disappeared. However, many of these avowed elements of 'national reconciliation' were not that different from what Karmal had proposed in the course of his failed attempts to legitimate the regime. And Giustozzi has rightly noted that 'most of what Najibullah was throwing away was *the dreams* of "modernizing" the Afghan countryside, rather than the reality' (Giustozzi, 2000: 168). Najibullah had hinted at this himself when he declared that 'We are weak in the tactical and practical sphere. Most of the grand thoughts and plans get drowned in mere words and remain on paper' (BBC *Summary of World Broadcasts* FE/8260/C/1–2, 16 May 1986).

Personnel changes were also part of the policy. The aim was essentially that of decapitating the opposition by coopting its key leaders into the regime. A first step was the induction of 'non-party figures' into ostensibly significant offices. On 26 May 1988, Dr Muhammad Hasan Sharq replaced Keshtmand as Chairman of the Council of Ministers. Much was made of his non-party background, but to most Afghan observers, Sharq was a longstanding fellow traveller with the *Parcham* faction, and it was almost certainly his reliability which led to his appointment. The Soviet Union regarded him with scorn – in a report to the Soviet Politburo on 23 January 1989, a high-level Soviet commission described the actions of Sharq and many of his ministers as 'Feeble, to say the least' (Hershberg, 1996–1997: 182). Sharq remained in office for less than a year. Other offices were identified as available to those prepared to join a 'government of national unity' as part of Najibullah's readiness 'officially and in practice, to share power' (BBC *Summary of World Broadcasts* FE/8622/C/2, 17 July 1987). A careful reading of the list showed that the Defence, Interior, and State Security ministries – what one might call the 'power ministries' – were excluded.

Finally, as part of the 'national reconciliation' policy, Najibullah announced a 'ceasefire' of six months from 15 January 1987, which in July he announced would be extended for a further six months. However, the fine print permitted 'crushing blows' in retaliation, and the resistance regarded the ceasefire as a complete sham. It certainly did not lead to any significant cessation of firing.

Obstacles to 'national reconciliation'

A number of serious barriers stood in the way of the policy of 'national reconciliation'. The policy was being pursued from a slender territorial and institutional base. In areas outside the regime's control, it was difficult for the regime to spread its message except through radio broadcasts, given the shortage of skilled cadres, and some important areas were so firmly under the control of particular resistance groups that they were to all intents and purposes inaccessible. But more seriously, the regime faced a problem of credibility. Memories of the boorish intrusions of party activists into rural areas in 1978–1979 were still relatively fresh, and did nothing to enhance the prospects for 'national reconciliation', although the specific content of the new messages was of course quite different.

A particular credibility problem arose from Najibullah's determination to retain effective control of events, which sapped 'national reconciliation' of any real political content. Part of his problem was that it was difficult to move at a faster pace than his patrons in the USSR: only on 13 March 1990 was 'the leading and guiding role' of the Communist Party expunged by the new Congress of People's Deputies from Article 6 of the *Soviet* Constitution. The limited scope of what Najibullah had to offer was apparent from his speeches, many of them broadcast to the Afghan people. In his speech to the PDPA Conference in October 1987, he argued that in a coalition administration 'the PDPA should not lose its leading role in all levels of the state sovereignty' and that 'the party's decision to keep the presidency for itself is logical' (BBC *Summary of World Broadcasts* FE/8707/C/7–8, 24 October 1987). In a December 1987 press conference, he stated that 'Our people attach great value to the peace-creating activities of the Soviet soldiers', hardly an observation likely to carry weight with the armed opposition. At the same press conference, asked whether he would retain both the presidency of Afghanistan and the position of General Secretary of the Party Central Committee, he replied that 'If I gave up the post of General Secretary of the PDPA, this would be an example of ingratitude to the party, which has placed such trust in me. However, it does not mean that the other parties will feel that I am being administratively selfish' (BBC *Summary of World Broadcasts* FE/0021/C/3, 9 December 1987). It is hardly surprising that 'national reconciliation' ran into difficulty.

The failure of 'national reconciliation'

Ultimately, the policy of 'national reconciliation' fell between two stools. It was too radical for the *Khalq* faction and for the *Parchami* supporters of Karmal; reading it as a surrender of all that they had sought to achieve, they manoeuvred quite effectively to thwart its implementation. But for the resistance, it was not nearly radical enough: its subtext was that those against whom the resistance had long struggled would remain in a dominant position, with the Mujahideen offered only crumbs from the PDPA's dining table. Not a single credible figure from Afghanistan's past was prepared to accept a power-sharing arrangement with the PDPA, and Zahir Shah, whom Najibullah had many times identified as a person with a role to play as part of 'national reconciliation', refused to have anything to do with it. Pluralism and freedom of speech existed on paper, but not in reality: when the Imam of the Pul-e Khishti mosque in Kabul denounced Najibullah in March 1989 – 'You have done nothing for your Creator, so you cannot do anything for his creatures' – he was promptly arrested (Rubin, 1995a: 166; Giustozzi, 2000: 159).

Despite all these problems, might there not be some basis for claiming that 'national reconciliation' was at least in part successful? After all, Najibullah survived the withdrawal of Soviet forces and remained in office until April 1992. However, as we shall shortly see, the strategies which Najibullah deployed in order to retain his hold on power had little to do with genuine 'reconciliation' – that is, with the generation of legitimacy – but rather with the purchasing of loyalty from important social groups, using externally supplied resources to do so. Here, Gorbachev's view of the situation in Afghanistan most likely diverged from that of Najibullah (and his conservative KGB backers such as Vladimir Kriuchkov). Halliday and Tanin have argued that the policy of national reconciliation 'turned out to be less extensive than Moscow hoped: Najib used military and economic means to win over tribes to his support, but this was very much in the manner of manipulation from the centre, rather than the political broadening envisaged by Moscow' (Halliday and Tanin, 1998: 1374). Yet it is hard not also to conclude that realistically, these manipulatory devices were the only tools he had available. The notion that with his gruesome background he could reconstitute himself as a pluralist was sheer fantasy. Rather, his KhAD background 'inherently disqualified him as the architect of national reconciliation' (Tsagolov and Harrison, 1991: 53). Gorbachev wanted him to save the PDPA regime. Najibullah probably realised he would be lucky if he could even save himself.

6

The Road to Soviet Withdrawal

In a radio broadcast on 8 February 1988, General Secretary Gorbachev announced the intention of the Soviet Union to begin the withdrawal of Soviet troops from Afghanistan by 15 May 1988. In his Vladivostok speech of 28 July 1986, he had signalled an intention to withdraw six regiments by the end of the year, but the announcement had met with widespread scepticism (Saikal and Maley, 1991: 91). The February 1988 commitment was of a totally different character: the proposal was for a complete rather than partial withdrawal, and was ultimately to lead to the signing in April 1988 of the so-called 'Geneva Accords' which provided a formal cover for the USSR's retreat. Gorbachev's announcement had not been widely anticipated: apart from the analyst Anthony Arnold, who had long argued that the USSR would be obliged to withdraw (Arnold, 1988), few observers had held out much hope that the Soviets would ever be prepared to accept that the gains of a Marxist-Leninist 'revolution' could be reversed. In this sense, the withdrawal from Afghanistan was a seismic development in world affairs, and the subsequent fall of the Berlin Wall and the collapse of the Soviet sphere of influence in Eastern Europe represented the extension and expansion of a principle which had already been conceded in the remote reaches of Southwest Asia.

This chapter is divided into three sections. In the first, I examine the making of the Soviet decision to withdraw, identifying the more important factors underlying the decision, and the key moments at which decisions were made. The second deals with the role of the United Nations in structuring negotiations between some – but, crucially, not *all* – of the parties to the conflict, and offers an assessment of the importance of this example of 'Good Offices' mediation. The third examines some specific developments during the course of the Soviet withdrawal itself. The previous chapter, of course, has dealt with some of the main military events of the withdrawal period; this chapter rather is concerned with the politics of the withdrawal itself.

The Soviet decision to withdraw

The foreign policy process under Gorbachev

During the Brezhnev period there developed a semi-convention on the need for consultation as part of the foreign policy-making process. This was to a significant degree shaped by the damage that the USSR had suffered on account of two decisions taken without widespread consultation: the October 1956 decision to invade Hungary, and the June 1962 decision to deploy SS-4 and SS-5 missiles to Cuba, a decision which led directly to the October 1962 Cuban missile crisis. By the time of the Soviet invasion of Czechoslovakia in 1968, a much more consultative process had come into play. This in part reflected Brezhnev's penchant for consensus-building, but also the fact that he had not yet established a position of secure dominance within the leadership. The ill-considered decision to invade Afghanistan was a departure from the earlier model, in part because Brezhnev's position in the leadership had altered, but also because Afghanistan specialists were not prominently represented among the foreign policy specialist community, the so-called *mezhdunarodniki*.

The advent of Gorbachev brought a number of significant changes to the foreign policy process. Apart from ideological innovation, and the sidelining of Andrei Gromyko, significant personnel changes occurred. Of particular importance was the retirement of Boris Ponomarev, the octogenarian party secretary who headed the Secretariat's International Department. Ponomarev was replaced by Anatoly Dobrynin, a very different figure. Whereas Ponomarev was a Comintern veteran, Dobrynin had served as Soviet Ambassador to the USA from 1962 to 1986, which gave him unrivalled insights into Western policy priorities, and injected a worldliness into leadership discussions which complemented that brought by Iakovlev following his decade in Canada. There was also a major reorganisation of the 'departmental' structure within the Foreign Ministry, which one observer argued 'had remained virtually unchanged since the time of Czar Nicholas II' (Miller, 1991: 57), and a shake-up of Soviet Ambassadors abroad. These set the scene for a different Soviet diplomatic image. A new information administration was established, headed by Gennadi Gerasimov, who proved to be a droll defender of Soviet positions. The new Foreign Minister also had a very different style from his predecessor. I recall seeing Eduard Shevardnadze, during an official visit to Australia, arriving at Parliament House in Canberra, and rather than ascending the front stairs on his left, instead turning right (to the consternation of security staff) and plunging into a crowd of Afghan refugees protesting the Soviet presence in their homeland. Such a spontaneous encounter with angry victims of Soviet policy would have been unthinkable from Gromyko.

But in addition to these high-level developments, other changes occurred in the making of policy. Specialists in relations between the Soviet Union and the Third World were increasingly candid in the views which they expressed about Afghanistan. Some did so under provocation, such as Academician Oleg Bogomolov. In response to an article by the conservative journalist Aleksandr Prokhanov which sought to pin the blame for the original invasion decision in part on poor advice from specialists on Islam and other experts, Bogomolov struck back, pointing out that his institute, the Institute for the Economics of the World Socialist System in the Soviet Academy of Sciences, had written to the leadership in January 1980 about the danger of the decision (Bogomolov, 1988: 10; Ostermann, 2003–2004: 243). Others did so out of deep conviction, such as Dr Nodari Simoniya of the Institute of Oriental Studies, who in interviews published in *The Times of India* in May 1987, described the Soviet intervention as a 'real tragedy' and stated that it 'was necessary to involve scientific and specialist circles before taking this decision. This was not done sufficiently in 1979. Today the government is trying to involve such specialists when deciding something important in a variety of fields including foreign policy' (Lifschultz, 1987).

The recognition of strategic failure

Glasnost', as I noted earlier, permitted all sorts of aspects of the Afghanistan war to be publicly exposed in the USSR. However, it did not take *glasnost'* for the Soviet leadership to become aware of the disaster area which Afghanistan had become. This became clear with Kim Tsagolov's 1988 interview with Artyom Borovik (Borovik, 1988). This interview cost Tsagolov his rank and his position (Mendelson, 1998: 113), but the substance of what he said was scarcely contestable. And his conclusions were devastating. Fundamentally, he addressed the position of the PDPA: 'The territory on which state power has been firmly and definitively established has barely increased in recent years. It is impossible to name a single province or district where the question of who is in charge (*kto kogo*) has been definitively decided in favour of state power.' He described the 'Saur Revolution' as a 'military coup' (*voennyi perevorot*), and observed that the 'party was unable to become an organically united political organisation'. Political work among the masses 'remained on paper' (*ostalas' na bumage*). He also spoke scathingly of the economic consequences of the conflict: 'As a result of the war a large number of enterprises, transport, electricity lines, communications and roads have been partially or completely put out of action.' He added that 'unemployment and inflation are growing. The living standards of workers are falling.' As more information became available in the post-Soviet period, it became clear that Tsagolov's views had been quite widely shared within key Soviet circles. However, the fact that his views were well grounded did not mean that all circles found them palatable – his own fate showed this rather clearly – and in reality there were significant groups which resisted the relabelling of the Afghanistan experience even though by the time Tsagolov's views appeared in print, the Soviet withdrawal was irreversibly in train. The pace of elite turnover meant that the views of those who were directly inculpated at the highest level in the original invasion decision were substantially irrelevant by the late 1980s; but the institutions which were involved both in the prosecution of the war and in the attempt to nurture the Afghan communists into some semblance of a viable political force stood to lose more from the exposure of their failings.

The role of Gorbachev

Here, it was of crucial significance that there was a new leader in place in the USSR. While formally elected by the Central Committee of the Communist Party of the Soviet Union, the General Secretary was in practice selected by the members of the Politburo from within their number. To some degree this limited the capacity of the Politburo rapidly to divest themselves of a General Secretary who proved unorthodox, since to do so would raise questions about the wisdom of having selected him in the first place. This gave Gorbachev scope for innovation, although only after a certain amount of consensus-building had been attempted. In fact, Gorbachev raised the Afghanistan issue even before the end of the year in which he acceded to office. On 17 October 1985, there was a Politburo discussion of Afghanistan, at a meeting which Dobrynin, who attended it, has described as 'the decisive one in determining our withdrawal'. He quotes Gorbachev as saying, 'It's time to leave', and adds that there was 'no objection', although the Politburo 'did not yet fix any concrete dates' (Dobrynin, 1995: 442). Chernyaev, who also attended the meeting, puts Gorbachev at centre stage, quoting him as saying that 'With or without Karmal's consent, we'll take a firm line on the matter of our rapid withdrawal from Afghanistan' (Chernyaev, 2000: 42). This approach took a certain amount of courage, for at this time, there were still Politburo members in place who had been in office at the time of the invasion – notably Gromyko, First Secretary of the Moscow City Party Committee Viktor Grishin, Ukrainian Party First Secretary Vladimir Shcherbitskii, and the First Secretary of the Kazakhstan Party organisation Dinmukhamed Kunaev.

13 November 1986

Dobrynin's view that the 17 October 1985 meeting was the decisive one is debatable. There can be much less debate about the significance of a Politburo meeting held on 13 November 1986. 'If there was a key decision', Halliday has written, 'then this was it' (Halliday, 1999: 684), a view shared by Henry S. Bradsher (Bradsher, 1999: 277). The details of the meeting became known in late 1992 when Michael Dobbs of *The Washington Post* obtained a declassified transcript of the meeting (Dobbs, 1992), and the transcript itself appeared in the journal *Voprosy istorii* in 1993. Interestingly, the official transcript carried the title 'On Zahir Shah', even though the former Afghan king received no mention in the actual Politburo discussion. The transcript in its mimeographed form was marked 'Top Secret' (*Sov. sekretno*), and there can be little doubt that the participants believed that what they said would indeed remain hidden from the wider world. Thus, while the views that they advanced certainly reflected underlying political calculations and rhetorical strategies, they are of remarkable value to the historian. During the meeting, Gorbachev expressed his views with uncompromising firmness: 'In Afghanistan we have already been fighting for six years. If the approach is not changed, the fighting will go on for another 20-30 years' (Grossman, 1993: 22) After referring to the October 1985 meeting, Gorbachev proposed that over a two-year period (*v techenie dvukh let*) the USSR should withdraw its forces from Afghanistan, with 50 per cent to be withdrawn in 1987 and the remaining 50 per cent in the following year (Grossman, 1993: 26). The members of the Politburo agreed.

Before concluding discussion of this decision, it is necessary to discuss one important thesis about it which has recently been advanced by Sarah E. Mendelson in her book *Changing Course: Ideas, Politics, and the Soviet Withdrawal from Afghanistan*. Mendelson notes three kinds of explanation for the withdrawal. The first looks at events in the

international system as a source of change. However, Mendelson main-
tains that these were indeterminate, as the Soviet leadership could have
responded to them in different ways. The second refers to different kinds
of learning. One interpretation might be that 'the Soviet image of the
opponents – both the mujahideen and the United States – changed as a
result of disconfirming and overwhelming information about the war
and the international system' (Mendelson, 1998: 25). Another might be
that the Soviet leadership withdrew on a 'tactical learning' basis 'simply because they were getting beaten' (Mendelson, 1998: 27). She finds
neither of these interpretations plausible in the light of her reading of
the evidence. Her preference is for a third explanation focusing on the
interplay of ideas and politics, which she concludes are 'necessary and
sufficient variables for explaining the change in Soviet foreign policy
in the 1980s and the Soviet withdrawal from Afghanistan' (Mendelson,
1998: 38). Here, she credits Gorbachev with using 'coalition-building
strategies... within traditional institutions to bring about change and the
empowerment of a dominant community of experts that helped ensure
an alternative source of legitimacy and power for the reformist agenda'
(Mendelson, 1998: 37).

There is clearly substance in the view that the foreign policy process
underwent significant change under Gorbachev, both in terms of personnel
and legitimating ideology. However, Mendelson's specific thesis about the
importance of *experts* does not stand up well in the face of the evidence (for
more detail, see Maley, 1999a). She writes that 'the bulk of the specialists
were not consulted until late 1986 and through the spring and summer of
1987' (Mendelson, 1998: 125), and concludes that 'the leadership's decision in principle to withdraw seems to have been reached in late spring
and summer 1987' (Mendelson, 1998: 125). But this conclusion is flatly at
odds with what we know about the November 1986 meeting. Mendelson is
aware of the meeting, and indeed quotes from the transcript (Mendelson,
1998: 112), but seems not to grasp its full implications for her case. While
that meeting did not address all the complexities involved in withdrawing
Soviet troops or overcome all resistance to withdrawal (see Bradsher, 1999:
280–3), it indisputably involved a decision 'in principle' to withdraw, and
within a specific time frame of two years. All in all, her 'tactical learning' explanation, suitably modified to encompass not just military defeat
but the deeper notion of political failure, seems far more effective in
explaining the Soviet withdrawal. Here, it is worth highlighting Marshal
Sergei Akhromeev's fundamental insight, which he expressed during the
November meeting: 'We have lost the battle for the Afghan people' (*My
proigraly bor'bu za afganskii narod*) (Grossman, 1993: 25).

The decision to withdraw Soviet troops from Afghanistan was not, however, a decision to abandon Dr Najibullah. November 1989, when in effect the USSR surrendered its Eastern European surrogates to their fate through what Gennadi Gerasimov somewhat flippantly called 'the Sinatra doctrine' (Brown, 1996: 240), was still years away. At the November 1986 meeting, Gorbachev repeated the need to pursue a 'widening of the social base of the regime' (Grossman, 1993: 26). Shevardnadze stated that Najibullah 'needs practical support' (Grossman, 1993: 24). The American Sovietologist Jerry F. Hough rightly argued just two months after the November 1986 meeting that 'There are a great many indications that Gorbachev, despite all the talk of flexibility and of a coalition government, will not accept anything less than a "coalition" that is dominated by the communists and a recognition of their rule in Afghanistan.' Unfortunately, Hough then went on to claim that 'Gorbachev has a winning hand in Afghanistan' and that 'When Gorbachev begins reducing the number of Soviet troops, it is a sign not of retreat but of victory' (Hough, 1987). The leadership in Moscow knew better.

The United Nations and the Geneva Accords

The development of negotiations under UN auspices

As noted earlier, the Soviet Union's status as a permanent member of the UN Security Council afforded it the capacity to veto any condemnation by that body of its invasion, let alone any forceful response of the type which Chapter VII of the United Nations Charter permits the Council to authorise in the event of a threat to international peace and security. Resolutions of the General Assembly, while powerful indicators of international opinion, could not bind member states as a matter of international law. Thus, there was effectively no mechanism available in the UN system by which to compel a Soviet withdrawal from Afghanistan. However, one avenue did exist to establish a process to facilitate Soviet withdrawal should the Soviet leadership feel compelled to change course. The avenue in point was a product of what are known as the 'Good Offices' of the Secretary-General, in which the UN mediates between parties to a dispute with a view to producing a peaceful resolution on terms satisfactory to the parties.

Such activity has a clear constitutional basis. The Secretary-General of the League of Nations (1920–1946) was very much an administrative officer, and the position of Secretary-General of the League was something of a graveyard for diplomats with promising political careers. When the UN Charter was being drafted, its authors understood that there could be advantages in enhancing the political capabilities of the UN Secretary-General. Article 99 of the Charter gave the Secretary-General a novel political capacity: 'The Secretary-General may bring to the attention of the Security Council any matter which in his opinion may threaten the maintenance of international peace and security.' In the hands of Dag Hammarskjöld, UN Secretary-General from 1953 until his death in a plane crash in 1961, the office on the basis of this Article developed a new salience (Newman, 1998: 21). Article 98 provided also that the Secretary-General should perform certain identified functions, and should perform 'such other functions as are entrusted to him' by the General Assembly, Security Council, Economic and Social Council, and Trusteeship Council.

Given the complexity of the world, it would be impossible for the Secretary-General personally to discharge all the functions which these organs might call upon him to perform. To assist in these tasks, the Secretary-General draws upon the UN's professional bureaucracy, the Secretariat, for analysis and activity in the field. However, it is also open to the Secretary-General to recruit mediators. A hierarchy has developed of special representatives, personal representatives, and envoys of other types who undertake mediation in the field with the Secretary-General's authority (see Skjelsæk, 1991; Hume, 1995). It can be crucial to the success of such endeavours that the mediator be seen as independent, rather than simply an agent of the Security Council or the Great Powers: indeed, one prominent mediator, Giandomenico Picco, who made it clear in Lebanon that he was acting for the Secretary-General, realised that he 'could have paid for it dearly' had he led his interlocutors to believe that he was acting for the Security Council (Picco, 1999: 161).

The Soviet leadership was not eager to see Good Offices mediation of this type develop. Its objective was rather to bring about direct talks between the Karmal regime and the regime of General Zia in Pakistan. In a letter to Cuban leader Fidel Castro dated 10 March 1980, Brezhnev made this quite clear, arguing that it 'seems inadvisable to us to have any degree of involvement on the part of the General Secretary (sic) of the U.N. in these affairs. This, among other aspects, would unavoidably be linked to the well-known anti-Afghan resolution of the General Assembly of the United Nations' (Hershberg, 1996–1997: 169).

The evolution of the Geneva Accords

The Geneva Accords were the product of a series of structured negotiations orchestrated by the UN between 1982 and 1988. Communications between Kabul and Islamabad were initiated in April 1981 by Javier

Pérez de Cuéllar of Peru, who had been appointed in February 1981 by UN Secretary-General Kurt Waldheim to be his Personal Representative. On 22 February 1982, following the election of Pérez de Cuéllar to the position of Secretary-General, the position was assumed by Diego Cordovez of Ecuador, who had been appointed Under-Secretary-General for Special Political Affairs on 1 August 1981. Between 1982 and 1984, the communications took the form of 'shuttle talks', with the mediator travelling between capitals to pass on the positions of the different parties. From August 1984, the negotiations took the form of 'proximity talks', in which the participating parties occupied rooms at the Palais des Nations in Geneva, between which UN officials oscillated. This peculiar arrangement was necessary because of Pakistan's resolute refusal to agree to any measure which might be interpreted as according *de facto* recognition to the regime put in place and sustained by Soviet troops (see Khan, 1991; Cordovez and Harrison, 1995; Rubin, 1995b).

The shape which the Geneva Accords were to take was foreshadowed – and some might go so far as to say determined – in a statement issued by the Karmal regime on 14 May 1980. The proposals of course originated from Moscow: three hours after the statement's broadcast in Pushto by Kabul Radio, an English text with additions was issued by the Soviet newsagency TASS. The statement outlined proposals for a 'political solution' to the 'tension that has come about in this region' (BBC *Summary of World Broadcasts* FE/6421/C/1–3, 16 May 1980). Cordovez subsequently observed that it was 'widely felt at the U.N. that the proposals should be ignored or rejected as insincere' (Cordovez and Harrison, 1995: 74). However, the programme which the 14 May statement proposed was mirrored in the agenda of talks under UN auspices, which covered the withdrawal of 'the foreign troops', non-interference in the internal affairs of states, international guarantees, and the voluntary repatriation of refugees.

The participation in the talks of delegations from the Kabul regime and the Government of Pakistan gave the talks a faintly surreal dimension, for the number of relevant parties was much larger. The Soviet Union, of course, was heavily involved just off-stage with its Afghan clients: Gromyko in March 1983 indirectly highlighted this when he observed to the Politburo that 'The Afghans, of course, must be given materials which would give them the ability to prepare well for the negotiations' (Hershberg, 1996–1997: 178). However, it would be a mistake to conclude that the Kabul delegation simply parroted instructions from Moscow: indeed, by September 1987, the Afghan delegation, well aware of the peril in which Najibullah's regime found itself, proved exceedingly obstreperous in Geneva (Cordovez and Harrison, 1995: 303–6). Similarly, the interests of Pakistan were in significant ways different from those of the USA and Iran, and by 1988 there were even important differences surfacing between President Zia and his prime minister, Mohammad Khan Junejo. But most fundamentally, the Afghan resistance was not directly involved in the negotiations, with consequences I will highlight shortly.

When one is dealing with complex political problems, the mere existence of negotiations in no way implies progress towards a negotiated settlement. Negotiators typically deal first with the least troublesome or intractable issues on an agenda, in the hope of building some confidence between the parties. It is thus quite common for an illusion of progress to develop, after which negotiations stall. Leadership change in the USSR added to this. Thus, in 1983, there was a flurry of optimism that the Andropov leadership might preside over a shift in Afghanistan (see Cordovez and Harrison, 1995: 100–5). However, it was not to be, and declassified documents raise real doubts as to whether the prospects at the time were at all bright. 'We are fighting', he argued at a Politburo meeting on 10 March 1983, 'against American imperialism which well understands that in this part of international politics it has lost its positions. *That is why we cannot back off*' (Hershberg, 1996–1997: 177, emphasis added). Given the nature of his audience, it seems reasonable to conclude that this represented Andropov's genuine conviction, and that his reported support for a settlement in a conversation less than three weeks later (Bradsher, 1999: 271) was a form of disinformation. Rather than concluding that the USSR had lost the battle for the Afghan people, Andropov pointed to the length of time it had taken the Red Army to subdue the Basmachi Movement in Central Asia in the 1920s and 1930s (Hershberg, 1996–1997: 177). The Soviets had an interest in the continuation of a negotiation process – to buy time, to play down their setbacks, to confuse the Afghan resistance, to mute international criticism, and to raise doubts about the wider value of aid to the resistance forces (Saikal, 1984a: 487). But ultimately, more than just time separated 1983 from 1988.

The finalisation and signing of the Geneva Accords

Bringing the Geneva Accords to a conclusion proved a complex task. The reason was that the draft accords dealt not only with the withdrawal of Soviet forces from Afghanistan, but also the discontinuation of external assistance – in effect, aid from Pakistan and the USA – to the

Afghan resistance. In a letter to Cordovez of 8 December 1985 and in a speech five days later, US Deputy Secretary of State John Whitehead had effectively accepted that US aid to the resistance would cease at the *beginning* of a Soviet withdrawal from Afghanistan, even though Soviet aid flows to the Kabul regime would be permitted to continue throughout (and beyond) the period of the withdrawal. This concession seems to have resulted from a certain degree of inattention in US circles at a time when there was little confidence that the Geneva process was leading anywhere. It appears that President Reagan had not been briefed on the details of the negotiations and knew nothing about Whitehead's speech (Cordovez and Harrison, 1995: 193). When Reagan was quizzed about the issue in a television interview in December 1987, he rejected the idea of cutting off aid to the resistance in exchange for a Soviet withdrawal, and in the face of outrage from Senators and members of Congress, this was formalised in a State Department statement on 4 March 1988.

Coming *after* Gorbachev's decisive statement of intention to withdraw from Afghanistan, this prompted an explosion from Gorbachev in Moscow (Matlock, 2004: 285–8). Yet those in the State Department who had promoted the December 1985 concession had no case for believing that they were being sabotaged. It should always have been apparent to them that the kind of arrangements which they were contemplating would be at odds with the President's intuitive commitment to back anti-Soviet forces in the Third World, and would be challenged by the Mujahideen's supporters. The impasse was overcome tacitly rather than explicitly: to coincide with the signing of the Accords, the US Administration issued a statement that 'The obligations undertaken by the guarantors [the USA and the USSR] are symmetrical. In this regard, the United States has advised the Soviet Union that the U.S. retains the right, consistent with its obligations as guarantor, to provide military assistance to parties in Afghanistan. Should the Soviet Union exercise restraint in providing military assistance to parties in Afghanistan, the U.S. similarly will exercise restraint' (*Department of State Bulletin,* 88, 2135: 55, June 1988).

In Pakistan too there was a hiccup, as President Zia became suddenly uneasy at the absence of any mechanism for transition in Afghanistan to a government with normative legitimacy. The Soviets' desire for an accord to provide a dignified cover for their retreat from Afghanistan gave Pakistan a certain amount of leverage, and Zia was keen to exploit it. However, once the US Administration decided to accept the Accords, it brought pressure to bear on Pakistan to do the same, also exploiting a sharp divergence of opinion on the matter between Zia and Junejo

(Rubin, 1995b: 89). (Zia dismissed Junejo on 29 May 1988.) The Accords were finally signed at a ceremony at the *Palais des Nations* on 14 April 1988. Najibullah's Foreign Minister Abdul Wakil signed on Kabul's behalf. Pakistan's signature was recorded by Pakistan's Foreign Minister Zain Noorani, and George Shultz and Eduard Shevardnadze represented the USA and the USSR respectively. The only speaker was the UN Secretary-General, Pérez de Cuéllar, and Noorani and Wakil avoided eye contact. The mood was funereal rather than euphoric, for the gaps in the Accords were almost as striking as their content.

The content of the Geneva Accords

The Accords consisted of four distinct but integrally related texts. The first was entitled *Bilateral Agreement between the Republic of Afghanistan and the Islamic Republic of Pakistan on the Principles of Mutual Relations, in Particular on Non-Interference and Non-Intervention*. Article I provided that 'Relations between the High Contracting Parties shall be conducted in strict compliance with the principle of non-interference and non-intervention by States in the affairs of other States.' Article II (4) committed each party 'to ensure that its territory is not used in any manner which would violate the sovereignty, political independence, territorial integrity and national unity or disrupt the political, economic and social stability of the other High Contracting Parties'. Article II (8) obliged each 'to prevent within its territory the training, equipping, financing and recruitment of mercenaries from whatever origin for the purpose of hostile activities against the other High Contracting Party, or the sending of such mercenaries into the territory of the other High Contracting Party and accordingly to deny facilities, including financing for the training, equipping and transit of such mercenaries'. Even more specifically, Article II (12) required each party 'to prevent within its Territory the presence, harbouring, in camps and bases or otherwise, organizing, training, financing, equipping and arming of individuals and political, ethnic and any other groups for the purpose of creating subversion, disorder or unrest in the territory of the other High Contracting Party and accordingly also to prevent the use of mass media and the transportation of arms, ammunition and equipment by such individuals and groups'.

The second was a *Declaration on International Guarantees*, signed by the USSR and the United States. Each committed itself 'to invariably refrain from any form of interference and intervention in the internal affairs of the Republic of Afghanistan and the Islamic Republic

of Pakistan and to respect the commitments contained in the bilateral agreement between the Republic of Afghanistan and the Islamic
Republic of Pakistan on the Principles of Mutual Relations, in particular
on Non-Interference and Non-Intervention'; and urged all states 'to act
likewise'.

The third was a *Bilateral Agreement between the Republic of
Afghanistan and the Islamic Republic of Pakistan on the Voluntary
Return of Refugees*. This was the least contentious of the documents,
providing in Article I that 'All Afghan refugees temporarily present
in the territory of the Islamic Republic of Pakistan shall be given the
opportunity to return voluntarily to their homeland in accordance with
the arrangements and conditions set out in the present Agreement', and
in Article VI that 'At the request of the Governments concerned, the
United Nations High Commissioner for Refugees will co-operate and
provide assistance in the process of voluntary repatriation of refugees in
accordance with the present Agreement.'

The final text was simply entitled *Agreement on the Interrelationships
for the Settlement of the Situation Relating to Afghanistan*. This text
provided in Paragraph 5 that

> The Bilateral Agreement on the Principles of Mutual Relations, in
> Particular on Non-Interference and Non-Intervention; the Declaration
> on International Guarantees; the Bilateral Agreement on the
> Voluntary Return of Refugees; and the present Agreement on the
> Interrelationships for the Settlement of the Situation Relating to
> Afghanistan will enter into force on 15 May 1988. In accordance with
> the time-frame agreed upon between the Union of Soviet Socialist
> Republics and the Republic of Afghanistan there will be a phased
> withdrawal of the foreign troops which will start on the date of entry
> into force mentioned above. One half of the troops will be withdrawn
> by 15 August 1988 and the withdrawal of all troops will be completed
> within nine months.

The limitations of the Geneva Accords

The merits of the Geneva Accords continue to be debated. Bokhari has
argued that the Geneva Accords 'were an important success story in
large part because of the way the negotiation process was conceived:
aims were kept limited, the art of the possible was stressed, and the
mujahideen were excluded from the process' (Bokhari, 1995: 261).
From a narrowly *diplomatic* perspective, this was certainly the case.

But a *conflict resolution* perspective yields a different evaluation. In 1989, I concluded a mournful assessment of the Geneva Accords with the warning that 'for many Afghans, they offered only the peace of the grave' (Maley, 1989b: 25). The years of bloodshed which were to follow highlighted their limitations. First, the Afghan resistance groups were neither party to the Accords, nor involved in any serious way in the negotiation process. There is no doubt that the difficulties in trying to involve elements of such a collection of combatants would have been considerable, not least because of the manipulative inclinations of their Pakistani hosts; but their absence left a hole in the process: a mark of a truly great mediator's dexterity is an ability to find ways of linking all *necessary* parties to a settlement, while excluding all *unnecessary* parties. Second, the Accords left a crucial issue in the Afghanistan conflict, namely the character of the country's rulers, unaddressed. The Secretary-General on 14 April 1988 stated that the Accords 'lay the basis for the exercise by all Afghans of their right to self-determination, a principle enshrined in the Charter' (United Nations, 1988: 1). This was precisely what they did *not* do. The hiatus here was not simply an aesthetic weakness, for such gaps mean that fundamental issues *in dispute* can remain unresolved (Randle, 1973: 487). To be fair to Cordovez, at the time at which he was working, a lesson that became clearer during the 1990s – that political reconstruction in disrupted states is a complex and laborious process, involving the rebuilding of trust, change in elite relations, relations with non-state actors, and efforts to bring about the institutionalisation of politics (Maley, 1995b; Maley, 2003) – was not so widely appreciated. Yet while this may excuse a mediator any moral blame, it does not make defective agreements any more meritorious.

The course of the withdrawal

UNGOMAP and UNOCA

The period of the withdrawal witnessed the first deployment in Afghanistan of what might broadly have been called a 'peacekeeping mission'. Peacekeeping is not a function explicitly entrusted to the UN under the United Nations Charter, but instead arose through creative diplomacy on the part of senior UN officials. Dag Hammarskjöld famously remarked that peacekeeping was authorised by 'Chapter Six-and-a-Half' of the Charter. Peacekeeping classically involves the deployment in a non-coercive mission of lightly armed, neutral personnel, serving with the permission of host countries, and under the formal authority of the Secretary-General acting pursuant to a resolution of the Security Council, to perform tasks such as observation, interposition, the maintenance of law and order, and the delivery of aid (Diehl, 1994: 4–10; see also Rikhye, 1984; James, 1990; Fetherston, 1994). The United Nations Good Offices Mission in Afghanistan and Pakistan (UNGOMAP) met these requirements, and was included by the UN in its fiftieth anniversary listing of peacekeeping operations (United Nations, 1998). It was UNGOMAP that was the first peacekeeping operation to monitor the actions of a superpower (Diehl, 1994: 166), and this alone makes it of some interest.

The UNGOMAP mission operated from May 1988 until March 1990. Its expenditures were modest, only US$14 million in total, drawn from the regular budget of the UN. It comprised 50 military observers, together with local support staff: its international personnel were drawn from Austria, Canada, Denmark, Fiji, Finland, Ghana, Ireland, Nepal, Poland, and Sweden. Cordovez, as Personal Representative of the Secretary-General, controlled the mission, with Major-General Rauli Helminen of Finland serving as his deputy during the withdrawal phase (Birgisson, 1993: 307). It had offices in Kabul and Islamabad, and permanently manned posts at Shindand airbase south of Herat, and at Hairatan and Torghundi on the border between Afghanistan and the USSR. Tasked with receiving complaints about violations of the Geneva Accords, it confronted a veritable deluge: Kabul lodged 7,545 complaints alleging violations, and Pakistan 1317 (Birgisson, 1993: 308). With such a small staff, there was manifestly little that UNGOMAP could do to handle such protests seriously. Nor did UNGOMAP possess a significant monitoring or observation capability: rather, it was a theatrical prop in the final scene of a drawn-out drama, part of the raft of measures designed to ease the USSR out of Afghanistan with minimum humiliation.

The signing of the Geneva Accords also triggered a rush to establish institutions for the delivery of postwar reconstruction assistance, with a particular focus on refugee repatriation. On 11 May 1988, the Secretary-General appointed Sadruddin Aga Khan, who had served as United Nations High Commissioner for Refugees from 1965 to 1977, to head the Office of the United Nations Coordinator for Humanitarian and Economic Assistance Programmes Relating to Afghanistan (UNOCA). On 10 June 1988, the Secretary-General issued an appeal for funds for Afghanistan, with targets of US$1.116 billion for relief and rehabilitation needs for 1988–1989, and a further US$839.6 million for rehabilitation and recovery in the period 1990–1993 (UNOCA, 1988: 14). The appeal in its details was quite detached from ground realities. For example, for mine action it solicited a meagre US$9 million, only a tiny fraction of what would eventually be required. But its greatest detachment from reality came with the claim that the Geneva Accords 'provide for a political settlement to enable the people of Afghanistan and the international community to embark on a major co-operative and co-ordinated effort to bring humanitarian relief and sound economic recovery to Afghanistan and all of its people' (UNOCA, 1988: 9–10). This was even more florid and inaccurate than the claim made by Pérez de Cuéllar on the day the Accords were signed – and markedly more dangerous. For in this case, scarce resources were being sought not because the need was manifest, but rather to substantiate the myth that the Geneva Accords had addressed all the fundamental issues over which Afghans were divided. The weaknesses of this approach were soon all too apparent: the expected repatriation of refugees did not occur, ongoing conflict blocked large-scale reconstruction, and donors rapidly became fatigued. The UNOCA mission became caught in ferocious turf battles between different UN agencies, and found its functions steadily reduced to the mundane. The problems by which UN development assistance was afflicted, searingly documented in 1969 by Sir Robert Jackson in a famous report (Jackson, 1969), were prominently on display, and conflict between different agencies within the UN 'family' was to contaminate the UN's approach to Afghanistan right through the 1990s and into the twenty-first century.

Manoeuvrings during the withdrawal

The withdrawal of Soviet forces was hardly a smooth process. Retreats rarely are. Najibullah seems to have had little faith at all that his regime would survive. On 28 April, he stated, probably more out of hope than conviction, that Soviet military advisers would remain in Afghanistan after the withdrawal. He seems to have taken little comfort from General Gromov's press conference in Kabul on 14 May (Gromov, 1994: 309), even though Gromov announced that $1 billion worth of equipment would be left behind for the regime, for Washington concluded that as a result, and pursuant to its 14 April declaration, aid to the resistance should proceed. In June, Najibullah visited Moscow. Chernyaev paints an unflattering picture of his demeanour during a meeting with Gorbachev: 'Gorbachev tried to impress upon him the concept for our withdrawal. Najibullah acted desperate, unbelievably primitive (compared to what I'd observed in him before). For example, he suggested organizing a joint campaign with the USSR, India, and Afghanistan against Pakistan, or a major Soviet operation against the Mujahideen. Gorbachev unceremoniously ridiculed both' (Chernyaev, 2000: 161–2).

This did not prevent Moscow from doing its bit to pressure the USA and Pakistan over their support for the resistance. On 23 July, Soviet Deputy Foreign Minister Vladimir Petrovskii in an interview with *The Washington Post* warned that the withdrawal might not meet the 15 February deadline unless aid to the Mujahideen was cut off (Cordovez and Harrison, 1995: 377). On 7 August, Shevardnadze threatened counteraction against Pakistan if 'crude violations' of the Geneva Accords continued. And on 4 November, Soviet Deputy Foreign Minister Aleksandr Bessmertnykh announced a suspension of the withdrawal. However, in all this there was a large dose of bluff (Rubin, 1988), for it remained fundamentally in the USSR's interest to extract itself from Afghanistan, whether Najibullah survived or not. The Soviet Union met the 15 August deadline for the withdrawal of half its force, and completed the full withdrawal on time as well.

Cordovez, who remained the personal representative of the Secretary-General, was involved at this time in putting forward a plan for a ceasefire and the replacement of Najibullah's regime with a transitional 'Council of Notables' to organise a Loya Jirgah, something for which he called in Islamabad on 9 July 1988 (Rubin, 1989). Cordovez in his memoir blames the failure of this approach in part on plotting by aides of the Secretary-General (Cordovez and Harrison, 1995: 382–3), and it is clear not just from this but from comments in Pérez de Cuéllar's own memoirs that relations between the Secretary-General and his personal representative had become frosty (Pérez de Cuéllar, 1997: 187). However, the problems with Cordovez's approach went much deeper. In principle it had a number of virtues, but in practice the time was not ripe for it. First, it was naive to believe that the leaders of Afghan political parties who saw themselves as the vanguard of a decade-long anti-communist struggle would agree to be thrust aside in favour of 'notables' of uncertain provenance. Cordovez described those supporting his approach as 'the silent majority who have not been heard throughout the war' (Cordovez and Harrison, 1995: 376), but without apparently appreciating that such a claim, even if it were true, would be offensive to resistance groups capable of thwarting the approach he was promoting, since the implication was that they were unrepresentative. Second, the prospects for a ceasefire were negligible, given that Afghanistan was awash with commanders independent of external control. Third, the term Loya Jirgah *at that particular time* was a controversial one among Afghans, with some viewing it as an instrument of Pushtun domination (Dupree, 1989: 46–7). Fourth, and most fundamentally, some (although not all) of the resistance leaders, and some of their key backers, believed that the battlefield offered a more promising theatre for the achievement of their interests than the negotiating table, and were deeply suspicious of Cordovez and the UN because of the way in which they had been excluded from the Geneva negotiations.

The death of Zia

Pressure from President Zia of Pakistan might have forced the more obdurate resistance leaders to shift ground, but on 17 August 1988, Zia was killed in an aircraft accident. His C-130 Hercules crashed shortly after taking off from the city of Bahawalpur, which he had been visiting with a high-level delegation to inspect M-1 tanks. Not only Zia died in the crash, but also 29 other senior figures, including former ISI Director-General Akhtar Abdul Rahman, and US Ambassador Arnold Raphel. The cause of the crash was never established, with theories ranging from a disabling gas smuggled aboard in a crate of mangoes, to sabotage of the plane's main and auxiliary hydraulic systems (Kaplan, 1989: Nawaz, 2008: 393–405). The effect on Pakistan's politics was dramatic. Elections had been scheduled following Zia's dismissal of Junejo, and Zia's successor, Senate President Ghulam Ishaq Khan, determined that they should proceed. Victory went to the Pakistan People's Party led by Zia's arch-enemy Benazir Bhutto, and it was no more in her interest to devote resources to investigating the death of a ruler she loathed than it was in America's interest to risk compromising relations with Pakistan's new leader by pursuing inquiries which could have unpredictable outcomes.

The death of Zia empowered the Director-General of ISI, Major-General Hamid Gul, and the new Chief of Army Staff, General Mirza Aslam Beg. Gul had been lucky to survive an early scandal, namely the explosion of an arms dump near Islamabad on 10 April 1988, which destroyed weapons that had been stockpiled for the resistance, and rained ordnance on the civilian population, killing around a hundred people and injuring over a thousand (Yousaf and Adkin, 1992: 220–33). Whereas Zia had shown some interest before his death in Cordovez's moves towards an internal settlement in Afghanistan to augment the Geneva Accords (Cordovez and Harrison, 1995: 378; Rubin, 1995b: 101), Gul, who came to the position from a cavalry background and with little grasp of Afghanistan's complexities, favoured highly structured conventional military operations, for which the Mujahideen were organisationally unsuited. Removed as head of ISI in 1989 and forced into retirement in 1992, he thereafter drifted into ever more extreme circles, ultimately surfacing as an ardent supporter of the Taliban. Capping a career marked by misjudgement, he graced them with his presence at their celebration of Afghanistan's Independence Day in Kabul in August 2001. General Gul in an interview even told his interviewer that 'You Americans will have to support the Taliban one day' (Frantz, 2001). It was Pakistan's misfortune that this limited man should ever have found himself in a position of influence. It was Afghanistan's misfortune even more.

Mujahideen positioning

In May 1988, the head of the Central Political Directorate of the Soviet armed forces, General Aleksei Lizichev, announced that 311 Soviet soldiers were 'missing in action' in Afghanistan. This highlighted the issue of missing Soviet soldiers and Soviet prisoners of war more generally, and gave a certain amount of leverage to the Afghan resistance, since they and they alone were in a position to satisfy the desire for information on the part of Soviet families. The result was a series of meetings between Soviet officials and resistance delegates. On 13 October, Iulii Vorontsov, a very senior official of the Soviet Foreign Ministry, was named Ambassador to Afghanistan – a position which normally would have been filled by a nominee somewhat below his rank of Deputy Foreign Minister. Rubin argues that Vorontsov had a mission 'to create a coalition government that would include the PDPA, the mujahidin, and representatives of the old regime and would take power after the Soviet withdrawal' (Rubin, 1995b: 102). On 27 November, a meeting took place at the Pakistani Foreign Ministry in Islamabad between four Soviet officials and two resistance officials: Engineer Abdul Rahim of the *Jamiat-e Islami*, and Ghairat Baheer of the *Hezb-e Islami* of Gulbuddin Hekmatyar. The meeting dealt mainly with the issue of prisoners and soldiers missing in action, but Engineer Rahim was reported to have stated that he and Baheer had 'sought to reassure the Soviet team that a future mujahideen-dominated government would be non-aligned and seek good relations with Moscow' (*Reuters*, 28 November 1988). A further meeting took place at a higher level, in Taif in Saudi Arabia on 3–4 December. Vorontsov attended from the Soviet side, and from the resistance, Burhanuddin Rabbani of the *Jamiat-e Islami* and Sebghatullah Mojadiddi of the *Jabha-i Milli-i*

Nejat-e Afghanistan took part, although not with any credible claim to be representing the entire resistance. However, it ended without any concrete outcome, and nor did anything of use emerge from a third round of talks with Vorontsov which was held in Islamabad from 6 to 9 January 1989. Ultimately, the gap dividing the parties was too great. Vorontsov's brief was to secure a coalition government, but this was exactly what the Mujahideen parties could not accept: covert contact with regime members was one thing, but overt acceptance of the legitimacy of the PDPA as a political force was something entirely different (Saikal and Maley, 1991: 113–14).

The focus of the Mujahideen's backers was instead how to take over Afghanistan after the expected collapse of Najibullah's regime. Yet in the measures that were taken to address this issue lay some of the seeds of the disarray which was ultimately to eventuate. In the mid-1980s, there had been concerted attempts to foster a semblance of unity among the Sunni, Pakistan-based parties, culminating in the 16 May 1985 establishment of the 'Islamic Alliance of the Mujahideen of Afghanistan'. The alliance existed mainly on paper, but it did serve to produce a resistance 'spokesman', with the leaders of the seven participating parties serving three-month rotating terms. In 1988, an effort had been made to put together an 'Interim Government', with members being announced on 19 June. The head was one Engineer Ahmad Shah, a member of Sayyaf's *Ittehad-e Islami Afghanistan*, who was married to an American convert to Islam, but widely regarded as a Wahhabi backed by Saudi Arabia. The list of members was reportedly drawn up by Hamid Gul (Rubin, 1995a: 249), and there is no doubt that the ISI was heavily involved in orchestrating the entire process (Khan, 1991: 259).

From the point of view of those closest to Ahmad Shah, namely Sayyaf and Hekmatyar, and their Saudi and Pakistani backers, what was needed was some device by which to clothe his 'government' with legitimacy. The strategy on which they settled was the holding in Rawalpindi of a *shura* or 'council', which ran from 10 to 24 February 1989 and overlapped with the completion of the Soviet withdrawal. Rather than projecting unity, it achieved the very opposite (Saikal and Maley, 1991: 122–5). Mojadiddi had travelled to Iran and reached an agreement whereby the Iran-based Shiite groups would occupy 100 shura seats (Akram, 1996: 291), but – realising that a combination of Shia and 'moderate' Sunnis would be able to out-vote the 'Islamist' parties if this went ahead – the Islamists rejected this on his return in favour of an arrangement which offered these Shia far fewer places. The Iran-based Shia then refused to take part, prompting the mercurial

Mojadiddi to remark at a press conference I attended on 18 February 1989, organised at short notice by his spokesman Hamed Karzai, that the *shura* represented *at maximum* 'one third' of the Afghan population.

Pakistan and Saudi Arabia manipulated the proceedings shamelessly, with Saudi intelligence reportedly spending US$26 million per week in an effort to secure its desired outcome (Rubin, 1991: 81). Prominent commanders within Afghanistan were severely underrepresented, and Ahmad Shah Massoud later stated that he had received an invitation to send representatives to the *shura* only two days before it started (*AFGHANews*, 15 May 1989: 7). In the face of deep divisions within the *shura*, a committee headed by Jalaluddin Haqqani devised seven groupings of offices for the 'Interim Islamic Government of Afghanistan', to be apportioned between the seven Sunni parties in accordance with the outcome of balloting. The balloting saw Mojadiddi elected 'Head of State', Sayyaf as 'Prime Minister', Muhammadi as 'Head of the Supreme Court', Hekmatyar as 'Defence Minister' and Rabbani as 'Foreign Minister'. However, Muhammadi then used a procedural device to opt for the 'Defence Ministry', which led an enraged Hekmatyar to claim the 'Foreign Ministry', displacing Rabbani to the position of 'Minister for Reconstruction'. This outcome verged on the farcical, for it marginalised the parties whose commanders were most effective in Afghanistan, and left as the external face of the 'Interim Islamic Government' one of the most unappetising Mujahideen figures, namely Hekmatyar, who later in the year was to be named in the British press as the likely owner of the world's largest heroin factory (Teimourian, 1989).

The 'Interim Islamic Government' secured recognition from only four states – Saudi Arabia, Sudan, Bahrain, and Malaysia (Talmon, 1998: 314) – and in March 1989 was granted Afghanistan's seat in the Organisation of the Islamic Conference (OIC). The USA in June 1989 appointed Peter Tomsen as Special Envoy to the Afghan Resistance with the personal rank of Ambassador, succeeding Edmund McWilliams, who (unlike Tomsen) had had to report to Washington through the US Embassy in Pakistan, and was repeatedly contradicted by the US Ambassador to Pakistan, Robert Oakley (see Rubin, 1991: 85; Coll, 2005: 180–4; Gutman, 2008: 29–30). But neither Pakistan nor the USA was prepared to grant the 'Interim Islamic Government' formal recognition, and Pakistan even abstained on the vote to grant it the OIC seat. Launching a government-in-exile is always a difficult undertaking. But few have failed on the launching-pad as spectacularly as this.

The completion of the withdrawal

As the final date for the withdrawal approached, the international isolation of the Kabul regime became ever more palpable. In the first week of January 1989, the Soviets closed their military hospital in Kabul and evacuated the patients. On 21 January, West Germany's diplomatic personnel left, and on 27 January, the United Kingdom, France, Japan, and Italy announced that they were withdrawing their diplomats. Finally, on 30 January, the United States formally closed its Embassy. It was not to reopen until December 2001, and the empty buildings in the Embassy compound through the 1990s stood as a cameo of the Afghan people's involuntary transition from Cold War heroes to post-Cold War 'failed state' pariahs.

The end of the withdrawal was a bloody affair. Bradsher reports that the 40th Army 'unleashed one final campaign of terror in an effort to prevent attacks on its last troops on the road, with Gorbachev's personal authorization' (Bradsher, 1999: 309). Unfortunately, this slaughter – a microcosm of the Soviets' activities for over nine years in Afghanistan – received far less attention than the photogenic spectacle of General Gromov crossing a bridge at Termez leading from Afghanistan to the USSR, and finally bringing Moscow's ground combat in Afghanistan to a conclusion.

Thus, the end of the Soviet involvement saw different illegitimate or enfeebled claimants to power pitted against each other, in a country whose 'state' had limited capacity to function autonomously without external backing. The illegitimate regime of Najibullah was challenged at the political level by the impotent Interim Islamic Government and its self-interested external promoters. The significant *legitimate* power of local and regional commanders was not integrated into effective organisational structures at the national level, around which ordinary Afghans could rally. With no processes in place to reconcile these antagonisms or relegitimate political power, the outcome could only be determined by political manipulation and battlefield combat. This set the scene for the second and third waves of the Afghanistan conflict.

7

Consequences of the Soviet–Afghan War

The completion of the Soviet withdrawal from Afghanistan was not a moment of rapturous joy for Afghans, although there were certain grounds for celebration. On the one hand, those who had battled Soviet forces since the December 1979 invasion felt overwhelming pride that a superpower had been forced into what they saw as a retreat. But on the other hand, the suffering which the people of Afghanistan had been forced to endure during a decade of occupation was enormous, and even on the most optimistic of scenarios, the damage which had been inflicted on the country would take years if not decades to put right. From the Soviet point of view, too, there was little about which to be satisfied. Thousands of young soldiers had perished in a harsh land for little gain, leaving grieving relatives to ponder how and why such a disastrous commitment had come to be undertaken. Yet the war affected the two states very differently, and the aim of this chapter is briefly to identify some of the more important of these effects, together with two particularly important lessons of the war. In Afghanistan, the war produced a multilayered destructuring of politics, economy, and society, in ways which remain massively apparent at the beginning of a new century. In the USSR, on the other hand, the burdens of the war contributed to the short-term delegitimation of Communist Party rule, and played a role in the breakdown of mono-organisational socialism and the disintegration of the USSR as a territorial unit. The new Russian Federation which emerged from the wreckage of the USSR has been able to reposition itself in the world, and substantially distance itself from the Afghanistan conflict of the 1980s. Afghanistan enjoys no such luxury.

Effects of the war on Afghanistan

The civilian population

The effects of the war on the civilian population were horrendous. While certain areas were insulated for most of the 1980s from the worst effects – notably Kabul, with its security belts – the rural areas in which the bulk of the population lived were acutely vulnerable to the kinds of weapons which the Soviet and Afghan Armies employed. A careful analysis of data collected in refugee camps relating to patterns of war-related mortality concluded that between 1978 and 1987, unnatural deaths in Afghanistan amounted to 876,825 (Khalidi, 1991: 107). On average, this represented over 240 deaths every day for ten years straight, or over 60 Afghan deaths for each Soviet soldier who died as a result of the war. In assessing the social effects of the war, however, it is necessary also to take into account the position of the injured and the disabled. In 1995, the World Health Organisation estimated the physically disabled as totalling 'nearly 1.5 million persons' (WHO, 1995: 1), and in a society as damaged as Afghanistan, providing even minimal support for the disabled is an awesome task (Miles, 1990). Furthermore, the scale of war-related psychological trauma could not but have been massive, although such trauma is easily overlooked, not only because of a dearth of vocabulary in Afghan languages pointing to depression (Waziri, 1973: 214), but also because of social pressure on the victims of trauma to hide their suffering.

To this must be added the effects of displacement. As noted earlier, at the beginning of the 1990s over 6 million Afghan refugees were outside the country. While Pakistan and Iran performed remarkably in hosting the vast majority of these people, the environment of the refugees was inevitably one in which skills acquired through daily exposure to economic activity in Afghanistan were lost. Thus, the refugee exodus was destructive not only of the psychosocial wellness of those driven into exile, but also of the ability of a new generation of Afghans to function as farmers, herdsmen, or traders. Such disruption to human capital formation can fuel a cycle of conflict in war-torn societies, since it is often easier to train unskilled youths to fight than to farm. In addition to external refugees, countless Afghans were internally displaced during the war (Maley, 1998b). Anecdotal evidence spoke of Kabul's population swelling during the 1980s as people sought to enter a heavily protected city to escape the effects of aerial bombardment of the countryside.

The effects of the conflict on Afghan women for the most part were especially devastating. Some women visitors to Kabul were impressed by what they were shown – one even reported enthusiastically that there 'were female employees (and several female volunteer soldiers) at Pol-e Charkhi prison' (Moghadam, 1994: 866). Given the abuse of women which regularly took place in the regime's prisons, this was akin to praising Heinrich Himmler as an equal opportunity employer because there were women guards at Belsen. But most observers saw through the facade. Noting the combat techniques deployed by the Kabul regime and its backers, Nancy Hatch Dupree observed that 'Women shared more than equally in these events; often only women with their children occupied the mud-brick housing flattened by air and ground fire' (Dupree, 1992: 31). A small number of determined women were actively involved in the resistance and were persecuted as a result (Ellis, 2000: 7–9). Furthermore, women in refugee camps in Pakistan, located in one of the most conservative parts of a conservative state, were forced to endure an existence that was stultifying in the extreme (Boesen, 1988; Mayotte, 1992: 147–89; Shalinsky, 1994: 129). Finally, women suffered from the disruption to their social existence which occurred with the loss of male relatives. In a society in which the family is a key unit and men are typically the breadwinners, the consequences of male war deaths will be very widely felt.

The economy

Afghanistan suffered extensive physical damage during the 1980s which severely affected the operations of the Afghan economy. Infrastructural assets were sometimes targeted directly, and in other cases decayed through lack of necessary maintenance. Mud-brick housing readily fell victim to bombs and artillery shells: it was simply not reinforced sufficiently to survive even relatively small detonations. By the early 1990s, approximately 60 per cent of Afghan schools had no building (UNO, 1994: Vol. I: 16). The road system was in a very poor condition, although – amazingly – buses continued to criss-cross the country (Maley, 1999b: 235).

Given the significance of agriculture, however, it was the deterioration of the agricultural sector that posed some of the greatest problems at the end of the 1980s. Before the communist coup, Afghanistan, as André Brigot and Olivier Roy put it, was 'a poor country but not a country of hunger' (Brigot and Roy, 1988: 10). During the war, this fortunate situation changed. Evidence surfaced of localised malnutrition (D'Souza, 1984), and a meticulous 1988 study (SCA, 1988: 29–31) confirmed earlier reports (Farr and Gul, 1984) of sharp falls in agricultural output. By 1987, output was only a third of what it had been in 1978 – a result of the loss of land for cultivation, 50 per cent falls in yields from land which *could* be cultivated, and the deaths of draught oxen. Much of this damage was a product of deliberate attacks designed to deny the resistance access to food in sensitive areas. The damage caused to irrigation systems was to have one unintended but shattering consequence, namely the encouragement of narcotics production. While it is a myth that the Afghan resistance flourished on opium revenues – according to Rubin, Gulbuddin Hekmatyar was 'the only leader to exploit opium profits systematically as a basis for a hierarchically organized party and conventional army' (Rubin, 1995a: 257) – many Afghan farmers nonetheless found it profitable to switch to a crop which could be easily irrigated from melting snows. In the Soviet attacks on the traditional irrigation systems of rural Afghanistan, notably the ingenious *karez* network of interconnected tunnels, lay the foundations of the illicit economy of the mid-to-late 1990s.

Given the fragmentation of markets as a result of war, to speak of an Afghan 'macro-economy' in the 1980s is to stretch the meaning of the term, except perhaps in the area of the money supply. Similarly, official data supplied by the Kabul regime to international agencies were no more reliable than data produced by its Soviet patron. It is clear, however, that Afghanistan faced a deteriorating balance of payments, as its exports fell and its imports rose. In 1980 Afghanistan had a trade deficit of US$69 million (or 9.8 per cent of exports). By 1990 this had risen to US$649 million (or 276.2 per cent of exports). As might have been expected, foreign debt also increased, from US$1.2 billion in 1980 to US$5.1 billion in 1990. Finally, Afghanistan suffered significant inflation: prices during the decade of the 1980s increased by 980 per cent (Marsden and Samman, 2001: 39–41). Such developments are not purely of abstract interest. If price rises are not matched by rises in income, the ability of individuals and families to maintain their living standards is compromised. Similarly, if the external value of the currency falls – a common result of an intractable payments deficit – prices of imported goods will rise, again affecting living standards.

Afghan politics

Finally, some remarks about the effects of the war on Afghan politics are in order. First, the Afghan state at the time of the Soviet withdrawal had lost its capacity to function with any significant degree of autonomy. By 1988, fully 84 per cent of government expenditure was routine rather than developmental, in contrast to the situation in 1978 when 53 per cent of expenditure was on development. Less than a quarter of government expenditure was funded by domestic revenue; more than three-quarters was funded by rentier income (foreign aid and sales of natural gas) and by domestic borrowing (Rubin, 1995a: 297). In practice, this amounted to a disguised form of *state collapse*, since domestic revenue fell far short of what was required even to cover ordinary state expenditure. If and when the state's financial life-support machine was disconnected, a crisis was unavoidable.

Second, the tools of politics were altered by the war. Politics had to a limited extent been institutionalised during the New Democracy period, but Daoud's coup undermined these achievements, and the April 1978 coup contaminated the institutions of the state by harnessing them to the service of a Marxist party. While bargaining and manipulation of interests remained an important political device, coercion through the deployment of force had surged in significance (Goodson, 2001: 97–104). Thus, the state was confronted not simply with fiscal challenges, but the challenge of how to re-institutionalise and re-legitimate the state after years of politics based on ideology, personality, and the threat of violence. It was a challenge it was to prove incapable of meeting.

Third, Afghanistan's political elites had been significantly reconfigured, with traditional authority figures to a significant degree displaced in favour of party cadres on the regime side, and militarised and militant activists on the resistance side (Rubin, 1995a), although with local variations according to the extent to which particular localities had been insulated from the wider war. Furthermore, the new elites were separated by a gaping chasm. Not a single resistance leader of significance regarded Najibullah as an acceptable formal partner in any political transition. Therefore, any such transition would at the very least require a restructuring of the PDPA elite. Yet given the persistence of antagonisms between *Khalqis* and *Parchamis*, and between different elements of the *Parcham* faction, any attempt to change the leadership was likely to have unpredictable ricochet effects. Should Najibullah show any sign of weakness, his party enemies would descend upon him like a pack of angry piranhas. This limited his own room to manoeuvre.

Fourth, ethnic shifts during the course of the war were of potentially momentous import. While the lack of hard data makes it perilous to offer firm conclusions, the fiercest bombardments, and the highest levels of mortality, appear to have been in the areas bordering Pakistan which were largely populated by Pushtuns. While many exercised the option of exit as refugees (Sliwinski, 1989b), others perished without having the chance to do so. The net effect may well have been to reduce the proportion of Pushtuns in the overall population. This shift was paralleled by increasingly politicised ethnic consciousness among groups such as Tajiks (for many of whom Massoud was a heroic and inspirational leader) and Hazaras (who to an unusual extent enjoyed a degree of insulation from external forces). This is not to say that there was a resulting loss in identification with the territory of a united Afghanistan as a natural homeland (see Schetter, 2005), but rather that groups which previously had been in a subordinate position were unlikely to agree to return to such status under a new political dispensation.

Fifth, despite the withdrawal of Soviet troops, Afghanistan remained an important venue for international competition. The Soviet Union's *troop* withdrawal did not amount to a complete disengagement from Afghanistan; on the contrary, an air-bridge unrivalled since the days of the Berlin blockade was shortly to be put in place to keep the regime supplied. At the same time as this was happening, Pakistan stood poised to extract returns from what key Pakistanis regarded as *their* victory in Afghanistan. And Iran, ever vigilant as to the well-being of Afghanistan's Shiite minority, had moves in mind to heighten its own influence. The years following the Soviet withdrawal would not be easy.

Effects of the war on the Soviet Union

The Afghan war and Soviet society

The war in Afghanistan impacted upon Soviet society in complex ways. Naturally, given the size of the USSR, there were many families who were not touched by the war at all. Furthermore, only on a small number of occasions, when resistance groups backed by ISI intruded across the Soviet border into the union republic of Tajikistan, was the effect of the war directly felt on Soviet soil. But that said, the effects were more widespread than some observers realised at the time. A first effect, noted earlier, was the creation of a cohort of disaffected veterans of the war in Afghanistan – the *afgantsy* – who in Kipling's memorable phrase had known the worst too young, and usually returned with little faith in the Soviet system, and considerable scorn for the politicians who had fathered the commitment. (In downtown Moscow in early 1989, I was presented with a mimeographed collection of poems by an *afganets* which on the cover bore a scathing cartoon of a doddering Brezhnev, with a bottle of vodka in his belt, directing a host of young conscripts to a flaming hell through an archway labelled 'Afganistan'.) This is not to suggest that the *afgantsy* became an organised political lobby with a high degree of influence, but given the relaxations associated with the policy of *glasnost'*, they were well positioned to articulate positions which subtly altered the climate of opinion towards decision making by the top party elite.

Here, it is worth noting that events such as the war in Afghanistan can have both immediate and metaphorical impacts. Immediate impacts are discernible in war-related mortality, bereavement, injury, and trauma. But metaphorical impacts can be just as potent in social and political terms. The sinking of the *Titanic*, in April 1912, became metaphorically important, because it symbolised the perils of a hubris which decreed that a maritime vessel was unsinkable. Neville Chamberlain's unfortunate speech referring to 'peace in our time' following the September 1938 Munich Agreement became the defining image of appeasement, symbolising the triumph of self-delusion over a realistic assessment of what had happened (Taylor, 1979: 1004). And for the intellectual supporters of Gorbachev, 'Afghanistan' became a metaphor capturing the evils of 'stagnation': it was no surprise that figures such as Academician Andrei Sakharov brought up the matter of Afghanistan very frequently (Sakharov, 1988).

Faith in the party leadership

A loss of faith in the party leadership was actually a very serious development in the Soviet system. Competitive party systems are typically defended as giving substance to democratic accountability, providing an alternative set of rulers to whom the public can switch their loyalties if the current rulers prove inadequate. One-party systems inevitably depend upon overt coercion or the fear of it, since this is necessary to quash attempts to establish alternatives, but usually defend themselves on different bases, either in terms of intraparty devices for consultation ('democratic centralism') or of the unique insight or understanding enjoyed by a party leadership by virtue of its character. In certain circumstances, however, such claims can be sorely tested, and manifest policy failure is one of these. Sometimes, the response to such failure is an escalation of coercion, so that no one dares point out the party's weaknesses. However, the situation becomes much more dangerous where the loss of faith occurs not at the mass level (or the mass level *only*), but penetrates the middle or even upper echelons of the party itself. This was what happened in the case of Afghanistan. The process by which the decision to intervene was taken was so much at odds with the informal norms of consultation which had built up during the Brezhnev era, and with any notion of intraparty consultation, that it was tailor-made for those within the party who wished to pursue a reformist course. It was *not* the only such issue, but it was probably the easiest to exploit. Failure in economic policy, for example, can have complex causes, and it may be difficult to sheet home the blame to a small leadership group. Where an invasion decision has been taken by a small group of hierarchs without 'proper' consultation, it is much harder to persuade oneself that the system which allows such decision making is beyond reproach.

The erosion of the Brezhnev Doctrine

The war in Afghanistan struck a fundamental blow to the Brezhnev Doctrine. The Soviet Union for decades previously had been prepared to use force outside its borders to defend what the Soviet leadership perceived as core interests. This use of force was not as rampant as some conservative analysts painted it as being, but it had permitted the consolidation in Eastern Europe of a glacis of dependent states whose populations, witnessing the invasions of Hungary in 1956 and Czechoslovakia in 1968, had few illusions about the fate that would await them if they too proved restive. But on occasion, a passionate desire for freedom could override such prudential calculations. In Poland in December 1981, this actually prompted a pre-emptive strike against the Solidarity trade union by a Polish military aware that a Soviet invasion might be the alternative (Saikal, 1984b).

The Soviet withdrawal from Afghanistan undermined the previously fundamental notion that the 'gains of socialism' were irreversible (Wiles, 1985). While the Soviet Union, as noted earlier, referred to Afghanistan after the 1979 invasion as a 'developing' rather than 'socialist' country, by the end of the 1980s, the ideological innovations of the Gorbachev period had stretched the notion of socialism so much in the direction of a kind of 'guided' welfare state that the notion of Soviet power being used to prop up socialist regimes was becoming decreasingly plausible. However, even in 1988, it struck one shrewd observer as inconceivable that the Soviet Union could have sanctioned the overt dismantling of the Najibullah regime as part of a settlement process in Afghanistan (Richardson, 1989: 167), and this suggests that the collapse of the Eastern European glacis, even at this stage, was below the horizon. Perhaps the Gorbachev leadership would have gravitated to the 'Sinatra Doctrine' in any case, but the withdrawal from Afghanistan may well have hastened the process.

Was Afghanistan the USSR's Vietnam?

The Vietnam War and the fall of Saigon in April 1975 did not lead to the breakdown of the US political system or the breakup of the USA as a political system. However, they did create a lingering sense of failure within the United States, which the humiliations of the Carter Presidency, notably the fall of the Shah of Iran and the subsequent hostage crisis (Saikal, 1980) significantly aggravated. It took the Reagan Presidency from 1981 to 1989 to remove this sense of impotence.

Some analysts have queried whether the experience in Afghanistan constituted a military 'defeat' for the Soviet Union (Jukes, 1989: 96–8; Galeotti, 1995: 153; Mendelson, 1998: 27), and by implication, whether an analogy between the US experience in Vietnam and the Soviet experience in Afghanistan could stand up. When the USA left Saigon in 1975, the image of a helicopter lifting off from the US Embassy in the besieged South Vietnamese capital was to haunt a generation of politicians. The Soviet leadership, and General Gromov, managed to avoid such imagery. However, those who challenge the Vietnam analogy tend to point to the lack of a decisive combat defeat for the USSR, and the relatively lighter character of the Soviet force commitment to Afghanistan compared with the US commitment to Vietnam. Mark Galeotti, for example, argues that 'had the USSR ever deployed the sort of forces the US had used in Vietnam, for example, where a ratio of 7 soldiers per square kilometre was reached, compared with Afghanistan's 0.7, the war could have been won.' He endorses the view that 'this was a war the Soviets never really tried to win' (Galeotti, 1995: 153).

Galeotti's argument invites three kinds of response. First, the argument is speculative and depends upon counterfactual assumptions. Second, it is not clear exactly what it means to say that the war could have been 'won'. Would the 'battle for the Afghan people', as Marshal Akhromeev put it, have been 'won' simply by increasing the number of despised invaders in the country? Third, as writers such as T. H. Rigby long ago emphasised, the defeat in the Afghan war was a *political* defeat (Rigby, 1989: 67). Douglas Borer has elaborated a response to Galeotti which deserves to be quoted at some length, as it goes to the heart of the issue:

In order to understand superpower war loss in Vietnam and Afghanistan, the focus should not be primarily on any analysis of the battlefield, but rather on the analysis of the politics that ruled the battlefield ... In every single major engagement, in both wars, US and

Soviet troops dominated their opponents. However, domination of the battlefield in a strict military sense did not produce political victory for the superpowers. Likewise, battlefield defeat was not equivalent to political failure for those resisting the superpowers in Vietnam and Afghanistan. We must remember that devoid of its ultimate political significance, war has no worthy moral, intellectual or social meaning. Without politics, war is simply murder on an aggregate scale. (Borer, 1999: 190–1)

Finally, it is worth noting an important point made by Borer. 'From a comparative perspective', he argues, 'it is clear that Afghanistan's impact on the ultimate fate of the Soviet Union was much greater than Vietnam's impact on the United States. The United States survived Vietnam, and the Soviet Union did not survive Afghanistan. Therefore despite multiple layers of analogy, in comprehensive terms Afghanistan was not the Soviet Vietnam; and mercifully, Vietnam was not the American Afghanistan' (Borer, 1999: 239). Here we find a genuinely novel argument: that Afghanistan was not the Soviet Vietnam, but something even *worse*.

Afghanistan and the disintegration of the Soviet system

Does this argument hold up? A superficial response to it might be that many factors contributed to the breakdown of the USSR, but that America's 'Vietnam syndrome' was mono-causal. However, that claim too is debatable. The USA's mid-1970s crisis of confidence was also a product of diverse factors. The failure in Vietnam was certainly one, but others included the collapse of the Bretton Woods international monetary system after President Nixon's suspension of US dollar convertibility into gold in 1971, and then, of course, Nixon's own enforced resignation in 1974 after the Watergate scandal (Arnold, 1988: 129). While the combination of these was debilitating, the stability of the US constitutional system was never remotely under threat, and in significant respects the last years of the Vietnam War and the immediate post-Vietnam period saw important progress in a number of areas of historical tension, notably the civil rights of African-Americans.

What role, then, did Afghanistan play in the demise of the Soviet system? Unquestionably, it was not the only factor at work, and no serious scholar has attempted to claim that it was. A new leader with unorthodox views, economic weakness, an intellectually impoverished ideology, rifts in 'world communism', and renewed competition with a superpower rival were all considerations of notable significance, helping to fuel the crisis of faith in the party leadership discussed earlier. But some of these factors were themselves heightened in significance as a result of the war in Afghanistan. Anthony Arnold has compared Afghanistan to a 'fateful pebble', tripping up a tired and stumbling walker (Arnold, 1993). In a useful article, Rafael Reuveny and Aseem Prakash have sought to identify different effects which the Afghanistan war had on Soviet politics. First, they note *perception* effects. The war, they argue, 'changed the Soviet leadership's perception of the efficacy of holding their diverse country together by using military force'. In the light of this development, within the USSR itself, 'non-Russian movements were emboldened to openly preach secession'. Second were *military* effects. 'Since the military', they argue, 'was an important pillar of the anti-*perestroika* camp, the reverses in Afghanistan weakened anti-reformists, hastened *perestroika*, and facilitated the collapse of the system.' The war 'created conditions for the demilitarizing of Soviet society'. Third were *legitimacy* effects: the war 'accentuated the cleavages between the non-Russian republics and the Soviet state'. Fourth were *glasnost'* effects: the war 'added new vigour to the forces unleashed by glasnost' (Reuveny and Prakash, 1999: 698–705). All these are plausible points, although debate over their weight compared to other factors will inevitably persist.

One final issue deserves mention, and that is the role of Afghanistan in the failure of the coup attempt in Moscow in August 1991. If there was a *coup de grâce* against both the Soviet sociopolitical order and the Soviet Union as a territorial unit, then the failure of the conservatives in the 'State Committee for the Extraordinary Situation' to seize and retain Soviet power was it. One of the key reasons why the coup failed was that the Soviet armed forces split, notwithstanding Defence Minister Iazov's having joined the 'State Committee' (see Sixsmith, 1991; Billington, 1992; Lepingwell, 1992). In part this may have reflected a heightened constitutional consciousness within the military, or a reluctance to follow the Bonapartist path on which Iazov had embarked, but it undoubtedly involved a breakdown in an hierarchical chain of command, with the commander of the Airborne Forces, General Pavel Grachev, taking a stand against the coup, as did significant groups of troops in the Moscow area. The Afghanistan debacle may have contributed to the willingness of key officers to think for themselves, rather than tell themselves that orders were orders.

Two lessons of the war

In conclusion, there were two lessons of the Soviet–Afghan War which stand as awful warnings to major powers contemplating interventions on the territory of smaller neighbours. The first lesson was that *wars cannot be fought to successful conclusions with unrealistic objectives.* In the Afghan case, the Soviet Union was trapped in a double bind: the more it supported the PDPA regime with armed force, the more it compromised the legitimacy of the beneficiary of its actions. This was a product both of the nature of Afghan society, the nature of the Soviet system, and the nature of the Soviets' clients. At the time of the Soviet invasion of Afghanistan, the bulk of Afghan society was *not* in crisis. Perverse as it may have seemed to detribalised Marxists in Kabul, rural dwellers for the most part felt that they had a lifestyle worth defending against external threats, and powerful norms of reciprocity ordained solidarity in the face of external attack. Furthermore, the Soviet Union was the very kind of external agent that would most effectively activate such norms. The explicit atheism of the Soviet order, based on the Marxist doctrine of dialectical materialism, was notorious in Afghan circles, and positive memories of Soviet–Afghan cooperation in the 1950s were nowhere near strong enough to cleanse the Soviets' reputation at the mass level. Finally, the People's Democratic Party of Afghanistan was an unworthy beneficiary of support. Henry S. Bradsher's cruel description of it as a party of 'teahouse political talk' (Bradsher, 1987: 339) perfectly encapsulated its weaknesses. An unpopular state which confronts a robust society in defence of undeserving surrogates is unlikely to find it a rewarding or happy experience.

The second lesson was that *moral conviction and external support can act as significant force multipliers which even the military capabilities of a superpower cannot match.* A great deal of evidence attests to the low morale of Soviet soldiers in Afghanistan, the bulk of them unwilling conscripts. I recall the manifest despondency of a company of Soviet soldiers I encountered in Uzbekistan in 1984, almost certainly destined for deployment in the USSR's southern neighbour. By contrast, the morale of the resistance was in general remarkably high, and *remained* remarkably high even in the face of terrible losses. Scorched-earth tactics left behind survivors who in many cases had nothing left to do *except* struggle against the communist regime and its backers. This was poignantly captured in the words of a young *mujahid* who remarked: 'I died five years ago when I left Kabul. My soul has gone to heaven; this is just my body' (Goodwin, 1987: 175). A resistance movement which can obtain external support is a different foe from one which is isolated and dependent purely upon indigenous networks for assistance. External supporters can supply not only armaments, ammunition, and *matériel* which would otherwise be unavailable, but also an added sense of legitimacy to a struggle by conveying to the resistants that their objectives are shared with other power holders, rather than eccentric and idiosyncratic. This in turn can be a significant morale booster.

In a very real sense, the Soviet–Afghan War had no winners. The Soviet Union was corroded by its political failure, and the struggle between the Afghan resistance and Afghan communists was remitted to the battlefield. It was not even a triumph for 'conflict resolution'. The Geneva Accords simply brought the first wave of the wars of modern Afghanistan to a conclusion. The 1990s were to prove a decade of misery and sorrow for the Afghan people. It is now time to examine why.

8

The Interregnum of Najibullah, 1989–1992

Few observers expected Najibullah's regime to last for very long after the Soviet withdrawal from Afghanistan. Yet over three years were to pass before it finally disintegrated, years of what Goodson called 'high intensity civil war' (Goodson, 1998: 480). These years were marked by a growing indifference to Afghanistan in the wider world, driven in part by the emergence of dramatic events elsewhere. The fall of the Berlin Wall, the collapse of communism and the end of the Cold War were momentous developments which overshadowed Afghanistan and the Afghans' contributions to political change in the Soviet bloc. The Bush Administration and its key policymakers were preoccupied with the careful management of transition in the Soviet Union (Beschloss and Talbott, 1993; Bush and Scowcroft, 1998), and then from August 1990 with the Iraqi invasion of Kuwait and its regional and international consequences. The situation in Afghanistan after the Soviet troop withdrawal appeared a minor concern when compared with these great events, and that unfortunately was how it was treated. Yet it was a period of great significance in the long run, for Afghanistan became the venue for a bitter transnational war which permitted groups such as Osama Bin Laden's to find a haven, and was brought to an end only in September 2001 when Pakistan, under intense US pressure, was forced to abandon the active promotion of its Taliban clients.

The aim of this chapter is to identify the factors which accounted for Najibullah's unexpected survival until April 1992, and the collapse of his regime at that point. The chapter is divided into four parts. In the first, I discuss the mechanisms which Najibullah exploited in order to hold on to office. The second deals with the problems which beset the organized resistance groups during this period and prevented them from operating in a concerted way to exploit the fruits of their anti-Soviet activities. The third examines attempts which the UN made during this period to orchestrate an orderly transition to a 'broad-based government'. The fourth traces the tumultuous events of late 1991 and early 1992 which led to the collapse of Najibullah's regime and his seeking refuge in UN offices in Kabul. A key point which emerges from this analysis is that while Najibullah showed considerable dexterity in identifying and exploiting non-legitimate forms of domination, he failed to develop broadly based normative support of a kind which could sustain his regime in the face of an acute crisis.

Mechanisms of regime maintenance

Continuing Soviet assistance

In Afghanistan from February 1989, even though Soviet troops had left, Soviet planes kept flying. This was absolutely crucial, since Kabul could not have survived as an isolated redoubt without such backing: cities do not feed themselves, and bread shortages have brought down large numbers of governments. Kabul needed food supplies of approximately 700 tonnes a day, and the Soviet leadership made sure that these stocks arrived (Burns, 1989). Military assistance also continued. In a May 1989 memorandum to the Politburo, Foreign Minister Shevardnadze, Defence Minister Iazov, KGB Chief Kriuchkov, and Party Secretary Zaikov recommended a 'search for additional reserves to accelerate delivery of armaments and ammunitions into Afghanistan, particularly the armament like R-17 missiles, air-defense equipment, and others' (Hershberg, 1996–1997: 184). The R-17 missile is more popularly known as the SCUD, a missile which won considerable notoriety when Iraq fired modified versions at Israel during the Gulf War in 1991. The SCUD missile had certain features which protected it from Stinger missiles in the hands of the resistance: it was a proper guided missile with mechanisms to correct ballistic trajectory, and its warhead hit at speeds well above the speed of sound (Cordesman and Wagner, 1990: 163). A detailed study of missile use in Afghanistan concluded that the number of missile launches between the signing of the Geneva Accords and the collapse of Najibullah's regime exceeded the total of 'all ballistic missiles fired in anger since the end of the Second World War' (Bermudez, 1992: 51). The total value of aid to the communist regime in the post-withdrawal period was credibly estimated at US$300 million a month (Isby, 1991), with one report suggesting that arms deliveries alone in the six months following the withdrawal were worth US$1.4 billion (Coll, 1989).

Militias and segmentary politics

Resources supplied from the USSR, together with the printing of more Afghan money, gave the regime some scope to buy off influential local commanders. As Rubin noted, this was extraordinarily expensive, with 'containers' of banknotes being sent to regime supporters (Rubin, 1995a: 161). Nonetheless, it worked in the short term, as a number of commanders were content to accept Kabul's money, secure in the knowledge that in the long term they retained the option to defect to the opposition. This reflects the fundamental fragility of support purchased with currency: it tends to last only as long as the currency flow can be sustained. To address this problem, Najibullah made use of militias drawn from ethnic or sectarian minorities. The two most significant of these were an Ismaili Shiite militia from Baghlan loyal to Sayed Mansur Nadiri, and the so-called 'Jawzjani' Uzbek militia loyal to Abdul Rashid Dostam, which technically functioned as the 53rd Division of the Army, but worked directly for Najibullah and consisted of volunteers who were paid in accordance with results (Dorronsoro, 2005: 205). In each of these cases, the lure of state patronage proved irresistible to groups which had been either marginalized or actively harassed by the state or its agents in the past. Dostam's militia was multiethnic (Rubin, 1995a: 160), but largely non-Pushtun. It was exceedingly brutal in combat, and this in part accounted for its solidarity: defection was not an option for its members, given the fate that would likely await them on account of their past behaviour.

Dostam was to become a significant political figure in the 1990s, and a candidate for the presidency in 2004. Born in an Uzbek peasant family near Shibarghan in 1955, he was at no time a member of the resistance. Rather, he rose to prominence by organizing self-defence units for the northern gas-fields. It was from these units that his militia emerged, and he received a range of material and symbolic rewards from Kabul, notably command of the 53rd Division in March 1990 and membership of the party Central Committee (Giustozzi, 2000: 222). In the 1990s it was to become clear that Dostam had ambitions which stretched beyond mere local or even regional significance. Unfortunately, these ambitions were not allied to a long-term, strategic, sense of direction, and Dostam was to disrupt a number of attempts to consolidate central political institutions, but without being able either to offer a credible national alternative, or even protect his own power-base in Mazar-e Sharif. While he was a moderately effective administrator in his own locality, at the countrywide level, Dostam was for years to come a spoiler rather than a builder, and his miscalculations were to cost him dearly at different times.

Rebadging the party

As well as relying on Soviet support and purchased loyalty, Najibullah attempted to make full use of nationalism as a new basis for popularity. This entailed jettisoning most of the party's ideological baggage, a move which Najibullah undertook with all the subtlety of a balloon pilot seeking to lighten his load as the burner runs low on gas. The most dramatic gesture was the mid-1990 change in the name of the party, to *Hezb-e Watan*, or 'Party of the Fatherland'. This was preceded by an abandonment of Marxist rhetoric, and intensified vilification of Pakistan and of Arab extremism. The party, in its new guise, was to be open only to 'believing and practising Muslims' (Rubin, 1995a: 166).

At this time, Najibullah also resumed his strategy of promoting 'non-party' figures. He had done this previously with the appointment of the ineffectual Dr Hasan Sharq as Chairman of the Council of Ministers in May 1988. However, Sharq had been unceremoniously removed on 20 February 1989 and replaced by his predecessor, Sultan Ali Keshtmand, who became Chairman of the Executive Committee of the Council of Ministers (although formally Najibullah was to chair the Council). On 7 May 1990, a dignitary from Herat who had served as Deputy Finance Minister under Daoud, Fazel Haq Khaliqyar, was appointed to succeed Keshtmand, who was increasingly at odds with Najibullah, and was subsequently to be severely injured in an assassination attempt. (Khaliqyar had been wounded *before* coming to office, in a spectacular Mujahideen attack in Herat on 6 April 1990 during a 'national reconciliation' ceremony.) Other figures, such as Muhammad Asghar, a prominent figure from the 'New Democracy' era (but also a recipient of a Soviet decoration on the centenary of the birth of Lenin) were given some scope to express some heterodox views. But realistically, all these changes were cosmetic rather than substantive. Najibullah was *not* a 'born-again' pluralist. He was simply prepared to adopt any approach that might help him retain his position.

Intraparty rivalries

What thwarted Najibullah's approach at this time, just as it had when he first preached 'national reconciliation' before the Soviet troop withdrawal, was the lack of consensus within the party elite on the appropriate course to take. Even after the October 1988 party purge, there were still numerous *Khalqis* in significant positions, and they tended to despise Najibullah and his policies in equal measure. It was a measure of Najibullah's lack of room to manoeuvre that on 17 August 1988, shortly before the purge, the Army Chief of General Staff, Lieutenant-General Shahnawaz Tanai, had been appointed Defence Minister, even though he was a *Khalqi*. Tanai had been involved as a young officer in the April 1978 coup, but came to prominence as a commander of the 37th Commando Brigade during operations in the Panjsher Valley. After the completion of the Soviet troop withdrawal, the relationship between Najibullah and Tanai deteriorated rapidly. In December 1989, Najibullah arrested 100 *Khalqi* officers who were charged with plotting to overthrow the regime. Finally, in March 1990, Tanai attempted a coup against Najibullah. The regime alleged it was prompted by fear that the *Khalqi* defendants might implicate him (Bradsher, 1999: 342). Others hypothesized that Soviet circles may have been involved (Hyman, 1990: Arnold, 1990). But in any case, it failed rather badly. Of the resistance party leaders in Pakistan, only Hekmatyar was prepared to throw his weight behind Tanai; the coup plan had called for Tanai's forces to open a route for *Hezb-e Islami* loyalists to enter Kabul (Rubin, 1995a: 253). The coup reflected disorganization on the part of the *Khalq*, and triggered a new purge. Zeray, Gulabzoi, Dastagir Panjsheri, and Asadullah Sarwari were all expelled from the party.

One other development caused trouble for Najibullah. On 20 June 1991, Babrak Karmal returned from Moscow, where he had been in enforced exile for over four years. During his years of exile, Karmal had been treated frostily by the Gorbachev leadership: the Soviets even refused to pay for a Karmal family wedding, on the grounds that Karmal had no friends to invite. Karmal made no secret of his resentment at the way in which he had been treated, and described the April 1978 coup as the 'greatest crime against the people of Afghanistan' (Snegirev, 1991). Rubin has suggested that his return may have been at the instigation of Kremlin hardliners looking to reassert a tough line in Afghanistan (Rubin, 1995a: 152); Najibullah apparently blamed Karmal's return on a KGB-CIA conspiracy (Halliday, 1999: 688). But it was by no means only hardline communists in Moscow who were hostile to Najibullah. Increasingly, Soviet commentators were critical of the continuing burden of supporting the regime. Just a week after Karmal's return to Kabul, a blistering critique of Najibullah appeared in the Soviet press. The author reported that it was Soviet economic and military aid that was keeping Najibullah in office; that 85 per cent of Afghan territory lay outside the regime's control; that Najibullah's offers of a coalition government would entail his party's retaining control of the most important ministries; and that continuing Soviet support for the regime was prompted by the fear that a free Afghan government would demand war reparations (Vasil'ev, 1991).

One analyst, Richard Weitz, has suggested that the USSR's strategy in Afghanistan 'proved remarkably successful', and was undermined only by the 'unplanned' collapse of authority after the August 1991 coup (Weitz, 1992: 25). Had Weitz known how swiftly Najibullah's regime would follow Gorbachev's into oblivion, he might not have offered so positive an assessment. The Moscow coup was not an 'Act of God', but rather the culmination of processes of institutional decay and elite fragmentation (Gill, 1994) which at some point would surely have seen an ongoing commitment to Najibullah discarded as an anachronism. The Soviet strategy bought Najibullah time, but very little else. Furthermore, his survival was to a considerable degree the result of misjudgements by some of his opponents.

Fracturing within the Afghan resistance

The completion of the Soviet troop withdrawal forced the Afghan resistance forces to reconsider the nature of their struggle. Traditional warfare, based on a politicized value system, had proved well fitted to denying the USSR the political objectives which it had invaded Afghanistan to pursue. But to some, it was necessary in the post-Soviet period to move to a more conventional form of combat, in which organized forces such as Hekmatyar's *Lashkar-e Isar* ('Army of Sacrifice') could flex their muscles. This proved to be a grave error, which had much to do with the failure of the Mujahideen properly to capitalize on the Soviet retreat. But the Mujahideen also suffered from a loss of international support, at a crucial juncture, which adversely affected their combat performance. Some fighters were simply war-weary, and less interested in eliminating remote Afghan communists than alien Soviet invaders (Rubin, 1995a: 247). Finally, Hekmatyar's ambitions thwarted efforts to act concertedly.

Resistance tensions: Jalalabad and Farkhar

A very clear indication that not all was well with the resistance came barely a month after the completion of the Soviet troop withdrawal, when an attempt to seize the city of Jalalabad failed badly. Initially, the attack led Najibullah to make a panicky request to the Soviet leadership for airstrikes from Soviet bases against the resistance (Chernyaev, 2000: 207). Given the widespread belief that Najibullah's days were numbered, the Jalalabad operation had an extremely adverse impact on resistance morale, and concomitantly boosted the morale of the regime. Predictably, the problem which thwarted the entire operation was one of coordination. Massoud later stated that he learned of the attack on Jalalabad only from a BBC broadcast, and that it took place 'when most of the country was covered with snow' (*AFGHANews*, 1 October 1989: 6). In the vicinity of Jalalabad, too, there were significant problems of communication between different groups of Mujahideen. The defensive positions of the regime held; convoys slipped through to the city, reducing pressure on the defenders; SCUD missiles had a psychological impact even though they were not especially accurate; and massacres of surrendering regime forces by Arab extremists in the attackers' ranks (Rubin, 1989–1990: 155) provided a disincentive for others to consider defection. After three to four months, the operation simply fizzled out, with the regime still in control of Jalalabad.

Were the Mujahideen leaders properly consulted before the operation? Some writers claim so (Yousaf and Adkin, 1992: 227), but Bradsher argues that the decision to launch the attack 'was taken in Islamabad on 5 March at a meeting of Pakistani officials attended by United States Ambassador Robert B. Oakley but not by any *mujahideen* officials' (Bradsher, 1999: 346). However, one source which he cites looked suspiciously like an ISI attempt to shift blame on to other policy circles, with the claim that General Naseerullah Babar, a close aide to Prime Minister Benazir Bhutto, was responsible (Kamm, 1989). While Babar was in time to prove himself at least as maladroit as General Hamid Gul as far as Afghan policy was concerned, it seems unlikely that he would have been able to outflank the head of the ISI on this issue, and other well-placed sources attest to Gul's involvement (Yousaf and Adkin, 1992: 227).

In any case, no one doubts that Pakistani misreading of the situation in Afghanistan had much to do with the shambles which eventuated. This partly reflected a misunderstanding of the capabilities of the resistance (see Yousaf and Adkin, 1992: 230–1), but also a certain blatancy as to objective: the refusal of many resistance groups to cooperate with the ISI arose, as Henry S. Bradsher put it, 'from a perception that Jalalabad was an ISI effort to defeat Najibullah so it could install its favourite, the Ghilzai Pushtun, Hekmatyar, in Kabul. Few Ghilzais outside his party, and still fewer Durrani Pushtuns, Tajiks, or other Afghans wanted to die for that' (Bradsher, 1999: 345–6). The ISI never seemed to learn that in Afghanistan, it is better to coordinate through consultation than through decree. The blame for the failure fell on General Gul, who was removed as Director-General of ISI and returned to an Army position.

The tensions which were smouldering at the time of the Jalalabad campaign flared openly on 9 July 1989, in what came to be known as the Farkhar massacre. Thirty commanders associated with Massoud's *Shura-i Nazar* – including Dr Sayed Husain, Commander Sar Malim Tariq, Commander Islamuddin, Commander Abdul Wadood, and Mawlawi Ezatullah – were murdered by a commander from Hekmatyar's *Hezb-e Islami* named Sayed Jamal. The killings occurred as they returned from a meeting which had planned an attack on Kunduz, and manifestly reflected Hekmatyar's desire to cripple a rival party (Weintraub, 1989). Faced with widespread condemnation by other resistance leaders, and the threat of formal expulsion from their ranks, Hekmatyar archly withdrew from the 'Interim Government', claiming that only through an election in Afghanistan could it become representative.

Several other attacks should be mentioned at this point. On 7 August 1989, the renowned 76-year-old Kandahar commander Haji Abdul Latif was poisoned, reportedly by agents of the Kabul regime (*AFGHANews*, 1 September 1989). In March 1990, Mulla Nasim Akhundzada, the Deputy Defence Minister in the Interim Government, was assassinated in Peshawar. Given Akhundzada's prominence in the opium trade, Hekmatyar's *Hezb* may again have been involved (Rubin, 1995a: 263). On 30 August 1991, Mawlawi Jamilurrahman, a former *Hezb* commander who in 1985 had established a puritanical 'mini-state' in Kunar but fled to Pakistan in the face of a *Hezb* attack, was assassinated in Pakistan by an Egyptian, Abdullah Rumi, who was then killed by bodyguards. (Kunar was perhaps the most disordered province in the entire country, and was the scene of a massive explosion in the provincial capital, Asadabad, on 20 April 1991, blamed on a SCUD missile attack.) And on 4 November 1991, the former king, Zahir Shah, was stabbed in Rome by a 'journalist' born in Angola and carrying a Portuguese passport.

Resistance consolidation

Not all was bleak as far as the resistance was concerned. On the ground, there were some military achievements, such as the capture of Khost in March 1991, which saw a resistance force under Jalaluddin Haqqani capture not only the town, but a number of senior regime generals, including Deputy Defence Minister Muhammad Zahir Solamal. However, the resistance proved unable to build on this gain: the ISI tried to claim it as a victory for *Hekmatyar*, and the political rewards of the conquest were entirely dissipated.

This reflected a new line of tension: between the parties and their backers in Pakistan, and field commanders in Afghanistan. From 7 to 9 May 1990, a first meeting of a 'National Commanders Shura' was held, followed by another from 22 to 25 June, and a major gathering on the border between Badakhshan and Kunar from 9 to 13 October. While the bulk of the participants were Pushtuns, the Shura served to affirm the rising status of Massoud, who in October 1990 paid a visit to Pakistan as its spokesman, his first trip outside Afghanistan since the beginning of the war. During the visit, he met with President Ghulam Ishaq Khan, Army Chief Mirza Aslam Beg, ISI Director-General Durrani, and also with Hekmatyar. The strategy adopted by the Shura was incremental: to divide Afghanistan into nine administrative regions and to target outposts of the regime. With the failure of the Pakistan-based 'Interim Government', the USA was prepared to support the new approach of aiding commanders directly, despite ISI's objections (Yousaf and Adkin, 1992: 208–9). One consequence was a resumption of aid to Massoud: as Olivier Roy has recorded, from November 1988 until October 1990, Massoud 'did not receive a single bullet from the US-sponsored programme' (Roy, 1991: 37).

As well as consolidation among Sunni commanders, there was also a degree of consolidation, albeit not exactly consensual, among Afghanistan's Shiite parties. It reflected in part the frustration of the Shia at their inability to secure appropriate representation at the 1989 shura in Rawalpindi (Harpviken, 1996: 101). As mentioned earlier, on 16 June 1990 the establishment of the *Hezb-e Wahdat* ('Party of Unity') was announced in Tehran. It did not reflect total unity among Shia. A significant chunk of the *Harakat-e Islami* of Asif Mohseni opted not to join. Mohseni, a Pushto-speaker from Kandahar, had maintained a certain ambivalence about his own identity, and may have felt that he could best maintain this position through retaining his independence. The *Hezb-e Wahdat* was based in Bamiyan, and while ultimately it was to develop fissures, it marked a considerable step forward in the articulation of the interests of Afghan Shia.

US disengagement

George Bush had been inaugurated as US President almost on the eve of the completion of the Soviet troop withdrawal. Yet despite two terms as vice-president to President Reagan, he did not bring a fixed vision of how to proceed in Afghanistan. His approach instead was to explore options, all the while giving priority to protecting the position of Gorbachev, whose continued dominance he saw as vital to USA–Soviet relations. This was a position to which he stuck firmly, even when Gorbachev's swing to the right in the late part of 1990 and the early part of 1991 (Brown, 1996: 269) raised the ire of conservatives in the Congress and his own Republican Party. Afghanistan was no longer a key East–West issue, and Bush largely left the crafting of policy to Secretary of State James A. Baker III, although Ambassador Oakley in Islamabad, reportedly known locally as 'The Viceroy' (Rashid, 2000: 172), also played an increasingly active role, which anticipated a delegation of policy responsibility to the US Embassy in Pakistan of a kind which was to prove quite dangerous in the years ahead. But it is important to emphasize that the Bush Administration did not set out to 'abandon' the Mujahideen. Certain glitches in the early days of the Bush Administration left the Mujahideen under-resourced at a time when steady resource flows (as envisaged by the USA's declaration at the time the Geneva Accords were signed) would have been of significant value (Saikal and Maley, 1991: 121–2), but these did not reflect any malevolent intent to cripple the resistance.

That said, certain important factors came into play in shaping policy, and ensured that uncritical support would no longer be on offer. One was disillusionment with Pakistan's handling of the Afghanistan issue. During the 1980s, Congress had been willing to vote in favour of very large disbursements to aid the resistance, for the greater good of blocking Soviet geopolitical ambitions. With those ambitions shrinking, more attention began to focus on the explicit anti-Americanism of some of the groups to which Pakistan had channelled funds (Goldman, 1992: 183–5). This was brought sharply into focus during the 1991 Gulf War, when Hekmatyar adopted a pro-Iraqi position. Another was a growing sense that Najibullah could be eased out of office by cooperative US–Soviet action, specifically of a kind which would result in a cutoff of supplies to his regime. Shevardnadze in February 1990 had outlined a framework for regime transition in Afghanistan which proved a workable basis for further US–Soviet dialogue (Shevardnadze, 1990), and in December 1990, the Soviets and the USA came very close to an agreement, with broad consensus on the need for a cutoff in weapons supplies, and a UN-sponsored transitional process. Under pressure from hardliners, Shevardnadze lacked the ability to close a deal by setting firm dates, and with his resignation later that month, the process came to a halt (Rubin, 1995b: 109–10). However, the outcome of the Gulf War was a striking setback not only for Saddam Hussein, but for figures such as Hekmatyar and in particular General Mirza

Aslam Beg, who had bizarrely misjudged what was likely to happen (Rubin, 1995b: 113–14). This weakening of those most strongly committed to a military solution set the scene for the United Nations to renew its involvement in the Afghanistan situation.

UN attempts to manage transition

In late 1989, Diego Cordovez relinquished his position as the Secretary-General's Personal Representative for Afghanistan in order to become Foreign Minister of Ecuador (which in October 1990 established diplomatic relations at ambassadorial level with Najibullah's regime). This briefly left the head of UNOCA, Sadruddin Aga Khan, as the UN's most prominent official dealing with Afghanistan. However, it was to prove an uneasy position to occupy. Funding problems rapidly became critical (Maley, 1989a: 126–7) as the expected mass repatriation of refugees to Afghanistan following the Soviet troop withdrawal simply did not occur. As an Ismaili Shia, Prince Sadruddin was regarded with a certain suspicion by various resistance groups, given the support which Nadiri's Ismaili Shiite militia had given to Kabul; and great offence sprang from the perception that UNOCA had vetoed the use of dogs in mine clearance operations on the grounds that 'animals' should not be put at risk to solve problems caused by humans, implying that Afghans were less valuable than dogs (McGrath, 2000: 150). His notion that one could establish 'Zones of Tranquillity' in 'the areas where fighting has ceased' (Sadruddin Aga Khan, 1990) was also poorly received by the resistance parties, who interpreted it as an attempt to limit their scope for tactical manoeuvre in the ongoing struggle against Najibullah's regime; in some cases it actually caused fighting to flare up (Donini, 1996: 37). Sadruddin finally resigned in frustration in December 1990. This provided an opportunity to attempt to unify the UN's political and humanitarian activities. On 15 March 1990, the Secretary-General had established the Office of the Secretary-General in Afghanistan and Pakistan (OSGAP), and appointed a UN official, Benon Sevan, to head it. From 1 January 1991, Sevan was also appointed to head UNOCA. He was to have an uncommonly interesting time in office.

The Secretary-General's May 1991 plan

On 21 May 1991, following extensive discussions between Afghan actors and Benon Sevan, Secretary-General Pérez de Cuéllar issued a new statement on Afghanistan (Pérez de Cuéllar, 1991). It was deliberately cast in general terms, with a good deal of material included that would be quite uncontroversial. The key paragraphs read as follows:

I believe that the following elements would serve as a good basis for a political settlement in Afghanistan, acceptable to the vast majority of the Afghan people:

1. The necessity of preserving the sovereignty, territorial integrity, political independence and non-aligned and Islamic character of Afghanistan.
2. The recognition of the right of the Afghan people to determine their own form of Government and to choose their economic, political and social system, free from outside intervention, subversion, coercion or constraint of any kind whatsoever.
3. The need for a transition period, details of which have to be worked out and agreed upon through an intra-Afghan dialogue, leading to the establishment of a broad-based Government.
   (a) The need, during that period, for transitional arrangements acceptable to the vast majority of the Afghan people, including the establishment of a credible and impartial transition mechanism with appropriate powers and authority (yet to be specified) that would enjoy the confidence of the Afghan people and provide them with the necessary assurances to participate in free and fair elections, taking into account Afghan traditions, for the establishment of a broad-based Government.
   (b) The need for cessation of hostilities during the transition period.
   (c) The advisability of assistance, as appropriate, of the United Nations and of any other international organization during the transition process and in the electoral process.
4. The necessity of assistance, as appropriate, of the United Nations and of any other international organization during the transition period and in the electoral process.
5. The recognition of the need for adequate financial and material resources to alleviate the hardship of the Afghan refugees and the creation of the necessary conditions for their voluntary repatriation, as well as for the economic and social reconstruction of Afghanistan.

The Kabul regime accepted the plan almost instantly (BBC *Summary of World Broadcasts* FE/1080/C2/1, 24 May 1991). From Najibullah's point of view the UN plan was attractive in that it did not explicitly demand that he quit his post, let alone set a timetable for him to do so. On 25 September 1991, with paragraph 3 (a) of the Secretary-General's statement plainly in mind, he proposed the formation of a 'national unity government, which will be based on the government of Khaleqiar, the Prime Minister of the Republic of Afghanistan, the transitional government based in Peshawar, with the participation of the nine-party alliance in Iran, the council of internal commanders, Afghan personalities living in Europe and the USA, associates of Mohammad Zaher, former king of Afghanistan' (BBC *Summary of World Broadcasts* FE/1189/B/2, 28 September 1991). Agreeing to the plan left him *in situ*, and turned pressure on Pakistan and the resistance parties to develop a response which would not leave them looking like obstreperous spoilers. For this very reason, the UN plan did prove divisive as far as the resistance parties were concerned.

Hekmatyar, whose views were echoed by Sayyaf, was predictably the most hostile to the proposal, later describing it as 'complicated, ambiguous and impractical'. He demanded that 'Najibullah step down, power be delegated to a regime acceptable to the mojahedin, Zaher Shah remain in exile and elections be held within a year after the formation of the transitional government' (BBC *Summary of World Broadcasts* FE/13 19/B/1, 3 March 1992). Gailani, Mojadiddi, and Muhammadi were the most in favour of the proposal, and in February 1992 stated that 'the UN talks – and not continued military pressure – offered the best way to resolve the conflict' (Coll, 1992a). This echoed the response of 500 commanders, meeting in Paktia, who released a statement to the effect that if the UN plan, after clarification, was 'not against the expectations of our jihad (holy war) and national interest and results in the establishment of Islamic government, it will not be opposed' (BBC *Summary of World Broadcasts* FE/1298/B/1, 7 February 1992). The *Hezb-e Wahdat* leadership adopted a similar position (BBC *Summary of World Broadcasts* FE/1323/B/1, 7 March 1992).

The weaknesses of the UN plan

The critical section of the Secretary-General's proposal was contained in the third paragraph, and Massoud and the *Jamiat-e Islami* responded with comments which went to some of the details of the proposal. Massoud, in an interview with a French journalist, remarked that 'UN efforts to bring peace to Afghanistan are appreciable, but as long as Najib is in power or has a share of power, in one form or another, UN efforts will not succeed' (*AFGHANews*, 15 July 1991). This echoed comments he had made a year earlier: 'I do not disagree with the elections to be held under auspices of the United Nations, or the Organization of the Islamic Conference. We consider elections to be a sound method of settling the Afghan issue. But elections will be possible only when the People's Democratic Party steps down and an Interim Government trusted by the Afghan people takes its place' (*AFGHANews*, 15 June 1990). Massoud's reference to Najibullah's having a 'share of power, in one form or another', highlighted his alertness to the crucial vagueness in the Secretary-General's proposals, and also the gulf which continued to divide Afghan power holders. It was a gulf which the UN was never able to bridge.

There were some other weaknesses in the proposal as well. An interesting commentary was issued by the *Jamiat*-controlled Information Department of the 'Interim Government', whose minister, Dr Najibullah Lafraie, held a PhD in political science from the University of Hawaii. Noting that the Secretary-General's plan called for 'transitional arrangements acceptable to the vast majority of the Afghan people', the commentary raised an obvious logical objection: 'before elections, who will determine that the arrangement is acceptable to [a] majority of Afghans'? (*MIDIA Monthly News Bulletin*, 1 June 1991). It also noted the need to clarify the meaning of terms such as 'Afghan traditions'. This was conceptually an important point to raise, for the Secretary-General's statement read as if 'Afghan traditions' are universal and fixed, whereas virtually all 'national traditions' are in a constant process of reformulation or even invention (see Hobsbawm and Ranger, 1983; Shils, 1997: 114–19), and 'traditions' which are normatively salient for one particular group (for example the *Loya Jirgah* among Pushtuns) may at particular times appear to other groups as 'norms of partiality' (Ullmann-Margalit, 1977: 173–6) entrenching the dominance of one group over another (Hanifi, 2004).

The evolution of the UN plan

The evolution of the situation on the ground, and especially shifts in the US and Soviet attitudes to Afghanistan which I will mention shortly, prompted efforts by the UN to give concrete shape to some of the more abstract principles contained in the Secretary-General's statement. There were two particular strands of activity. One was concerned with the departure of Najibullah. This was largely a matter of timing. All the international actors appreciated that Najibullah would have to go, but as to the timing of his disappearance, there was no consensus until

October 1991, when Pérez de Cuéllar reported that 'some of the controversial personalities concerned would not insist on their personal participation, either in the intra-Afghan dialogue or in the transition mechanism' (quoted in Rubin 1995b: 126). The reference here was sufficiently oblique that it had no immediately explosive effect. Five months later, when the same point was made explicitly, the effect was altogether different.

The other strand of activity was concerned with the precise composition of a 'credible and impartial transition mechanism'. Attracting potential 'neutrals' to such a body was a major undertaking for Sevan and some of his political officers, notably Huseyin Avni Botsali. Yet the difficulties of finding 'neutrals' were to prove significant. In a hard-fought conflict, neutrality becomes a matter of perception, and partisans are likely to interpret the silence of 'neutrals' as amounting to tacit support for the enemy. In January 1992, the new UN Secretary-General, Dr Boutros Boutros-Ghali, inaugurated a laborious procedure to bring together an assembly of Afghans acceptable to the Afghan parties, from which a smaller committee would be selected to carry out wider consultations. However, it ground to a halt when Zahir Shah, the Islamist Sunni parties, and Najibullah all declined to provide names of recommended participants. As events gathered pace on the ground, the UN came up with the idea of a 'pre-transition council' (Coll, 1992b), which the Kabul regime immediately accepted (*The New York Times*, 12 April 1992). This unravelled on 15 April 1992 and was buried in the wreckage of Najibullah's regime – leaving behind, among other things, a significant number of badly disappointed 'neutrals'.

The collapse of the regime

In August 1991, Najibullah reiterated that he 'would not resign to allow an interim government to be established prior to elections, a consistent demand of the Americans' (Thomas, 1991). At the time, I wrote that 'Najibullah is well aware, however, that his regime cannot survive without out Soviet aid' and that 'his moment of truth is approaching' (Maley, 1991c: 15). His grasp that the writing was on the wall was reflected not in his public statements, but in his treatment of his immediate family. In 1989, when Eduard Shevardnadze had suggested that Najibullah's family move to Moscow, Najibullah's wife Fatana, a former schoolteacher and a member of the royal line of King Amanullah, had responded: 'We would prefer to be killed on the doorsteps of this house rather than die in the eyes of our people by choosing the path of flight from their misfortune. We will all stay with them here to the end, whether it be happy or bitter' (Shevardnadze, 1991: 69). In 1992, Fatana and her children left for Delhi (Rashid, 2000: 49). What brought this about was a fundamental change in the position of the regime as a result of developments in Moscow.

The August 1991 coup and Soviet aid

In summer 1991, Moscow simmered with discontent. Gorbachev's swing to the right had alienated his liberal supporters, but failed to appease his hardline critics, who felt betrayed by his failure to back a military crackdown on independence movements in Lithuania and Latvia. On 23 July 1991, the newspaper *Sovetskaia Rossiia* printed an article enti-tled *Slovo k narodu* ('A Word to the People') which called on the Soviet armed forces to act as 'reliable guarantors of security'. The signato-ries included two generals closely associated with Afghanistan – Boris Gromov and Valentin Varennikov – as well as two other conservatives who were shortly to gain considerable notoriety, Aleksandr Tiziakov and Vasilii Starodubtsev. Four weeks later, the blow finally fell, as Gorbachev, vacationing in the Crimea, was detained at the instigation of the self-designated 'State Committee for the Emergency Situation'. The coup collapsed within two days, and then the recriminations began. The implications for Afghanistan were considerable, for two reasons. First, the 'State Committee' (consisting of Vice-President Gennadii Ianaev, Prime Minister Valentin Pavlov, Defence Minister Dmitrii Iazov, Interior Minister Boriss Pugo, and KGB Chief Vladimir Kriuchkov, as well as the hapless Tiziakov and Starodubtsev) had included in its ranks a number of those most committed to continuing support for Najibullah, most importantly Kriuchkov. The fall of the 'State Committee' blew a gaping hole in Najibullah's support network in Moscow. Second, the fail-ure of the coup shifted the balance in Soviet politics decisively away from Gorbachev (who had been responsible for promoting a number of the plotters to the positions which they then used to move against him), and in favour of his rival, the popularly elected President of the Russian Soviet Federative Socialist Republic (RSFSR) within the USSR, namely Boris El'tsin. As early as 14 July 1990, El'tsin had argued that supplies of arms from Russia to Afghanistan had to be stopped, and in September 1990, his envoy Iona Andronov had invited Mujahideen leaders to visit Russia for talks (Maley, 1991c: 13). A clear sign that times had changed came on 10 November, when a resistance delegation, led by Rabbani and including Muhammadi, Asif Mohseni, Sayed Hamed Gailani, and

Dr Hashmatullah Mojadiddi, arrived in Moscow and held direct, high-level discussions with Russian officials on Russian soil. The final communiqué agreed on the need 'to pass all power in Afghanistan to an Islamic interim government' (*TASS*–15 November 1991). Hekmatyar was so alarmed that he sent a message to Najibullah, via Libyan leader Muammar Qaddafi, that 'You and I could do something in Afghanistan' (Rubin, 1995b: 130, 172).

The most important policy development, however, came on 13 September 1991, and it signed the death warrant of Najibullah's regime. On that day, a joint statement was issued by the new Soviet Foreign Minister, Boris Pankin, and US Secretary of State Baker, in which they announced that the two countries would cease to deliver 'lethal material and supplies' to parties in Afghanistan from 1 January 1992. And this was exactly what happened. Ironically, the Soviet Union itself ceased to exist on that date. Najibullah could at least claim to have outlasted the power on which he had depended for so long. But for him it was little comfort.

The revolt in the north

Shorn of resources, Najibullah turned to the manipulation of ethnicity as a way of boosting his position. It proved to be a serious mistake, although his options at the time were extremely limited. In January 1992, he attempted to replace the Tajik commander of the Hairatan Garrison, General Abdul Momen, with an ethnic Pushtun *Khalqi*, General Rasul. Momen had been providing intelligence to Massoud and aid to Dostam (Rubin, 1995a: 269), which did give Najibullah some rationale for trying to replace him, but the result was instead that Dostam joined Momen in opposition to Najibullah, and for good measure lured Sayed Mansur Nadiri's Ismaili militia in Baghlan into opposition as well. The consequence was an unravelling over the next two months of the regime's military position in most of northern Afghanistan, and a significant nationwide shift in the correlation of forces. On 18 March, Mazar-e Sharif fell to the anti-regime forces.

Splits in the regime and the Afghan Army: ideology and ethnicity

On 18 March, Najibullah finally signalled that he would step down, agreeing 'that once an understanding is reached through the United Nations process for the establishment of an interim government in Kabul, all powers and executive authority will be transferred to the interim government as of the first day of the transition period' (Gargan, 1992a). He made this statement under great pressure from Sevan, who in turn acted with the support of Secretary-General Boutros-Ghali. The aim was to clear the way for agreement on the specifics of the UN plan, and in part it did do this. However, Najibullah's announcement also prompted numerous people in his regime to recalculate what was in their *own* best interests, and few of these found much in the UN plan that offered them anything at all. Instead, they began to build bridges to different resistance groups, and the result was the emergence of new power formations which appeared to key resistance leaders to offer better prospects of delivering their objectives than a still only vaguely specified UN plan.

Ethnicity ostensibly determined the destination of defectors, but ideology may have been equally important, since the two poles of attraction, Massoud and Hekmatyar, not only came from different ethnic backgrounds, but also had different political orientations, with Massoud being a moderate Islamist while Hekmatyar, in Olivier Roy's phrase, was an 'Islamo-Leninist' (Roy, 1994: 113; see also Edwards, 1993). *Khalqi* Pushtuns for the most part gravitated towards Hekmatyar's *Hezb-e Islami*. This was hardly surprising, since Hekmatyar's embrace of Tanai in March 1990 had shown that he was willing to form tactical alliances with anyone who could be of use to him. The most important such defectors were the *Khalqi* Interior Minister Raz Muhammad Paktin, and the Defence Minister Aslam Watanjar. On the other hand, Tajik *Parchamis* tended to shift towards Massoud. The most important of these were Foreign Minister Abdul Wakil, who had been working for Massoud for quite some time, and Farid Mazdak, a youthful party leader who had also established ties with Massoud. Nearly as important were three generals whose defection disrupted any unified command system within the Afghan Army: Deputy Defence Minister Muhammad Nabi Azimi; Army Chief of Staff Muhammad Asif Delawar; and Kabul garrison chief Baba Jan. On 21 March, just three days after Najibullah announced his intention to quit, Azimi had quietly made contact with Dostam.

The collapse of the UN plan

In early 1992, Pakistan appeared to be moving to support the Secretary-General's plan. The Foreign Ministry had initially welcomed it (BBC *Summary of World Broadcasts* FE/1080/C2/2, 24 May 1991); on 4 January 1992, Pakistan's Army Chief of Staff, General Asif Nawaz Janjua held a symbolically significant meeting in Rome with Zahir Shah's son-in-law, General Abdul Wali; and on 27 January, the Foreign Minister of Pakistan announced that his government had decided 'to support the UN Secretary-General's efforts to convene an assembly of Afghan leaders to decide on an interim government acceptable to the Afghans and to facilitate the convening of such an assembly' (BBC *Summary of World Broadcasts* FE/1290/A3/1, 29 January 1992). That this marked a change of policy was confirmed when the ISI Director-General, Major-General Asad Durrani, was replaced on 1 March (*The Economist*, 7 March 1992). These developments held out the possibility of concerted pressure by Pakistan on the Peshawar-based parties to agree to the plan as it took more concrete shape. They did not, however, guarantee the support of internal commanders; and nor did they ensure that Hekmatyar would not make a bid for power with the backing of those ISI elements with whom he was most closely allied.

The regime finally collapsed on 15–16 April 1992. These were momentous days in both Islamabad and Kabul. In Islamabad, at a meeting at Prime Minister Nawaz Sharif's residence, the UN plan began to crumble as participants from both Rabbani's and Mojadiddi's parties expressed a preference for the immediate establishment of an Islamic government, rather than the UN's transitional approach. These blows to the UN plan, it should be noted, came from both an 'Islamist' *and* a 'moderate' party in the ranks of the Sunni resistance, and from a Pushtun-dominated as well as a Tajik-majority party. Sevan, who had developed a plan to fly to Kabul with members of the 'pre-transition council', and to fly Najibullah out on the same aircraft, left on his own for Kabul, which he reached in the early hours of Thursday 16 April.

By then, he was in another world. His plane was not cleared for landing by the Khwaja Rawash airport control tower, and when it made a first pass, it was hit by gunfire (Picco, 1999: 38). On Wednesday 15 April the airport had changed hands. Azimi, possibly in cooperation with Babrak Karmal's brother, had flown between 600 and 1,000 of Dostam's troops from Mazar-e Sharif to Kabul in order to seize it (Rubin, 1995b: 173; Bradsher, 1999: 379). During a meeting that day, Najibullah had confronted Azimi, Delawar, and other senior figures, who were accused of treason (Bradsher, 1999: 379). They probably held the same view of him. Najibullah then headed for the airport, possibly because of panic that Azimi had assumed control of his security detail (Bradsher, 1999: 379). But he never made it. A well-placed account captures some of the drama of what must have been a truly remarkable event:

> 'He passed through two checkpoints. But close to the airport, where Sevan's UN plane was supposed to land, he encountered a third checkpoint. The car was stopped, and Najibullah was asked

the password. He gave the wrong one and immediately realized he was trapped by people who were not from his own Pashtu tribe. His driver executed a screeching U-turn, doubled back at high speed, and made for the UN compound, the only place that could guarantee his safety' (Picco, 1999: 38; for a more detailed account see Corwin, 2003: 88–92).

With Najibullah off the scene, it remained only to arrange a transfer of power. Two distinct processes played out. The first process was a standoff in the Kabul area, where both Massoud and Hekmatyar had forces. Massoud, wary of accusations of Bonapartism, especially from Pushtun commanders from within the National Commanders Shura (Akram, 1996: 385–6), resisted the temptation to enter Kabul, but did commence discussion with Wakil, who had scathingly denounced Najibullah, after his attempt to leave the country, as 'a hated dictator who had been an obstacle to peace' (Gargan, 1992b), and Mazdak, who had taken over as *Hezb-e Watan* leader. Hekmatyar, on the other hand, was desperate to seize Kabul as his capital. The second process was a prolonged series of negotiations in Peshawar between the different Sunni party leaders to reach an accord on power sharing in a new government. The two processes came together in the last week of April. Late on Friday 24 April, a partial agreement was reached by all the main Sunni leaders – except Hekmatyar – for a transition process. But on the same day, Hekmatyar had begun to smuggle troops into Kabul in cooperation with *Khalqis* in the Interior Minister, and the next day, as Bradsher puts it, he 'claimed control of Kabul, said there was no need for coalition leaders to come to the capital, and warned he would shoot their plane down if they tried' (Bradsher, 1999: 381–2). Mojadiddi then issued a communiqué naming Massoud as 'Defence Minister' of the 'Islamic Interim Government of Afghanistan', and requested that he 'urgently begin to work' (Maley and Saikal, 1992: 30). With an explicit pledge of support from Azimi (BBC *Summary of World Broadcasts* FE/1365/C1/2, 27 April 1992), Massoud did just that, securing the city and ejecting the *Hezb-e Islami* forces. On 26 April, full agreement was reached and announced between the Sunni leaders – except Hekmatyar – and on 28 April, Sebghatullah Mojadiddi arrived by car in Kabul, as head of a new regime.

   Giandomenico Picco, who in March–April 1992 was Assistant Secretary-General for Political Affairs, argues that it was a 'devastating error of judgment' on the part of the Secretary-General to pressure Najibullah to announce his intention to relinquish power, since it had the potential to create 'a vacuum that could be filled only by a more devastating civil war'. He reports that Sevan stated that the 'men in Peshawar will help fill the vacuum with Pakistani help' (Picco, 1999: 37). To believe in such circumstances that the ISI would not seek to promote Hekmatyar at the expense of other party leaders and internal commanders was to indulge in large-scale fantasizing. Boutros-Ghali's memoirs are entirely silent on the details of this episode, which he even puts in the wrong year (Boutros-Ghali, 1999: 301), but Picco was clearly haunted by what happened. 'To this day', he writes, 'I believe we were responsible for much of what ensued in that tragic place' (Picco, 1999: 39). Yet one can plausibly argue that the demand that Najibullah leave came not prematurely, but *much too late*. By 18 March 1992, his regime was manifestly coming apart at the seams: his announcement aggravated and accelerated the process, but did not cause it. The time for such an announcement was at the time of the Pankin-Baker statement, before the regime had lost its external income source, and before Najibullah's attempts at the manipulation of ethnic segmentation had triggered the gross fragmentation of the military that came after the January 1992 northern crisis. Sevan's mistake was to overestimate Najibullah's personal authority, putting off until too late in the day the task of pressuring him to go. Sometimes strong leaders are not all that they seem.

Was a workable UN plan derailed at the last minute by ambitious commanders from the north? Some scholars have implied that this was the case (Rais, 1994: 221; Kakar, 1995: 274; Ahady, 1995: 626), and an active conspiracy theory to this effect was to flourish for years among émigré Pushtuns who resented the rise of non-Pushtun leadership figures (see Misdaq, 2006: 323 n.24). However, the evidence to support it is not in the least compelling. Massoud actually *rejected* an offer from Wakil to enter Kabul as head of state, and ultimately moved his forces into the city only on 25 April when a takeover of Kabul by Hekmatyar – in alliance with *Khalqis* and with support from Pakistan – seemed imminent (Rubin, 1995b: 132–3; Bradsher, 1999: 381–2). Within the Mujahideen, it was Hekmatyar rather than Massoud who was uncompromising: on 22 April, three days *before* Massoud entered Kabul, Hekmatyar's official spokesman, Nawab Salim, was reported round the world as saying 'Hekmatyar can't agree to anything that includes Ahmed Shah Massoud' (*International Herald Tribune*, 22 April 1992). The UN plan was fatally overwhelmed by the collapse of the regime, and Sevan lacked the personal authority to rescue it: in the eyes of commanders (with whom Sevan had had far too little contact), he had been too gentle with Najibullah, and for too long, to have any real credibility. Here, Rubin's verdict merits repetition: 'When state institutions unravel, and armed factions emerge as the main form of collective action, interim governments offer no quick solution to the problem of political order. No government can compensate for the dissolution of the state' (Rubin, 1995c: 236). Unfortunately, this curse applied not only to Najibullah, but also to his successors.

9

The Rise and Fall of the Rabbani Government, 1992–1996

The period from 1992 to 1996 is one of the more misunderstood in modern Afghan history. It is all too frequently depicted as a period of unmitigated despair during which undisciplined 'warlords', seemingly determined to establish that they were even less appetising than the communist regime, battered each other for no obvious purpose at hideous cost to the civilian population. The vocabulary of 'tribal warfare', of 'honour' and 'revenge', and of the 'blood feud' is deployed to give a semblance of anthropological respectability to such claims.

These images are in need at very least of careful qualification, and in some respects should be discarded altogether. To a considerable extent they are the product of an urban bias in reporting. The southern suburbs of Kabul were largely destroyed during this period, but in rural areas, the kinds of bombardments which caused such massive casualties during the 1980s largely ceased: as a result, the average levels of mortality in the post-communist period across the country as a whole were sharply lower than those of the 1980s – and no reputable scholar has ever sought to argue to the contrary. But the popular images also reflect a failure to understand the politics of this period in a wider context. It was indeed a misfortune that Massoud put his faith in the Peshawar-based party leaders to craft a government (Nojumi, 2002). But the turmoil after the collapse of the communist regime was fundamentally rooted in the collapse of the state, in the exposure of Afghanistan's domestic politics to external manipulation, and in the rationality of the spoiler. In a penetrating analysis of this period, Gilles Dorronsoro corrected some of the misreadings of what was going on: 'This new war's frequently shifting alliances give the impression of irrationality and chaos, but everything that has happened since 1992 has been the result of a rigorous political logic. The Afghan civil war is not "primitive" or "tribal," but strongly political' (Dorronsoro, 1995: 37).

This chapter is divided into five sections. In the first, I discuss the attempt to provide a new foundation for political power through the crafting of elite settlements, and show why these various endeavours failed to bear fruit. In the second, I discuss the battle for Kabul, its twists and turns, and its consequences. The third briefly examines the situation beyond Kabul. The fourth deals with efforts made by the new 'UN Special Mission to Afghanistan' to contribute to a settlement, and shows why these efforts failed. The fifth, without going into great detail about the nature of the Taliban movement, traces the undoing of the Rabbani government, culminating in its retreat from Kabul as the Taliban closed in on 26 September 1996.

The failure of elite settlements

The nature of elite settlements

In the aftermath of the collapse of the communist regime, the need for a functioning political system was considerable. The task of reconstruction was enormous, and the end of communist power had triggered the largest and fastest spontaneous repatriation of refugees in modern history. By the end of 1992, fully 1.4 million refugees had returned to Afghanistan since the beginning of the year (Ruiz, 1992). Yet the search for workable political institutions remained in its infancy, and one of the reasons was that the new Afghan political elite was severely divided.

The problem of elite division is one which has afflicted many political systems, and has attracted a considerable amount of attention in recent times in writings on 'democratic transitions'. However, it is just as pertinent when one is discussing the political reconstruction of war-torn societies, which very often have run into difficulty in the first place because of the crystallisation of division within national elites. National elites consist of competitors for control of the central government (as opposed to local elites, who entertain no such aspirations). Elite disunity can have lethal effects, as the following account makes clear:

> Communication and influence networks do not cross factional lines in any large way, and factions disagree on the rules of political conduct and the worth of existing political institutions. Accordingly, they distrust one another deeply; they perceive political outcomes in 'politics as war' or zero-sum terms; and they engage in unrestricted, often violent struggles for dominance. These features make regimes in countries with disunified elites fundamentally unstable, no matter

whether they are authoritarian or formally democratic. Lacking the communication and influence networks that might give them a satisfactory amount of access to government decision-making and disagreeing on the rules of the game and the worth of existing institutions, most factions in a disunified elite see the existing regime as the vehicle by which a dominant faction promotes its interests. To protect and promote their own interests, therefore, they must destroy or cripple the regime and elites who operate it. Irregular and forcible power seizures, attempted seizures, or a widespread expectation that such seizures may occur are thus a by-product of elite disunity. (Burton, Gunther and Higley, 1992: 10)

The picture they paint is so grim that one wonders how problems of elite disunity might ever be overcome. However, several routes of escape are available. Elite *convergence*, a step-by-step process of reconciliation through electoral politics, depends upon the existence of a relatively stable institutional framework (Higley and Burton, 1989) which was precisely what post-communist Afghanistan lacked. *Elite restructuring* comes about when the employment of force produces a beneficial change in the composition of the national elite, either through the elimination of parties or a fundamental change in the nature of their power (Maley, 1997a: 172). *Elite settlements* are 'relatively rare events in which warring national elite factions suddenly and deliberately reorganize their relations by negotiating compromises on their most basic disagreements'. They tend to occur in response to two developments: 'recent elite experience of costly, but also essentially inconclusive conflict', and 'the occurrence of a major crisis which provokes elite action' (Burton and Higley, 1987: 295, 298). They differ from the intergroup pacts which have been widely discussed in democratic transition literature in that they are more inclusive (O'Donnell and Schmitter, 1986: 37–9; DiPalma, 1990: 86–90). It was through elite settlements that the attempt was made to overcome the burden of fragmentation within the resistance, but the burden proved too heavy to bear. Ultimately, it was to take almost a decade, and the US war against terrorism, to bring about some degree of elite restructuring.

The Peshawar Accord

The first attempt at an elite settlement came in the Peshawar Accord of April 1992, which provided for the 'structure and process for the provisional period of the Islamic State of Afghanistan' (United Nations,

1992: 34–5). It was a very brief text, of only 12 paragraphs. Paragraph 1 provided that Mojadiddi would for two months head a 51-person body (*Shura-i Intiqali*) to 'take over power from the present rulers of Kabul', and would serve as President. After this, according to Paragraph 2, Rabbani was to take over the presidency, and serve as President and Head of the *Shura-i Qiyadi* ('Leadership Council') for a further four months, a period not to be extended 'even by a day' (Paragraph 3). The Accord then distributed offices, to be held by 'second grade members' of the parties: the prime ministership to Hekmatyar's *Hezb*, the Defence Ministry to the *Jamiat-e Islami*, and the Foreign Affairs Ministry to Gailani's party. After six months a Council of Supreme Popular Settlement (known by the Islamic legal term *Shura-i Ahl-e Hal va Aqd*) would be convoked to form an interim government which would organise elections to be held after 18 months.

This agreement faced a number of fundamental challenges. Hekmatyar, who resented Massoud's appointment as Defence Minister, resorted to the strategy of 'spoiling'. Hekmatyar was a classic example of what Stephen J. Stedman has called 'total spoilers': individuals 'who see the world in all-or-nothing terms and often suffer from pathological tendencies that prevent the pragmatism necessary for compromise settlements of conflict' (Stedman, 1997: 10–11; for a differing perspective see Greenhill and Major, 2006–2007). The logic of spoiling is quite straightforward: as an Australian politician once put it, if you can't run a meeting, wreck it. Hekmatyar refused the offer of the prime ministership for his party, and instead denounced the new administration as 'communist'. It was indeed the case that Dostam and various generals from the Najibullah era had emerged as prominent figures, but the wider allegation was preposterous, not only because most members of the old communist elite had fled (Arnold, 1994: 67–8), but also because Hekmatyar at the very time he made these charges was continuing to work with *Khalqis* whose human rights records were as bad as his own. Once Rabbani took over as president – after a certain amount of manoeuvring by Mojadiddi, who had hoped to prolong his term (Rubin, 1995a: 273) – Hekmatyar upped the stakes, (even though one of his functionaries, Abdul Saboor Farid, who was eventually assassinated in Kabul on 2 May 2007, briefly occupied the premiership). In August, the *Hezb-e Islami* launched a rocket attack on Kabul in which over 1,000 civilians were killed. It was at this point that Rabbani dubbed Hekmatyar a 'dangerous terrorist who should be expelled from Afghanistan' (BBC *Summary of World Broadcasts* FE/1461/B/1, 17 August 1992). In December 1993, a *Shura-i Ahl-e*

Hal va Aqd met in Kabul and endorsed Rabbani's remaining in office for a further 18 months, until 28 June 1994. Rabbani's opponents, many of whom boycotted it (Akram, 1996: 415–16), claimed that he had manipulated it to his advantage (Rubin, 1995a: 273), but its problem was actually a deeper one, which would have exposed it to denunciation by whoever was disappointed by the outcome: as an unelected body, it could not claim to be representative.

The Islamabad Accord

With casualties rising in Kabul, and the wider world largely indifferent to what was happening, Rabbani's government faced a real dilemma. On the one hand, it could continue to strike at Hekmatyar's forces. On the other, it could seek some sort of accommodation with him. Under intense pressure from Pakistan to compromise, Rabbani signed an agreement in Islamabad on 7 March 1993 with Hekmatyar and the representatives of five other resistance groups, providing for Hekmatyar to assume the office of prime minister and form a Cabinet 'in consultations with the President, and leaders of Mujahideen parties' (United Nations, 1993a). It was much more professionally drafted than the Peshawar Accord, but still failed to address the root causes of the ongoing instability (see Maley, 1993b: 388–90).

First, the Accord did not address Hekmatyar's spoiling capacity by putting in place a mechanism for the monitored removal of his armed forces from the Kabul area. Second, the Accord was not the product of consensus among Afghanistan's elites, but of external pressure, especially from Pakistan and Saudi Arabia. Third, the Accord failed to develop a workable set of interim political arrangements. It assumed the existence of consensus when in fact there was none. By creating two ostensibly 'strong' executive offices, it invited further conflict. By mid-April 1993, *Hezb-e Islami* rockets were again falling on Kabul, and Hekmatyar was again threatening war if his desire to marginalise Massoud by putting the Defence Ministry under collegial control were not granted (BBC *Summary of World Broadcasts* FE/1664/B/1, 16 April 1993). Rabbani finally buckled on 20 May, when a compromise reached in Jalalabad provided for the Defence and Interior Ministries to be placed under the control of 'commissions' for two months, after which ministers would be elected by a meeting of resistance commanders. Of course, the deadline passed without any such elections being held. Finally, the symbolism of the March 1993 agreement was lamentable. The message it supplied was that spoilers could expect to be rewarded. Unless one is sure that there is only *one* spoiler to appease, this is an exceedingly dangerous message to broadcast.

Distrust and manipulation in the absence of a state

The attempt to ground political power in an elite settlement failed for three reasons. The first was that the level of distrust within the elite was too high, especially between Hekmatyar and Massoud (Edwards, 2002: 243–4; 288). In Hekmatyar's case, the explanation was largely pathological: Stalin once remarked 'I trust no one, not even myself', and there were definite echoes of this in Hekmatyar's approach to the world. In the case of Massoud, the explanation was more rational. Trust is a product of expectations (Maley, 2003), and Hekmatyar had given Massoud excellent grounds to be wary, not only through the killing of commanders in 1989 and his spokesman's candid anti-Massoud statement in April 1992, but through a sustained and documented record of using violence to eliminate or intimidate those in the Afghan resistance who would not subordinate themselves to him (see Human Rights Watch, 1991: 101–3, 110–11).

The second problem for an elite settlement was the impact of external powers, which affected the identities of the *participants* in the settlement. Officials in Pakistan, the host of the talks which led to the Peshawar and Islamabad Accords, had long held the view that Afghan opinion should be articulated through political parties. But by 1992–1993, other actors – such as Dostam, Ismail Khan in Herat, and diverse shuras in different parts of the country – had emerged on the scene, and their absence from the negotiations undermined the legitimacy of the final output. Those groups which felt marginalised were more likely to seek foreign patrons than accept the dictates of a body which they had played no great role in assembling. This Dostam did.

But the third, and most critical, problem was the absence of a state. The fragmentation of the Afghan Army (Davis, 1993a) meant a government could not even remotely hope to secure an immediate monopoly over the means of large-scale violence, although in the long run it was Massoud's aim as Defence Minister to establish such a monopoly. The collapse of state instrumentalities meant that securing a ministerial position was no guarantee of *institutional* power. In an atmosphere of rampant distrust, prudence would dictate the adoption of other strategies to secure one's position. Much of the violence that smashed parts of Kabul reflected rationally self-interested decision making by leaders, parties and militias *in a situation in which there was no state to provide an overarching*

guarantee of security. It also reflected the interest of some of these decision makers *in preventing any such state from taking shape.*

The bombardment of Kabul

The symbolism of the capital

Where the state has collapsed, control of the symbols of the state may be
all that combatants can realistically aspire to attain. This helps explain
why petty bureaucratic requirements, such as the demand that foreign
visitors obtain exit visas, were rigorously enforced under the Rabbani
government: the right to make such a demand was a symbolic marker of
sovereignty, even though it had no effect on foreign combatants flowing
across Afghanistan's borders, and only impacted on legal visitors whose
goodwill it sorely tested. Unfortunately, there were other symbols which
it was easier for Rabbani's opponents to contest. The most important of
these was Kabul as a capital city. This helps explain the strategies of
the parties in the battle for Kabul. Massoud on occasion trained wither-
ing fire on the southern and western suburbs of Kabul, but his use of
firepower was fundamentally different from that of Hekmatyar's commanders. Their objective was to undermine the symbolic authority of
the Rabbani government by highlighting its inability to protect civilians
in its own capital. Massoud, plainly, had no interest in doing any such
thing.

The division of Kabul between militias

While forces under Massoud's authority had effectively ejected the *Hezb-e
Islami* from Kabul in the days before Mojadiddi's arrival on 28 April,
this did not mean that all the forces which had entered Kabul at the time
were exclusively loyal to Massoud. Indeed, the opposite was the case. A
range of forces found their way into the capital, and their loyalties shifted
in accordance with changing incentive structures. The key forces were
those loyal to Massoud's *Shura-i Nazar*; to Sayyaf's *Ittehad-e Islami*; to
Dostam's *Jumbesh-e Melli Islami* ('National Islamic Movement'); and
to the *Hezb-e Wahdat*, led by Abdul Ali Mazari. The two former parties
were ideologically committed to a strong state. By contrast, the *Hezb-e
Wahdat* feared a strong state would weaken the relative autonomy of the
Hazaras, while the *Jumbesh* represented Dostam's aspiration to control
an autonomous fiefdom in the north: each had an interest in blocking
the development of a strong state. The greatest antagonism was between

the *Hezb-e Wahdat* and the *Ittehad*: apart from different conceptions of the state, *Wahdat* was an Iran-backed Shiite party, whereas *Ittehad* was a Saudi-supported Sunni party, bitterly hostile both to Shiism and to Iranian influence. It was between these two that fighting within the city initially broke out, on 2 June 1992 (Harpviken, 1996: 113). *Hezb-e Wahdat* forces occupied west Kabul; Massoud's the north; Dostam's the area around the Bala Hissar fortress and Teppe Meranjan; and Sayyaf's the Paghman area.

In January–February 1993, the relations between Massoud and *Hezb-e Wahdat* reached a critical point. In the hope of promoting a state monopoly on the means of violence, Massoud had moved to disarm the *Hezb-e Wahdat* militia in December 1992. *Hezb-e Wahdat* responded by denouncing the *Shura-i Ahl-e Hal va Aqd*, in which it refused to take part. On 24 January 1993, *Wahdat* forces attacked Massoud's while they were occupied with combating Hekmatyar's *Hezb-e Islami* (Gille, 1993; Akram, 1996: 418); Rubin states that during this month, Hekmatyar 'signed a formal alliance' with *Hezb-e Wahdat* (Rubin, 1995a: 273). On 11 February, citing *Wahdat* predations against the civilian population (Dorronsoro, 2005: 242–3), *Ittehad* and *Shura-i Nazar* forces struck massively against *Hezb-e Wahdat* supporters. The operation did not eliminate *Wahdat*: instead, *Wahdat* allied itself with Hekmatyar, although in autumn 1993 it reached a short-lived rapprochement with Massoud (Dorronsoro, 1995: 39).

The main damage to Kabul came from 1 January 1994. On that day, a new alliance, the so-called *Shura-i Hamahangi* ('Council of Coordination'), consisting of Hekmatyar, Dostam, and *Hezb-e Wahdat*, with Mojadiddi as a loose associate, launched a huge rocket and artillery attack on the capital. While the expatriate staff of the International Committee of the Red Cross remained at their posts, UN international staff were evacuated on 8 January, an abandonment which the government felt very keenly, since it assisted the attackers' strategy. For some government members also, this was the moment to leave: the Foreign Minister, a Gailani supporter who was abroad at the time, simply did not return to Afghanistan, and faded into temporary insignificance. Dostam feared Massoud's rising power, which he realised would weaken his own position, and therefore threw in his lot with Hekmatyar and *Wahdat*. It did not save him: in a remarkable display of nerve, Massoud and his forces survived the onslaught and ejected most of Dostam's forces from their positions in an operation in June 1994 (*The New York Times*, 27 June 1994).

The final chapter in this struggle for Kabul took place in February–March 1995. By then, the Taliban movement had emerged as a force, occupying Kandahar in November 1994. Coming towards Kabul from the south, it seemed more immediate a threat to Hekmatyar's position in Charasiab, from which Kabul had been rocketed, than it was to *Shura-i Nazar* forces in north Kabul. And this was what it proved to be. On 13–14 February, Hekmatyar fled to Sarobi, leaving his Charasiab headquarters in a disordered state. His 'Radio Message of Freedom' disappeared from the airwaves (BBC *Summary of World Broadcasts* FE/2229/A/3, 16 February 1995). This triggered a number of further significant developments. On 8 March, two days after Massoud launched a full-scale offensive against *Hezb-e Wahdat*, the *Hezb-e Wahdat* leadership allowed Taliban forces into their frontlines in western Kabul, with a view to triggering conflict between the stronger Taliban and *Wahdat*'s opponent Massoud. There were indeed some clashes, but, against the *Wahdat* leadership's expectations, some of its own fighters defected to a splinter faction of *Wahdat* led by the Qizilbash Sheikh Muhammad Akbari, and attacked the Taliban. Government forces then struck hard on 11 March, taking over west Kabul and driving the Taliban from the city. The Taliban, in the belief that they had been betrayed by *Wahdat*, seized and killed *Hezb-e Wahdat* leader Mazari, together with a number of other members of the *Wahdat* Central Committee (Davis, 1998: 56–9). Dostam's last forces headed north. This left Massoud finally in control of Kabul, backed by Sayyaf's *Ittehad*, and for the moment, the Taliban advance was halted.

Rocket attacks and atrocities

The rocketing of Kabul reduced large tracts of the city to rubble, but not the entire city. On the contrary, the north of the city was to a considerable extent protected from ballistic projectiles by a large hill, *Koh-e Asmai*, which bisected the city. But frontline areas such as Jadi Maiwand Avenue suffered awesome damage, as did the southern suburbs, and the human toll was dreadful, not only in terms of deaths but also injuries, population displacement, and psychological trauma. The scale of mortality is difficult to calculate. Drawing from a range of sources, Gille offers a figure of at least 9,800 killed and 56,100 wounded for the period from April 1992 to March 1995, but notes the variability of different sources (Gille, 1996: 4). A representative of the Afghan Red Crescent Society reportedly concluded that 10,000 had been killed in 1993 alone (United Nations, 1993b: para. 26), and in late 1994, the Special Rapporteur of the UN Human Rights Commission estimated that at least 3,500 people had been killed since the beginning of the year (United Nations,

1994a: para. 17). Amnesty International offered a figure of 25,000 dead (Amnesty International, 1995: 33). Given the types of weaponry involved, there is no doubt that the *Hezb-e Islami* of Hekmatyar was directly responsible for the bulk of the deaths.

When Kabul first fell, there was no mass purge of communists comparable to the liquidation of collaborators (*épuration*) that broke out in France following the liberation from the Germans and the obliteration of the Vichy regime in 1944 (United Nations, 1992: para. 41). However, the small Hindu and Sikh communities were targeted by extremists (*Les Nouvelles d'Afghanistan*, 63, 1994: 21–2), who associated them with India's support for both Karmal and Najibullah. Once war began in earnest, there were a number of grisly massacres during the course of combat in the city (Afghanistan Justice Project, 2005; Human Rights Watch, 2005; Maley, 2008a). One was the Afshar massacre of 11 February 1993, which claimed the lives of hundreds of Hazaras. One writer, who quotes an estimate of 700 dead, has stated that the forces who carried out the massacre were 'under the direct order of President Rabbani and his chief commander, Massoud' (Mousavi, 1997: 198), but it is not clear whether by this he means that Rabbani and Massoud ordered the massacre, or simply that they headed the hierarchy of which the troops were a part. The Special Rapporteur of the UN Human Rights Commission reported between 200 and 300 people killed in west Kabul (United Nations, 1993b: para. 58), but appeared to fix the blame principally upon forces of Sayyaf's *Ittehad*. The savagery of the attackers was appalling (Griffin, 2000: 30). There is no doubt whatever that women and children were among the victims, and among emigré Hazara communities, a graphic videotape was circulated that depicted what had happened (Akram, 1996: 419–20). There were also documented cases of rampaging *Shura-i Nazar* soldiers in March 1995 in west Kabul. As well as pillage, there was targeted looting of the Kabul Museum in mid-1993 when the suburb in which it is located was controlled by *Hezb-e Wahdat* (Dupree, 1996: 45) – although the skill of the looters in choosing what to take suggested the involvement of agents for dealers in stolen artworks, rather than thieving Mujahideen. Finally, politically motivated killings took place, notably the 29 July 1994 murder of the BBC correspondent Mir Wais Jalil, whose fearless reporting had outraged the *Hezb-e Islami* (Dorronsoro, 1994; Amnesty International, 1995: 41).

A particularly difficult issue to pin down relates to rape and sexual assault. There is abundant and significant anecdotal evidence of rape of women by armed males (Amnesty International, 1995: 62–5), and given the stigma which can so unjustly be attached to the victim, it would be exceedingly surprising if there were not many cases that went unreported. However, determining the actual scale of such violations is well-nigh impossible, both because rumour undoubtedly magnified the fears which women felt, and because the mere accusation that members of particular groups sanctioned the 'dishonouring' of women was a lethal charge to level in Afghan society, and therefore an attractive one to a partisan seeking to discredit his opponents.

The peace of March–October 1995

Some defenders of the Taliban were to laud the peace which they allegedly brought to Kabul when they finally occupied it in September 1996 (Fergusson, 1997). Given that the Taliban had been rocketing Kabul in a merciless fashion for months before they occupied the city, this was akin to arguing that Hitler brought peace to Warsaw when his forces overran it in late September 1939. However, there *was* a period of remarkable peace in Kabul: from March to October 1995. It is so frequently overlooked in histories of Afghanistan that it at least deserves mention. During this period, the city was completely free of rocket attacks, and movement around the city was easier than it had been for years. A UN official whom I interviewed in Kabul in May 1995 described the situation only two months earlier as 'another world' compared to May. Reconstruction projects were beginning to get underway, and among aid agencies, there was a sense of considerable optimism. As it turned out, this period represented the calm before the storm. It came to an end when the Taliban made their way back to the outskirts of the city and began to rocket it in a fashion indistinguishable from that of the *Hezb-e Islami* (Davis, 1998: 64). But it showed that there was an alternative to Taliban power as a way of bringing a better life to the people of Kabul.

Beyond Kabul

Thus far, I have concentrated on the situation in Kabul, for its symbolic importance made it the focal point of struggle. With the collapse of Najibullah's regime and the fragmentation of the Afghan Army, new power centres emerged in different parts of the country (although in the Hazarajat, the situation remained much as it was before the regime collapsed). In some places, local commanders struggled for influence or exercised control over limited tracts of territory; while in other parts regional 'strongmen' emerged, either from the ranks of the Mujahideen or from the wreckage of the Kabul regime, who benefited from the autonomy which the disorder in Kabul indirectly conferred on them. Where 'strongmen' emerged, they tended to appropriate the surviving 'trenches' and 'dispersed field offices' of the state in order to administer state functions. In Pushtun areas, the assets of the old state were more likely to be divided as booty between different groups. 'Among Pashtuns,' Rubin writes, 'the only modernized military force that survived was Hikmatyar's, precisely because it had no regional or tribal base to fragment it' (Rubin, 1995a: 275). Where local commanders jostled for power, there was a sharp increase in predatory warlordism, as 'taxing' – in effect, *robbing* – those using the roads became a key income source to sustain the commanders' patronage networks. This was particularly a problem in southern Afghanistan.

Eastern and southern Afghanistan

Jalalabad and Kandahar each found themselves controlled by groups of Pushtun notables. However, the pattern of rule in the two areas proved quite different. In Jalalabad, after a certain amount of tussling, Haji Abdul Qadir, a prominent member of the Arsala family which also included the Kabul-area Pushtun commander Abdul Haq, emerged to head a local shura which controlled the city. A pragmatist, Qadir sought to maintain civil relations with both Rabbani and Hekmatyar (Gille, 1994: 5). His pragmatism also extended to tolerating the cultivation of opium, and the training of Arab extremists, in the vicinity of the city (Rubin, 1995a: 277). It was here that Osama Bin Laden settled when he returned to Afghanistan in May 1996 (Bergen, 2001a: 93).

In Kandahar the situation was more complicated. In different parts of the province, various commanders carved out particular areas of territory over which they held sway, and in the city itself a number of armed groups were present: adherents of the *Jamiat*, the *Ittehad* and Gailani's party clashed from time to time (Dorronsoro, 1993: 5). In 1992, the situation in the Kandahar area was relatively quiet, but it deteriorated sharply in 1993 and 1994. Haji Abdul Latif's son Gul Agha was formally the governor, but lacked his father's leadership skills (Davis, 1998: 47). The *Jamiat* leader, Mullah Naqib, was ultimately to surrender Kandahar to the Taliban without a fight, prompting suspicions that he had been bought, but there is also evidence that he was following Rabbani's instructions: unusually, he remained in Kandahar for some two months under the Taliban before returning to his home district (Davis, 1998: 49–50). He was to resurface in 2001, perhaps confirming the prudence of his approach.

Northern and western Afghanistan

Mazar-e Sharif became Dostam's main power-base. He ran an administration which purported to be liberal, although hardly in the classical sense. Lower-level *Parchamis* found a niche there, and local Mujahideen commanders were brought under Dostam's control (Dorronsoro, 1993–1994). The relative stability of the north, and its proximity to access routes through Uzbekistan, led to something of a boom, with UN offices and foreign consulates being established. Dostam used these to consolidate his autonomy. By collecting customs duties at Hairatan, he established a fiscal basis for his exercise of power, and employed tax farmers to collect revenue in towns under his control. He also appointed local administrative officials: in 1997, I visited a court in Balkh at which a *qazi* (judge), appointed by Dostam, was hearing civil cases. Nonetheless, his administration was not without its problems. Dostam diverted scarce resources to establishing a palatial lifestyle for himself, and included some brutally unattractive figures, notably the Uzbek Rasul Pahlavan, in his administration.

Herat under Ismail Khan was generally well administered and reconstruction proceeded apace (Dupaigne, 1993–1994). Ismail successfully established a monopoly of force, eliminating some militias and accommodating others. From 20 to 25 July 1994, he hosted a large gathering of notables, including President Rabbani, former prime minister Dr Yousuf, and a son of the late King Amanullah (d'Afghanistan, 1994). The meeting was notable for being Afghan-organised (in contrast to the gatherings which produced the Peshawar and Islamabad Accords), but its conclusions, calling for a new process of political transition (United Nations, 1994a: Appendix), were soon outdated as the Taliban appeared on the scene. Only when Ismail overreached himself in September 1995 against the Taliban was his administration finally overthrown. Herat was at this time still a notably peaceful and stable region, giving the lie to the Taliban claim that they only sought to promote peace and stability, but Ismail's popularity had been weakened by his use of conscription, at a time when many Heratis felt that customs revenues could have been used to fund a proper regular force.

The reappearance of the UN

In June 1992, Benon Sevan had relinquished his position, and moved on to other duties in the UN system. A gap then followed in UN political activity in Afghanistan. However, on 21 December 1993, the General Assembly in Resolution 48/208 requested the Secretary-General 'to dispatch to Afghanistan, as soon as possible, a United Nations special mission to canvass a broad spectrum of the leaders of Afghanistan, soliciting their views on how the United Nations can best assist Afghanistan in facilitating national rapprochement and reconstruction, and to submit its findings, conclusions and recommendations to the Secretary-General for appropriate action'. On 14 February 1994, Secretary-General Boutros-Ghali appointed the former Foreign Minister of Tunisia, Mahmoud Mestiri, to head the Special Mission. Mestiri assembled a fresh team of advisers, of whom one of the most influential was an American, Charles Santos, who had worked with Cordovez (Cordovez and Harrison, 1995: 375) and who after ceasing to work for the Special Mission maintained his interest in Afghanistan, even accompanying Dostam during a visit he paid to New York. Santos, according to Ahmed Rashid, came to be 'intensely disliked by all the Afghan leaders, especially the Taliban' (Rashid, 2000: 171).

Initially, the Special Mission worked in a low-key fashion. Its mandate, after all, was to inquire and recommend rather than mediate directly. In a report of 1 July 1994, it made a number of important points: that 'the people widely identify themselves, first and foremost, as Afghans and Muslims'; that they wanted 'to ensure the territorial sovereignty of Afghanistan'; that 'most of the country, at least two-thirds, was at peace'; and that the Mission was repeatedly told 'that the majority of those fighting were doing so for money since this was one of the only ways to earn a living, especially in Kabul' (United Nations Special Mission, 1994: paras. 23(e), 13, 16). If this had led to a programme of pressure on those states fuelling the conflict to *desist*, the Mission might have played a very useful role. Instead, it became entangled in the morass of Afghan internal politics, recommending in Paragraph 40 (c) that the United Nations 'begin serious and in-depth consultations with the various Afghan leaders on the establishment of a viable transitional authority and a complete and total cease-fire'. Fatefully, this idea was adopted by the UN. In November 1994, the President of the UN Security Council issued a statement welcoming

the acceptance by the warring parties and other Afghan representatives of a step-by-step process of national reconciliation through the establishment of a fully representative and broad-based Authoritative Council which would: (i) negotiate and oversee a cease-fire, (ii) establish a national security force to collect and safeguard heavy weapons and provide for security throughout the country, and (iii) form a transitional

government to lay the groundwork for a democratically chosen government, possibly utilizing traditional decision-making structures such as
a 'Grand Assembly' (United Nations Security Council, 1994).

Unfortunately, Mestiri at this point proceeded in a manner which was
utterly detached from the ground realities in Afghanistan. When the members of the *Shura-i Hamahangi* moved with massive force against Rabbani
on 1 January 1994, one of the things which they did in the process was tear
up the Peshawar and Islamabad Accords. Having done so, but then having
failed in their efforts to oust Rabbani by military means, they were hardly
in a position to resurrect the two accords and demand that Rabbani stand
down in mid-1994 in accordance with their provisions. Yet this essentially
was the position that Mestiri was to adopt. Indeed, he went so far as to
express to journalists the view that he confronted 'a very difficult task – to
wrest power from Mr Rabbani' (*Reuters*, 18 March 1995). There was no
prospect whatever that this would happen. Mestiri had no capacity himself
to wrest power from anyone, and because he had failed up to that point
to secure *any* commitment from the Taliban to accept the UN's plans,
Rabbani would have been mad to accede to his demands.

Oddly enough, there may have been at this time a small opening for
negotiation between Rabbani and some elements of the Taliban (Maley,
1998d: 192), but Mestiri made no effort to exploit it. Instead, he rounded
on Rabbani, and at a Donors' Conference for Afghanistan held in
Stockholm in June 1995 by the United Nations Development Program,
he managed with one speech to destroy his own credibility. He did not
appear to have had proper speech notes; in the text which was supplied
to foreign missions, some passages hostile to Rabbani and Massoud
were crossed out, but remained clearly legible, including a recommendation for 'challenging the legitimacy of those who claim to be in power'.
He claimed the Kabul government had 'no legal basis', which was a
startling assertion given that it had been granted Afghanistan's UN seat
on the recommendation of the Credentials Committee of the General
Assembly. And while offering no criticisms of Dostam and the Taliban,
he voiced his disapproval of the idea of a settlement between Massoud
and Dostam, on the grounds that it could provoke 'further ethnic tensions'. The spectacle of a UN official discouraging parties in conflict
from reaching a compromise was an unusual one even for seasoned diplomats: most participants in the meeting were aghast at his intervention.
As Saikal has written: 'One tragic consequence of these indiscretions
may have been to help divert Rabbani's opponents from any thought of
compromise, and to encourage further meddling by external forces, the

Pakistan-driven seizure of Herat in September 1995, and the resumption of rocket attacks on Kabul a month later' (Saikal, 1996: 24).

From this point Mestiri lost all credibility and his mission effectively came to an end, although he continued to talk to the various parties, and retained his position until May 1996. His mediation miscarried because he failed properly to grasp three essential features of the situation. First, the Rabbani government was confronted not by 'normal' politicians, but by a 'total spoiler' (Hekmatyar up to February 1995) and an unpredictable movement with at least some 'total spoilers' at its heart (the Taliban from February 1995). In such circumstances, it is not sufficient for the UN simply to be *moral* guarantor of a transition mechanism; security guarantees are required from a neutral security force (Walter, 1997: 129; King, 1997: 77–8; Walter, 2002). This Mestiri never offered, and as far as a 'national security force' was concerned, the Secretary-General stated that 'the most that the Afghanistan parties can expect is the establishment of a voluntary trust fund for which I would solicit contributions from Member States interested in supporting the peace process in Afghanistan' (United Nations, 1994b: para. 79). Second, Mestiri took inadequate account of the role played by neighbouring states in prolonging the Afghan conflict: without some understandings to insulate Afghan politics from wider regional rivalries, his plans had little hope of succeeding. Third, he offered no solution to the problem of *state* collapse.

Regime decay

From its high point in 1995, Rabbani's government embarked on a process of decay, which culminated in its displacement by the Taliban in September 1996. Four factors accounted for its failure. The first, but least important, was factionalism within the *Jamiat-e Islami*. The second was a failure to find moderate Pushtuns with whom to ally. The third was Rabbani's serious error of judgement in reaching a rapprochement with Hekmatyar. The fourth, and most significant, was backing for the Taliban from Pakistan and from Osama Bin Laden for a further bid to take over Kabul, at a time when Rabbani lacked a committed external patron and the USA was indifferent to his fate.

Politics in Kabul

The absence of a functioning state gave rise to a politics in Kabul based not so much on institutions as on personal connections. Within the

Jamiat-e Islami there were a number of factions, based on attachments to particular individuals. The strongest group consisted of Panjsheris loyal to Massoud, many of whom had spent years working with him in the Panjsher Valley. Rabbani, who had spent most of the war in Pakistan, had a following of his own, from the *Jamiat* party bureaucracy and 'Interim Government'; these tended to be non-Panjsheris, with a number coming from Rabbani's old province of Badakhshan (Saikal, 1998a: 34–7). There were also some very talented non-aligned persons, reflecting the attraction that the *Jamiat* had held for moderate Islamist intellectuals. Unfortunately, while there were some highly skilled and dedicated figures in the upper echelons of the regime, who never lost sight of their duty to assist ordinary Afghans, there were also some who were singularly unattractive: one such minister even kept a mistress in New Delhi. The able ministers had to spend an excessive amount of time covering their backs, and this not only prevented creative attempts to commence a process of state-building, but disrupted a flow of shrewd political advice to Rabbani, who it turned out needed all that he could get.

The failure to find moderate Pushtun allies

A further problem for Rabbani's government was that moderate Pushtuns shied away from supporting it against Hekmatyar, opting in general for a studied neutrality. In some cases this was understandable, especially among those who walked away from engagement in the political conflict because they were revolted by the Afshar massacre. The moderate Pushtun Abdul Haq, who had been designated Kabul Police Chief in the post-communist distribution of offices, felt that he was totally undermined by the power of the *Shura-i Nazar* forces, although the real problem may have been that the policing function remained difficult to discharge seriously when the law-and-order problems of the city were the product of a wider anarchy. And he was not the only moderate Pushtun to feel that he was being marginalised, or even excluded: where there is no functioning state, those who hold offices without institutional power will almost inevitably develop such feelings. In other cases, the stance taken by 'Pushtun moderates' simply suggested that they were more Pushtuns than moderates when it came to the crunch – a conclusion which no social anthropologist would find surprising, given that individuals' identities consist of complex and not necessarily compatible strands of values and affinities. For some, denouncing Rabbani and Massoud as power-hungry 'fundamentalists' was a way of reconciling the tension between ethnic and ideological strands of identity, although it did involve a certain cognitive dissonance since, whatever else one thought of the pattern of rule under Rabbani and Massoud, it did *not* reflect a serious attempt to establishment a 'Government of God'.

Others simply viewed Rabbani and Massoud as ineffectual, although the irony of Pushtuns blaming Tajiks for not suppressing predatory warlordism among Pushtuns – especially when the Tajiks were themselves being attacked by a Pushtun extremist – was not lost on all observers. A more frequent charge, not made only by moderate Pushtuns, was that Massoud showed a lack of political judgement to match his military skills, with the rift with *Wahdat* especially in mind (Griffin, 2000: 30). However, it is not otherwise clear what alternative strategy the critics would have recommended for a Defence Minister confronted by an externally backed total spoiler in circumstances of state collapse. There are rarely magic solutions to such problems.

The Rabbani–Hekmatyar rapprochement

One way *not* to proceed was illustrated by Rabbani. Although Rabbani in 1992 had called Hekmatyar a dangerous terrorist, at times he seemed willing to treat him as if he were little more than a wayward Kabul University student. May 1996 was one of those times. In that month, the two reached an agreement at Mahipar (BBC *Summary of World Broadcasts* FE/2685/A/1–2, 8 August 1996; BBC *Summary of World Broadcasts* FE/2686/A/1, 9 August 1996), providing for Hekmatyar once again to become prime minister, an office he duly assumed on 26 June. The architects of this rapprochement were the Pakistani politicians Qazi Hussain Ahmad of the *Jamaat-e Islami*, and General Hamid Gul. The agreement caused fury among various *Jamiat* supporters, and the Taliban welcomed Hekmatyar to Kabul with a ferocious rocket barrage during his swearing-in ceremony (Gélinas, 1997: 118–19). Rabbani seems to have felt that bringing Hekmatyar into the government would 'broaden its base' through the granting of a key position to a Pushtun. But Hekmatyar was not the kind of Pushtun Rabbani needed, since his base had never been regional or tribal.

Hekmatyar could be brought back only because he was *weak* (Rubin, 1997b: 287), too weak to function as a 'total spoiler'. The agreement was attractive for Hekmatyar, since it rescued him from the political abyss into which he had been thrust by the Taliban in February 1995. It also embarrassed the Taliban's Pakistani supporters. But for ordinary Afghans it had very little appeal: the people of Kabul had gone through hell in 1993 and 1994 to *avoid* having Hekmatyar controlling their lives, and on arriving in Kabul that was what he set out to do, issuing Taliban-like decrees on women's dress which were at odds with the relatively relaxed atmosphere that Massoud had cultivated. The dangers which the Mahipar agreement held for Rabbani became clear within four months. Not only did the return of Hekmatyar tarnish the legitimacy of the Rabbani government within Kabul, but more importantly, it prompted all-out Pakistani support for the Taliban, which proved crucial in their ability to overwhelm Kabul in September 1996. It also led Rabbani to pressure Massoud into the militarily dangerous step of expanding his defensive lines to cover Hekmatyar's bases (Davis, 1998: 65–6). When the final Taliban attack came, Massoud's forces were simply spread too thinly.

The international context

What ultimately proved fatal to Rabbani's government was the strength of its opponent, both in terms of military capability and access to resources. As Davis has written, the Taliban 'were pre-eminently a military organisation rather than a political movement' (Davis, 1998: 69). There is no doubt that Pakistan played a pivotal role in making them a military instrument (Saikal, 1998b). This was in the context of the failure of its client Hekmatyar to deliver the outcomes which the ISI had desired, and the bitter resentment towards Pakistan which had built up among the victims of Pakistan's strategy, most notably displayed in an attack on Pakistan's Embassy in Kabul on 6 September 1995 following the use of force by Pakistan at the Afghan Embassy in Islamabad to end a still-mysterious hostage crisis. With arms supplied by Pakistan, and money from Osama Bin Laden, the Taliban were well positioned to capitalise on disillusionment with Rabbani by making a new thrust towards Kabul.

This came at a time when the government's position was increasingly stretched. When the communist regime fell, Massoud, alone among the Mujahideen commanders, 'lacked a powerful foreign patron' (Rubin, 1995a: 274). This did not substantially change over the intervening period: in 1995 a well-informed observer could write that 'Jamiat-e Islami is the only party involved which, so far, is without any permanent foreign ally. The government, which is controlled by Jamiat, has received some deliveries of aviation petrol and other petroleum products from Saudi Arabia, but the organization itself does not, as far as it is known, obtain any military supplies from abroad' (Fänge, 1995: 23). By 1996, the position had improved somewhat, with new supplies coming in from Russia and Iran

(Rashid, 1996), and after the death of Mazari, Iran sought to improve relations with Kabul across the board. But this brought few direct benefits, and actually caused a chill in relations with the United States, which Massoud was keen to develop. In August 1996, US Assistant Secretary of State for South Asia, Robin Raphel had demanded that Iran 'should stop supplying Kabul' (*Crosslines Global Report,* nos 22–3, 1996: 13). Only the Taliban stood to benefit from such a demand.

The end came suddenly. Jalalabad was occupied by the Taliban on 11–12 September. They pushed on at high speed and took Sarobi on 24 September. The situation for Kabul was now critical, and at 3 p.m. on 26 September, Massoud ordered his forces to evacuate the capital, an exercise which was accomplished with brilliant dexterity. The door was open for the Taliban, and they roared through it. On 27 September 1996, Kabul awoke to a new era. It was to be a new era for the wider world as well.

10

The Rise and Rule of the Taliban, 1994–2001

On the morning of 27 September 1996, the residents of Kabul awoke to a grisly spectacle. Two dead bodies were hanging from a traffic police-man's pylon in a downtown square. The dead men were Dr Najibullah and his younger brother. Just a few days earlier, during a meeting with UN Under-Secretary-General Marrack Goulding, Najibullah had declined to leave Kabul. 'He had no fear of the Taliban, he said; his only enemy was Ahmed Shah Masood' (Boutros-Ghali, 1999: 301). It was the worst, and the last, mistake of his life. Photographs of the spectacle were flashed around the world, and although the exact identity of the killers was never firmly established, it was universally interpreted as a manifestation of the Taliban character.

Yet who were these Taliban? The word itself is a common one, simply the Persianised plural of an Arabic word for student, *talib*. Students of this sort were well-known figures around the North-West Frontier and in Afghanistan. Winston Churchill in 1898 had referred in his book *The Story of the Malakand Field Force* to 'a host of wandering *Talib-ul-ilms*, who correspond with the religious students in Turkey [and] live free at the expense of the people' (Churchill, 1990: 7). However, the Taliban who seized Kabul were more than a mere collection of students: they were a militarised force with a proper name, in Pushto *Da Afghanistano da Talibano Islami Tahrik*, or the 'Islamic Movement of Taliban'. The emergence and advent to dominance of the Taliban movement was one of the oddest things ever to happen to modern Afghanistan, and their pattern of rule was one of the strangest to be witnessed in the mod-ern world, perhaps because it was so determinedly anti-modernist. The Taliban found themselves increasingly at odds with the world, and the final, cataclysmic clash of late 2001, which saw them driven from office and crushed into fragments, was perhaps unavoidable. But it has left

Afghanistan deeply scarred, and defined an agenda of responsibilities for the international community which it will take years properly to discharge.

This chapter deals with the rise and rule of the Taliban, and is divided into four sections. The first deals with the origins and spread of the Taliban movement, together with their campaigns to subordinate the north of Afghanistan to their rule. The second discusses the objectives and policies of the Taliban. The third deals with the human rights record of the Taliban, which rapidly became the focus of global attention, and the fourth deals with the Taliban's troubled relations with the wider world.

The origins and spread of the Taliban

Pakistan's search for clients

In 1994, with the failure of the *Shura-i Hamahangi*'s attempt to oust Rabbani, Pakistan found itself in an awkward position. Hekmatyar had proved incapable of seizing and controlling defended territory: in this respect he was a bitter disappointment to his patrons. There had also been a change of government in Pakistan, with Benazir Bhutto returning to the prime ministership in 1993. On resuming office, she installed as her Interior Minister the retired Major-General Naseerullah Babar, who had been her father's adviser on Afghanistan. If anyone deserved the dubious title of 'Godfather' of the Taliban, it was he. Babar referred to the Taliban as 'our boys', which infuriated Pakistani diplomats intent on covering Pakistan's tracks (Murshed, 2006: 45). At odds with ISI, and keen to assert control over Afghanistan policy, he activated a cell within his own Interior Ministry to advance his stratagems. Bhutto, whose own responsibility for the rise of the Taliban should not be underestimated, later stated that 'We have striven for an Afghanistan that should be free of factions' (BBC *Newshour*, 4 October 1996). This was true only in the sense that she wanted a pro-Pakistan faction to eliminate other power holders in Afghanistan. In 1996, she again lost office, to Nawaz Sharif, and subsequent revelations about misrule during her tenure (Burns, 1998) made her return to power in the foreseeable future unlikely. But by then, her government had let loose forces in Afghanistan which were to have a profound effect not only on that country, but also her own.

Whether the Interior Minister or individual talibs made the first move to establish a new political force is almost impossible to determine, and may be lost forever in the mists of time: none of those involved is likely to be a reliable witness. The Taliban, in explanation of their emergence as a movement, stated that a Ghilzai Pushtun mulla from Sangisar, Mulla Muhammad Omar, formerly attached to the *Hezb-e Islami* of Younos Khalis, had a dream in which he was called to lead a campaign by 'pure' young students to cleanse Afghanistan of the corruption and debauchery of warring commanders (Sirrs, 2001b: 44). There is no doubt that corruption and debauchery existed aplenty in the Kandahar area, but the Mulla's 'dream' had all the hallmarks of a foundational myth concocted to legitimate a force which took shape for other purposes. It contributed to a sentimental image of the Taliban which was advanced by some eccentric Taliban defenders in the USA, notably the journalist Nancy DeWolf Smith, whose preposterous 'analysis' now makes embarrassing reading (Smith, 1995). General Babar was certainly involved from the outset in Taliban activities in Afghanistan. On 20 October 1994, he had taken a group of Western ambassadors (including the US Ambassador to Pakistan John C. Monjo) to Kandahar, without even bothering to inform the Kabul government, even though it manned an embassy in Islamabad (see Rashid, 2000: 27; Kux, 2001: 335). France, to its credit, declined the invitation (Dupaigne, 1995: 13). On 29 October 1994, a convoy of trucks, including a notorious ISI officer, Sultan Amir (known by the *nom de guerre* 'Colonel Imam'), and two figures who were later to become prominent Taliban leaders, entered Afghanistan. The convoy was held up by a group of commanders on 2 November. The very next day, a group of Taliban, well armed with weapons obtained from the Pasha arms depot on 12 October (Davis, 1998: 46), miraculously materialised to free the convoy. They then moved on to Kandahar city, and spread outward from there.

While key figures in the Taliban were Afghans, and the movement to some degree built on local resonances in Afghanistan which groups such as Hekmatyar's *Hezb-e Islami* never succeeded in achieving (Harpviken, 1997: 280–2), it was ultimately not a manifestation of resurgent Afghan tradition, but rather an example of 'creeping invasion', albeit one in which the ability to exploit existing tensions in Afghanistan played an important role (Sinno, 2008b). Creeping invasion occurs when a middle power uses force against the territorial integrity or political independence of another state, but covertly and through surrogates, denying all the while that it is doing any such thing; and this use of force is on a sufficient scale to imperil the exercise of state power, by the state under threat, on a significant part of its territory, and is designed and intended to do so (Maley, 2002a). A very large proportion of those Taliban who fought in Afghanistan were not Afghans. According to Ahmed Rashid, 'Between

1994 and 1999, an estimated 80,000 to 100,000 Pakistanis trained and fought in Afghanistan' (Rashid, 1999: 27). This is an astonishing figure by any standard. Pakistan was not the only state whose nationals were to join the Taliban, but its support was much the most important (Sirrs, 2001a: 62), and could accurately be described as 'massive' (Byman, 2005: 195). A July 2001 report by Human Rights Watch recorded in great detail the nature of Pakistan's military backing for the Taliban:

> Of all the foreign powers involved in efforts to sustain and manipulate the ongoing fighting, Pakistan is distinguished both by the sweep of its objectives and the scale of its efforts, which include soliciting funding for the Taliban, bankrolling Taliban operations, providing diplomatic support as the Taliban's virtual emissaries abroad, arranging training for Taliban fighters, recruiting skilled and unskilled manpower to serve in Taliban armies, planning and directing offensives, providing and facilitating shipments of ammunition and fuel, and on several occasions apparently directly providing combat support.

As many as 30 trucks a day crossed the border into Afghanistan 'carrying artillery shells, tank rounds, and rocket-propelled grenades'. The report also noted evidence 'that Pakistani aircraft assisted with troop rotations of Taliban forces during combat operations in late 2000' (Human Rights Watch, 2001a: 23, 26). According to one credible source, a 'number of senior officers' from Pakistan 'were seconded to the Taliban' (Abou Zahab and Roy, 2004: 56); another equally credible source numbered these in the hundreds (Hussain, 2005: 204).

Pakistan's backing for the Taliban was explained in different ways. Some commentators saw in it a relentless searching for 'strategic depth' in the event of a conventional war between Pakistan and India. Others saw it as driven by economic concerns, notably the belief that there were profits to be made from oil and gas pipelines from Central to South Asia through a stable Afghanistan. Still others defended the policy in terms of ethnic factors, in terms of the alleged 'need' for Afghanistan to be ruled by Pushtuns, but not Pushtuns of a nationalist stripe. This argument carried some weight with General Pervez Musharraf, who overthrew Nawaz Sharif in a military coup in Pakistan on 12 October 1999: in an interview with the BBC, he claimed that 'our national security compulsion as far as Afghanistan is concerned is that the Pakhtoons of Afghanistan have to be on Pakistan's side' (BBC *Talking Point*, 2 August 2000). With the exception of several diplomats (Judah, 2002) and some courageous journalists – notably Ahmed Rashid and

Ejaz Haider (Haider 1998; Rashid, 2000) – few Pakistanis seemed to have grasped just how perilous it was to embrace a transnational force such as the Taliban, which had the potential to cause enormous damage to Pakistan itself (Maley, 2001a). In September 2001, the Pakistan leadership finally came face to face with the scale of its folly.

The composition of the Taliban

The Taliban were a military force. As Anthony Davis has demonstrated, it is a myth that they came to power with scarcely a shot being fired (Davis, 1998). They did not originate from a standard military training programme, however, but from a complex mixture of social and political contexts which went some way towards explaining their character (Dupaigne, 1995; Moshref, 1997; Glatzer, 1997; Maley, 1998c; Marsden, 1998; Rashid, 2000; Griffin, 2004; Cornell, 2006: 264). The Taliban were *not* simply an example of villagers coming to the cities. Their values were not the values of the village, but the values of the village *as interpreted by refugee camp dwellers or madrassa students who typically had not known normal village life.* They were a *pathogenic* force, whose view of the world conspicuously omitted the pragmatic moderation which historically had muted the application of tribal and religious codes in Afghan society (Barfield, 2005). Bernt Glatzer once quoted a tribal leader remarking that 'a shame that nobody talks about is no shame' (Glatzer, 1977: 158). Willem Vogelsang quotes an equally vivid observation from an elder: 'One half of the Koran is fine, the other half we write ourselves' (Vogelsang, 2002: ix). Neither of these observations could have come from a talib. Nor were the Taliban at all representative of Afghanistan's social complexities: they were an overwhelmingly Sunni Pushtun group, and many of them were fiercely hostile to Afghanistan's ethnic and Shiite minorities.

'Beware of the beggar who becomes king', runs a well-known Afghan proverb. The undisputed leader of the Taliban, from its inception to its collapse, was Mulla Muhammad Omar. He had little mass charismatic appeal, and was a poor speaker, but was respected for his piety by the top leadership of the movement. He had lost an eye as a combatant during the war against the Soviets, and plainly found his injury mortifying: he did not allow himself to be photographed, and in a meeting with one senior visitor kept twisting his head to hide his disfigurement. Omar, with the carefully managed acclamation of a group of ulema, took the title of *Amir al-Momineen* ('Commander of the Faithful'), and to legitimate his authority, appeared in public with one of Afghanistan's most sacred treasures, the Cloak of the Prophet Muhammad (*Khirqa-i mubarak*) (Maley, 1998c: 19). Following this nomenclature, the Taliban re-titled their country 'The Islamic Emirate of Afghanistan'. The deployment of this title was symbolically significant: it marked a claim to absolute authority, and a decisive repudiation of power sharing, or indeed of politics. When one knows one is right, there is no reason to give scope to others to propagate error.

Widely recognised as deputy leader of the Taliban, and in the view of some a moderating influence, was Mulla Muhammad Rabbani (*not* a relative of President Rabbani), who was to die of cancer on 16 April 2001. Initially, Omar was advised by a Supreme Shura of other mullas, but as time passed, Taliban decision-making, always an obscure process, became more and more opaque, with most Taliban excluded from the decision-making circle. By mid-2001, the picture of the leadership was as follows:

> Shura meetings are no longer held, and the Kabul ministers are rarely consulted about key decisions. Mullah Umar has become much more isolated. The core group around him includes some Qandahari ulama and judges of the Supreme Court of Qandahar (who are all above 70 years old, have never traveled outside Qandahar, and are extremist and simplistic in their views); a few powerful, hard-line individuals from the Taliban structure such as Mullah Nuruddin Turabi, Minister of Justice and head of the Religious Police, Chief of Army Staff Mullah Mohammed Hasan, and Commander Dadullah; individual Afghans working in Umar's office who were educated in Pakistani madrasas and who have a strongly expansionist and jihad-ist view of the Taliban's role in the Muslim world; Usama Bin Ladin and other Arabs who advise Umar on foreign policy (some Afghans from Qandahar even claim that Bin Ladin is consulted on domestic issues such as the Buddhas); and Pakistani ISI officers. (Rubin, Ghani, Maley, Rashid and Roy, 2001: 12)

Within the Taliban, there were a number of distinct groups. The leaders were not young students, but like Omar himself had typically been combatants in Mujahideen parties, most commonly the *Hezb-e Islami* of Khalis, and the *Harakat* of Mawlawi Muhammadi (who strongly supported the Taliban). The madrassa students who gave the movement its name, on the other hand, were often too young to have fought against the USSR. Many were orphans from refugee camps who had been recruited into madrassas and had lacked any normal family or home life. To a large extent they were victims of the Soviet–Afghan War, and their inadequate socialisation in significant measure accounted for their ability to do things which would have been unthinkable in traditional Afghan society, such as rain blows on women in the street. The movement also contained *Khalqis* who had joined the Taliban out of ethnic solidarity, whom the prominent talib Mulla Muhammad Masum Afghani described as 'communists... who have abandoned their old ideas' (BBC *Summary of World Broadcasts* FE/2234/A/1, 22 February 1995). In addition, as the Taliban continued to spread through the country, a large number of people prudentially switched to their side, providing them with an ostensibly large, but in fact rather fragile support-base. Finally, the Taliban attracted some moderate Pushtuns who clung to the hope that the Taliban would pave the way for the return of Zahir Shah. Moderates of this ilk were hardly ISI's cup of tea, given their attachments to the Afghan regime which had been at odds with Pakistan over Pushtunistan, but they did perform the useful function of reassuring the Americans that there were Taliban supporters with whom they could deal.

The Deobandi heritage

The backing which they received from Pakistan did not come only from Babar and from the ISI. As well, the Taliban received support from trucking mafias and drug barons (who benefited from easy movement on roads in Afghanistan) and from provincial governments. They also had a ready supply of manpower, and here, the mushrooming network of Deobandi madrassas in Pakistan (associated with a Pakistani political party, the *Jamiat-e Ulema-i Islam*) was of crucial importance. The term 'Deobandi' derives from the town of Deoband in India, where in 1867 an institute by the name of Dar ul-Ulum Deoband was established (Metcalf, 1982). Deobandi ideas were very influential in Afghanistan, where madrassas of Deobandi orientation provided the bulk of the Afghan ulema (Roy, 1990: 58). On occasions in the twentieth century, the Afghan ulema had emerged as a potent political force, especially in the last years of King Amanullah's rule (Nawid, 1999), but in general they were neither of high social status nor central to day-to-day politics.

In Pakistan, however, where the Taliban movement was nurtured, a process of distinct radicalisation had been occurring over a number of years (Nasr, 2008). The growth of sectarianism, both Sunni and Shiite, is abundantly documented (Zaman, 1998; Nasr, 2000a). From the mid-1980s, Sunni–Shia clashes became much more common. Sunni extremists such as the *Sipah-i Sahaba* ('Army of the Companions') and the *Lashkar-e Jhangvi* ('Army of Jhangvi') engaged in terrorist acts; in 1999, the *Lashkar-e Jhangvi* even attempted to kill Prime Minister Nawaz Sharif. The key development facilitating this was the growth of radicalised Deobandi madrassas. One careful study reported that the number of madrassa students in the Punjab increased *ninefold* between 1960 and 1995 (Zaman, 1999: 322; see also Zaman, 2002); and madrassa networks similarly expanded in Baluchistan and the North-West Frontier Province. Nasr has argued that there 'appears to be a region-wide radical Deobandi resurgence in the making – something akin to the Wahhabi explosion in the eighteenth-century Arabian peninsula – extending in the form of an arc from India through Pakistan and Afghanistan into Central Asia' (Nasr, 2000a: 179). These networks proved to be of use to the Pakistani state: as Nasr elsewhere wrote, the government of Pakistan in 1994–1996 'organized militant Sunni seminary students into Taliban and *Harakat ul-Ansar* units for Pakistan-backed operations in Afghanistan and Kashmir' (Nasr, 2000b: 179). Of critical importance as a supplier of these students was a madrassa in the North-West Frontier Province, the Dar ul-Ulum Haqqaniyya, headed by Sami ul-Haq, leader of one faction of the *Jamiat-e Ulema-i Islam* (Rashid, 2000: 90–2). It was from madrassas such as these that the Taliban poured out in their thousands (Abou Zahab, 1996).

The USA and the Taliban

There was one world capital that one might have expected to be thoroughly alarmed by the Taliban's rise to power and ultimate occupation of Kabul: Washington DC. Yet this was not the case. Some saw in it an opportunity: Zalmay Khalilzad, who was to be sent to Kabul in January 2002 by President George W. Bush as his Special Envoy to Afghanistan, published an article in *The Washington Post* arguing that it was time for the USA to re-engage Afghanistan, maintaining that 'the departure of Osama Bin Laden, the Saudi financier of various anti-U.S. terrorist groups, from Afghanistan indicates some common interest between the United States and the Taliban' (Khalilzad, 1996). Once it became clear that Bin Laden had *not* left Afghanistan, but indeed had been a principal financier of the Taliban's final thrust to Kabul (LeVine, 1997), Dr Khalilzad distanced himself from this position (see Khalilzad and Byman, 2000). The State Department's reaction caused more controversy. The acting spokesman, Glyn Davies, remarked that 'the United States finds nothing objectionable in the policy statements of the new government, including its move to impose Islamic law' (*Voice of America*,

27 September 1996). A week after the Taliban seized the Afghan capital, Assistant Secretary of State for South Asia Robin Raphel stated that 'We have no quarrel with the Taliban in terms of their political legitimacy or lack thereof' (BBC *Newshour*, 3 October 1996).

Comments such as this prompted widespread suspicions that the State Department, driven by an anti-Iranian zeal, had directly masterminded the Taliban takeover. No credible evidence to support such a strong thesis ever surfaced, but there was a good deal of evidence to support a weaker and in some ways no-less-damning claim, namely that the Clinton Administration had culpably misread the situation in Afghanistan, and that yet again, Washington was being led by Islamabad down a very treacherous pathway. This was not for want of intelligence: declassified cables and reports from the US Embassy in Islamabad released by the National Security Archive at George Washington University show that US diplomats were well aware of Pakistan's activities in support of the Taliban (Elias, 2007). Indeed, to any informed observer, it was no secret: the US 9/11 Commission bluntly described Pakistan's ISI as 'the Taliban's primary patron' (9/11 Commission, 2004: 123) Between 1994 and 1996, Ahmed Rashid has argued, 'the USA supported the Taliban politically through its allies Pakistan and Saudi Arabia, essentially because Washington viewed the Taliban as anti-Iranian, anti-Shia, and pro-Western' (Rashid, 2000: 176). On occasion, this led US officials to make quite fatuous assertions about the Taliban, such as the comment made by one State Department staffer to the writer and filmmaker Richard Mackenzie: 'You get to know them and you find they really have a great sense of humour' (Mackenzie, 1998: 97). US policy throughout this period reflected a profound failure to grasp the nature of the political forces that had been let loose in Afghanistan (Coll, 2005; Gutman, 2008).

The Clinton Administration's initial position seems to have been driven by an argument something like the following: 'Afghanistan's problem is the lack of order. The solution is to establish a common national power. The Taliban are the right people to fill this void. They are Pushtuns, from whose ranks Afghanistan's rulers must be drawn. They are Sunnis, and hostile to Iran. They are not anti-Western, and may well invite the former King to return. And once they restore order, the Taliban will withdraw from politics as they have promised. US energy corporations can construct oil and gas pipelines through Afghanistan, and rents from these pipelines will fund reconstruction.' At least some elements of this Hobbesian thesis found supporters (Goldsmith, 1997; Magnus and Naby, 1998: 195), but as a whole it was spectacularly at odds with Afghan realities. The belief that the Taliban would willingly relinquish political power to anyone was mindboggling in its naiveté, as was the belief that Afghanistan's substantial non-Pushtun minorities would willingly accept Taliban domination. The faith in energy companies as engines of reconstruction – in the absence of a proper institutional framework to receive and manage revenues generated by their activities – was particularly absurd: such a situation is tailor-made for spoiler activities, and is more likely to foster patronage networks than serious postwar reconstruction (Maley, 1998). Most seriously of all, the argument entirely overlooked the brutality of the 'order' which the Taliban had brought. As Tacitus wrote in the *Agricola*, they had made a wilderness and called it peace. It was because of this last reality that the case for supporting the Taliban was soon to fall apart. The Taliban by their own activities scared the Administration away from any kind of embrace. With the passage of time, the Clinton Administration became more aware of the dangers which the Taliban posed, but it did not prove capable of devising and implementing policies that could respond effectively to the threat (see Clarke, 2004; 9/11 Commission, 2004: 174–214). Nor did the new Bush Administration which, until the September 11 attacks, was preoccupied with other issues that it saw as more pressing than threats emanating from Afghanistan. As one insider starkly put it, 'When the United States was attacked on September 11, 2001, our government had on the shelf no war plan to destroy al Qaida in Afghanistan or to overthrow the Taliban government' (Feith, 2008: 88).

Military developments after September 1996

The events of late September 1996 left three main power centres out of Taliban control. One was north-east Afghanistan, essentially the area occupied by Massoud's forces following their retreat from Kabul. The second was the Hazarajat region. And the third was Dostam's fiefdom based on Mazar-e Sharif. Dostam, in an act of almost unparalleled foolishness, had sought to appease the Taliban in 1995 by reaching an agreement with them pursuant to which he provided technicians who repaired the aircraft they had captured in Kandahar when they took it over. This gave them access to air power (Rashid, 2000: 39). But on 10 October 1996, he struck a new alliance with Massoud, Rabbani, and the Shiite leader Muhammad Karim Khalii. With Mohseni's *Harakat* and Sayyaf's *Ittehad*, this came to be known officially as the *Jabha-i Muttahed-e Islami Milli bara-i Nejat-e Afghanistan* ('National Islamic United Front for the Salvation of Afghanistan'), but colloquially as the

Northern Alliance. From Dostam's point of view, entering such an alliance was a rational move, since it was inconceivable that the Taliban would have accommodated him for more than a brief period, but it did mean that he joined their list of targets.

In May 1997, the Taliban made their move. On 19 May, rumours began to circulate that Dostam's foreign affairs spokesman, General Abdul Malik Pahlavan, had switched sides and joined the Taliban. I was in Mazar-e Sharif at the time and can bear witness to the electrifying effects of the rumours. Dostam was widely believed to have been behind the assassination of Malik's brother Rasul Pahlavan in June 1996. Ismail Khan was in Malik's territory at this time, and Malik sought to establish his new credentials as a Taliban ally by handing Ismail over to the Taliban. But it was clear that Pakistan was behind the changes, since Malik would not have defected unless he had received stronger guarantees than the Taliban could give that he would remain in charge after Dostam was removed. On 24 May, fighting flared inside the city, and Dostam fled to Turkey. On 25 May, Pakistan's Foreign Minister Gohar Ayub Khan announced that Pakistan would grant diplomatic recognition to the Taliban. (He subsequently revealed that this was done under ISI pressure (Khan, 2007: 289).) But just three days later, on 28 May, the arrangement unravelled. Young Taliban – obviously not privy to the subtler details of the Taliban's deal with Malik – tried to disarm some of Malik's force, who returned fire. More Taliban were killed by an anti-tank missile as their truck headed towards the city centre, and a bloodbath occurred as Taliban were hunted down by enraged locals. Hundreds were killed. By nightfall, the alliance between Malik and the Taliban was dead, even though Malik had done his best during the day to stop the fighting. A subsequent UN investigation pointed out that an alarming amount of ethnically motivated violence was triggered by these events: 'It appears that everybody was butchering everybody up there', a UN official reportedly said (*Associated Press*, 13 December 1997). A large number of Taliban prisoners in Malik's hands were killed, possibly in revenge for Taliban killing of *Jumbesh* prisoners after a flare-up of fighting in September. The Taliban did eventually take the city. On 12 September 1997, Dostam returned from Turkey and resumed control, displacing the treacherous Malik with relative ease. He even managed to resist a renewed Taliban attempt to take the city. But his aura of competence had been very seriously compromised, and this worked to his disadvantage in August 1998, when the Taliban struck again. This time, the Taliban took no chances, and Dostam was forced to flee for a second time. An orgy of slaughter then ensued.

The Taliban approach to the Hazarajat combined a blockade to prevent the entry of foodstuffs (Rashid, 1997a), and military assaults directed at breaking the Hazaras' military capabilities. The Hazaras remained a significant force, and held Bamiyan longer than Dostam held Mazar. Bamiyan was still under *Hezb-e Wahdat* control on 21 August 1997 when Abdul Rahim Ghafoorzai, a talented Pushtun diplomat who had represented the Islamic State at the United Nations and whom the anti-Taliban forces had agreed should become their prime minister, was killed there in a plane crash. On 13 September 1998, the Taliban took Bamiyan; *Wahdat* regained it on 21 April 1999, but the Taliban took it back on 9 May (Rashid, 2000: 67–79), killing a significant number of civilians in the process (Amnesty International, 1999a). Thereafter, the Taliban concentrated on hunting down groups of opponents in more remote parts of the Hazarajat, often using barbaric tactics to do so. Bamiyan was briefly retaken by anti-Taliban forces on 13 February 2001, but changed hands yet again a few days later – with dire consequences for Afghanistan's cultural heritage.

Massoud was never eliminated on the battlefield. For much of the period between 1996 and 2001, forces under his control remained surprisingly close to Kabul, often controlling large tracts of land in the fertile Shomali Valley to the north of Kabul, which housed Bagram air base, as well as the town of Charikar. The Shomali Valley became a target for ferocious Taliban attack, and changed hands on a number of occasions. Two Taliban attacks were particularly destructive. On 16 January 1997, the Taliban launched a major assault on the valley, producing population displacement, and destruction of houses and crops. It was this attack which first led to widespread allegations of 'ethnic cleansing' by the Taliban, since the bulk of those displaced were Tajiks. Even more destructive was a scorched-earth attack in August 1999. On 14 August, the United Nations reported that the Taliban were 'intentionally setting homes on fire', which prompted UN Secretary-General Kofi Annan to state that 'The parties responsible for such disasters cannot, cynically, commit such criminal acts, then turn to the United Nations and the international community as a whole to help save their own people from disasters provoked by those who claim to be their country's leaders' (UNOCHA *News Release*, 14 August 1999). Within a fortnight, it was clear that the Taliban were systematically demolishing the agricultural infrastructure in the valley (*Agence France Presse*, 27 August 1999), and after the Taliban were overthrown, pitiful reports on the condition of the valley and its people began to emerge (Waldman, 2002). Yet these tactics did not ultimately deliver secure control of the valley. By

September 2001, the frontline between Taliban and anti-Taliban forces was next to the Bagram air base. Massoud also faced attacks further north. He lost the town of Taloqan, to which he had shifted his headquarters, but managed to reestablish his headquarters to the east, ultimately in the town of Khwaja Bahauddin. Massoud concentrated on methodical organisation of his forces. From the point of view of international politics, Massoud's ongoing resistance had two significant implications. One was that Rabbani's government was in a position to retain Afghanistan's UN seat, which would have been difficult had it controlled no territory in Afghanistan. The other was that it provided a potential Afghan partner for international operations against the Taliban. This was to prove crucial in October–November 2001.

The objectives of the Taliban

The Taliban were above all an *anti-modernist movement*. Their anti-modernist character suffused their approaches to policy, while the fact that they were a movement rather than a Leninist party gave a certain looseness to the implementation of decisions. Negotiating with the Taliban, one observer reported, was like 'grasping smoke' (Keating, 1997: 11–12). The result was that some international aid staff who interacted with particular Taliban on a day-to-day basis found that they could strike pragmatic compromises with them to achieve particular objectives, while those who had to deal with the Taliban over matters of principle found them impossible (compare Kleiner, 2006; Donini, 2004; Donini, 2007). There were notable differences in the Taliban's approach to cities and to the countryside. They tended to see urban centres such as Kabul as Cities of Sin, to be ruled with a strong hand. Rural areas, especially populated by Pushtuns, were of less interest to them. They felt more secure there, and perhaps as a result, allowed the rhythm of rural life to go on largely uninterrupted.

The Taliban and security

The Taliban defended their approach to rule above all else in terms of *security*. Mulla Afghani in February 1995 stated that the leadership took the view that the 'most important issue in the current situation was security and the prevailing mayhem, in addition to the absence of Islamic government'. He went on to say that 'Our programme is to continue jehad until we achieve security and stability, until Islamic law is applied, and until Afghanistan becomes strong internally and externally', and that 'We want a weapons-free Afghanistan' (BBC *Summary of World Broadcasts* FE/2234/A/1–2, 22 February 1995). However, the Taliban's notion of security proved difficult to pin down. In March 1998, a correspondent laconically reported that while a Taliban spokesman had said in a statement that there was 'complete peace and security' in the provinces controlled by the Taliban, 'at the same time, he told reporters that a lack of adequate security is another serious problem in providing education to female students' (*Voice of America*, 19 March 1998).

There is no doubt that many Afghans did sincerely welcome the Taliban as providers of 'security', although how many is impossible to ascertain. Drug traffickers certainly did (Rubin, 2000: 1795). What is quite clear, however, is that the Taliban's notion of 'security' intersected at best partially with the ideas of 'human security' which now figure prominently in discussions of security in Western circles, and barely at all with any notion of human dignity. It was based on fear, not the rule of law. Human security, Ramesh Thakur has argued, 'refers to the quality of life of the people of a society or polity' (Thakur, 2000: 231). Many aspects of human security in this sense – for example access to the wherewithal to avoid squalid poverty – interested the Taliban not at all. In 1998, Nancy Hatch Dupree, a longtime observer of Afghan society, noted that 'For the first time in its history, beggars roam the streets of Kabul or huddle outside relief agencies', and continued: 'One wonders how the authorities can countenance the sight of so many destitute female beggars while still maintaining that a pillar of their existence is to guarantee the dignity of women' (Dupree, 1998: 155).

The Taliban and Sharia law

The Taliban's 'answer' to the issue of security was rigorous application of Islamic law (*Sharia*). Their conception of law was a simple one: rather than seeing law as a complex tradition or discourse subject to evolution and reinterpretation (Krygier, 1986), they viewed it as a rigid code of rules including penalties to be enforced. They showed little if any awareness of the subtleties of Islamic jurisprudence (see Hallaq, 2005; Amanat and Griffel, 2007), and the message that there should be no compulsion in religion, contained in the Qur'an (*Sura al-Baqarah*, 2: 256), carried no weight with them.

The agency for the enforcement of law was the religious police, or to give it its full title, *Amr bil-Maroof wa Nahi An il-Munkir*, the department responsible for 'the Promotion of Virtue and the Suppression of Vice', an expression derived from the Qur'an. The religious police proved to be one of the best organised of the Taliban's agencies, and also one of the most vicious. The combination of police powers and religious zealotry is a frightening one, as European populations learned during the times of the Inquisition, and under the Taliban the mere existence of such an agency served the purpose of deterring resistance. In September 1997, the Taliban official Sher Muhammad Abbas Stanekzai admitted that it 'is a fact our rules are obeyed by fear', which he justified by claiming that 'people are addicted to sin' (*Agence France Presse*, 23 September 1997). In 1997 in Kabul, I often heard Afghans whisper the word *wahshat* ('terror') to describe the situation in what had once been a remarkably cosmopolitan city, and other reportage confirmed this (Burns, 1997). People bitterly resented what they saw as double standards, for example the toleration the Taliban displayed for a serial rapist in their ranks (Khan, 2000). The religious police had no concept of due process, let alone a sense that accused persons were innocent until proved guilty. Those who fell into their hands could expect to be treated abominably (Amnesty International, 1999b; Sullivan, 2002).

In common with most totalitarian movements, the Taliban recognised no such thing as a 'private' sphere of life, lying beyond the reach of public authorities. However, they differed from totalitarian regimes such as those found in Nazi Germany and the Soviet Union in the 1930s in that they did not control the kind of state instrumentalities that were at the disposal of Hitler and Stalin. The period of Taliban rule was one in which, for once, the absence of a state-building agenda might actually have been a blessing in disguise.

The Taliban and the state

The Taliban's approach to rule was one in which the state did not play as central a role as one might have thought. They needed a radio station to propagate their decrees and a religious police to enforce them, but beyond this, the 'Islamic Emirate' went through the motions of 'state-like activity' but did not make any serious attempt to mobilise resources systematically with a view to redistributing them in accordance with policy guidelines. The boundaries between the Taliban as a *movement* and the 'Islamic Emirate' as a *proto-state* were ill defined, as one would have expected given the role of Mulla Omar as superordinate authority.

The nature of the economy under the Taliban contributed to this. The Taliban were not even able to control the Afghan currency (Rubin,

2000: 1797). Instead, they presided over a criminalised economy in which the revenues which they obtained, apart from $10 million from Pakistan to pay salaries, came largely from activities that the wider world viewed as illicit. One source of revenue was the exploitation of 'transit trade' and other smuggling between Afghanistan and Pakistan. Under the Afghan Transit Trade Agreement of 1965, certain goods could be imported into Afghanistan through Pakistan, free of Pakistani customs duties. It is clear that a significant proportion of the goods thus imported were then smuggled into Pakistan, where they were sold in smugglers' markets. Under the Taliban, this trade was augmented by the transportation into Pakistan of goods imported into Taliban-controlled areas of Afghanistan from Dubai and other trading ports in the Persian Gulf. The value of this trade was estimated in a World Bank study at $2.5 billion, and the profit to the Taliban as high as $75 million, although it was not pooled so as to permit efficient budgeting (Naqvi, 1999: 1).

Another source of revenues was opium, of which Afghanistan under the Taliban became the world's largest producer. It is a myth that opium was the main crop cultivated in Afghanistan under the Taliban. In 1998, on the eve of drought, cereal production totalled 3.85 million tonnes (FAO/WFP, 1999: 5), compared to 2,600 tonnes of opium (Rubin, 2000: 1796) Opium was nevertheless a vital source of income for the Taliban. The involvement of the Taliban in the drug trade was plain almost from the outset of their rule. In a 1996 interview, Mullah Omar admitted that the Taliban received revenue from a tax on opium (Maley, 2000a: 17), and by 1999, 97 per cent of Afghanistan's opium crop was from Taliban-controlled areas, (Rubin, 2000: 1795). Eyewitness testimony pointed to Taliban involvement not only in compelling farmers to grow opium, but in distributing fertilizer for the crops (Meier, 1997: 4), and the USA concluded that there was 'evidence that the Taliban, which control much of Afghanistan, have made a policy decision to take advantage of narcotics trafficking and production in order to put pressure on the west and other consuming nations' (US Department of State, 1998). In 1999, according to a UN report, 'the production of opium increased dramatically to 4600 tonnes, almost twice the average production of the previous four years' (United Nations, 2001a: 35). However, on 27 February 2000, doubtless with an eye to their international standing, the Taliban ordered a total ban on cultivation of the poppy; the output for 2000 fell to 3,276 tonnes, and for 2001 to just 185 tonnes (United Nations, 2001d: para. 79). The ban was resented by farmers, for whom no alternative income sources were provided, and won the Taliban surprisingly little kudos, in part because of the suspicion that the ban was driven by the desire not to add to what was already a large stockpile, and that output falls owed much to the drought by which Afghanistan had been gripped, the worst since 1971.

The Taliban and human rights

The Taliban's human rights record attracted relatively little attention after they took over Kandahar and Herat. The killing of Najibullah changed all that. The unusual spectacle of a former president gruesomely murdered was sufficient to attract correspondents from around the world, and once they had filed stories on the death of Najibullah, they searched for other things to report. They did not have far to look. The Taliban were by a wide margin the least feminist movement on the face of the earth, and their immediate implementation of repressive policies towards women guaranteed them a blast of adverse publicity. It was a blast from which they were never to recover. Their gender policies became a metaphor for all that was wrong in their extremism (see Hosseini, 2007).

Women's rights to education and health

The Taliban were profoundly aggrieved by the ways in which their policies towards women were received. From their point of view, Afghanistan before their emergence had been wracked by violence and disorder, of which women were the main victims. Their obligation as men and as Muslims was to protect women's 'honour'. Their solution was to confine women in the home, where they would be surrounded only by children, other women, and men who by virtue of being relatives could be expected to treat them honourably. They saw absolutely nothing wrong with this. But restrictions on women served a wider purpose as well, symbolically asserting the right to interfere in even the most intimate aspects of individuals' lives (Dupree, 1998: 151). Indeed, the very triviality of the Taliban's early decrees on personal conduct – which banned cassette tapes, beard trimming, kite flying, pictures and portraits, dancing at wedding parties, the playing of drums, and 'British and American hairstyles' (United Nations, 1997: Appendix I) – pointed to this deeper agenda. Such decrees were *not* universally enforced – without a state, universal enforcement was impossible – but citizens always ran the risk of falling foul of the Religious Police, and this was sufficient in most cases to produce compliance. Only in rural areas was the situation more relaxed;

there, the indefatigable Swedish Committee for Afghanistan ran a robust network of girls' schools (Najimi, 1997).

Decrees issued by the religious police banned women from travelling unless accompanied by a close male relative (*mahram*), and swathed in a tent-like garment, the *burqa*. These restraints on personal freedom were stifling enough for educated women, but two other developments were arguably even more grave in their impact. One was the immediate exclusion of women from most paid employment (Skaine, 2002: 61–86). During Rabbani's government, as I witnessed on many occasions, women lectured at the University of Kabul, provided 70 per cent of schoolteachers (Dupree, 1998: 154), and played an important role in the health sector. Some of these women were widows, of whom there were 50,000 in Kabul in January 1997 (Dupree, 1998: 155), and did not have male breadwinners to whom they could look for support. The consequences for these women and their children of loss of paid employment were therefore catastrophic. While some women health workers were subsequently allowed back to work, the health consequences for women remained grim, since female patients were also segregated (Amnesty International, 1999c: 4–5). Reports by Physicians for Human Rights documented the scale of women's suffering as a result of these policies (Physicians for Human Rights, 1998a; Physicians for Human Rights, 2001).

The other development was the emergence of the practice of forcing young girls into marriage with Taliban. I heard of this practice from informants in Kabul shortly after the Taliban took the city (Maley, 2000a: 18), and it was subsequently noted in a UN report (United Nations, 2000, para. 12). On the basis of interviews in Kabul after the Taliban left, Matthew Campbell concluded that 'hundreds of women were abducted, forcibly married, raped or sold into sexual slavery by Taliban fighters' (Campbell, 2001). Since sex within a forced marriage is actually a form of rape, such behaviour violated the very principles which the Taliban leaders purported to be defending. It was also deeply hypocritical, given that the Taliban were quite willing to stone women for the 'crime' of adultery (Burns, 1996). Such hypocrisy is typical of neofundamentalists such as the Taliban (Roy, 1994: 197).

Political freedoms

Since the Taliban did not recognise any realm of legitimate political contestation, political freedom did not exist in the areas over which they held sway. This was well illustrated in a comment made about

Ismail Khan by Taliban Information Minister Qudratullah Jamal following Ismail's sensational escape from Taliban custody on 26 March: Jamal said that 'Khan was a criminal because he fought against the Taliban' (*Agence France Presse*, 30 March 2000). Media of communication were equally subject to control. Television broadcasts were discontinued, and television sets banned. Radio broadcasts were limited to prayers and propaganda. Reporters sans Frontières accurately described Afghanistan under the Taliban as 'a country with no news or pictures' (Reporters sans Frontières, 2000). The Taliban's early promises to withdraw from public life had long been forgotten.

Massacres: Mazar-e Sharif and Yakaolang

The Taliban did not hesitate to massacre those whom they defined as enemies, although it should be noted that the worst massacres occurred when significant numbers of radicals from other countries were in their frontlines, especially *Sipah-i Sahaba* activists. Pakistanis rather than Afghans were responsible for some of the more notorious murders that occurred under the Taliban, such as the murders in August 1998 of Iranian consular staff in Mazar-e Sharif, and of a Military Adviser to the UN Special Mission to Afghanistan, Lieutenant-Colonel Carmine Calo (Maley, 2000a: 24).

When the Taliban occupied Mazar-e Sharif on 8 August 1998, they embarked on a three-day massacre which Ahmed Rashid described as 'genocidal in its ferocity' (Rashid, 2000: 73). The most conservative estimate of the number killed was 2,000 and others went much higher (see Cooperation Centre for Afghanistan, 1998; Human Rights Watch, 1998; Winchester, 1998; Cooper, 1998). In an article protesting how little attention it received at the time, Rupert Colville of UNHCR, writing in his personal capacity, described some of the things that happened to the Hazara victims:

> Some were shot on the streets. Many were executed in their own homes, after areas of the town known to be inhabited by their ethnic group had been systematically sealed off and searched. Some were boiled or asphyxiated to death after being left crammed inside sealed metal containers under a hot August sun. In at least one hospital, as many as 30 patients were shot as they lay helplessly in their beds. The bodies of many of the victims were left on the streets or in their houses as a stark warning to the city's remaining inhabitants. Horrified witnesses saw dogs tearing at the corpses, but were

instructed over loudspeakers and by radio announcements not to remove or bury them. (Colville, 1999)

In one of the most poignant events of the massacre, a Pushtun woman who had hidden eight Hazara women was shot along with all of those she had tried to help. The massacre was supervised by Mulla Abdul Manan Niazi, a fanatical Pushtun chauvinist from the Shindand area who incited his troops to further action through incendiary speeches over loudspeakers in which he denounced Shiite Muslims as unbelievers. In a step reminiscent of Mengele at Auschwitz, Niazi personally oversaw the selection of prisoners to be moved in containers (Human Rights Watch, 1998). This frenzy of killings was in all probability the worst single massacre in the entire history of modern Afghanistan.

Yakaolang in the Hazarajat was also the scene of massacres of Hazaras, this time under the supervision of the extremist Commander Dadullah, a close adviser of Mulla Omar. The worst was in January 2001. Amnesty International estimated the number of victims at over 300. Some 73 women, children, and elderly men were killed when the Fatematuzahra mosque in the Kata Khana area of Yakaolang, in which they had sought sanctuary, was attacked with two rockets (Amnesty International, 2001: 3, 4). The Taliban also killed two delegations of Hazara elders who had sought to intercede with them (Human Rights Watch, 2001b). The Hazaras must have wondered how their torment could ever end.

Protection of cultural property

The identities of communities and the meanings of the lives of their members often owe much to cultural practices and cultural property. The Taliban were prepared to disrupt the former and destroy the latter if they thought it necessary to do so. One manifestation of this was the prohibition of music, which struck particularly hard given the popularity of music in Afghanistan and the richness of its musical traditions (Baily, 2001). But much the most spectacular episode, which earned the Taliban worldwide condemnation, was the destruction on 10 March 2001 of Afghanistan's two greatest archaeological treasures, the giant statues of Buddha carved in the cliffs above Bamiyan (Marigo, 2001; Centlivres, 2001). Commander Dadullah was the supervisor of this staggering piece of cultural vandalism, but it was ordered by Mulla Omar in a decree of 26 February directed against statues; pursuant to this decree, two Taliban ministers smashed their way through the Kabul Museum (McGrory and

Alberge, 2001). The Buddhas had come under serious threat in 1997 (Thomas, 1997), and on 18 September 1998, a commander fired shells at one of the statues (Rashid, 2000: 76; Griffin, 2004: 164), but the decision finally to dynamite them in 2001 provoked considerable speculation as to the motive. Various possibilities, not necessarily incompatible with each other, surfaced in commentaries on what had happened. Taliban spokesmen were later to claim that the Buddhas were destroyed in reaction to the hypocrisy of Western statesmen who cared about statues more than near-destitute Afghans. Since the Taliban had shown no interest in developing policies to alleviate the plight of near-destitute Afghans, this bore all the hallmarks of a clumsy *ex post facto* rationalisation. Some saw the destruction as a primal scream prompted by international isolation or as an attempt to force the international community to enter discussion with the Taliban. Others inferred a desire to punish the Hazaras, in whose land they were located, and possibly deprive them of future tourism revenue; or a symbolic display of power (Spillmann, 2001). Still others sensed the influence of Osama Bin Laden, or other Islamic radicals, a possibility for which some tantalising evidence later surfaced (DiGiovanni, 2001). But it is unlikely that we will ever know exactly why the Buddhas were blasted out of existence.

The Taliban and the world

The impact of gender

The Taliban's treatment of women became an international issue within days of the occupation of Kabul, and attracted the attention of prominent feminists. On 29 September 1997, the European Union Commissioner for Humanitarian Affairs, Emma Bonino, was detained by the Taliban during a visit to what had been designated by the Taliban as a women's hospital. The resulting publicity was damning (Amanpour, 1997). Bonino became a frontline critic of the Taliban and the European Parliament adopted 'Flowers for the Women of Kabul' as a slogan for the following International Women's Day, 8 March 1998. The resulting demonstrations led Taliban radio to describe International Women's Day as a 'conspiracy' by 'the infidels of the world under the leadership of Emma Bonino' and to complain of 'the provocation which has been launched by Christendom against the Islamic Emirate of Afghanistan' (BBC *Summary of World Broadcasts* FE/3172/A/1, 11 March 1998). Then, on 18 November 1997, during a visit to an Afghan refugee camp in Pakistan,

US Secretary of State Madeleine Albright described Taliban policies towards women as 'despicable' (*Reuters*, 18 November 1997). This was a heavy blow for the Taliban, as it made clear that domestic political pressure on the issue of gender had forced the Clinton Administration to abandon its muted response to the rise of the Taliban in favour of overt criticism. This process had actually begun within days of their takeover (Sciolino, 1996).

For the Taliban, time was out of joint. The UN International Women's Conference in Beijing in September 1995 endorsed a reform agenda profoundly out of step with the policies of the Taliban, and a strong network of pressure groups was committed to giving effect to that agenda. The Feminist Majority Foundation under Eleanor Smeal took a strong lead in criticising the Taliban, with help from American celebrities such as Mavis Leno and Lionel Richie (Waxman, 1999; Mann, 1999). These US groups cared deeply about their *own* government's response to the Taliban's demands for acceptance, as an important symbol of the Clinton Administration's seriousness about gender issues. But the Taliban treated women as they did not because it was in their interest to do so, but because it was in their nature. Thus, an unbridgeable gulf opened between the Taliban and those states in which gender equality was taken seriously. The tensions over the gender issue actually reflected a deeper tension – between a vision of the world as governed by rules of an evolving international society, and a vision of the world as ruled by the word of God. In late December 1997, Mulla Omar claimed that the United Nations had 'fallen under the influence of imperialist powers and under the pretext of human rights has misled Moslems from the path of righteousness'. Increased rights for women would lead to adultery and herald 'the destruction of Islam'. 'We do not', he continued, 'accept something which somebody imposes on us under the name of human rights which is contrary to the holy Koranic law'. The holy Qur'an, he concluded, 'cannot adjust itself to other people's requirements; people should adjust themselves to the requirements of the holy Koran' (*Agence France Presse*, 29 December 1997).

Seeking recognition

Despite this uncompromising repudiation of the norms of international society, the Taliban were desperately keen to secure international status. Upon taking Kabul, they immediately demanded both recognition from other states as the government of Afghanistan, and Afghanistan's seat in the UN General Assembly. However, they received neither. As far as recognition was concerned, the explanation was political. The reactions in Western states to reports coming out of Kabul in the days following the Taliban takeover were extremely adverse, both at mass and elite levels. As a result, states such as the USA, France, the United Kingdom, and Australia in which the Rabbani Government had diplomatic or consular agents opted in the first instance to leave the *status quo* in place. There was a firm legal basis for this: as Sir Hersch Lauterpacht observed of revolutionary forces, 'So long as the revolution has not been fully successful, and so long as the lawful government, however adversely affected by the fortunes of the civil war, remains within national territory and asserts its authority, it is presumed to represent the State as a whole' (Lauterpacht, 1948: 93). In due course the Taliban were granted recognition by Pakistan, Saudi Arabia, and the United Arab Emirates, but they had wanted far more.

The Taliban faced similar problems at the UN. The UN General Assembly on 14 December 1950 had adopted Resolution 396 (v), which provided that 'wherever more than one authority claims to be the government entitled to represent a Member State in the United Nations and this question becomes the subject of controversy in the United Nations, the question should be considered in the light of the Purposes and Principles of the Charter and the circumstances of each case'. This worked to the disadvantage of the Taliban, whose invasion of UN premises to seize Najibullah displayed little commitment to the purposes and principles of the Charter, and whose treatment of women shocked many member states. Thus, in 1996, 1997, 1998, 1999, 2000, and 2001, the Credentials Committee of the UN General Assembly opted to preserve the *status quo,* which left the Rabbani Government in control of Afghanistan's seat, a valuable symbolic asset.

Finding friends

Of course, the Taliban's main backer was Pakistan, aided financially by Saudi Arabia. But this did not deter the Taliban from seeking other supporters. For the first four years of its life, the Taliban movement was courted by a number of optimistic energy corporations. In October 1995, the US corporation UNOCAL and the Saudi corporation Delta Oil signed a memorandum of intent with the government of Turkmenistan, which anticipated the construction of a gas pipeline through Afghanistan to Pakistan. 'The US and Unocal', according to Ahmed Rashid, 'wanted to believe that the Taliban would win and went along with Pakistan's analysis that they would' (Rashid, 2000: 179). When the Taliban took

Kabul, a UNOCAL vice-president, Chris Taggart, reportedly termed it a 'positive development' (*Reuters*, 1 October 1996). UNOCAL put Robert Oakley on its board, and Delta employed Charles Santos to advance its interests. Neither was to benefit from the connection.

For both UNOCAL and the Taliban, the relationship proved frustrating. For the Taliban, the relationship with UNOCAL delivered neither a stream of income nor wider American support. Their expectations were hopelessly unrealistic: according to Rashid, they expected 'the company which wins the contract to provide electricity, gas, telephones, roads – in fact, virtually a new infrastructure for a destroyed country'. The Taliban's negotiating team with the oil companies was made up of 'half a dozen mullahs with a madrassa education and one engineering student who has never practiced engineering', and the Taliban's Minister for Mines and Energy 'was a carpet dealer in Saudi Arabia before joining the movement' (Rashid, 1997b: 10). From UNOCAL's point of view, the Taliban proved unable to deliver the level of security which would be required to permit such a project to go ahead – and given the vulnerability not only of the pipeline itself, but also the expatriate staff who would inevitably have been involved in its construction, that level of security was extremely high. As a result, according to another UNOCAL vice-president, Marty Miller, 'lenders have said the project at this moment is just not finance-able' (*Reuters*, 11 March 1998); and in August 1998, the company suspended its involvement in the project. In the face of these problems, the Taliban sought to maintain lines of communication with one of UNOCAL's competitors, the Argentinian company Bridas, but ultimately that avenue proved unrewarding as well, and the Taliban's hopes of securing a free revenue stream through bargaining with major multinational consortia simply slipped away (Rashid, 2000: 157–82).

The UN and the Taliban

The UN as an organisation found the Taliban extraordinarily difficult to handle, not least because of its own character. The 'United Nations' is a network of loosely connected and weakly coordinated bodies, with their own interests to pursue. The Taliban proved unexpectedly adept at playing one part of the UN system off against another. For example, the Secretary-General in his September 1999 report to the Security Council on Afghanistan wrote that he was 'deeply distressed over reports indicating the involvement in the fighting, mainly on the side of the Taliban forces, of thousands of non-Afghan nationals, mostly students from religious schools and some as young as 14 years old'. He went on to 'appeal to all parties to respect the Convention on the Rights of the Child' (United Nations, 1999: para. 40). Within days, he was contradicted by the UN's relief coordinator in Islamabad, who after a visit to Taliban frontlines in the company of Taliban officials, commented, 'Generally these types of statements are sound bites and taken by the press as catchy headlines' (*Reuters*, 1 December 1999), adding that 'he regretted the Taliban believed Annan was personally responsible for the report, which he himself had not actually written' (*Agence France Presse*, 2 December 1999). The impertinence of this intervention was lost on the coordinator, who in an interview with a *New York Times* correspondent in January 2000 engaged in his usual pastime of detecting specks of light at the end of a tunnel which other observers found completely black (Crossette, 2000).

The result was a growing contempt for the UN. This was clearly manifested in the Taliban blockade to prevent food supplies reaching the central Hazarajat region, implemented despite high-level pleas from the UN that it not go ahead, and enforced by the bombing of Bamiyan airport on 1 January 1998 when a clearly identified UN plane was on the runway. After a series of provocations, culminating in an assault on a UN official by the Taliban Governor of Kandahar Mulla Muhammad Hasan, on 23 March 1998, the UN ordered the withdrawal of its expatriate staff in Kandahar and suspended its humanitarian activities in the south of the country. Ambassador Lakhdar Brahimi, the UN Under-Secretary-General for Special Assignments, was in Pakistan at the time of the withdrawal, and sent a very firm message: if the UN could not operate as it did in all other member states, 'we should pack up and go'. He added that the 'international community has a standard and if you want to be a member of the club you have to abide by the rules' (*Associated Press*, 28 March 1998). The UN Under-Secretary-General for Humanitarian Affairs, Sergio Vieira de Mello, demanded 'written assurances that international humanitarian law and principles will be respected' (*Agence France Presse*, 24 March 1998). Some such written assurances were given in a Memorandum of Understanding signed in Kabul on 13 May 1998 by the Taliban 'Planning Minister', Qari Din Muhammad, and the UN Deputy Emergency Relief Coordinator. In other respects, however, the document proved a disaster for the UN, since Article 13, in a section entitled 'Access to Health and Education', stated that 'women's access to health and education will need to be gradual' (for the full text, see *International Journal of Refugee Law*, 10, 3: 586–92). This prompted a scathing attack from the Executive Director of Physicians for Human Rights, Leonard S. Rubinstein, who stated that the UN 'endorsement of

Taliban restrictions on women's basic rights to education and health care is a betrayal of international human rights standards and of the female population of Afghanistan' (Physicians for Human Rights, 1998b). It is one thing to recognise that progress on gender issues will be slow and may involve some uneasy compromises, but it is another thing altogether to endorse such compromises in advance. This specific issue, however, took a back seat when US 'Tomahawk' cruise missile strikes in August 1998 prompted a temporary UN withdrawal from Afghanistan.

Despite these difficulties, the UN had one significant success in the political realm – not in terms of inducing the parties to negotiate a settlement, but in terms of assembling a strong team to manage mediation should the situation on the ground change. After the resignation of Mahmoud Mestiri, the UN Special Mission had been headed by a German diplomat, Dr Norbert Holl (see Holl, 2002), who made no progress and failed to energise the Mission. However, on 28 July 1997, the Secretary-General appointed Ambassador Lakhdar Brahimi as his Special Envoy for Afghanistan. Brahimi was a markedly more senior and experienced figure than any mediator since Cordovez. Formerly Foreign Minister of Algeria, he had headed UN peace missions in Haiti (after the US intervention) and South Africa (in the run-up to the 1994 election), and was widely regarded as one of the most skilled negotiators in the UN. His appointment signalled a new seriousness on the UN's part. On 20 October 1999, after over two years of intense involvement with the Afghanistan issue, he announced his intention to 'stand aside', but added 'if things change next week I shall be happy to come back'. The Secretary-General then appointed another senior and highly respected UN official, Francesc Vendrell of Spain, to head the Special Mission as his personal representative, with the rank of Assistant Secretary-General. During his sabbatical, Ambassador Brahimi went on to chair a high-level panel which produced a major report on UN peace operations, but it was clear that he had not given up working on Afghanistan; rather, he was conserving his considerable personal authority for the moment when the conflict might somehow ripen for a settlement. As things turned out, he did not have long to wait.

Terrorism and sanctions

The catalyst for change in Afghanistan, and the fatal mistake of the Taliban, was their decision to provide hospitality to the Saudi extremist Osama Bin Laden. He abused their hospitality in a shameless fashion, and they paid the ultimate price. His presence in Afghanistan surfaced as a matter of concern for the USA shortly after the Taliban takeover of Kabul, when it became clear that Bin Laden was still in Afghanistan under Taliban protection. But it was in August 1998 that the problem became acute. On 7 August, suicide car bombers blew up the US embassies in Kenya and Tanzania (Bergen, 2001a: 105–26). The USA concluded that Bin Laden was to blame, and on 29 May 2001, four associates of Bin Laden were convicted by a US court of offences related to the bombings (Bergen, 2001b). Almost two weeks after the attacks, on 20 August, President Clinton ordered that terrorist training camps run by Bin Laden near Jalalabad be hit with 'Tomahawk' cruise missiles. The strikes killed a number of militants – Afghans, Arabs, Pakistanis, and Kashmiris – but Bin Laden escaped unscathed. Indeed, Bergen concludes that they turned Bin Laden 'from a marginal figure in the Muslim world into a global celebrity' (Bergen, 2001a: 125).

A certain amount of public debate then took place in Washington over how further to address what was obviously becoming a major problem. While Taliban apologists such as Laili Helms continued to argue for engagement (United States Institute of Peace, 1998: 4–5: Roddy, 2002), a major study for the Afghanistan Foundation recommended 'a much tougher policy toward the Taliban' (Khalilzad, Byman, Krakowski, and Ritter, 1999: 17–18). It was the latter approach which the Administration adopted, and the result was a hail of sanctions against the Taliban. On 7 July 1999, the Clinton Administration imposed a range of *unilateral* sanctions on the Taliban, freezing all Taliban assets in the USA and banning commercial and financial ties between the Taliban and the USA (*Federal Register*, 64, 29, 7 July 1999). These were augmented by mandatory 'Chapter VII' sanctions imposed by the UN Security Council, binding on all UN member states pursuant to Article 25 of the UN Charter. In Resolution 1267 of 15 October 1999, the Security Council demanded that the Taliban turn over Bin Laden 'to appropriate authorities in a country where he has been indicted, or to appropriate authorities in a country where he will be returned to such a country, or to appropriate authorities in a country where he will be arrested and effectively brought to justice'. Failing such a handover, the resolution required states to deny permission for any aircraft 'to take off from or land in their territory if it is owned, leased or operated by or on behalf of the Taliban', except on the grounds of 'humanitarian need', and then only if approved in advance by a special Committee of the Security Council. It also contained a wide-ranging requirement for states to freeze 'funds and other financial resources' belonging to the Taliban or available for their use.

The Taliban categorically refused to comply with the demands of the resolution, and this led directly to further measures in Resolution 1333 of 19 December 2000. This moved from economic to military sanctions. The key operative paragraphs, 5 (a) and 5 (b), dealt not simply with the actions of states, but required states to prevent 'the direct or indirect supply, sale and transfer to the territory of Afghanistan under Taliban control ... by their nationals or from their territories, or using their flag vessels or aircraft, of arms and related materiel of all types including weapons and ammunition, military vehicles and equipment, paramilitary equipment and spare parts for the aforementioned' and to prevent 'the direct or indirect sale, supply and transfer to the territory of Afghanistan under Taliban control ... by their nationals or from their territories, of technical advice, assistance or training relating to the military activities of the armed personnel under the control of the Taliban'. These measures put Pakistan in a very difficult position. Pakistan responded in two ways. First, it protested that the sanctions were having dire humanitarian consequences. This claim was tested and found wanting by a UN study: the Secretary-General advised that while 'there are adverse humanitarian effects from the current sanctions regime', those effects 'are limited, and their scope and magnitude is greatly exceeded by the effects of the other factors causing humanitarian suffering, most notably the unprecedented drought, the continuation of the conflict and the widespread deprivation of human rights' (United Nations, 2001b: para. 67). Second, Pakistan sought to evade the terms of Resolution 1333: this was made clear, albeit obliquely, by an expert UN committee which in May 2001 concluded that to 'believe that the Taliban are still surviving on former stocks is naïve' (United Nations, 2001c: para. 31). The USA was reluctant to pressure Pakistan over its violations: some in Washington apparently still held to the belief that Pakistan might use its good offices to moderate the Taliban. This illusion collapsed in September 2001. If American officials had laughed or slept through the rise of the Taliban, by the evening of 11 September they were deadly serious and wide awake.

11

The Fall of the Taliban

On 9 September 2001, some Arab journalists carrying Belgian passports arrived in Khwaja Bahauddin to conduct an interview with Ahmad Shah Massoud. It proved to be anything but a normal interview. They presented Massoud with a list of 15 questions typed in French. Two questions might have provoked more caution than they did: 'Why do you call Osama Bin Laden a killer?' and 'If you take Kabul, what will you do with him?' But nobody spotted anything out of the ordinary, until the Afghan Ambassador to India, Masood Khalili, happened to notice that the cameraman had a 'nasty smile on his face'. It was too late: an instant later, a bomb hidden in the camera exploded. Khalili said that he saw 'a dark blue, thick fire rushing towards us' (Dugger, 2001). Within a short space of time, Massoud was dead, although his death was not officially announced until 15 September. Such an assassination had no precedent in Afghan circles. Suspicion immediately fell on Osama Bin Laden (Fitchett, 2001), and what looked like proof positive finally surfaced at the end of 2001, when computer files in Kabul belonging to Bin Laden's organisation *Al-Qaida* ('The Base') were found by Western journalists to contain the list of questions presented to Massoud, typed out in May 2001 (Cullison and Higgins, 2002).

This was one of the most momentous events in recent Afghan history (Anderson, 2002), but it was overshadowed internationally by what happened just two days later (9/11 Commission). At 8.45 a.m. on 11 September, American Airlines Flight 11, which had left Boston's Logan Airport for Los Angeles an hour earlier, slammed into the North Tower of the World Trade Center in New York. Although it was a cloudless day, the cause was not immediately apparent: after all, in 1945 a plane had crashed into the seventy-eighth floor of the Empire State Building. At 9.05 a.m., however, it became all too clear. At that instant, United Airlines Flight 175, which had left Boston for Los Angeles at 7.58 a.m., smashed into the World Trade Center's South Tower. The United States was under terrorist attack. Two other planes that day did not reach their destinations. At 9.39 a.m., American Airlines Flight 77, which had left Washington Dulles for Los Angeles at 8.10 a.m., struck the Pentagon Building, headquarters of the US Department of Defense, and at 10.10 a.m., United Airlines Flight 93, which had left Newark for San Francisco at 8.01 a.m., crashed near Pittsburgh, Pennsylvania, apparently after passengers overpowered those who had hijacked their aircraft. The structures of the World Trade Center suffered lethal damage: the South Tower collapsed at 10 a.m., and the North Tower at 10.29 a.m. The total dead from the plane crashes and attacks on the Center totalled 2,973 (9/11 Commission, 2004: 311) . The 19 hijackers were led by an *Al-Qaida* activist, Mohamed Atta. The spectacle was captured by television cameras which flashed it to households throughout America and screens all around the world. As a disaster it caused a psychological shock comparable to the sinking of the 'unsinkable' ship *Titanic* on 15 April 1912, and the fiery destruction of the airship *Hindenburg* on 6 May 1937, but with one difference: They had been accidents, whereas the attacks of September 11 were indubitably deliberate, with Bin Laden the instigator (DeYoung and Pincus, 2001; Dobbs, 2001). The closest parallel was with the bombing of Pearl Harbor on December 7 1941, which President Roosevelt described as 'a date that will live in infamy'. That was how the United States saw September 11, 2001, and it spelt the end for the Taliban regime.

This chapter details the events which followed. It is divided into three sections. The first gives a brief overview of Bin Laden, his organisation, and his links with the Taliban, who became increasingly radical as a result of his influence. The second traces the military campaign by which the Taliban were obliterated as a political and military force, and discusses the factors which contributed to their rapid collapse at the very time when some observers were predicting a prolonged campaign and warning that the United States could find itself trapped in a new Vietnam. In the final, I examine the Bonn Agreement of 5 December 2001, which defined a path for the establishment of new political arrangements in Afghanistan and led to the inauguration of a post-Taliban Interim Administration on 22 December.

Osama Bin Laden and the Taliban

Bin Laden's background

Osama Bin Laden was born on 10 March 1957 in Riyadh, Saudi Arabia, the son of a building magnate of Yemeni origin, Muhammad Bin Laden, who made a fortune as an entrepreneur in the kingdom before his death in a plane crash (Bergen, 2001a: 45). The young Osama was a student at the King Abdul Aziz University in Jedda (Kepel, 2000: 310), where he fell under the influence of the Palestinian Dr Abdullah Azzam. Following the Soviet invasion of Afghanistan, Bin Laden made his way to Peshawar, and devoted his energies to supporting the struggle against the Soviet occupation: from 1984, he ran a guesthouse for Arab volunteers entitled the *Beit al-Ansar* ('House of Supporters'). There is no credible evidence to suggest that he was supported in this by the United States, and nor does it seem particularly likely, since Saudi support for such activities was readily forthcoming at that time, and Bin Laden was personally wealthy. According to Peter Bergen, author of one of the most detailed and reliable studies of Bin Laden's operation, he 'would form his closest ties with the ultra-Islamist Hekmatyar and with Sayyaf, an Afghan leader who was fluent in Arabic and had studied in Saudi Arabia' (Bergen, 2001a: 54). In 1986, he established a base in the Jaji area of Paktia, known as *Maasadat Al-Ansar* (Rubin, 1997a: 196), and in 1989, he formed the *Al-Qaida* organisation. But shortly thereafter, in the wake of the Soviet withdrawal from Afghanistan and the assassination of Abdullah Azzam, he returned to Saudi Arabia, from which he was then not allowed to leave (Kepel, 2000: 313).

It was there, during the Gulf War and the deployment of US forces in Saudi Arabia as part of Operations Desert Shield and Desert Storm, that a rage seems to have gripped him. As early as 1988 he had reportedly described it as the duty of every Muslim 'to prepare himself to defend Mecca and Madina from the "Jews"' (Rubin, 1997a: 196). The Western deployment seems to have struck him as the very violation he was called upon to resist. He was finally permitted to leave Saudi Arabia in April 1991, but by then he had developed an obsessive detestation of both the Saudi regime, which had permitted non-Muslims to deploy on the soil of the kingdom, and of the USA, which had supplied the bulk of those troops. This obsession was mixed, however, with another obsessive conviction, namely that the experience of the Soviets in Afghanistan had proved the vulnerability even of superpowers when confronted with true believers. With no direct experience of the United States or indeed of Western countries, he was poorly placed to detect the perils in assuming that the USA was a mirror image of the USSR. After leaving Saudi Arabia, he revisited Afghanistan and Pakistan, before making his way to Sudan, where he settled in late 1991. In April 1994, he was deprived of Saudi citizenship; in May 1996, he left Sudan for Afghanistan – in time to aid the Taliban in their push to Kabul.

Bin Laden and the Taliban leaders

One wonders whether the Taliban appreciated just what they were embracing when they decided to permit Bin Laden and his associates to remain on their territory. The obligation which Omar and his key advisers manifestly felt towards Bin Laden could be interpreted in a number of different ways. Some saw it as personal, citing the rumour – never supported with credible evidence – that the two had been linked by the marriage of Bin Laden to Omar's daughter. Others saw it as religious: both were Sunni Muslims. However, Islam ordains punishment, not hospitality, for those who engage in criminal acts. Two explanations were more plausible. One pointed to the power in Pushtun society of the norm of hospitality contained in the Pushtun tribal code. The other pointed to obligations of reciprocity, springing from Bin Laden's support for the Taliban to overthrow Rabbani's government. It is in this context that the assassination of Massoud can also be viewed, as a measure to shore up Bin Laden's support from the Taliban on the eve of an *Al-Qaida* attack which might give them an excellent reason for bringing the relationship to a close.

Here, it is worth noting that the relationship was not without its tensions. The Taliban were not a unified force, and on occasion issues arose as to how to proceed. Bin Laden's presence seems to have been one of those issues. Not all Taliban were necessarily sympathetic to Bin Laden: some commentators saw the late Mulla Rabbani as a moderating force, and one less sympathetic to the *Al-Qaida* connection than Omar himself (Rashid, 2001a). Others cast the Taliban 'Foreign Minister', Wakil Ahmad Muttawakil, in a similar role, but this was probably a misreading, since Muttawakil was little more than a mouthpiece, with no power base of his own: he was hardly a 'force'. In addition, some evidence surfaced that even the relationship between Bin Laden and Omar was not without its tensions. Peter Bergen hints at a crisis in relations in February 1999 over Bin Laden's anti-American statements, and notes that in June 2001, Omar stated that Bin Laden had no authority to issue a *fatwa*, or authoritative ruling, of a kind that might undermine his own position (Bergen, 2001a: 164). Recently captured computer files also point to an earlier crisis, before July 1998 (Cullison and Higgins, 2002). What these materials all suggest is a tension in the Taliban's attitudes between calculations of international *political* interest, on the one hand, and norms of identity on the other. After September 1996, the Taliban obtained almost no international political benefit from association with the Bin Laden organisation, but to have surrendered him would have violated deeply internalised norms which defined how a good Pushtun should behave. There is some evidence that the Taliban received significant cash payments from *Al-Qaida* (Woodward, 2001), which would have supplied an additional reason for the Taliban to persist in aiding him, but other sources point to a cash-strapped *Al-Qaida* organisation (Bergen, 2001b; Cullison and Higgins, 2002).

The radicalisation of the Taliban

That said, from mid-1999, indications began to appear that the Taliban were becoming more radical. In one sense, they had always been radical, in that their anti-modernist image of a good society was not the same as the complex reality of Afghanistan, but from 1999 they moved in a more radically anti-*Western* direction. On 13 July 1999, just six days after the USA imposed unilateral sanctions on the Taliban, Abdul Ahad Karzai, moderate leader of the Popalzai Pushtun tribe, was assassinated in Quetta. Karzai had been a prominent member of the *Meshrano Jirgah*, the upper house of the Afghan Parliament, during the New Democracy period, and had also served in a four-member contact group set up by Mahmoud Mestiri when he was head of the UN Special Mission. This murder was a clear indication that moderate Pushtuns, once useful to the Taliban, had become expendable. In December 1999, the Taliban facilitated the escape of militants who had hijacked Indian Airlines Flight IC814 to Kandahar after it had taken off from Kathmandu on a flight to New Delhi. While there is no evidence that the Taliban had advance notice of the hijacking, their actions at a number of key points worked to the hijackers' advantage (see Chipaux, 2000; Misra, 2000). And further evidence of radicalisation came with a raft of measures in 2001 directed at non-Muslims: the 10 March destruction of the Buddhas of Bamiyan, a 21 May decree from Mulla Omar that Hindus should wear an identifying yellow patch, and the 5 August arrest of eight expatriate Christian aid workers from the NGO Shelter Now International on a charge of proselytesation. Bin Laden's influence may have been at work here, but a desire to reinforce the Taliban's ranks by energising impressionable madrassa students in Pakistan may also have been a significant consideration, and perhaps even the wish to drive Western NGOs from the country, of which there had been some evidence since July 1998 (Maley, 2000a: 24–5). The United Nations was acutely aware of this radicalisation, to which it was exposed on a daily basis. In a December 2001 report (United Nations, 2001d), the Secretary-General noted that throughout the year, 'the Taliban became increasingly uncooperative as the influence of extremists closely linked with al-Qa'ida network grew. The number of foreigners fighting for the Taliban surged, and their role in helping the Taliban carry out massacres of civilians, particularly in the Hazarajat region of central Afghanistan, and in serving as shock troops for Taliban military offensives against the United Front was significantly enhanced' (para. 87).

He also noted that 'it became clear over the year that the tone of Mullah Mohammed Omar's decrees and statements had evolved from concern with just Afghan issues to notably greater support for a global jihad, as promoted by Bin Laden' (para. 88).

September 11: the logic of messianic terror

Some analyses of the September 11 attacks depicted them in instrumental terms, as means to a rationally calculated end. Anthony Sampson, for example, argued that 'he must have planned this terrifying act, not as an end in itself, but as part of a much broader strategy against his enemy', that being to provoke a US reaction which would 'inflame the Saudi fundamentalists who felt so humiliated by the Gulf War' (Sampson, 2001). There is no doubt as to Bin Laden's hostility to the Saudi state (Simon and Benjamin, 2001–2002: 8), but this approach may over-rationalise the mindset of messianic terrorist groups, which typically mix religious inspiration with cognitive dissonance, conspiracy theorising, and a denial of social and political realities. They are sustained by an image of a world populated by enemies (Juergensmeyer, 2000: 171–8; Kimball, 2002), and by the 'faith that there will be a day in which history of life on this earth will be transformed totally and irreversibly from the condition of perpetual strife which we have all experienced to one of perfect harmony that many dream about' (Rapoport, 1988: 197). In the luggage of Mohamed Atta, the US Federal Bureau of Investigation found a note in Arabic which encapsulated perfectly a version of the messianic *Weltanschauung*: 'Purify your heart and clean it from all earthly matters ... The time of judgment has arrived ... You will be entering paradise. You will be entering the happiest life, everlasting life ... We are of God and to God we return' (*The Washington Post*, 28 September 2001). Bin Laden may have been more calculating than those he sent to their deaths: leaders of such groups usually are. But he probably had no sense at all of what would befall him as a result of the September 11 attacks. His hapless Taliban protectors would have been taken even more by surprise.

The obliteration of the Taliban regime

The 'War on Terrorism'

At a memorial service in Washington DC a few days after the September 11 attacks, the congregation sang a song composed during the Civil War which would have been known to most Americans – Julia Ward Howe's stirring anthem *The Battle Hymn of the Republic*. One line in particular should have made the Taliban tremble: 'He hath loosed the fateful lightning of his terrible swift sword.' It is not only religious fundamentalists who can be gripped by fervour. In the United States, the attacks of September 11 produced a righteous and awesome wrath which demanded prompt retaliation. *Al-Qaida* and the Taliban were the targets.

The key decision-makers in the United States – President George W. Bush, Secretary of Defense Donald H. Rumsfeld, and Secretary of State Colin L. Powell, together with the Chairman of the Joint Chiefs of Staff, General Richard B. Myers – were of course all fully aware of the disaster that had befallen the Soviet Union in Afghanistan, and from the outset were determined to avoid becoming involved in a large-scale land war in Afghanistan in which the frontline combat role would be played by US personnel (see Woodward, 2002). The terrain militated against the kind of lightning land campaign that had proved so effective at the end of Operation Desert Storm in 1991, and Afghanistan's landlocked character created significant practical problems, especially given the hostility to the USA of significant figures in Afghanistan's western neighbour, Iran. This suggested a need for allies of two types: first, states to assist in various ways in the conduct of the more limited operation that would be required, and second, partners on the ground in Afghanistan to spearhead an ultimate ground assault against the Taliban.

As to the former, there was no shortage of sympathetic states whose own nationals had perished in the ruin of the World Trade Center. The United Kingdom under Prime Minister Tony Blair moved rapidly to stand by the United States, and other European allies followed. The US's partners in the NATO alliance took the unprecedented step of formally invoking the provisions of Article 5 of the April 1949 North Atlantic Treaty, which provided that an 'armed attack against one or more of them...shall be considered an armed attack against them all'. Small-to-middle powers also pledged support: the Australian Prime Minister, in Washington DC on 11 September, and due to go to the polls within a matter of months, supplied 'Special Air Service' troops to serve in Afghanistan with US commandos.

The state which it was most important to bring into line was Pakistan. Here, what the USA needed was not active support so much as a complete and immediate end to Pakistan's support for the Taliban. Given the scale of the pressure which Washington brought to bear on Islamabad – reportedly including the demand that Pakistan declare itself either a friend or a foe (*Dawn*, 19 September 2001) and a threat to return Pakistan to the 'Stone Age' (Musharraf, 2006: 201) – it was hardly surprising that President

Musharraf, in an address to the nation on 19 September, came out in firm support of the US position. However, he had reasons of his own to take the same position. First, for some months, he had been verbally very critical of religious extremism, protesting that 'religious groups are surfacing who are trying to spread their faith to other countries and providing an opportunity to some nations to declare Pakistan a terrorist country, thus tarnishing our image and deterring foreign investments' (Borchgrave, 2001). Second, a large number of Muslims, some of them Pakistanis, had died in the attacks on the World Trade Center. 'These were capable Pakistanis', said Musharraf, 'and I would like to convey my deep sympathy to their family members' (*Dawn*, 19 September 2001). On 28 September, Musharraf sent the ISI Director-General, Lieutenant-General Mahmood Ahmed, to Kandahar to try to persuade the Taliban to hand Bin Laden over (Burns, 2001), but nothing came of the exercise, and amid stories that ISI freelancers had visited Kandahar without permission to offer advice to the Taliban (Rashid, 2001b; Frantz, 2001), Musharraf obtained his resignation two weeks later (*Jang*, 8 October 2001), and replaced him with the reportedly more moderate Lieutenant-General Ehsanul Haq.

The other types of allies required were organised military forces on the ground in Afghanistan (see Andres, Wills and Griffith, 2005–2006). Here, there was only one realistic option, namely to work with the United Front forces based in the north-east of the country and the northern reaches of the Shomali Valley near Kabul. The claim that the Taliban 'controlled' large tracts of Afghanistan was misleading, since the Taliban presence in rural areas was light (Dorronsoro, 2005: 281), but the tribes in those areas were fragmented and not organised for conventional war against the Taliban. In a display of what one observer has called 'staggering negligence, or myopia' (Davis, 2002: 7), the United States had long kept the United Front forces at arms' length, and reasoned cases for supporting them (Gerecht, 2001) had fallen on deaf ears. Several kinds of argument were advanced to justify the arms' length approach. One, mounted by the historian S. Frederick Starr, seemed to come straight out of the Cold War: he wrote of the anti-Taliban forces in dismissive tones, and maintained that in opposing the Taliban, the United States had made itself 'the junior partner in a Russian-Indian crusade against Muslim Afghanistan and Pakistan' (Starr, 1999). This argument attracted a stinging retort from US Undersecretary of State for Political Affairs Thomas W. Pickering (Pickering 1999), but it hardly slowed Starr in his tracks: on 21 March 2001, he actually hosted a Taliban adviser to Mulla Omar, the 24-year-old Sayed Rahmatullah Hashimi, at his institute, and he continued his attacks on the United Front ('this sinister alliance') well after 11 September (Starr, 2001). Another argument for the arms' length approach was outlined in an article in *Foreign Affairs* by Milton Bearden, who had served as CIA Station Chief in Islamabad from 1986 to 1989. This article – which managed to discuss the course of the Afghan conflict without making a single reference to Gulbuddin Hekmatyar – argued that there was 'no reasonable guarantee' that the 'now leaderless' Northern Alliance forces could dislodge the Taliban, and that 'the most likely consequence of a U.S. alliance with the late Masoud's fighters would be the coalescing of Afghanistan's majority Pashtun tribes around their Taliban leaders and the rekindling of a brutal, general civil war that would continue until the United States simply gave up' (Bearden, 2001: 29).

The Bush Administration fortunately was not swayed by such arguments, which was just as well, as they were remote from Afghanistan's ground realities, although not from a line of propaganda being sedulously promoted by Pakistani sources. The Taliban *were*, of course, dislodged, and Afghanistan did *not* slide into civil war, although it came to face a growing threat from radical insurgents operating from sanctuaries in Pakistan. Given that Massoud had favoured institutional rather than patrimonial rule, his death did not trigger a fragmentation of the *Shura-i Nazar* component of the United Front. The likelihood of an American assault on the Taliban gave those who survived Massoud an excellent incentive to work cooperatively, at least in the short run. Three individuals emerged as Massoud's successors. General Muhammad Qassem Fahim, one of Massoud's closest lieutenants, succeeded him as military commander. Younos Qanuni, who had long been his principal political plenipotentiary in dealings with other groups, continued to play the role of negotiator. Dr Abdullah, by training a medical practitioner, and onetime secretary to Massoud, filled the position of Foreign Minister. One of their first steps was to renew contact with former King Zahir Shah in Rome. This had two merits. First, it held out the prospect of broadening the base of the anti-Taliban forces by attracting a symbolically significant Pushtun to their cause. Second, it confirmed the marginalisation of Hekmatyar, who had smouldered in frustration in Tehran since the retreat from Kabul in 1996: in August 2001, Hekmatyar had described Mulla Omar as 'a hundred times better than Zahir Shah' (*Les Nouvelles d'Afghanistan*, 94: 30). At the conclusion of the talks, a communiqué in Rome announced an agreement in principle to set up a 'Supreme Council of National Unity' (United Nations, 2001d: para. 37).

The war begins

Towards the end of September, President Bush approved covert aid to anti-Taliban groups (Gordon and Sanger, 2001). His Administration also pursued the isolation of the Taliban: the United Arab Emirates severed ties with the Taliban on 22 September, followed by Saudi Arabia three days later. The US signalled its own intentions through the prepositioning of forces. While officials on 26 September stated that a military strike was 'not imminent' (Sipress and Ricks, 2001), preparations were underway for just such a strike. Aircraft carriers were deployed in the northern reaches of the Indian Ocean, and on 5 October, 1,000 US troops were flown into Khanabad airbase in Uzbekistan on C-17 transport aircraft (Sanger with Gordon, 2001).

On 7 October, exactly four weeks after Massoud's death, the US launched 'Operation Enduring Freedom' – a massive attack on Taliban and *Al-Qaida* positions in Afghanistan (see Cordesman, 2002; Martel, 2007: 232–7), using 15 land-based B-52 bombers and B-1 'Stealth' bombers, flown respectively from Whiteman Air Force Base near Kansas City and from the island of Diego Garcia in the Indian Ocean, together with 25 strike aircraft (F-14 Tomcats and F-18 Hornets) from the aircraft carriers USS Enterprise and USS Carl E. Vinson. In addition, 50 Tomahawk cruise missiles were fired from British and American submarines and four US ships, the USS McFaul, the USS John Paul Jones, the USS O'Brien, and the USS Philippine Sea. The bulk of the ordnance used in this first attack consisted of 500-pound Mark 82 bombs directed against training camps; 2,000-pound 'Joint Direct Attack Munitions' guided with Global Positioning system references were used against radars and military headquarters (Ricks and Loeb, 2001; Tyler 2001).

This was the first blast of a campaign which was to continue through to the end of the year and into 2002, as remnants of the Taliban and *Al-Qaida* in different parts of the country were systematically targeted. On 17 October, President Bush stated that the enemies' air force and air defences were being demolished, 'paving the way for friendly troops on the ground to slowly but surely tighten the net to bring them to justice' (Gordon and Shanker, 2001). While Defense Secretary Rumsfeld had at first downplayed the importance of airpower by suggesting that Afghanistan was not a 'target-rich environment' (Gordon, 2001), airpower was to prove devastating in its effects, not least because reactions by the Taliban to an opening strike often assisted the USA to identify new targets. The B-52 bombers could be tasked to strike particular targets by Special Operations Forces on the ground attached to anti-Taliban forces. Unpiloted drones (notably the RQ-1 Predator) were used to good effect, as was the AC-130 gunship, an armoured and armed aircraft which rained a blistering fire on Taliban targets. According to one report, Taliban and *Al-Qaida* prisoners confirmed that 'the precise bombing from planes they often could not hear or see broke the will of battle-hardened troops' (Schmitt and Dao, 2001). Especially terrifying was the 15,000-pound BLU-82 bomb known as the 'Daisy Cutter', used sparingly – on only four occasions, three times against Taliban frontlines, and on 9 December against a cave in eastern Afghanistan – but with great effect given the force of the pressure wave created by its detonation. Also effective, but deeply worrying because of the long-term risk they posed for civilian populations, were the CBU-103 'Combined-Effects Munitions', which scattered cluster bombs. By the time the Bonn Agreement was signed, approximately 12,000 bombs had been dropped, 6,700 of them precision-guided (Bender, Burger and Koch, 2001: 20). Estimating the number of casualties from the attacks is virtually impossible, but there is no doubt that on occasions bombs struck targets for which they were not intended, either because of mechanical defects or because of intelligence failures. One example was the village of Madoo in eastern Afghanistan (Bearak, 2001). These problems of implementation blunted some of the effects of a very careful and cautious approach to targeting, designed to ensure that the conduct of the war did not violate the law of armed conflict (see Cryer, 2002; Bellamy, 2006: 180–98).

On the ground things did not initially proceed so smoothly. Even before 7 October, there was evidence of panic in Kandahar (Moore, 2001), and once attacks began, refugees began to flee in their thousands (Neilan, 2001). A commando operation in the Kandahar area on the night of 19 October ran into difficulties when it encountered ground fire, fuelling suspicions that the Taliban may have been forewarned by ISI sympathisers of what was about to happen. Even more serious was the capture and murder by the Taliban on 26 October of the prominent moderate Pushtun Abdul Haq, a highly respected figure who many had hoped would be able to rally Pushtun support against Mulla Omar. Abdul Haq, whose wife and young son had been murdered in Peshawar some years previously, had been living in Dubai, but had returned to Afghanistan with the support of several private American activists. Again, the suspicion remains that he was betrayed by Taliban supporters in ISI. Finally, the sense began to develop among the United Front forces that the USA was reticent in striking Taliban frontlines through which they could then have driven (Rohde, 2001a), possibly because of Islamabad's obvious fear that the United Front would recover a dominant position, leaving Pakistan's Afghanistan strategy in ruins.

Nor did things proceed altogether smoothly in the political realm. Pakistan remained a problem. On 25 September, Foreign Minister Abdul Sattar warned that any move by foreign powers 'to give assistance to one side or the other in Afghanistan is a recipe for great suffering for the people of Afghanistan' (Apple, 2001). The United Front found this breathtaking in its hypocrisy, given that this was exactly what Pakistan had been doing for years. A more serious political glitch arose when Secretary of State Powell, during a visit to Islamabad, appeared at a press conference with Musharraf and seemed to suggest that moderates within the Taliban could be persuaded to join a future Afghan government (Constable, 2001). The statement was at best somewhat innocent, as the Taliban movement constituted only a tiny fragment of the Pushtun ethnic group (Schetter, 2001). It startled key allies (Chandrasekaran, 2001). It also alarmed the United Front – Dr Abdullah responded that there was 'no such thing as moderate Taliban elements' (Filkins, 2001a) – and disposed its leaders to seize any opportunities which they might encounter, rather than simply be a tool of US strategy.

They did not have long to wait, for within the space of four days in November, key cities fell to anti-Taliban forces in a cascade. Cascades occur when one event leads observers of what has happened to recalculate what is in their best interests, and they shift allegiance accordingly. This was what happened in November. On 9 November, Mazar-e Sharif fell to groups led by Dostam, the Shiite leader Ustad Mohaqqeq, and Commander Atta Muhammad. The following day, United Front forces launched simultaneous attacks across northern Afghanistan, in Khwajaghar, Eshkamesh, Baghlan, Pul-e Khumri, Nahrin, Aibak, and Bamiyan. All fell, as did Hairatan and Shibarghan to Dostam's forces. Maimana fell on 11 November, and Herat on 12 November. On the same day, the *Shura-i Nazar* forces launched an attack on the frontlines north of Kabul. Pakistani spokesmen urged the United Front not to enter Kabul – from the United Front's perspective an impertinence akin to retreating Germans urging de Gaulle not to enter Paris in August 1944 – but the following day the Taliban fled the city, looting the main currency market and the Da Afghanistan Bank as they left (Richburg, 2001). The United Front then occupied Kabul unopposed. This was criticised by Zahir Shah's adviser Abdul Sattar Sirat (*Reuters*, 13 November 2001), but in reality there was no alternative: disorder would have broken out in the city had the forces not made their move. There were scenes of ecstatic celebration in Kabul as the new forces arrived. 'Almost all people in Kabul regard the demise of the Taliban as a liberation', reported the BBC's Kate Clark (BBC *Newshour*, 13 November 2001). Huge crowds gathered shouting 'Death to the Taliban' and 'Death to Pakistan'. On 22 November, Pakistan bowed to the inevitable and closed down the Taliban Embassy in Islamabad (Glasser and Khan, 2001).

The main battles of the war were not quite over. The cascade had ended Taliban rule in most of the areas in which Pushtuns were numerically less significant, but except in Jalalabad, which fell the day after Kabul, the fall of the main Pushtun centres took a little longer. A prison riot by captured Taliban fighters in Mazar-e Sharif cost the life of a CIA agent on 25 November before it was ruthlessly suppressed (*Associated Press*, 28 November). In the north, hard-core Arab fighters had retreated into the city of Kunduz. On 26 November, after relentless pounding by B-52s, the city was taken by United Front forces: most of the remaining Taliban forces either fled or surrendered, although some intriguing reports hinted that planes, most likely from Pakistan, had been evacuating Pakistani Taliban every night for nearly two weeks with US consent (Filkins, 2001b; Hussain, 2001). There were a large number of Arabs in Kunduz, and the anti-Taliban forces showed them little mercy: if anything, their loathing of the Arabs and Pakistanis led them to treat Afghan Taliban a little less harshly than they might otherwise have done. By the time the battle for Kandahar loomed, the Taliban were on the point of collapse. Forces loyal to Hamed Karzai, who had succeeded his father Abdul Ahad Karzai as Popalzai tribal leader following the older Karzai's assassination in July 1999 formed one bloc threatening the city, from the north; in addition, forces still loyal to Haji Abdul Latif's son Gul Agha Sherzai took up positions to the east. A dispute broke out between two power holders of an earlier era, Gul Agha Sherzai and Mulla Naqib, but Karzai succeeded in brokering an agreement between the two. Finally, on 9 December, exactly nine weeks after the bombing campaign had begun, Karzai entered Kandahar in an unarmed convoy (Rohde with Schmitt, 2001). The era of Taliban rule was over. And on 16 December, Secretary of State Powell stated that 'We've destroyed al Qaeda in Afghanistan, and we have ended the role of Afghanistan as a haven for terrorist activity' (Kifner with Schmitt, 2001). The top Taliban leadership fled to Pakistan.

Why did the Taliban fall so quickly?

The swift fall of the Taliban was the result of a number of different factors. One was the loss of most support from Pakistan, which left the Taliban bereft. Their military machine was significantly affected, as was the flow of resources that could have been used to bolster support. The Taliban's religious backers in Pakistan were unable to mobilise large-scale demonstrations in support of Omar and his colleagues, of a kind that would bring real pressure to bear on Musharraf. United States' pressure on Pakistan effectively denied the Taliban and their supporters any significant fallback haven on Pakistani soil. But more significant was the weak legitimacy of the Taliban movement. Had the Taliban been an organic outgrowth of Afghan society, they would have survived much longer, and a campaign of harassment of the new power holders would have begun immediately. This simply did not happen. And most important of all was the sheer might of the USA, which confronted the Taliban with an opponent formidable beyond their darkest dreams.

The notion that Afghanistan would be a graveyard for the Americans in much the way it unquestionably proved to be for the Soviets was quite misleading. The nineteenth and twentieth centuries are unreliable guides to Afghanistan in the twenty-first, given how much change recent decades have wrought. Afghans do not automatically resent foreigners: much depends upon what foreigners actually seek to do. 'The intervention of foreign troops in any country', said Zahir Shah in an interview for the BBC, 'is something that's not easy to accept. But if it's an intervention such as we witnessed in Europe with the Second World War when the British, the Americans and the Canadians came down in France to get rid of the Nazis, this is different' (BBC Radio 4 *Today*, 25 September 2001). The internal situation in Afghanistan on the eve of the US campaign was radically different from that which prevailed in late 1979. At the time of the Soviet invasion, most of Afghanistan was *not* in crisis, and inhabitants of the Afghan countryside united to resist what they interpreted as a threat to a way of life which they valued. By contrast, in 2001, most of Afghanistan *was* in crisis, as a result of two decades of massive destruction and population displacement, augmented by Taliban repression and the effects of drought. For many Afghans, the only way left to go was up, and the US intervention created an opportunity for the reordering of the political space. Thus viewed, Operation Enduring Freedom was not an attempt to destroy their religion or their culture, but rather a welcome manifestation of an international responsibility to protect people in dire need (International Commission on Intervention and State Sovereignty, 2001: 69–75). None of this is to deny that foreign forces might outstay their welcome, but if they do, it will be as a result of how they have behaved, rather than simply what they are.

The Bonn Conference and its aftermath

The Bonn Agreement

On 3 October 2001, the UN Secretary-General appointed Lakhdar Brahimi to be his Special Representative, with 'a widened mandate entailing overall authority for the humanitarian and political endeavours of the United Nations in Afghanistan' (United Nations, 2001d: para. 2). On his shoulders fell the responsibility of trying to nurture agreement between the different groups that aspired to exercise power after the fall of the Taliban. In the first instance it was important to build consensus between Afghanistan's neighbours, Russia and the US (the so-called '6 + 2') on how to proceed. The '6 + 2' meetings had historically been notable for their insincerity, given the destructive roles which Afghanistan's neighbours had played in its politics, but the changed situation on the ground had reconfigured their interests. On 12 November, after a high-level '6 + 2' meeting in New York, the participants agreed to 'the establishment in Afghanistan of a broad-based, multi-ethnic, politically balanced, freely chosen Afghan administration representative of their aspirations and at peace with its neighbours' (United Nations, 2001d: Annex). This was admirably vague, and the challenge was to put in place a process which would come up with concrete mechanisms for transition, in line with the '6 + 2' consensus, that relevant Afghan parties would deem acceptable. With the endorsement of the Security Council, which he briefed in an open meeting on 13 November, Brahimi set about to bring together the representatives of a number of key Afghan groups – the United Front, the 'Rome Group' associated with Zahir Shah, the 'Peshawar Group' associated with Pir Gailani, and the small 'Cyprus Group' associated with Homayoun Jareer – to craft a transition.

With the strong support of the German Government, a meeting was held from 27 November to 5 December 2001 near Bonn between key representatives of these groups. No Taliban were invited (Fielden and Goodhand, 2001: 20). A parallel meeting of representatives of Afghan 'civil society' was held nearby with the support of the Swiss Peace Foundation, in order to feed ideas into the formal meeting. The negotiations between the parties proved extremely taxing. Zahir Shah was not present, and neither was Burhanuddin Rabbani, still formally the President of the Islamic State of Afghanistan. Dostam did not take part, and Haji Abdul Qadir and Karim Khalili left, protesting what they saw as lack of representation for their particular interests. Still, the participants were a stellar group by Afghan standards, with women as well as men taking part. American and European officials were active on the fringes of the meeting, with Zalmay Khalilzad and James F. Dobbins of the USA intensively engaged in conveying to the Afghan participants the desire of Washington and other key donors to see the negotiations result in an agreement.

The final result was the 5 December 'Agreement on Provisional Arrangements in Afghanistan Pending the Re-establishment of Permanent Government Institutions'. It was endorsed the following day by United Nations Security Council Resolution 1383. It was not a peace agreement, since the participants in the Bonn meeting were not at war with each other, but rather a road map for the re-establishment of rudimentary state structures. It did not provide for an Interim *Government*, but for an Interim *Administration* (with a 'chairman' and 'members' rather than 'prime minister' and 'ministers'). It consisted of a principal text and three annexes. At the beginning of the principal text, the signatories expressed their appreciation 'to the Afghan mujahidin who, over the years, have defended the independence, territorial integrity and national unity of the country and have played a major role in the struggle against terrorism and oppression, and whose sacrifice has now made them both heroes of jihad and champions of peace, stability and reconstruction of their beloved homeland, Afghanistan' and to 'His Excellency Professor Burhanuddin Rabbani for his readiness to transfer power to an interim authority which is to be established pursuant to this agreement'. They also recognised 'the need to ensure broad representation in these interim arrangements of all segments of the Afghan population, including groups that have not been adequately represented at the UN Talks on Afghanistan', and noted that 'these interim arrangements are intended as a first step toward the establishment of a broad-based, gender-sensitive, multiethnic and fully representative government, and are not intended to remain in place beyond the specified period of time'. The text then set out the substance of the agreement which had been reached. It provided that 'An Interim Authority shall be established upon the official transfer of power on 22 December 2001', consisting of 'an Interim Administration presided over by a Chairman, a Special Independent Commission for the Convening of the Emergency Loya Jirga, and a Supreme Court of Afghanistan, as well as such other courts as may be established by the Interim Administration'. Upon the official transfer of power, it went on, 'the Interim Authority shall be the repository of Afghan sovereignty, with immediate effect. As such, it shall, throughout the interim period, represent Afghanistan in its external relations and shall occupy the seat of Afghanistan at the United Nations and in its specialized agencies, as well as in other international institutions and conferences.'

It then dealt with the processes to be followed thereafter, providing that 'An Emergency Loya Jirga shall be convened within six months of the establishment of the Interim Authority. The Emergency Loya Jirga will be opened by His Majesty Mohammed Zaher, the former King of Afghanistan. The Emergency Loya Jirga shall decide on a Transitional Authority, including a broad-based transitional administration, to lead Afghanistan until such time as a fully representative government can be elected through free and fair elections to be held no later than two years from the date of the convening of the Emergency Loya Jirga.' The Interim Authority, it continued, 'shall cease to exist once the Transitional Authority has been established by the Emergency Loya Jirga'. It also provided that 'A Constitutional Loya Jirga shall be convened within eighteen months of the establishment of the Transitional Authority, in order to adopt a new constitution for Afghanistan. In order to assist the Constitutional Loya Jirga prepare the proposed Constitution, the Transitional Administration shall, within two months of its commencement and with the assistance of the United Nations, establish a Constitutional Commission.' With respect to the judicial function, it stated that 'The Interim Administration shall establish, with the assistance of the United Nations, a Judicial Commission to rebuild the domestic justice system in accordance with Islamic principles, international standards, the rule of law and Afghan legal traditions.'

It then outlined the shape of the Interim Administration, which was to be 'composed of a Chairman, five Vice Chairmen and 24 other members. Each member, except the Chairman, may head a department of the Interim Administration.' Importantly, it provided that 'No person serving as a member of the Interim Administration may simultaneously hold membership of the Special Independent Commission for the Convening of the Emergency Loya Jirga.' The Interim Administration was to be 'entrusted with the day-to-day conduct of the affairs of state', and had 'the right to issue decrees for the peace, order and good government of Afghanistan'. It also provided that 'the Interim Administration shall have full jurisdiction over the printing and delivery of the national currency and special drawing rights from international financial institutions. The Interim Administration shall establish, with the assistance of the United Nations, a Central Bank of Afghanistan that will regulate the money supply of the country through transparent and accountable procedures.' Finally, it made provision for two important Commissions: the Interim Administration was to establish, with the assistance of the United Nations, an 'independent Civil Service Commission to provide the Interim Authority and the future Transitional Authority with shortlists of candidates for key posts in the administrative departments, as well as those of governors and uluswals, in order to ensure their competence and integrity'; and an 'independent Human Rights Commission, whose responsibilities will include human rights monitoring, investigation of violations of human rights, and development of domestic human rights institutions'.

The last substantive section of the principal text dealt with the 'Special Independent Commission for the Convening of the Emergency Loya Jirga'. This body was to be 'established within one month of the establishment of the Interim Authority'. It was to 'consist of twenty-one members, a number of whom should have expertise in constitutional or customary law' and 'selected from lists of candidates submitted by participants in the UN Talks on Afghanistan as well as Afghan professional and civil society groups'. It would

> have the final authority for determining the procedures for and the number of people who will participate in the Emergency Loya Jirga. The Special Independent Commission will draft rules and procedures specifying (i) criteria for allocation of seats to the settled and nomadic population residing in the country; (ii) criteria for allocation of seats to the Afghan refugees living in Iran, Pakistan, and elsewhere, and Afghans from the diaspora; (iii) criteria for inclusion of civil society organizations and prominent individuals, including Islamic scholars, intellectuals, and traders, both within the country and in the diaspora. The Special Independent Commission will ensure that due attention is paid to the representation in the Emergency Loya Jirga of a significant number of women as well as all other segments of the Afghan population.

In Annex I, the participants in the talks requested 'the assistance of the international community in helping the new Afghan authorities in the establishment and training of new Afghan security and armed forces', and further requested the Security Council 'to consider authorizing the early deployment to Afghanistan of a United Nations mandated force' to 'assist in the maintenance of security for Kabul and its surrounding areas'. They anticipated that such a force 'could, as appropriate, be progressively expanded to other urban centres and other areas'. Annex II outlined the role of the special representative of the Secretary-General. Finally, in Annex III the participants requested that 'the United Nations and the international community take the necessary measures to guarantee the national sovereignty, territorial integrity and unity of Afghanistan as well as the non-interference by foreign countries in Afghanistan's internal affairs', and that 'the United Nations conduct as soon as possible (i) a registration of voters in advance of the general elections that will be held upon the adoption of the new constitution by the constitutional Loya Jirga and (ii) a census of the population of Afghanistan'.

The Interim Administration

The composition of the Interim Administration was one of the most contested issues in Bonn, but ultimately a consensus was reached. Abdul Sattar Sirat had long been considered a likely candidate for chairman, but his criticism of the United Front for moving into Kabul undermined his claims. Instead, the position of chairman went to the moderate Pushtun Hamed Karzai. Born in 1957, he had graduated with an MA degree from the University of Himachal Pradesh in India and spoke fluent Pushto, Persian, and English (see Mills, 2007). While the Taliban had initially sought to coopt him, he had become one of their fiercest critics, and a critic of Pakistani meddling in Afghanistan as well (Maley, 2008b). He had a longstanding interest in the complexities of tribal politics (Karzai, 1988), but an ability to work comfortably with non-Pushtun Afghans, and with the United States, where members of his family had lived for many years. The vice-chairmen included members of the different groups which had taken part in the Bonn talks. One, Dr Sima Samar, was both a woman and a Hazara, a major symbolic development given the sufferings of women and Hazaras under the Taliban. But the influence of the United Front was obvious. General Fahim was one of the vice-chairmen, and headed the Department of Defence. Younos Qanuni headed the Department of the Interior, and Dr Abdullah the Department of Foreign Affairs. Finance was headed by Hedayat Amin Arsala, a former Foreign Minister and World Bank official, Education by the well-known writer Abdul Rasul Amin, and Public Health by Dr Sohaila Seddiqi, who had won fame as both a surgeon and a general under a string of governments.

The UN Security Council on 20 December adopted Resolution 1386, which authorised the establishment of an International Security Assistance Force (ISAF), with a 'Chapter VII' enforcement mandate. It was not a 'UN peacekeeping force' under direct UN authority, or even a 'peacekeeping force' designed to stabilise a ceasefire through interposition, but – as its title suggested – a security assistance force, to secure Kabul and assist the process of developing a unified national army. Its expenses were to be met by the participating member states. The lead in this respect was taken by the United Kingdom, with Major-General John McColl as ISAF Force Commander. Within a short space of time it became clear that the force would be largely European.

The Interim Administration took office, as scheduled, at a dignified ceremony in Kabul on 22 December attended by nearly 2,000 men and women, with British Royal Marines patrolling outside. An empty chair with Massoud's photograph on it stood at the centre of the stage. Around it sat numerous people whose lives had intertwined with his – Rabbani, Mojadiddi, Pir Gailani, Dostam, Ambassador Brahimi – as well as General Tommy R. Franks, who had commanded the US campaign that wiped out the Taliban, and the Foreign Ministers of Iran, India, and Pakistan. Karzai was sworn in by the acting Chief Justice. Ismail Khan arrived during the ceremony, and Karzai greeted him with the salutation 'My brother'. At the end, Rabbani signed a transfer-of-power certificate, and described Afghanistan as 'thirsty for peace' (*Associated Press*, 22 December 2001). The Foreign Minister of Belgium, Louis Michel, said, 'I am sure that Mr Massoud is proud of his nation today' (Rohde, 2001b).

One event darkened the day. The night before, at Sato Kandaw, 15 miles south of Gardez, US bombers strafed a convoy of vehicles, leaving 65 dead. The USA maintained that it was a group of Bin Laden supporters. Locals maintained that they were tribal elders heading for Kabul to attend the swearing in ceremony. Ruling Afghanistan was not going to be easy. But the Bonn Agreement, focused on state-building rather than a division of spoils, constituted a promising start, indeed the best hope that Afghanistan had had for many a long year. Finally, there was light at the end of the tunnel.

12

Post-Taliban Afghanistan

The overthrow of the Taliban regime confronted Afghanistan with a substantial new set of challenges, and the years which followed were largely devoted to meeting them. Yet the outcomes, perhaps inevitably, were mixed, with a notable gulf between the formal requirements of the 2001 Bonn Agreement, and the wider needs of ordinary Afghans in Afghanistan itself. Positive developments such as improvements in the position of at least some women (Azerbaijani-Moghaddam, 2006; Azerbaijani-Moghaddam, 2007), a major currency reform, the drafting of a new constitution, and the holding of presidential and parliamentary elections were interspersed with darker developments such as major bombings, serious attempts on the life of the president in 2002 and 2008, the brazen assassination of Vice-President Haji Abdul Qadir on 6 July 2002, and mounting violence in the south and east of the country. The story of the years since 2001 is one of notable achievements mixed with tragically missed opportunities, often as a result of short-sighted decisions taken beyond Afghanistan's borders. By April 2008, Afghanistan was once again a focus of international alarm, dominating discussion at President George W. Bush's final NATO Summit held in the Romanian capital of Bucharest (Yaqub and Maley, 2008; Maley, 2008c). The hopes that Afghanistan's problems would rapidly be solved had proved to be ill-founded, and the threat of a sudden upsurge of violence continued to hover like an ominous storm-cloud over the daily lives of many Afghan people. One of the tragedies of this situation is that most of the problems that have afflicted Afghanistan's transition were identified early in the process by analysts, commentators, and Afghans themselves (see Maley, 2003–2004; Rubin, 2006a). It was Afghanistan's misfortune that those who had the capacity to respond effectively to these emerging threats for the most part failed to do so. The perils of wishful thinking have rarely been so prominently on display.

This chapter discusses key developments in the period since the over-throw of the Taliban regime, and maps the successes and failures in post-Taliban Afghanistan. It is divided into nine sections. The first sets out some of the particular challenges of the post-Taliban period. The second examines the complexities and idiosyncrasies of post-Taliban politics. The third deals with issues of reconstruction and development, and the fourth and fifth with challenges of security and security-sector reform. The three following sections address Afghanistan's relations with the wider world, including the United States and its partners in NATO; with Pakistan; and with Iran. The final section offers some observations on factors shaping future directions which Afghanistan might take.

Challenges in post-Taliban Afghanistan

Given the tortured history of Afghanistan in the years with which this book is primarily concerned, it is hardly surprising that the chal-lenges which it faced after 2001 proved daunting (see Maley, 2001b, 2002b, 2006a). Post-conflict transitions of their very nature are likely to be extremely complicated (Maley, 2006b). However, the post-2001 era brought an additional challenge with which a range of actors were to struggle, namely that of coordinating the varying strategic and tact-ical objectives of a range of different actors. This in turn gave rise to major questions as to the nature of sovereignty (Ghani and Lockhart, 2008). While President Bush was happy to celebrate the emergence of Afghanistan as a young democracy, the reality of the situation on the ground was that President Karzai of Afghanistan was more subject to the whims of foreign donors than of any Afghan political institution. The whole question of whose interests Afghanistan's transition has actually been driven to serve remains a troubling one.

Reconstituting the state

The reconstitution of the Afghan state – involving both the design of new institutions, and their progressive legitimation – was and is a central requirement of an effective transition, something which the participants at the Bonn conference had readily accepted. Such a process, however, is a more profound challenge at the conceptual level than is often rec-ognized. Too often, popular discussion of 'state-building' can proceed as if there is a 'one-size-fits-all' model of 'the state' that can readily be applied in all circumstances. Such a view is highly misleading, and overlooks the diversity of historical state structures (Fukuyama, 2004). States can vary significantly in both what they attempt to do, and how they go about doing things. A standardized model of 'the state' also overlooks the need for some 'fit' between state structures and local political and cultural expectations if a new state is to take root. If this were simply an analytical misconception, it could be addressed without too much difficulty. However, the problem runs deeper: to a significant degree, actors in the wider world approaching a transition such as Afghanistan's carry with them expectations that a state-building process will lead to state structures with which they can comfortably interact. This tends to privilege the position of bureaucracies based in a capital city staffed by English-speaking officials familiar with the 'international community', at the expense of investment in structures of local government working hand-in-hand with locally legitimate political actors and governance structures. In the long run, this can lead to serious frustration, and even a crisis of legitimacy (Suhrke, 2006).

The rebuilding of trust and the establishment of security

A second challenge for post-Taliban Afghanistan has been the rebuilding of trust (see Misztal, 1996; Maley, 2003a; Tilly, 2005). When a country has gone through decades of conflict, trust between those who lack face-to-face or lineage relationships is a likely casualty. This can militate against the achievement of a consensually unified elite. In Afghanistan, levels of trust have long been low: Afghan politics has had too large a share of treachery and duplicity for distrust to seem anything but rational. Where trust is limited, it is important to facilitate an environment in which people can re-experience the benefits of trusting and being trusted, and in which the costs of misplaced trust will not be too high. A neutral security force – supporting an interim government, but neutral as between its factional components – offers one way of minimizing those costs. Just as important, however, is the re-establishment of a *policing* capacity. Community policing is a device by which order and justice are guaranteed in local communities, and is designed to give substance to the notion of the rule of law (see McFarlane and Maley, 2001: 186–8). Once the environment is a safer one, working together for the achievement of some superordinate goal can rebuild trust between individuals (Leslie, 1995). Social capital does not result from *diktat*: it is a product of iterated engagement between actors who learn that it is beneficial to cooperate (Fukuyama, 2001).

The problem of rebuilding trust is intimately related to the bringing of security to the lives of ordinary people. A state that delivers an atmosphere of ambient security is well placed to win generalized normative support; a state that is incapable of doing so is likely to be regarded with scepticism and even suspicion. Yet the challenge of rebuilding security institutions is often profound. Effective military and police forces are not made simply by training personnel in basic skills; it is equally important that there be adequate middle-management structures, and an ethos of loyalty to civilian political authority rather than to other social forces with some claim to legitimacy.

Establishing foundations for reconstruction

A third challenge has been to lay foundations for reconstruction after decades of conflict. This is a multilayered challenge. Again, a basic prerequisite for reconstruction is security, especially a sense of security in the everyday lives of ordinary people. If the climate in a country remains deeply insecure, then distrust will remain pervasive, investment opportunities will stagnate (at least in the legal sectors of the economy), and people will have no confidence in the justice system, since insecurity arises from the power of others to act outside the law with impunity. And if such a sense of insecurity prevails for any length of time, it will likely undermine the legitimacy both of new political arrangements and new rulers (Rubin, 2005). But a further dimension of the challenge of reconstruction is to devise coherent plans for reconstruction, and effective mechanisms for implementing them. Here, it is important to note that in transitions from autocracy there are fundamental questions about the roles and responsibilities of the state, as well as about the resourcing of state policies, to which there are no uncontentious answers; political theory is replete with vigorous debates over just how such issues should be addressed. One of the responsibilities of new rulers is to develop a vision of how to take a country forward, and inspire the population to support this vision. This is something easier said than done.

Retaining international attention

For people caught up in major transitions, almost nothing can be more important than the question of whether the transition succeeds or not. Unfortunately, not everyone cares about Afghanistan as much as Afghans do. A sad lesson of history is that the concerns of one state can easily be overshadowed by developments in another. The immediate cause of the outbreak of the Second World War was the German invasion of Poland in September 1939, but by the end of the war in Europe in May 1945, it was beyond the capacity of the United States and United Kingdom to resist the desire of the Soviet Union to establish a Soviet-controlled regime in Warsaw. It was more than four decades before Poland became free again. General de Gaulle once remarked that Great Powers are cold monsters. He might well have added that they have limited attention spans as well. A vast challenge for Afghanistan in 2001 was simply to retain the attention of the major powers.

Politics in post-Taliban Afghanistan

Post-Bonn politics has passed through a number of different phases. In the immediate aftermath of the Bonn meeting, the United Front leaders and especially Massoud's successor Muhammad Qasim Fahim held dominant positions, not only because of formal office – Defence Minister in Fahim's case – but because forces loyal to them controlled Kabul. This led to much talk of a problem of Pushtun alienation (International Crisis Group, 2003a). But over time this changed. International forces took over control of the capital, and within barely two years, the United Front was on the defensive politically. The popular election of Karzai as president in 2004 provided him with the opportunity to reorganize his Cabinet, and soon thereafter it very much bore his stamp, with most key positions by late 2008 – Finance Minister, Defence Minister, Interior Minister, Education Minister, and National Security Adviser – held by members of his own Pushtun ethnic group. Indeed, as Schiewek noted in 2007, 'In a gradual process starting from the Emergency Loya Jirga of mid-2002, the biggest share of the cabinet positions and key ministries was acquired by educated returnees from the pre-war establishment, who happened to be nearly all Pashtuns. By December 2004 most power positions within the cabinet had been occupied by Pushtuns. Also a majority of the governors and the biggest groups of officers in the army and police are now Pashtun' (Schiewek, 2007: 211). Significant elite fragmentation became the order of the day, and from late 2005, the newly elected parliament, in which the United Front figure Younos Qanuni became Speaker of the Lower House, was often at odds with the president and his circle. This tension was not what the international backers of the Bonn Agreement had hoped to see.

Strategies of legitimation

The Bonn Agreement was a very sophisticated compact, much more subtle than a number of its critics appreciated (Maley, 2008e). It did not overlook issues of political legitimacy, as some observers have claimed (Starr, 2006), but it *was* premised on the notions that no single strategy of political legitimation would be salient for all components of the Afghan population, and that it would therefore be necessary to weave together a range of different strategies to exploit their combined effects (Maley, 2004). Thus the traditional authority of Zahir Shah, who returned to live in Kabul in 2002 and remained there for most of the period until his death in 2007, was placed at the service of a charismatic and personable Chairman of the Interim Administration, with the Loya Jirgas designed to add both traditional authority and the fruits of consultation with diverse sectors of Afghan society. In a formal sense, the objectives that were set in Bonn were met. An Emergency Loya Jirga from 11 to 19 June 2002 converted the Interim Administration into a Transitional Administration; a Constitutional Loya Jirga held from 14 December 2003 to 4 January 2004 led to the adoption of a new Afghan Constitution; and elections were successfully held on 9 October 2004 and 18 September 2005, with the former confirming Hamid Karzai as president with 55.4 per cent of the popular vote, and the latter putting in place a new Lower House (*Wolesi Jirga*) in a bicameral parliament, as well as establishing the membership of Provincial Councils.

But that said, the outcome of this exercise ultimately proved to be somewhat ambiguous (Maley, 2008h), and there are lessons for future transition processes that can be drawn from Afghanistan's experience (Maley, 2009b). Legitimacy in a fraught and fractious situation will be highly dependent upon the capacity of a new system, and of power-holders within it, actually to deliver the goods. In consolidated systems, institutions have a strength of their own that can ride out weak performance. But in fragile systems in transition, this is not the case. Institutions move through phases of infancy and adolescence before they reach maturity, and these early phases are beset with dangers. Infant institutions can easily be strangled in their cradles. The Emergency Loya Jirga showed that tensions between different Afghan groups remained high (Rashid, 2008: 138–42), with the Afghan-born US special envoy Dr Zalmay Khalizad intervening somewhat tactlessly to head off the schemes of partisans of former king Zahir. Furthermore, within the Afghan political elite, different ideas about the sources of legitimacy were to be found. United Front supporters and other former Mujahideen, especially non-Pushtuns, saw their power-claims as legitimated by the roles they had played in resisting militarily both the Soviet Union during the 1980s and the Pakistan-backed Taliban before September 2001 (Bhatia, 2007). This cut little weight with 'technocrats' who had returned from Western countries in which legitimacy was generated by legal-rational procedures, let alone émigré Pushtun nationalists.

Pathologies of new state structures at central and local levels

The Bonn process, for all its subtlety, contained three significant flaws. The first was that the Interim Administration was established not on the basis of a root-and-branch appraisal of what kind of state Afghanistan required, but rather through the allocation to political factions of different departments almost as rewards for participation in the process (see Dobbins, 2008: 96). This ensured a degree of ethnic balance in the Administration, but set the scene for dysfunctional central politics. Since most Afghan factions were patronage networks rather than 'parties' in the Western sense of the term, this laid the foundations for rampant nepotism – which widespread distrust of all but immediate associates was in any case likely to encourage. Furthermore, since most 'departments' existed largely on paper and donor funds were going to be needed to build them up, new 'ministers' had strong incentives to denigrate and discredit their competitors as a way of increasing their own share of the donor dollar. This set the scene for poisonous interagency relations in Kabul, at the very moment at which cooperation and coordination were particularly important.

The second flaw – not something for which the Bonn participants could be blamed, since it lay beyond their control – was that the Agreement of itself could not guarantee security throughout Afghanistan. The deployment of ISAF was designed to address this deficit. The rapid despatch of ISAF troops to different parts of the country was strongly recommended by Ambassador Brahimi on behalf of the UN, and by a number of other well-informed observers as well (Rashid, 2002; International Crisis Group, 2002; Olson, 2002). However, in a blunder of horrendous proportions, this was publicly blocked by the Bush Administration (Sipress, 2002), with some backing from United Front circles (Saikal, 2006a: 528). There could have been no move more calculated to undermine the positive momentum of Afghanistan's transition. In many parts of the country, Karzai – denied the benefit of ISAF expansion – had little option but to offer state positions to thuggish potential spoilers as a way of averting immediate spoiler action. The long-run effect, however, was to contaminate the reputation of the state as a result of its ostensible association with the predatory behaviour of such figures, and to disenfranchise traditional tribal leaderships (see Chayes, 2006).

The third flaw, perhaps unavoidable given the politics of the time, was that the process inaugurated in Bonn accommodated a number of political actors who in other circumstances might have been strong candidates for prosecution for crimes against humanity. The whole question of justice in a transitional period is a difficult one to handle, since it sets an ethic of absolutes against an ethic of consequences (Maley, 2008: 106), and international experience of promoting transitional justice has been less than satisfactory. But it is quite clear that impunity for offenders can send wretched signals about what kind of behaviour is acceptable (Mani, 2003; Niland, 2004). Nonetheless, the problems of impunity and transitional justice cannot easily be detached from a wider issue, namely rebuilding the rule of law through a clean and effective judiciary and penal system (Maley, 2007a). This is yet to happen in Afghanistan, which is why attempts to deal with some dark figures from the past, such as Asadullah Sarwari, proved to be farcical (Human Rights Watch, 2006).

The Afghan state has also suffered through its association with corruption. This is often seen as a product of individual moral failing, but it is more plausible to see it as reflecting the complicated incentive structures which Afghanistan's transition has created, and the stark lesson of decades of conflict which have fostered short-term rather than long-term thinking, and immediate self-interest rather than altruism (Maley, 2008d). The phenomenon of corruption is complex (see Alatas, 1990; Johnston, 2005; Uslaner, 2008), but involves unjust enrichment through exploitation of office and abuse of power. As Jonathan Goodhand has pointed out, 'not all forms of corruption are equally harmful or equally wrong in the eyes of most Afghans... It seems probable the people will tolerate corruption if the state can deliver some tangible benefits to them and their families' (Goodhand, 2008: 416). Pinning down the exact nature and scale of corruption is more difficult. There is no doubt that corruption is perceived within Afghanistan to be a major problem, but ordinary citizens typically see corruption as most extensive at the national level, rather than at local or provincial levels where they have direct experience (see Asia Foundation, 2004; Asia Foundation, 2006; Asia Foundation, 2007, Asia Foundation, 2008). This may reflect the power of Afghanistan's free media in reporting widely on dramatic cases of abuse of power, such as the building of glitzy residences in the Kabul suburb of Sherpur for powerful political figures (Reeves, 2003). The judiciary has long been seen as particularly compromised; certainly there is abundant anecdotal evidence, especially from Kabul, as to how difficult it is to make use of the court system to redress any kind of grievance without having to pay bribes (Watson, 2006).

Constitutional reform

The adoption of a new Afghan Constitution by a Constitutional Loya Jirga was seen as a major device by which to ensure Afghan 'ownership' of a new political system. Constitution-drafting is a complex exercise (Lane, 1996; Lutz, 2006), and an elaborate process was put in place to ensure expert advice was available to a Constitutional Commission of 35 members. The Constitution (*Qanun-e Asasi-i Afghanistan*) was ultimately finalized by an assembly of 502 delegates, most elected through an indirect but popular process, but some appointed by Karzai (see Rubin, 2004). The final text was an impressive document replete with many human rights guarantees, although there was some risk to these guarantees in Article 3 which provided rather vaguely that no law could contravene the 'beliefs and provisions' (*motaqidat wa ahkam*) of Islam (for the full text see Yassari, 2005: 269–329). It was particularly notable for guaranteeing substantial female representation in the lower house of parliament.

However, both the process by which the Constitution was drafted and the broader shape of the political system it ordained were to have longer-term consequences. One effect of the Constitutional Loya Jirga was to heighten tensions along lines of ethnicity within the Afghan political elite. It broadly pitted former Mujahideen, many of them non-Pushtuns, against returnee technocrats, many of them of Pushtun background, with the former advocating a parliamentary system, and the latter a presidential model. Ultimately, it was the advocates of a presidential system who prevailed, but at considerable cost (Schmeidl, 2007: 78–9). Tensions at the final stage of the drafting process were very high (Gall, 2004), and ultimately the delegates appointed by Karzai were crucial in ensuring that his preferred model was adopted.

The presidential system adopted in the constitution proved to have severe limitations (Saikal and Maley, 2008; Ruttig, 2008). The strength of presidential systems is that they provide an obvious national 'leader', and a single point of executive contact for the wider world (Maley, 2003b). However, presidential systems have notable weaknesses as well. In fractured or divided societies, they risk polarizing political life, since they create one winner and many losers. More seriously, in Afghanistan the position of president is perhaps too exacting for any occupant to perform satisfactorily. An Afghan president is not just symbolic Head of State, but also heads the executive government, and in addition becomes the ultimate point of appeal in the event of rivalry or clashes between subordinate actors and officials. If things go wrong, everyone knows whom to blame. In practice, President Karzai proved a personally attractive and conciliatory figure, notably courageous and keen to address the needs of long-marginalized groups such as women and ethnic Hazaras. However, he had grown up politically in a state-free realm, which meant that he was dependent on others for detailed policy development, and he was poorly served by the circle around him, in which even former Hekmatyar supporters were to be found. A mixed system with not just a president but also a prime minister based in the parliament might have served Afghanistan better.

Elections

The two sets of elections held in Afghanistan were a near-miracle from a logistical point of view, and did much to boost confidence about the country's prospects. The presidential election saw some minor technical problems relating to the mistaken use of non-indelible markers instead of the indelible ink designed to stain voters' fingers and prevent multiple voting, but while this caused a flurry of concern on polling day, it was not remotely on a scale that could have affected the final outcome.

The story of the legislative elections was different. Here, significant problems flowed from the choice of a notoriously perverse electoral system (see Bowler, Farrell, and Pettitt, 2005), the so-called 'Single Non-Transferable Vote', or SNTV. Electoral systems matter (see Rae, 1967; Maley and Saikal, 1992; Powell, 2000; Reilly, 2001; Norris, 2004; Reilly, 2006). Under SNTV, seats were allocated to provinces in accordance with their estimated populations, voters simply voted for a single candidate at province level, and seats were allocated to individual candidates in order of the number of votes received. The perversity of such a system is that if, for example, a strong, moderate candidate emerged in a province with ten seats and won 90 per cent of the vote, he or she would still only win one seat. The remaining 90 per cent of *seats* would be allocated to candidates who *in total* secured only 10 per cent of the votes. Much critical commentary has surrounded the question of how this system came to be chosen (see Reynolds, 2006; Johnson, 2006; Suhrke, 2008a), but one underlying consideration seems to have been President Karzai's hostility (shared by many Afghans) to political parties. It is very difficult for parties to flourish under SNTV unless they have extraordinarily well-disciplined blocs of supporters, and the likely outcome of an election which uses it is a kaleidoscopic legislature with other bases of identity such as ethnicity being activated to try to create cohesive groupings. This was what eventuated in 2005 (Ruttig, 2006: 43) A detailed post-election study pointed to grave fragmentation, with some very unsavoury characters successfully exploiting the peculiarities of the system to obtain seats (Wilder, 2005: 14)

At one level, Afghanistan's elections were a triumph. No one who witnessed the queues of voters waiting to cast their ballots on the early morning of 9 October 2004 could have failed to be moved by the spectacle, and there is an enormous amount to be said for political processes that allow ordinary people to choose and change their rulers without bloodshed. However, elections on their own cannot guarantee a democratic political culture, statesmanlike elite, or the institutionalization of political processes (Maley, 1995b). Unless things go well after voting concludes, they may end up fuelling cynicism about what democratization really has to offer (see Tadjbakhsh and Schoiswohl, 2008). And victory can blind victors, or their influential backers, to the need for inclusiveness in their choice of colleagues. Following Karzai's election as president, he restructured his Cabinet by replacing the dynamic but explosive Finance Minister (Dr Ashraf Ghani), the Defence Minister (Fahim), and ultimately the Foreign Minister (Dr Abdullah). The consequence was that by 2006, very few of those figures who had been most actively opposed to the Taliban before September 2001 had any roles to play in the government. The removal of Fahim was understandable, given his disposition to make thinly veiled threats against other Afghan political actors, but the replacement of Dr Abdullah, an exceptionally effective voice for Afghanistan in the wider world, went one step too far. The result was an increasingly bitter political environment in Kabul, at the very time when growing security threats made a truly national approach to government more important.

Reconstruction and development

The tasks of reconstruction that confronted Afghanistan in the post-Bonn environment were vast and daunting (United Nations Development Program, 2004). Very little had been done between 1992 and 2001 to address the consequences even of the Soviet–Afghan war, and significant further damage had accrued in the post-communist era, especially in Kabul. However, what made the situation even more pressing was the likelihood, very swiftly realized, that the overthrow of the Taliban would lead to significant, rapid return of refugees. This indeed occurred, emburdening the new authorities with responsibilities well beyond their capacity to cope (see Turton and Marsden, 2002). Nonetheless, many Afghans threw themselves with gusto into the process of rebuilding their country, and scored a range of striking achievements in areas such as GDP growth, reductions in infant mortality, the improvement of access to basic health care, and the building of schools.

The process of reconstruction, however, was notably tangled. What one witnessed in the months and years that followed Bonn was a multiplicity of agents seeking in a somewhat perplexing and confused environment to achieve a range of desirable outcomes, some of them mutually incompatible and many of them either having unanticipated consequences or involving the sacrifice of one good in order to attain another. In a real sense this also highlighted the tension between the donor desire for rapid, demonstrable progress, and the Afghan desire for capacity-building and the expansion of local sovereignty. Perhaps this is the standard story of complex responses to complex situations (see Jenkins and Plowden, 2006), but it inevitably complicates the process of legitimating new ways of doing things on the basis of performance. However, this experience pointed to a deeper challenge as well. 'Reconstruction' is not a simple technical exercise. It involves choices or decisions about what reconstruction should involve, how it should be resourced, and by what agents it should be implemented. The very making of these choices will create both winners and losers. As a result, reconstruction will almost always be a contentious process, shot through with politics from top to bottom. It can stir up tensions which otherwise might have remained dormant. Astri Suhrke, for example, has pointed to similarities between post-Bonn Afghanistan and the experience of Afghanistan under Amanullah, where a top-down programme of rapid modernization did not resonate sufficiently with its intended beneficiaries (Suhrke, 2007; see also Suhrke and Strand, 2005).

Agents of reconstruction

The agents of reconstruction in Afghanistan have been particularly diverse. The Afghan state has been one agent. A whole range of central ministries and agencies in Kabul have had reconstruction activities of some sort as an explicit part of their responsibilities, and others are charged with handling matters such as health and education where reconstruction of damaged facilities and retraining of staff is necessary

if any progress is to be made. But even here, recalling Migdal's cat-
egorization of different levels of the state, it is important to recognize
the diverse ways in which components of the state can impact on reconstruction (see Evans, Manning, Osmani, Tully and Wilder, 2004). Much
implementation must proceed in areas far from Kabul, as it is in those
areas that the majority of the population dwells, and this means that
the condition of sub-national governance in Afghanistan has been a
matter of real concern. Furthermore, specific policies can themselves
involve creative development of institutions to facilitate effective implementation of what particular communities want. For example, through
the so-called 'National Solidarity Program', grants of up to US$60,000
have been made available to 'Community Development Councils' which
actually function as a point of interstitial engagement of state and society
(Boesen, 2004).

But the state is paralleled by a range of other actors. These include
components of the United Nations system; the International Committee
of the Red Cross; international NGOs; local Afghan NGOs; and a large
number of private commercial contractors. Indeed, 'paralleled' may be too
gentle a word to use, for a large proportion of funding for 'state-like'
activity in Afghanistan is provided directly by donors to such 'non-state'
actors, while the Afghan Government must rely on its own revenue rais-
ing, and more limited funding through the Afghanistan Reconstruction
Trust Fund, for its recurrent and developmental spending. The UN system, NGOs, and private contractors function almost as a 'second civil
service' (World Bank, 2005: 47), drawing skilled Afghans away from
the 'real' state with offers of pay and conditions that the state itself cannot hope to match. The performance of these non-state actors has varied from the first-rate to the appalling, with a particular problem being
either projects that are unsustainable, or projects that involve shoddy
workmanship, often at extravagant cost (see Stephens and Ottaway,
2005; Nawa, 2006).

One fortunate development in Afghanistan's reconstruction was the
energetic role played by Dr Ashraf Ghani, Finance Minister between
June 2002 and December 2004. He and his team put great store on developing an effective budget process, which was a gargantuan achievement
given the ruins that the Taliban had left behind (see Carnahan, 2004:
123). Across a wide range of issues, including a remarkable currency
reform process, tax reform, treasury management, and banking law, they
laid a foundation for effective fiscal management (see Ghani, Lockhart,
Nehan and Massoud, 2007). The fruits of this process are still being
seen: a 2008 appraisal of public financial management in Afghanistan by

a World Bank team reported very positively on what had been achieved. Particularly striking was an improvement in domestic revenue collection, which increased from 4.7 per cent of GDP in 2004–2005 to 7.5 per cent of GDP in 2006–2007 (World Bank, 2008b: 3). However, to put this in context it is important to note that in the years 2002–2004, approximately 66 per cent of funding bypassed the state, and by the 2007–2008 fiscal year the figure was still approximately 56 per cent (see Ghani, Lockhart, Nehan and Massoud, 2007: 158; World Bank, 2008b: 49). As the World Bank put it, 'some recurrent spending and most public investment occurs outside national budgetary channels and procedures ... Donors are not subject, through their donor agreements, to plan, report and operate in line with Government procedures' (World Bank, 2008b: 49).

Donor priority-setting and national sovereignty

This has given rise to what some have called the sovereignty gap, but it could equally be seen as a significant pathology of Afghanistan's democratic transformation. Responsibility without power inevitably complicates the life of a leader, and this is substantially what President Karzai has faced. However, several factors complicate the search for a solution to this dilemma. The first is the absorptive capacity of the state. It is by no means clear that the various ministries of the new state are sufficiently equipped with either the administrative systems or the expertise to manage complex programmes effectively. The second is the stringency of audit and appropriation requirements in donor countries, which may act as a barrier to the transfer of funds to infant bureaucracies without established records of effective financial management. It is also the case that in a number of Afghan ministries, the dysfunctional bureaucratic procedures of the past rose like ghosts to blight the prospects for reform. In many spheres of official life, it is still necessary to acquire signatures of approval from a wide range of offices and officials, and this not only makes for excruciatingly slow processes, but also multiplies the prospect that at some point one will be asked to pay a bribe. Some notable progress has been made in administrative reform (World Bank, 2008a), but there is still a long way to go.

   The formal framework within which reconstruction and development have been attempted comprises the *Afghanistan National Development Strategy* and the *Afghanistan Compact*, both of which were formally endorsed at a donor's conference held in London on 31 January–1 February 2006 and re-endorsed in the Paris Declaration of

12 June 2008 (United Nations, 2008: para. 3) This framework involved comprehensive coverage of security, governance, the rule of law, human rights, and economic and social development, and a Joint Coordination and Monitoring Board (JCMB) to monitor performance and achievements. By 2006 the gulf between donor promises and donor action had become achingly obvious. The performance of donors in the early post-Bonn years was quite instructive. Figures compiled by the Center on International Cooperation at New York University showed that while a total of US$5.2 billion had been pledged for Afghanistan in January 2002, the total funds committed by May 2003 came to only US$2.6 billion, reconstruction disbursements came to only US$1.6 billion, and the value of projects actually completed was only US$192 million (Rubin, Hamidzada, and Stoddard, 2003: 19). Furthermore, the US *Emergency Supplemental Appropriations Act for the Reconstruction of Iraq and Afghanistan* of November 2003 approved just US$1.2 billion for reconstruction in Afghanistan, a figure dwarfed by the US$18.6 billion which the same bill appropriated for reconstruction in Iraq – a measure of the shift in US priorities during 2003.

By 2004, even US government agencies were recognizing the scale of the problem (General Accounting Office, 2004). In preparation for a major meeting held in Berlin on 31 March–1 April 2004, the Afghan government circulated an extremely detailed set of proposals which were directed, in Finance Minister Ghani's vivid phrase, at lifting the people of Afghanistan to the level of 'genteel poverty'. The central conclusion of the report was that 'Afghanistan will require total external assistance in the range of US$27.6 billion over seven years on commitment basis. A minimum of US$6.3 billion of external financing will be required in the form of direct support to the national budget – preferably more, since budget support helps build the State and its legitimacy' (Government of Afghanistan 2004: 11). Donor promises fell far short of this, totalling only $8.2 billion for the period March 2004–March 2007, and $4.4 billion for March 2004–March 2005. In early 2006, the Afghan government published the new *Afghanistan National Development Strategy*, building on the detailed analysis in the 2004 proposals. The conclusions were stark. Over five years, Afghanistan would require US$18.865 billion to cover development needs; but domestic revenue was anticipated to amount to US$4.489 billion, not enough even to cover non-development recurrent costs of US$5.453 billion. Therefore US$19.829 billion, or just under US$4 billion per year over five years, would be required in the form of assistance from the wider world. Nothing like this was pledged. Future donor commitments made at the London conference totalled a mere

US\$10.5 billion, barely half the figure Afghanistan needed (Gardiner 2006). This arguably has left Afghanistan in the worst of both worlds: under-funded but dependent.

Reconstruction in the provinces: building a civil economy

A 'civil economy' is a 'market economy operating within a clear legal framework' (Rose, 1992: 14). Afghanistan's economy is much more complex, with legal, in-kind, extralegal, irregular and illegal elements all in play (McKechnie, 2007: 103–4). The less formal sectors of the economy, embracing such activities as the granting of credit and the transfer of funds through the so-called *hawala* system, are very important lubricants of economic activity (see Maimbo, 2003; Fischer, 2005: 78; Klijn and Pain, 2007). However, to survive in what are extremely difficult times, Afghans have had to engage in a wide range of economic activities, often in an environment in which inadequate protection of property rights works against entrepreneurialism (see Wily, 2004; Beall and Schütte, 2006). In many parts of Afghanistan, local economic conditions have driven farmers to augment their cereal crops with plantings of a much more controversial plant, the opium poppy. This has had enormous ramifications for security, and increasingly, the fear that Afghanistan might become a 'narco-state' is being given voice.

Security threats in post-Taliban Afghanistan

Insecurity in Afghanistan since 2001 has come in many forms. It ranges from the threat to Afghanistan as a territorial unit posed by insurgents who want to deny the central government effective control of Afghanistan's territory, to the threat of violence that haunts the everyday lives of many ordinary people. Between these extremes are many different variants. The following remarks seek to identify some of the key agents of insecurity in Afghanistan, and to outline the kind of threats that they pose. It is important at the outset to note that not all armed groups in Afghanistan are security threats. Some may provide security, although it is also the case that a group may simultaneously offer security to one part of the population and threats to some other. The scholar Michael Bhatia, who himself was tragically slain by an improvised explosive device in May 2008, highlighted three ideal-typical armed groups: political-military organisations, community militias, and warlords and strongmen (Bhatia and Sedra, 2008: 73). I shall come to some of these shortly, but first it is necessary to deal with some externally based sources of insecurity.

Al-Qaida

It is notoriously the case that Osama Bin Laden managed to escape the attempts to apprehend him after the September 2001 attacks (Riedel, 2008). He slipped through the Coalition's fingers at Tora Bora in December 2001 (Katzman, 2005: 25). For years thereafter he was to taunt his pursuers through audiotapes and videotapes released to news outlets. Scholars and analysts have differed, sometimes fiercely, over whether *Al-Qaida* remains an organized threat with global reach. However, given the near-universal suspicion that Bin Laden found safe refuge in the tribal areas of Pakistan, there seems little doubt that he and his associates remain a threat to the nearby territory of Afghanistan. Hodes and Sedra argue that 'Contrary to the commonly held view that al-Qaeda has become merely an idea or brand-name, it is still extremely active in Afghanistan, and the rise of suicide attacks there bears the hallmarks of al-Qaeda's tactics' (Hodes and Sedra, 2007: 31). Suicide bombing in Afghanistan was the subject of a meticulous UN study in 2007. It showed that from 2005 the tactic had become increasingly common, and that attackers were often young, poorly educated, and drawn from madrassas in Pakistan – very much the profile of the original Taliban (United Nations, 2007: 85–91). The co-location of Taliban and *Al-Qaida* in the tribal areas has proved highly combustible.

The Neo-Taliban

The emergence of the 'Neo-Taliban' proved very destabilizing (see Giustozzi, 2007; Tarzi, 2008), and a disaster for ordinary Afghans. A typical report of Taliban activity in 2004 gives one a sense of what was involved:

> KABUL, June 28 (AFP) – Most of the 16 people killed in a bloody attack by suspected Taliban in south-central Afghanistan were recently returned refugees who wanted to participate in upcoming elections, the government said Monday.
> The group was pulled from their vehicle in Uruzgan province on Friday and shot dead, apparently for carrying voter registration cards, according to officials.

The Neo-Taliban incorporated not just the remnants of the old Taliban under the leadership of Mulla Omar (International Crisis Group, 2006b: 9), but also Gulbuddin Hekmatyar and his supporters; a network operating from the Parachinar region led by Serajuddin Haqqani, son of the Mujahideen commander Jalaluddin Haqqani; and *Al-Qaida* elements (Hoffman and Jones, 2008: 47–50) The rhetoric of these groups was directed against the foreign presence in Afghanistan, the effects of air strikes on civilians, and state corruption (International Crisis Group, 2008b). The Taliban were not able to create havoc throughout Afghanistan. As in the past, they secured far less traction among non-Pushtuns than in areas in which Pushtuns predominated. However, they proved quite adept in allying themselves with disaffected elements, or at exploiting local grievances, particularly those of non-elite Ghilzai Pushtuns directed against Durranis, and at stoking up grievances (for example by supporting Ghilzai nomads in 2008 seeking to take their flocks into parts of the Hazarajat). By doing this, and by engaging in asymmetric attacks against international forces using improvised explosive devices, they were able to create a mounting sense of insecurity, especially in provinces such as Helmand, Kandahar, Uruzgan, Ghazni, and Paktia. This did not win much support from locals, but it did disincline them from throwing their weight strongly behind the local agents of the Karzai government. In Afghanistan, it rarely pays to back what might be a loser.

'Warlords'

Another kind of insecurity in post-Bonn Afghanistan was sheeted home to actors described as 'warlords'. This proved to be a highly contentious area of debate, since the terminology of 'warlordism' was often used in a tendentious and politicized manner. The way in which the campaign against 'warlords' was pursued also had unfortunate consequences: some larger problems slipped below the radar while this one took centre-stage. Since the emergence of military strongmen in parts of China after the fall of the Ching dynasty in 1911, the phenomenon of 'warlords' has been much discussed. However, defining warlordism has proved more difficult (see Mackinlay, 2000; Lezhnev, 2005: 1–12); it is, after all, a 'highly heterogeneous phenomenon' (Biró, 2007: 41). A recent definition by Marten nonetheless succeeds in capturing key elements of the idea: 'First, trained, armed men take advantage of the disintegration of central authority to seize control over relatively small slices of territory. Second, their actions are based on self-interest, not ideology. Third, their authority is based on charisma and patronage ties to their followers. Fourth, this personalistic rule leads to the fragmentation of political and economic arrangements across the country, disrupting the free flow of trade and making commerce and investment unpredictable' (Marten, 2006–2007: 48).

In Afghanistan after 2001, the term was rapidly applied to figures such as Fahim, Dostam, and Ismail Khan in Herat (Giustozzi, 2009), and eventually they were subject to campaigns to detach them from their power-bases and marginalize them politically. The campaign was most successful where Fahim was concerned. In June 2004, he was dropped as Karzai's vice-presidential running mate, and five months later he was replaced as Defence Minister by Abdul Rahim Wardak, a long-time associate of Pir Gailani. He had a soft landing: he was appointed to the Upper House of Parliament, the *Meshrano Jirga*, after the 2005 elections, and was granted the rank of 'Marshal'. Where Ismail and Dostam were concerned, the outcome was more ambiguous. Dostam contested the presidential election, and won the backing of many Uzbeks. It was in Herat, however, that the situation proved messiest. Ismail Khan administered the city autocratically but efficiently (Johnson and Leslie, 2008: 180). However, in March 2004, his son was killed in a clash with a militia leader, and Ismail himself was subsequently displaced on 11 September 2004, in a move allegedly backed by the United States which had regarded him as pro-Iranian (Hersh, 2004: 158). He moved to Kabul to take up the position of Minister of Water and Power.

The fixation with confronting such figures proved multiply-damaging, for two reasons. First, it added to ethnic tensions. It could have escaped no one's attention that the figures being most vociferously denounced as 'warlords' were all non-Pushtuns; the whole vocabulary of warlordism came to be seen by non-Pushtun figures as a rhetorical device to legit-imate the establishment of Pushtun domination. This may not have been the intention of those who denounced warlordism, but it was easy to depict in such terms. But second, and more seriously, the preoccupation with fig-ures such as Fahim, Dostam, and Ismail distracted attention at a critical moment from the way in which lesser-known actors in the south and east of Afghanistan were creating fertile ground for a Taliban resurgence through their predatory and repressive behaviour. Some had been given state pos-itions to discourage them from total spoiling; others commanded sufficient force to be dominant in their localities. Many of these so-called 'American warlords' enjoyed the protection of the United States, which believed that they were essential sources of intelligence in the hunt for *Al-Qaida*. The most spectacular example was Gul Agha Sherzai in Kandahar, a Barakzai Pushtun who was re-installed with US backing (see Maass, 2002). A great deal of variety existed on the ground, and in places such as Paktia the tribal leadership structure and its traditional *arbaki* community police remained important (Schetter, Glassner, and Karokhail, 2007: 146–8), but over time, the activities of at least some of the armed figures in the south and east proved enormously damaging to Afghanistan's prospects for stability.

Criminality and narcotics

One reason why the 'American Warlords' were dangerous was that narcotics production flourished on their watch. As noted earlier, under the Taliban in 2001, opium production had fallen to just 185 tonnes. By 2008 it totalled 7,700 tonnes. Helmand, an area of vigorous Taliban activity, contained 66 per cent of the land on which opium poppies were grown. An estimated 2.4 million persons were involved in opium cultivation (United Nations Office on Drugs and Crime, 2008). Of the total export value of opium in 2007 (US\$4.0 billion), 75 per cent went in profit to Afghan traffickers; the total 'farm-gate' value of opium production was only US\$1 billion, and the per capita opium income in opium-growing families was US\$303 (United Nations Office on Drugs and Crime, 2007: 7). There is, however, a great deal of local variation in motivations for cultivation, and in production and trading practices, even within provinces (see Mansfield, 2007; Hafvenstein, 2007; Higgins, 2007; Macdonald, 2007; Rubin and Sherman, 2008). Opium supports livelihoods not just through income from sales, but via wage income for poor labourers and by facilitating access to credit, with opium being cultivated in repayment of a prior loan (World Bank, 2005: 118–19). The United States was not prepared to move against the revival of opium cultivation in the immediate aftermath of the overthrow of the Taliban, when the target was small and the signal sent would have been effective. The perception was that such a move would compromise the 'Global War on Terror' (Felbab-Brown, 2005). Now, when US officials speak blithely of crop eradication (Schweich, 2008), it strikes terror into the hearts of poor people who have become dependent on income from opium, and makes them easy pickings for Taliban recruiters. The political benefit to the Taliban from such reckless talk probably exceeds by far the financial benefit which they get from involvement with opium. The opium problem is very serious and needs to be addressed, but with nuanced solutions, sensitive to local complexities, that will prove sustainable in the long run (Felbab-Brown, 2009; Peters, 2009: 215–33).

'Collateral damage' in the War on Terror

One final point, often overlooked, is that Afghans also feel insecure because of the risk of injury from aerial attack directed against Taliban on the ground, a problem documented by Human Rights Watch in considerable detail (Human Rights Watch, 2008). President Karzai persistently raised this as a matter of grave concern, and on 25 August 2008, the Afghan Cabinet took up the issue after large numbers of civilians – 60 children, 15 women and 15 men – were reportedly killed in an air strike that struck a village in the Shindand region of western Afghanistan (Gall, 2008b). The choice of this kind of instrument to respond to the Taliban threat works against reliable intelligence-gathering. As one very well-informed observer put it, 'Why would an Afghan villager report on a Taliban presence in his village if he knew that would lead to ISAF operations with the strong possibility that 500-pound bombs could be dropped' (Stapleton, 2008: 29). But more seriously, casualties of this sort are a godsend for the Taliban, which uses them to paint the Karzai government as a puppet regime (Thier and Ranjbar, 2008). This has led some observers to argue that increasing troop numbers in Afghanistan might deliver tactical victories but prove more broadly counterproductive (Suhrke, 2008b). Yet on its own, to hold troop numbers steady or scale them down might well heighten a sense among Afghans that they were on the verge of being abandoned entirely. One proposal that has been outlined to respond to this dilemma is to replace ISAF and allied forces with a new Muslim force under UN control (Lafraie, 2006).

Building security in post-Taliban Afghanistan

Counter-insurgency challenges

The largest security forces in Afghanistan remain those of ISAF and the United States. The Afghan Government lacks control over how these forces are used, but bears the political costs if they cause 'collateral damage' to innocent civilians as part of operation against extremists. Much will depend upon the doctrines, rules of engagement, and standard operating procedures that shape their behaviour. Contrary to what is often claimed, the militaries operating in Afghanistan are extremely conscious of the constraints imposed by international humanitarian law, but even the best of systems can misfire on occasion.

One difficulty in Afghanistan relates to intelligence. In 2001, Western militaries were pitifully short of linguists familiar with the languages of Afghanistan, and improvement has been very slow. (Pushto, which is grammatically much more complex than Persian, is a particular challenge.) This has left international forces highly dependent on local partners and local translators. This can be a problem. An interpreter can be paid by the United States, but his principal loyalty may still be to a local political actor. And such actors, seeking to wipe out their opponents or competitors, may well be tempted to seek to mobilize the military might of ISAF or the United States against them. Some of the most egregious examples of air power causing harm to civilians may have been the product of deliberately misleading information being fed to such forces (see Rondeaux and DeYoung, 2008).

More broadly significant is the conception of the international forces' tasks. A 'War against Terrorism' could be carried out in a number of different ways. The overthrow of the Taliban used military power in a very conventional fashion, and while the continued employment of air strikes in part reflects a shortage of manpower on the ground, as well as a desire to minimize combat casualties, it also accorded with Secretary Rumsfeld's conception of the shape of future warfare. In the aftermath of the Iraq and Afghanistan conflicts, the whole notion of a 'War on Terrorism' has been heavily criticized, both for misconceiving the nature of the struggle against groups such as *Al-Qaida*, and for skewing the choice of instruments to pursue it in the direction of 'hard' military power. One unintended consequence has been to expose very effectively the limits of American power (Bacevich, 2008). An alternative approach, probably the most relevant to terrorist cells in Western countries, is better policing. Certainly this has the advantage of defining those who kill innocent civilians as grubby criminals rather than as participants in a cosmic struggle, which is doubtless the very way in which figures like Bin Laden would like to be depicted. But another approach again emphasizes the importance of counter-insurgency strategies and tactics, but modernized to take account of some distinct features of modern extremist groups (see Kilcullen, 2006–2007; US Army and Marine Corps, 2007; Kilcullen, 2009; Roberts, 2009). This puts fresh emphasis on the political consequences of local actions, on high-quality analysis and diagnosis, and cultural awareness rather than secret intelligence gathered with sophisticated technology. The US Army has actively supported counter-insurgency training for the Afghan National Army, but it remains to be seen how rewarding this will prove to be.

Demilitarization, demobilization and disarmament

Any process of transition after conflict is likely to involve the elimination of armed militias through a process of demobilization, disarmament and reintegration (DDR), and their replacement with a professional standing army and police force. This is likely to be difficult and may not even be desirable in all cases. Shahrani has argued that 'disarming local communities is not only dangerous for the long-term security of such communities vis-à-vis other belligerent and hegemonic forces, and/or oppressive and autocratic central governments, but also for national defence against foreign threats' (Shahrani, 1998: 238). Furthermore, attempts to eliminate militias may come to naught if the structures, attitudes and values which fostered them remain intact (Makinda, 2003).

The formal framework for DDR was the 'Afghan New Beginnings Program', funded by Japan, which was formally inaugurated in April 2003 and ran from October 2003 to June 2006. It was not focused on former Taliban, who could reconnect with the new state through the 'Program for the Strengthening of Peace', essentially a reconciliation rather than demobilization exercise. Rather, it was concerned primarily with anti-Taliban groups. Its achievements were mainly in the area of decommissioning of heavy weapons (International Crisis Group, 2003b), but in other areas it proved quite patchy. The Program led to 63,380 soldiers being disarmed and demobilized, but these figures 'belie the reality that many militia units have remained intact' (Bhatia and Sedra, 2008: 130). The Afghan New Beginnings Program was succeeded by a distinct process of Disbandment of Illegal Armed Groups (DIAG). This proved largely unsuccessful (see Bhatia and Sedra, 2008: 134–46). The reasons for this failure were complex, but the deteriorating security situation in different parts of Afghanistan undoubtedly made many groups reluctant to go down anything like a disarmament path. Giustozzi has argued that behind the bureaucratic façade of both these programmes, a lack of political will on the part of key Afghan partners undermined what was being attempted (Giustozzi, 2008). This suggests that it may be naive to expect too much of top-down DDR programmes if developments on the ground suggest that it may be unrewarding or imprudent to relinquish one's weapons or demobilize one's supporters.

Building a new Afghan National Army

So-called 'Security Sector Reform' (SSR) is often dominated by the establishment of new armed forces, although its ambit is somewhat wider, embracing police reforms as well. Effective reform, however, should be attuned to the specific needs of a given country (Maley, 2005), and needs to be informed by a long-term vision and sense of what is likely to be sustainable (Sedra, 2006). The creation of the new Afghan National Army was essential not just as a means of reconstituting a core state function, but also to lay the foundations for the eventual withdrawal of international forces.

The United States assumed the lead in the re-establishment of the Afghan National Army, and invested heavily in its creation. On 2 December 2002, Karzai announced a target of 70,000 for the ANA (Lander, 2002); in 2006 there was a flurry of concern as signals from the Bush Administration seemed to suggest an intent to reduce this target to 50,000 (Serchuk, 2006); but by mid-2008, the Army had a total of 76,000 personnel, and the US Secretary of Defense was reported as proposing its expansion to 120,000 (Shanker, 2008b), at a cost of US$20 billion over five years. This points to a serious problem for the future, namely that of sustainability from Afghan resources. As Barnett R. Rubin has argued, 'If the state cannot sustain the recurrent costs of its security forces, its stability will be at risk. Nor can any state long survive the funding of its army and police by foreign powers' (Rubin, 2005: 99). It is also the case that the size of an army does not necessarily provide a good measure of its quality. In the Afghan National Army, many soldiers are non-literate: the Corps Commander in Kandahar, for example, reported in early 2006 that 80 per cent of his soldiers were non-literate, as were 50 per cent of his officers (Baldrauf, 2006).

On the whole, assessments of the ANA's achievements have been positive. As Sedra put it, despite the 'many problems that the ANA has faced, it is widely viewed as a "success story" in the SSR process, particularly when compared with the state of reform in the police and the judiciary. The ANA has displayed a high degree of discipline, professionalism and combat effectiveness and, due to the institution of ethnic quotas, is largely representative of the country's ethnic composition' (Sedra, 2006: 97). The complete test of its consolidation, however, will come only when it is deployed in a major operation in which its personnel are required to act against persons of similar background – ethnic, regional, or *qawm* – to themselves. National sentiment can bind soldiers together when confronting an external enemy, but the situation is different where internal security operations are concerned.

Building a new Afghan National Police

Civilian policing is essential to deal with threats that fall below major challenges to civic order (for which the military must take responsibility), but exceed what can be dealt with at the community level by informal social mechanisms. The Afghan National Police force, however, is widely seen by outside observers as a disaster area, and the police building process a costly failure (Murray, 2007; International Crisis Group, 2008c). Oddly enough, popular assessments of the police seem to be somewhat more favourable (see Asia Foundation, 2006, 2007, 2008), but while this may reflect pride in a new local institution, or respect for young recruits targeted by the Taliban, it might also reflect a fear of respondents to speak of it with candour.

Germany accepted 'lead-nation' responsibility for police reform, but approached the task in a highly formalistic manner, focusing on the development of a National Police Academy to train senior police officials. The downside was that recruiting for lower-level positions was thoroughly corrupted. As Mani put it, 'faction leaders and commanders who seized power in late 2001 also took control of police stations and in most cases installed commanders loyal to them as police chiefs.' (Mani, 2003: 18; see also Hodes and Sedra, 2007: 63). A recent report paints a harsh and graphic picture of what ordinary Afghans have to face: 'Corruption in the ANP is likely widespread and has undermined the legitimacy and utility of the police in the eyes of the Afghan populace. Extortion at checkpoints, demanding money in exchange for necessary documents, or taking bribes to ignore criminal acts are commonplace. Abuse of position is also manifested in the crimes and brutal acts that police commit, only some of which are ever reported' (United Nations Development Program, 2007: 84). Many police have become drug addicts (International Crisis Group, 2007: 16). In 2006, a separate 'Afghan National Auxiliary Police' was established in the light of the Taliban resurgence, for which members receive ten days' initial training and then go into service. However, this has been criticized as a device to give some cover of legitimacy to armed militias, but with a very real risk of penetration by the Taliban (Wilder, 2007: 13–17).

Security, justice and the rule of law

All this said, it is important also to recall Ibn Balkhi's aphorism about the importance of justice. One factor that works in the Neo-Taliban's favour is the perception that they are less corrupt than the agents of the state, and that if they control a district, they may bring order through the brutal but prompt punishment of criminals, even ones with powerful patrons. Restoration of the rule of law is thus not just an abstract ideal; it is an essential component of any meaningful strategy to legitimate the new Afghan state and the post-Taliban order more broadly. This, unfortunately, is a classic example of the difficulty of fitting Western standards to conflict-ridden societies. A well-run system of punitive justice requires the integrated functioning of police, courts, witness protection programmes, and prisons and penal institutions. A weakness in any one of these spheres will likely be enough to cause the whole system to fail. The weaknesses of the Afghan National Police are already well documented, but the courts are nearly as defective, and witness protection is virtually non-existent. Some scholars concerned with restorative rather than simply punitive justice have turned their attention towards traditional Afghan institutions (Wardak, 2004; United Nations Development Program, 2007: 91–110), and even Sharia law has received favourable mention in this context as an alternative dispute resolution mechanism (see Suskind, 2008: 345–6).

Post-Taliban Afghanistan and the world

The US and the 'War on Terror'

The principal ally of the Afghan government since 2001 has of course been the United States, and managing the relationship with Washington is one of Kabul's most significant responsibilities. It is a more complex relationship than is often appreciated, since Afghan and US perceptions and objectives can easily diverge. In a speech in 2006, Ambassador James Dobbins looked back at the Bonn process and remarked that 'my instructions didn't say anything about democracy ... We wanted a government that would work with us to track down remaining Al-Qaeda elements ...' (Dobbins, 2006). The Afghan government, by contrast, looked for assistance for the reconstitution of state capacity so that security and justice could be made available to ordinary people. Quoted in 2007, Dr Robert P. Finn, an outstanding career diplomat who was US Ambassador to Afghanistan from March 2002 to November 2003, noted that from the outset of his posting he had complained that 'we didn't have enough money and we didn't have enough soldiers'; he added that 'I'm saying the same thing six years later' (Rohde and Sanger, 2007). Nor was Karzai much helped by Dr Finn's successor, Dr Zalmay Khalilzad, who served from 2003 to 2005. His approach was so interventionist and domineering that it compromised Karzai's reputation in many Afghan eyes. While the perception that he was Washington's preferred choice may have helped him win the presidential election, this was a mixed blessing: some Afghans at the time of the election said to me that they were voting for Karzai because the Americans would not let anyone else win.

In fact, Karzai was not a puppet, but as any Afghan president would have found, his freedom of action was sharply constrained by a lack of resources of his own on which to draw. He was more a hostage than a puppet – hostage to the reconstruction priorities of donors, and hostage to the wisdom of his allies. This was especially a problem with the US treatment of prisoners. This left much to be desired, and one particular scandal, surrounding the death in US custody of a young taxi driver named Dilawar (whose tragic fate was poignantly depicted in the Oscar-winning 2007 documentary *Taxi to the Dark Side*), was all too reminiscent of some of the abuses that occurred at the Abu Ghraib prison in Iraq (see Golden, 2005). This highlighted a broader problem – that US forces in Afghanistan pursued their own objectives, without necessarily reconciling them with either the wider political objectives of US diplomacy, or the wishes of the Afghan government. Here, the obsessions of Secretary of Defense Rumsfeld proved highly destructive, especially his conviction that high-technology could allow post-intervention stabilization to be accomplished with relatively limited manpower resources. Rumsfeld was arrogant and blind to complexity, but he was also extremely energetic, and a seasoned Washington insider. He found it easy to overwhelm both the gentlemanly Secretary of State, Colin L. Powell, and the light-weight National Security Advisor, Dr Condoleezza Rice. Ultimately, some of the costs of his approach were carried by American families: by August 2008, 362 US combat personnel had been killed in action in Afghanistan as part of 'Operation Enduring Freedom', and 2,378 had been wounded. These figures are substantial, but pale by comparison with US casualties in Iraq: 3,362 killed and 30,016 wounded. No reliable data exist on the scale of Afghan losses as a consequence of the 'War on Terror'.

The Iraq War and its effects

What proved shattering, however, was the loss of focus on Afghanistan that accompanied the US invasion of Iraq in March 2003, and the years of difficulty that followed as post-Saddam Iraq proved more difficult to stabilize than policymakers in Washington had expected (see Dodge, 2003; Record, 2004; Phillips, 2005; Diamond, 2005; Packer, 2005; Chandrasekaran, 2006; Ricks, 2006; Hashim, 2006; Allawi, 2007; Roy, 2008). The effect on Afghanistan was quite direct: as the Chairman of the Joint Chiefs of Staff, Admiral Michael G. Mullen, put it in December 2007, 'In Afghanistan we do what we can. In Iraq we do what we must' (Burns, 2007). There could be no starker indication of where Afghanistan sat in the Bush Administration's priorities.

However, Iraq affected Afghanistan in adverse ways not just because of the distraction that turmoil in Iraq provided for US military and reconstruction activities. The Iraq invasion was deeply unpopular in Europe, and Afghanistan suffered from the disposition of US officials to link the two. As recently as July 2007, President Bush's Homeland Security Adviser Frances F. Townsend publicly stated that 'These are clearly a single conflict by a single determined enemy who's is looking for safe haven' (Townsend, 2007). This was not only a grossly misleading characterization of very complex situations, but an approach almost calculated to induce European publics to resist involvement in Afghanistan as much as involvement in Iraq – something which the new US Defense Secretary Robert Gates ultimately recognized (Shanker, 2008a). Perhaps even more seriously, as time went by, the military tactics that had been used with such lethal effect by anti-American forces in Iraq began to surface in Afghanistan as well. These included, most perilously, the despatch of suicide bombers, and the use of roadside or other stationary improvised explosive devices (IEDs). This may have been coincidence, or it may have been due to the physical movement of extremists between the two theatres of operations, but it could just as easily have been the product of a learning process: anyone with access to mass media could easily see how effective such tactics had proved (see Kilcullen, 2005: 600–1). Iraq's poison had spread very far indeed.

NATO and Provincial Reconstruction Teams

As noted earlier, NATO countries rallied to support the United States in the aftermath of the September 2001 attacks, and over time, NATO forces became more and more heavily involved in Afghanistan (Yaqub and Maley, 2008; Maley 2008c). Indeed, NATO has become *so* heavily involved that its future significantly depends on success in the Afghanistan theatre of operations. If Afghanistan comes to be seen as a failure, the credibility of the NATO alliance will suffer a very heavy blow (see Noetzel and Scheipers, 2007; Bet-El and Smith, 2008; Kober, 2008).

NATO's involvement came in stages. On 9 August 2003, NATO assumed responsibility for ISAF, essentially to improve continuity at the level of ISAF leadership, which had been rotating between contributing countries. With Security Council Resolution 1510 in October 2003 finally authorizing ISAF expansion beyond Kabul, NATO's role was further enhanced; it deployed forces into the north of Afghanistan in 2004, into the west in 2005, and into the south and east in 2006. By mid-2008, there were approximately 52,700 troops serving with ISAF, from 40 different countries, 26 of them NATO members. The largest component was American (23,550), followed by the British (8,530), the Germans (3,370), the Canadians (2,500), the Italians (2,350), the Dutch (1,770), the French (1,670), the Polish (1,140), and the Australians (1,100). (There were other US troops in Afghanistan, involved in counter-terrorism missions, but Secretary Gates reportedly favoured bringing these under the US commander of NATO forces in Afghanistan (Shanker, 2008b).) These ISAF troops find themselves frequently in the line of fire, and this has made the deployments controversial in a number of NATO states, where the initial commitments were seen as part of an exercise in peace-building rather than war-fighting. The result has been endless public agonizing about the viability of commitments, the explicit setting of deadlines on the timing of deployments, and NATO summits at which the demands of the NATO Secretary-General for more troops and equipment are not fully met. All this goes on in full view of ordinary Afghans. They are unlikely to feel inspired by what they see, although in some parts of Afghanistan, excellent reconstruction work has been carried out by personnel from NATO countries.

Perhaps the most imaginative NATO contribution has come in the form of so-called 'Provincial Reconstruction Teams' (PRTs), which emerged from January 2003 to attempt to cover the gaps that the blocking of ISAF expansion had created. PRTs were envisaged as mixed teams of military personnel and civic affairs specialists, who would contribute to reconstruction and boost stability as the benefits of reconstruction spread like an ink-spot on blotting-paper. Given the nature of Afghanistan's problems, this was always likely to be a difficult task. The PRT model assumed that PRTs would be an adjunct to the state, but in many areas, the state amounted to very little, which threw PRTs back on their own devices (Stapleton, 2007). In addition, it became rapidly clear that there was no single 'PRT' model; rather, the PRTs differed according to the specific local circumstances by which they were faced, and to the contributing countries' distinctive military-organizational cultures and senses of what the objectives of their missions should be. It was also the case that some NGO staff resisted what they saw as an undesirable blurring of the distinction between military and humanitarian roles, fearing that attacks on NGO staff might result (Dziedzic and Seidl, 2005). What merits further evaluation is the success or otherwise of PRTs as agents of development. Many have focused on working cooperatively with provincial governors and officials, but they of course have their own interests (notably to be seen to be capable of bringing resources into the province), and this can militate against PRT activities fitting in with broader strategic objectives of the Afghan National Development Strategy (Piiparinen, 2007).

The UN and Afghanistan

The UN Security Council, by Resolution 1401 of 28 March 2002, established a United Nations Assistance Mission in Afghanistan (UNAMA), which has served as the overarching agent of UN engagement with and assistance in Afghanistan. In proposing the establishment of UNAMA, the Secretary-General recommended that 'UNAMA should aim to bolster Afghan capacity (both official and non-governmental), relying on as limited an international presence and on as many Afghan staff as possible, and using common support services where possible, thereby leaving a light expatriate "footprint"' (United Nations, 2002: para. 98). This very much reflected the wishes of the United States (Dorronsoro, 2008: 462). Since the establishment of UNAMA, it has been headed by four separate special representatives of the Secretary-General: Lakhdar Brahimi of Algeria (2002–2004); Jean Arnault of France (2004–2006); Tom Koenigs of Germany (2006–2007); and Kai Eide of Norway (from 2008). UNAMA had two critical 'pillars' of action: supporting the political process, especially the meeting of the benchmarks in the Bonn Agreement; and aid coordination. The experience of UNAMA exposed both the strengths and the limitations of such missions (see Thier, 2006: 508–41). The most significant limitation of all, as Thier put it, was that UNAMA 'stood deep in the shadow of the Coalition' (Thier, 2006: 540), but over-dependence on expatriates rather than local capacity-building was another, although some officials, such as Professor Reginald Austin, the Chief Electoral Adviser in the Secretariat of the Joint Electoral Management Body that ran the presidential election, went out of their way to see that local capacity-building proceeded. Brahimi, because of his standing in both Washington and New York, was able to provide strong leadership for UNAMA. He was decorated by President Karzai at an emotional ceremony to farewell him when he finished his term in early 2004, and granted honorary citizenship of Afghanistan. It proved difficult for his successors to achieve the same standing.

Afghanistan, Pakistan and the Taliban threat

Pakistan's ongoing support for the Taliban

As noted earlier, the Taliban in 2001 were obliterated as a regime, but not eliminated as a military force. The top Taliban leadership escaped to Pakistan, and many Taliban fighters escaped as part of Pakistan's airlift of personnel from Kunduz. This laid the foundations for a resurgence of some Taliban activity with Pakistani support. This surfaced much earlier than is often realized. In September 2002, a bomb blast killed large numbers of Afghans in downtown Kabul near the Spinzhar Hotel, and on 27 March 2003, a Red Cross worker, Ricardo Munguia, was murdered by the Taliban near Kandahar (Maley, 2003c). As noted earlier, there were other such incidents, and they all sent unsettling signals about the ability of the Taliban to strike at vulnerable targets (see Maley, 2003–2004). But at this time, there was still great optimism about Afghanistan's transition, and the US was committed to supporting the regime of President Musharraf. It thus turned a blind eye to what Weinbaum and Harder have called Pakistan's 'two-track foreign policy toward Afghanistan', with the second track involving entanglement with radical Islamists (Weinbaum and Harder, 2008: 27). Instead, it delivered US$10 billion in aid to Pakistan in the years following the September 11, 2001 attacks, but at the end of the day, it had little to show for its efforts (Cohen, 2007; Cohen and Chollet, 2007). In international politics, money does not buy love, and the willingness of Washington to continue supporting Musharraf as his standing plunged with his fellow countrymen led to a surge in anti-American sentiment.

A number of factors help explain why Pakistan continued to use the Taliban as a tool (see Grare, 2006: 8–15; Tellis, 2008: 12; Maley, 2008f). The Pakistan military had long been beyond the reach of effective checks and balances, as was graphically demonstrated when the black market nuclear technology dealings of the Pakistani scientist A. Q. Khan were exposed in 2003 (Corera, 2006). The upper ranks of the ISI contained many officers who had been radicalized as young soldiers during the time of General Zia, and some of them felt affinity with the Taliban's religious message. In January 2009, the Director-General of ISI, quizzed about the activities of Afghan Taliban leaders in Quetta, reportedly responded 'Shouldn't they be allowed to think and say what they like? They believe that jihad is their obligation. Isn't that freedom of opinion?' (Koelbl, 2009). Others saw the Taliban as a force in which to invest for the future once the Americans lost interest in Afghanistan; in May 2008, the Army Chief, General Ashfaq Kayani, in a conversation with Musharraf reportedly described Jalaluddin Haqqani as a 'strategic asset' (Sanger, 2009: 248). The blocking of ISAF expansion fostered just such a mindset. Furthermore, as Afghan–Indian relations improved, this became an additional source of frustration for Pakistan. And as time went by, President Karzai was increasingly surrounded by nationalist Pushtuns of exactly the ilk that had upset the Pakistanis during the heyday of the Pushtunistan dispute. With the major powers preoccupied after early 2003 by events in Iraq, the costs of ramping up harassment of the Karzai government did not appear high. Finally, the weakness of new Afghan state structures provided a good working environment for insurgents (Jones, 2008a), and maladroit US measures such as the threat to engage in mass opium eradication, combined with civilian casualties from air operations, created a pool of disgruntled Afghans whose support could be solicited.

Pakistan and the spread of insurgency

The spread of insurgency in southern and eastern Afghanistan was most strikingly obvious in the aftermath of the September 2005 parliamentary elections. Increasingly from this point, observers began to point to a threat from the 'Neo-Taliban'. By 2007, the role of sanctuaries in Pakistan was being more candidly discussed. In a report to the US Congress in January 2007, the US Director of National Intelligence described Pakistan as a country 'where the Taliban and al-Qa'ida maintain critical sanctuaries' (Negroponte, 2007: 5). In August 2007, President Musharraf admitted what had long been known when during a visit to Kabul he stated that 'There is no doubt Afghan militants are supported from Pakistani soil. The problem that you have in your region is because support is provided from our side' (Shah and Gall, 2007). Some of Musharraf's political allies in Pakistan were deeply involved in delivering such support (Norell, 2007).

At one level, this said all that needed to be said. As a sovereign state, Pakistan has duties as well as rights, and one such duty is to prevent its territory from being used to mount attacks on a neighbouring state. But in Western capitals, there remained a reluctance to press Musharraf on this point unless a 'smoking gun' exposed direct ISI complicity. Of such complicity informed commentators had long had little doubt, and a raft of press reports had highlighted strong circumstantial evidence to this effect (see Gall, 2006; King, 2006; Gall, 2007a). Carlotta Gall, a prominent correspondent for *The New York Times*, was beaten up by Pakistani intelligence agents in January 2007 (Gall, 2007b) when investigating Taliban activities in the Pushtunabad neighbourhood of Quetta, a well-known Taliban refuge (Rashid, 2008: 249–51).

By mid-2007, this was emerging as an expert consensus: as the RAND researcher Seth Jones put it, 'there is virtual unanimity that Pakistan's Directorate for Inter-Services Intelligence (ISI) has continued to provide assistance to Afghan insurgent groups (Jones, 2007: 15; see also Gregory, 2007; Jones 2008b). Finally, in 2008, the Bush Administration seemed to accept the core of this consensus as well. US generals had already spoken quite candidly about the problem when testifying before Congress (Tyson, 2007), and by 2008, the US was fast running out of options in Pakistan. The straw that broke the camel's back may have been the 7 July 2008 bombing of the Indian Embassy in Kabul (Wafa and Cowell, 2008). Rumours abounded that India had warned the US that if Washington was not prepared to act, then New Delhi would be. Within a matter of days, press reports surfaced that the ISI was involved in supporting the Taliban (see Mazzetti and Schmitt, 2008a), and that according to US government officials, 'members' of the ISI 'helped plan' the embassy bombing (Mazzetti and Schmitt, 2008b).

Talibanization of the tribal areas and Pakistan's internal crises

One reason why Washington may have opted for a more candid and direct approach to perfidy on Islamabad's part is that Pakistan itself had been slipping deeper and deeper into internal crisis, making the option simply of backing President Musharraf less and less appealing. The most dramatic manifestation of this crisis was the emergence of a strong Pakistani Taliban movement (*Tehreek-e-Taliban*), inspired by and operating in parallel with its Afghan counterpart. This development provided a classic example of chickens coming home to roost. In the late 1990s, a very senior UN official put it candidly to then Pakistani Prime Minister Nawaz Sharif: 'You send these young men into Afghanistan, telling them that Ahmad Shah Massoud is not a good Muslim. What makes you think that they will not return saying that *you* are not a good Muslim?' However, the crisis in the tribal areas reflects not just the influence of the Afghan Taliban, but the accumulated effects of underdevelopment, of poor governance, and of exploitation of the region for the training of militants as a tool of Pakistan's geopolitical strategies (see International Crisis Group, 2006a; Markey, 2008; Filkins, 2008; Pakistan Policy Working Group, 2008: 13–19). The activities of the Pakistani Taliban, led by Baitullah Mehsud, have been augmented by other radicals in the same area: Chechens, Uzbeks, and Uighurs (Williams, 2008). Mehsud reportedly swore allegiance to Mulla Omar in 2001 (Gannon, 2008). The result has been a fierce insurgency embracing significant parts of the Federally Administered Tribal Areas, and increasingly making its presence felt in the settled areas of the North-West Frontier Province (such as Swat) and beyond – most spectacularly . . . in the bombing of the Marriott Hotel in the centre of Islamabad on 20 September 2008 (Gall, 2008d). This prompted a harsh judgement on the Pakistani authorities from the security analyst Talat Masood: 'If they don't rise to this challenge, they are finished' (Hussain and Constable, 2008).

The US response to this problem has relied dangerously upon cooperation from the Pakistan military (Government Accountability Office, 2008), but Pakistan itself has not managed to identify a coherent approach to the problem. This is partly because it has been confronted by what Schaffer has called 'the double menace of violent extremism and institutional atrophy' (Schaffer, 2008: 9), but it is also because its military has historically been configured for conventional war with India rather than for counter-insurgency. It has therefore opted on occasion to deal with the enemy, as on 5 September 2006 when an agreement was struck in North Waziristan (International Crisis Group, 2006a). The agreement did not last, but in any case its main short-term effect was simply to displace radical activity across the border into Afghanistan's Paktia province, whose Governor, Hakim Taniwal, was killed by a suicide bomber five days later (Rubin, 2006b). In its own interest, Pakistan has little option but to confront these forces. To give them what they demand would simply invite them to demand still more, one reason why an agreement with radicals in Swat in 2009 was widely condemned.

But ultimately, Musharraf's limitation in confronting extremism lay not in the weaknesses of the Pakistan military, but in his own diminishing legitimacy. For added to the problem of insurgency was a multi-pronged domestic crisis that rolled out through 2007 and into 2008. It began with Musharraf's attempt to dismiss the Chief Justice of Pakistan, Iftikhar Muhammad Chaudhry, on 9 March 2007, and reached a kind of terminus on 18 August 2008 with Musharraf's resignation as president. The intervening 17 months had witnessed massive demonstrations by lawyers in support of the Chief Justice, his restoration by a judgement of the Supreme Court on 20 July, and then a sweeping move by Musharraf on 3 November not only to remove the Chief Justice again, but for good measure to suspend the Constitution, and remove many of the Chief Justice's fellow judges, and replace them with Musharraf supporters. The result was a collapse in Musharraf's popularity (Rashid, 2008: 391). This was augmented by a crisis in Islamabad, when on 8 July 2007 the military was sent in to dislodge extremists who had taken over the Lal Masjid ('Red Mosque') in the centre of the city. This led to large loss of life, and left the residents of the capital deeply shaken. The US, aware of Musharraf's declining popularity but unwilling to abandon him, instead pressured him to allow former prime minister Benazir Bhutto to return from exile, in the hope that she could become prime minister after scheduled elections and work in tandem with Musharraf as president. Bhutto indeed returned on 18 October 2007, and on 28 November Musharraf relinquished the position of Army Chief to General Kayani. But on 27 December 2007, Bhutto was assassinated at a rally in Rawalpindi (International Crisis Group, 2008a), and this left Washington's strategy in ruins, something confirmed when at the 18 February 2008 elections, Musharraf's supporters suffered a disastrous electoral defeat, not only in voting for the National Assembly but also for Pakistan's Provincial Assemblies as well (Rashid, 2008: 390–1). In this new environment, a move to impeach Musharraf gained increasing momentum, and it was this that finally prompted his resignation. Whether his opponents will be able to work together effectively to address Pakistan's other problems remains to be seen.

Talking with the Taliban

As Taliban assaults have caused more and more grief for ordinary Afghans and their supporters, it is perhaps not surprising that calls have surfaced for negotiation with the Taliban as an alternative to combat. This was long a staple of Pakistani policy advice. On 29 September 2007, following an especially nasty suicide bombing in Kabul, Karzai made the startling offer to leave the capital to talk with 'Esteemed' Mulla Omar, and 'Esteemed' Gulbuddin Hekmatyar. Nothing eventuated, but the call for talks with 'moderate Taliban' recurred, with some voicing regret that the Taliban had not been engaged in a political process from the time of the Bonn meeting and thereafter. This embodied a high level of fantasy. There would have been no Bonn meeting if Taliban had been invited, such was the fury of the United Front at the recent slaying of Massoud. More generally, it is doubtful whether talks could either be organized in a meaningful fashion, or lead to anything useful. It is not clear for whom Taliban 'negotiators' might speak, or whom their promises would bind. Negotiations with extremist groups can sometimes prove fruitful, but they can also prove very costly. This was demonstrated by dealings with Hekmatyar in the 1990s. Rewarding those who misbehave creates a classic moral hazard problem. The signal it sends is that misbehaviour is likely to be rewarded, and this encourages others to follow the same path. And even discussion of the idea of negotiating with the Taliban is likely to destabilize still further the already strained relations within the Afghan political elite, as well as confuse ordinary Afghans as to what their leaders are seeking to achieve (Maley, 2007b; see also Saikal, 2007; Tellis, 2009). It seems as if the lessons of past unrewarding attempts to negotiate with the Taliban have been largely forgotten.

Afghanistan and Iran

Iran, although it has a long border with Afghanistan, has historically been much less directly involved than Pakistan, doubtless because the Afghan Shia with whom it shares most in common are only a minority of the population. Nonetheless, on occasion it has been drawn into involvement, and in certain circumstances this could become much more active. In 2001, Iranian representatives took part in the Bonn meeting, and the US representative James Dobbins found them 'particularly helpful'; this engagement was facilitated by authorization to Dobbins from Secretary of State Powell 'to meet anywhere, anytime, on any matter with any Iranian official, as long as our discussions related to Afghanistan' (Dobbins, 2007). This positive atmosphere was undermined by Bush's January 2002 reference in his State of the Union speech to Iran as being part of an 'Axis of Evil'. A cynic might see this as no more than a vindication of George Monbiot's harsh judgement that the US does not really have a foreign policy but 'a series of domestic policies it projects beyond its borders' (Monbiot, 2008), but the effect was to derail international cooperation over Afghanistan at a crucial moment (Milani, 2006: 248–9).

The Iranian political system

The Iranian political system is curious to say the least. The Iranian revolution produced a diverse range of political ideas (Lafraie, 2009), and Iran's post-Revolution constitution embodied two radically conflicting models of legitimacy. One, derived from the doctrine of 'Guardianship of the Islamic Jurist' (*velayat-e faqih*) developed by the revolutionary leader Ayatollah Ruhollah Khomeini, underpins the office of 'Supreme Leader', a position held by Khomeini until his death in June 1989, and thereafter by Ayatollah Ali Khamanei. However, the constitution also provided for the election of a president who could serve two consecutive four-year terms. The president is subordinate to the Supreme Leader. Khamanei was president from 1981 to 1989; he was succeeded by Ali Akbar Rafsanjani (1989–1997); Mohammad Khatami (1997–2005), and, from 2005, Mahmoud Ahmadinejad. Rafsanjani was often labelled a pragmatist, but Khatami was a far more liberal figure (see Rabinovich, 2007), whose emergence near the apex of the political system was a remarkable development. It was during his presidency, in May 2003, that a proposal backed by both Khatami and Khamanei was transmitted to the US via the Swiss

Ambassador in Teheran for a wide-ranging exchange in which all aspects of Iranian action that had been criticized by the US would be on the table (Parsi, 2007: 243–57). The proposal proved to have a short life-span: it was killed by Vice-President Cheney and Defense Secretary Rumsfeld. For Afghanistan, this was profoundly unfortunate, since a rapprochement between Teheran and Washington could only work to Kabul's benefit. Yet the fact that the proposal was made remains of interest, since it points to the capacity for pragmatic policy calculations in Iran, of the kind which many in Washington might seek to deny.

The Ahmadinejad presidency

It was in this context that the 2005 Iranian presidential elections took place, and the outcome startled many observers. Former President Rafsanjani recontested the position but he was defeated by the populist Mayor of Teheran, Mahmoud Ahmadinejad (see Ansari, 2007; Naji, 2008). Ahmadinejad was soon to become a controversial figure in much of the world, for on 23 October 2005, he gave a speech which secured almost iconic status as an example of internationally unacceptable behaviour. The subject was Zionism, and in his speech, Ahmadinejad took up a familiar theme from Khomeini's pre-1989 rhetoric, stating that 'our dear Imam [Khomeini] proclaimed that the occupier-regime of Jerusalem should be effaced from the page of time' (*Imam-e aziz-e ma farmudand keh in rezhim-e ashghalgar-e Quds baid az safheh-i ruzgar mahv shavad*). In policy terms he may have intended no more than a recapitulation of Khamanei's own position of June 2005, namely 'the defeat of Zionist ideology and dissolution of Israel through a "popular referendum"' (Sadjadpour, 2008a: 20). However, his words were translated as a direct threat to 'wipe Israel off the map', and a storm broke out in both Israel and the United States, in which the complexities of cross-cultural translation (see Sharifian, 2007) were completely lost. Ahmadinejad subsequently did himself and Iran no good by hosting in December 2006 a gathering of crackpot Holocaust deniers (Naji, 2008: 162–74). Ahmadinejad may prove to be a transient figure: as one observer has put it, 'Far from detracting from the significance of civic and democratic values, the Ahmadi-Nejad interlude is likely to render them more urgently appealing' (Azimi, 2008: 411). However, the sense that he is a second Hitler will likely persist in some circles, and Iran's ability to be integrated as a constructive actor in its region and the world will suffer as a result.

Iran's interests in Afghanistan

Ironically, Iran in the aftermath of the US invasion of Iraq is in its strongest position regionally since the Iranian revolution. In Iraq, the Sunni regime of Saddam Hussein was replaced by a Shiite-dominated regime in which friends of Iran are prominently represented. Furthermore, in the 34-day Israel–Lebanon war of July–August 2006, the Iranian-backed Hezbollah, while hardly a victor, nonetheless succeeded in depriving Israel of the reputation for military competence on which it had drawn so heavily since its crushing victory in the 1967 Six Day War (see Norton, 2007; Harel and Issacharoff, 2008). This did not set the scene for the emergence of a single Shiite entity spanning the region under Iranian domination, but it did make Iran a force with which to reckon. This was clearly reflected in the approach to Iran taken by the Karzai government. This emphasized cordial relations and the potential benefits of regional cooperation, with a rail-link between eastern Iran and western Afghanistan being a concrete manifestation. Iran has good reasons to reciprocate, one obvious one being the need for cooperation to stem the flow of narcotics from Afghanistan into Iran, which faces serious problems of drug addiction.

Iran and the Taliban

Iran has no reason to desire an unstable Afghanistan on its doorstep, and although it has been prepared to use its relations with groups such as Hezbollah and Hamas to advance its interests, it has not since 1979 been a rampantly-aggressive power. Iran has not invaded another country since the nineteenth century; on the contrary, as one observer has put it, 'Iran has been on the strategic defensive for two hundred years' (Ansari, 2006: 240). If anything, despite its strong position in the aftermath of Saddam's removal, it feels surrounded by threats, with significant US ground forces deployed to the west (in Iraq) and to the east (in Afghanistan).

It is in this context that reports of Iranian weapons finding their way to the Taliban should be seen. These reports began to surface in 2007, when the Chairman of the US Joint Chiefs of Staff, General Peter Pace, stated that mortars and plastic explosives had been seized near Kandahar. But perhaps reflecting the more measured response of the new US Defense Secretary, General Pace explicitly added that it was not clear 'which Iranian entity is responsible' (Gordon, 2007). Further reports of arms seizures were published later in the year (Albone, 2007; Wright, 2007). While it was ironical that US officials would take up this issue when by any measure the support to the Taliban from circles in Pakistan was vastly more extensive, they did not add up to a campaign to implicate the Iranian government in Afghanistan's troubles. This may have been because the failure of weapons of mass destruction to materialize in Iraq had made US media sources much more sceptical about claims that could be exploited as a *casus belli* by conservatives and neo-conservatives in Washington. It may have been because the Karzai government plainly had no desire to back up any such claims (Mazzetti, 2007). However, it may have also reflected a genuine conviction that the weaponry seized in Afghanistan was being bought by the Taliban through criminal smuggling networks rather than supplied as part of an assistance package. But that said, it is by no means beyond the bounds of possibility that such weapons came from some part of the Iranian state structure, not because anyone in Iran wanted to see the Taliban emerge triumphant, but rather because US pressure on Iran made it useful for Iran to signal its ability in return to stir up some trouble in areas of vital strategic significance for the United States.

Iran's nuclear programme: implications

This points to the overarching challenge posed by Iran's nuclear programme. What could fundamentally destabilize the Afghanistan–Iran relationship would be a major international crisis over Iran's pursuit of uranium enrichment. This links back to the issue of Ahmadinejad's attitudes to Israel. As well as being alarmed by the Iranian president's reported rhetoric and by the company he has kept, Israel has long had a substantial nuclear weapons capability (Cirincione with Wolfsthal and Rajkumar, 2002: 221), and naturally would like to retain such a monopoly. It has therefore agitated vigorously for active measures to be taken to prevent Iran from going nuclear. Yet Iran is equally committed to uranium enrichment. It insists that such enrichment is purely for peaceful purposes, and no definitive evidence has surfaced to prove the contrary. However, Iran's own strategic situation is such that it would be unsurprising if it wished to possess a nuclear deterrent. As the eminent Israeli analyst Martin van Creveld has written, 'Remembering what happened to Saddam Hussein, who was attacked and destroyed for no very good reason, some would say that, if ever a country had good reason to go nuclear as fast as it could, it was Iran in 2003' (van Creveld, 2004: 121–2). Ironically, a US National Intelligence Estimate in November 2007 concluded 'with high confidence' that Iran in 2003 had 'halted its nuclear weapons program' and with 'moderate confidence' that Iran 'had not restarted its nuclear weapons program as of mid-2007' (National Intelligence Council, 2007: 5). This to some degree defused the fear of an immediate US or Israeli strike against Iran's nuclear facilities. It was also clear that senior US military figures had no appetite for such a strike while they were already overstretched in Iraq and Afghanistan (see White, 2008). The election of Barack Obama to the US presidency in November 2008 may have increased the likelihood of serious attempts to engage the Iranian leadership diplomatically (see Sadjadpour, 2008b; Sharp, 2008). Nonetheless, the possibility of attacks on Iran remains alive. The consequences for stability in Afghanistan would likely be catastrophic.

Afghan futures

For Afghanistan, 2008 was not a happy year. Afghan dismay at insensitivity on the part of Afghanistan's supporters seemed to be on the rise (DiManno, 2008). At the 27 April commemoration of the Mujahideen overthrow of Najibullah's regime, there was a brazen attempt on President Karzai's life (Gall and Wafa, 2008). On 13 June, a sensational Taliban attack on the main prison in Kandahar allowed many Taliban prisoners to escape (Smith, 2008a; Gall, 2008c). The bombing of the Indian Embassy on 7 July further unsettled a city that had been shaken by a terrorist attack on the Serena Hotel on 14 January (Wafa, 2008), and even earlier by a major riot in May 2006 (Maley, 2006a: 137–8). And the killings on 13 August of women aid workers serving the International Rescue Committee (Gall, 2008a), followed by a Taliban assault that killed ten French paratroopers near Sarobi on 19 August (Gall and Rahimi, 2008), created the impression of a situation sliding out of control. 'Friends' of Afghanistan added to this impression. In early October 2008, the British Ambassador in Kabul was reported to have privately remarked that the best solution for Afghanistan would be an 'acceptable dictator' (Sciolino, 2008), and a British commander in Afghanistan, in comments that would have been music to the ears of ISI officers, remarked that 'We're not going to win this war' (Lamb, 2008). Observations of this sort are of limited assistance in mapping Afghanistan's complexities – after all, the famous military strategist Basil Liddell Hart was equally, and erroneously, defeatist in early 1940 (Mearsheimer, 1988: 154) – but they contribute to the climate of fear by which Afghanistan is increasingly gripped.

On top of all this, jockeying in the context of the presidential election scheduled for 2009 led to the appearance of a range of stories in Western media either questioning the achievements of Karzai (Cooper, 2008) or openly denigrating him, often on bases that reflected more the zealotry and naiveté of the critics (see Marlowe, 2008; Schweich, 2008). Even the NATO Secretary-General, perhaps sensitive to criticisms of NATO's incoherent performance, sought to shift the blame for Afghanistan's problems onto the Afghan government (Scheffer, 2009). It is hardly surprising that ordinary Afghans in opinion surveys offered increasingly sombre views of the situation confronting them. In 2004, 64 per cent of respondents in an Asia Foundation survey felt that things in Afghanistan were going in the right direction. By 2006 this figure had fallen to 44 per cent, by 2007 to 42 per cent, and by 2008 to 38 per cent. The percentage of those who felt that things were going in the wrong direction rose from 11 per cent in 2004 to 21 per cent in 2006 to 24 per cent in 2007 and 32 per cent in 2008 (see Asia Foundation, 2004, 2006, 2007, 2008). While some observers might be relieved that less than one third of the respondents chose the most negative option available to them, the trend is not an encouraging one, and it remains unclear whether it will be reversed. What is clear, however, is that there are a number of specific factors which will shape Afghanistan's future prospects. It is with these factors that it is appropriate to conclude this book's overview of the wars of modern Afghanistan.

Tensions in Afghanistan's internal politics

Afghanistan's internal politics have not served it well in the period since the overthrow of the Taliban. The constitutional system has been dysfunctional in significant respects, political actors have often proved less than statesmanlike, and the burden of distrust within the political elite remains heavy. Nonetheless, the constitutional framework has provided a context for political competition, and the course that that competition takes in the immediate future is likely to have significant implications for the longer run. Three particular issues deserve attention.

The first is the impact of new elections for the presidency and the *Wolesi Jirga*. President Karzai in 2004 benefited from a strong public profile, the support of the United States, and a powerful sense that Afghanistan was heading in the right direction. Much has changed since then, and the elections scheduled for 2009 (Kippen, 2008; Danspeckgruber and Maley, 2009) may be far more ferociously fought, with the outcomes being anything but certain. The second issue is the future of the 2004 Constitution itself. An intense public debate over the

Constitution is unlikely to be immediately fruitful, as it would likely produce simply a rhetorical revisiting of the earlier debate in which Pushtuns lined up behind a presidential system and moved to block a parliamentary model. But a lesson of recent experience is that parliamentary systems have significant strengths as mechanisms of inclusion and reconciliation (Hartzell, 1999). Much will depend on the willingness of those who narrowly benefit from the present Constitution to reflect on whether it works well for Afghanistan as a whole. The third issue is the future of political parties as formal elements of the political process. One advantage of recognizing parties as political actors is that a legal framework can be established to shape the ways in which they engage in political activity. Moving to exclude political parties as formal actors does not eliminate the malign effects of factional networking. It simply drives it underground, perversely protecting it from scrutiny and benefiting some of the least attractive and most aggressively manipulative characters on the Afghan political scene. This was something that the early American Federalists appreciated all too well (Hamilton, Madison and Jay, 1961: 78).

Donor activities

The nature of ongoing international donor support for Afghanistan will likely shape its future in significant ways. The hopes of a Marshall Plan for Afghanistan died not long after the Taliban regime's overthrow, and the flow of resources into the country has been sporadic, poorly coordinated, and often so tardy as a result of constitutional and administrative procedures in donor states that no political benefits have resulted. With large elements of 'state-like' activity being carried out by non-state actors with direct external funding, the Afghan state is well placed to receive the blame for what goes wrong, but not the credit for what goes right. This may be an endemic problem in complex transitions, but the costs in the Afghan theatre of operations are likely to be high. The Afghanistan Compact and the Afghan National Development Strategy Secretariat have represented an attempt to streamline the process, but the downside has been a marginalization of line ministries and managers. The result is a process in which Afghans and donors both expect the Afghan government to be accountable to them; and serving two masters simultaneously is never an easy task. Some Afghans claim that Afghans are in the driving seat, but 'the problem is we have Afghans who cannot drive' (see Goodhand and Sedra, 2007: 54). To this other Afghans reply that

Afghans are in the driving seat, but are driving a taxi. There is no easy solution to these problems, which lie at the heart of ongoing dialogue between Afghanistan and its supporters, but without improvements in the aid-delivery system, and more strategic targeting of more abundant resources, the current system will continue to fall short of Afghans' expectations.

International attention

The Afghanistan transition was brutally derailed by the Bush Administration's intervention in Iraq. With the passage of time the consequences became all too clear. Resurgent violence in Afghanistan finally caught the attention of Washington policymakers, but by the time the Bush Administration began to give to Afghanistan more of the attention it deserved, Mr Bush was approaching the twilight of his presidency, never the best of times in which to mobilize fresh support for a campaign that had been allowed to stall. Nonetheless, Afghanistan is one of the main issues on the agenda of the Obama Administration (see Maley, 2008g), and a key question will be the willingness of that president, and Washington's principal allies, to signal by deed as well as word that there can be no going back to Afghanistan's grim past. The prospects that the new US leader will stand firm are perhaps better than one might think, for it should be clear by now that consigning Afghanistan to a Pakistani sphere of influence cannot work as a strategy for stabilizing the region, and that the Talibanization of West Asia through the creation of a 'Badlands' zone embracing the tribal area of Pakistan and the south and east of Afghanistan (Burke, 2007) would simply recreate on a grander scale the very conditions that led to the terrorist attacks of September 2001. Afghans will look to President Obama for positive indications that the region's problems will be confronted. As Giustozzi has written, 'the inability of the Americans to bring sufficient pressure to bear on the Pakistan government to force it to stop the insurgents' activities might have resulted in a belief among Afghans that being on the pro-Pakistan side in the conflict was wiser, as Pakistan was going to be involved in Afghanistan much longer and more effectively than the United States' (Giustozzi, 2007: 27). But Pakistan also has legitimate concerns for its own security, and much will turn on whether new strategies and architectures of regional cooperation can be developed which help overcome the interlocking regional security dilemmas that have proved so destructive (Rubin, Ghani, Maley, Rashid and Roy, 2001; Rubin and Rashid, 2008; Maley, 2009a).

Pakistan as a threat to regional and global stability

In the end, however, we come back to developments in Pakistan, a country with which Afghanistan's fate has been entangled for more than half a century. Afghanistan is once again experiencing a creeping invasion from Pakistan. As Johnson and Mason have argued, 'the key to success or failure in Afghanistan lies below its southern border, in northern Pakistan. As long as insurgents are virtually free to cross the border at will and Pakistani Frontier Corps elements aid and abet their movements, the insurgency cannot be shut down in Afghanistan' (Johnson and Mason, 2007: 89; see also Saikal, 2006b). Ordinary Afghans, *and ordinary Pakistanis,* have been ill served by the dominance in Pakistan of a military establishment in large measure prisoner of its own nightmares, and prone to engage in proxy wars in a reckless and short-sighted fashion. In no sense can one say that a demand to Pakistan that it abandon its engagement with extremism is a demand that it commit national suicide. Its embrace of the Taliban has proved a disaster for both Afghanistan and Pakistan, and it is far from clear that the forces liberated by this embrace will not end up fuelling a conflagration in Pakistan of truly catastrophic proportions. Terrorist attacks in Mumbai in November 2008 and in Lahore in March 2009 (Perlez and Sengupta, 2008; Perlez and Gillani, 2009) powerfully demonstrated just how destructive such forces can be, not only for Pakistan's neighbourhood, but for Pakistan itself.

For far too long, Western leaders naively put their trust in rulers such as Zia ul-Haq and Pervez Musharraf, rather than in institutions that would allow ordinary Pakistanis to rule themselves. This was sometimes rationalized through the belief that pressure on repressive rulers could undermine them and lead to an even worse outcome, but the consequence was that exceedingly dangerous forces took root and flourished under the patronage of the very leaders on whom Western statesmen chose to rely. It is such a gradual process of Talibanization, rather than a sudden collapse, that poses the greatest threat to Afghanistan, to Pakistan, and to the wider world, and Western policy should be directed at pressing Pakistan to address this problem before it spins totally out of control. This problem needs to be addressed on the basis of stern realism, not wishful thinking (Grare, 2007). As one senior UN official reportedly put it, the act of denying Pakistan's role in fomenting conflict in Afghanistan is akin to 'pretending that Niagara Falls doesn't flow' (Smith, 2008b.)

It is right and proper to support a civilian government in Pakistan, but to merit lasting support it must move swiftly to abandon its predecessor's ruthless and destructive destabilization of Afghanistan. Both morally and strategically, the Afghan people are entitled to demand nothing less. In this they deserve the full support of their Western allies. However, it remains to be seen whether Afghanistan's allies, in choosing how to deal with Pakistan, prove capable of choosing wisely.

References

Abou Zahab, Mariam (1996), 'L'origine sociale des Tâlebân', *Les Nouvelles d'Afghanistan,* 74–5: 24–6.

Abou Zahab, Mariam, and Olivier Roy (2004), *Islamist Networks: The Afghan-Pakistan Connection* (London: Hurst & Co.).

Afghanistan Justice Project (2005), *Casting Shadows: War Crimes and Crimes against Humanity 1978–2001* (Kabul: Afghanistan Justice Project).

Ahady, Anwar-ul-Haq (1995), 'The Decline of the Pashtuns in Afghanistan', *Asian Survey,* 35, 7: 621–34.

Ahmad, Ishtiaq (2004), *Gulbuddin Hekmatyar: An Afghan Trail from Jihad to Terrorism* (Islamabad: Society for Tolerance and Education).

Ahmed, Akbar S. (1997), *Jinnah, Pakistan and Islamic Identity: The Search for Saladin* (London: Routledge).

Ahmed, Ishtiaq (1996), *State, Nation and Ethnicity in Contemporary South Asia* (London: Pinter).

Akhromeev, S. F., and G. M. Kornienko (1992), *Glazami marshala i diplomata: Kriticheskii vzgliad na vneshniuiu politiku SSSR do i posle 1985 goda* (Moscow: «Mezhdunarodnye otnosheniia»).

Akram, Assem (1996), *Histoire de la guerre d'Afghanistan* (Paris: Éditions Balland).

Alatas, Syed Hussain (1990), *Corruption: Its Nature, Causes and Functions* (Aldershot: Avebury).

Albone, Tim (2007), 'Iran gives Taliban hi-tech weapons to fight British', *The Times,* 5 August.

Alexeyeva, Ludmilla (1985), *Soviet Dissent: Contemporary Movements for National, Religious, and Human Rights* (Middletown, CT: Wesleyan University Press).

Alexievich, Svetlana (1992), *Zinky Boys: Soviet Voices from a Forgotten War* (London: Chatto & Windus).

Allan, Pierre, and Dieter Kläy (1999), *Zwischen Bürokratie und Ideologie: Entscheidungsprozesse in Moskaus Afghanistankonflikt* (Bern: Haupt Verlag).

Allawi, Ali A. (2007), *The Occupation of Iraq: Winning the War, Losing the Peace* (New Haven: Yale University Press).

Allison, Roy (1988), *The Soviet Union and the Strategy of Non-Alignment in the Third World* (Cambridge: Cambridge University Press).

Amanat, Abbas, and Frank Griffel (eds) (2007), *Shari'a: Islamic Law in the Contemporary Context* (Stanford: Stanford University Press).

Amanpour, Christiane (1997), 'Tyranny of the Taliban', *Time,* 13 October.

Amnesty International (1983), *Democratic Republic of Afghanistan: Background Briefing on Amnesty International's Concerns* (London: Amnesty International, ASA 11/13/83).

—— (1984), *Summary of Amnesty International's Concerns in the Democratic Republic of Afghanistan* (London: Amnesty International, ASA 11/07/84).

—— (1986), *Afghanistan: Torture of Political Prisoners* (London: Amnesty International, ASA 11/04/86).

—— (1995), *Afghanistan: International Responsibility for Human Rights Disaster* (London: Amnesty International, ASA 11/09/95).

—— (1999a), *Afghanistan: The Human Rights of Minorities* (London: Amnesty International, ASA 11/14/99).

—— (1999b), *Afghanistan: Cruel, Inhuman or Degrading Treatment or Punishment* (London: Amnesty International, ASA 11/15/99).

—— (1999c), *Women in Afghanistan: Pawns in Men's Power Struggles* (London: Amnesty International, ASA 11/11/99).

—— (2001), *Afghanistan: Massacres in Yakaolang* (London: Amnesty International, ASA 11/08/2001).

Anderson, Jon Lee (2002), *The Lion's Grave: Dispatches from Afghanistan* (New York: Grove Press).

Andres, Richard B., Craig Wills, and Thomas Griffith Jr. (2005–2006), 'Winning with Allies: The Strategic Value of the Afghan Model', *International Security*, 30, 3: 124–60.

Andrew, Christopher, and Vasili Mitrokhin (1999), *The Sword and the Shield: The Mitrokhin Archive and the Secret History of the KGB* (New York: Basic Books).

—— (2005), *The World Was Going Our Way: The KGB and the Battle for the Third World* (New York: Basic Books).

Ansari, Ali M. (2006), *Confronting Iran: The Failure of American Foreign Policy and the Next Great Crisis in the Middle East* (New York: Basic Books).

—— (2007), *Iran under Ahmadinejad: The politics of confrontation* (London: Adelphi Paper no. 393, International Institute for Strategic Studies, Routledge).

Apple, R. W., Jr. (2001), 'Issue Now: Does US Have a Plan?', *The New York Times*, 27 September.

Arnold, Anthony (1983), *Afghanistan's Two-Party Communism: Parcham and Khalq* (Stanford, CA: Hoover Institution Press).

—— (1985), *Afghanistan: The Soviet Invasion in Perspective* (Stanford, CA: Hoover Institution Press).

—— (1988), 'Parallels and Divergences between the US Experience in Vietnam and the Soviet Experience in Afghanistan', *Central Asian Survey*, 7, 2–3: 111–32.

—— (1990), 'Behind Afghanistan Coup Plot', *San Francisco Chronicle*, 28 March.

—— (1993), *The Fateful Pebble: Afghanistan's Role in the Fall of the Soviet Empire* (San Francisco: Presidio Press).

—— (1994), 'The Ephemeral Elite: The Failure of Socialist Afghanistan', in Myron Weiner and Ali Banuazizi (eds), *The Politics of Social Transformation in Afghanistan, Iran, and Pakistan* (Syracuse, NY: Syracuse University Press): 35–71.

Aron, Raymond (1966), *Peace and War: A Theory of International Relations* (London: Weidenfeld & Nicolson).

Asia Foundation (2004), *Democracy in Afghanistan 2004: A Survey of the Afghan Electorate* (Kabul: The Asia Foundation).

—— (2006), *Afghanistan in 2006: A Survey of the Afghan People* (Kabul: The Asia Foundation).

—— (2007), *Afghanistan in 2007: A Survey of the Afghan People* (Kabul: The Asia Foundation).

—— (2008), *Afghanistan in 2008: A Survey of the Afghan People* (Kabul: The Asia Foundation).

Augoyard, Philippe (1985), *La prison pour délit d'espoir: médecin en Afghanistan* (Paris: Flammarion).

Azerbaijani-Moghaddam, Sippi (2006), 'Gender in Afghanistan', in *Promoting Democracy under Conditions of State Fragility: Afghanistan* (Berlin: Heinrich Böll Foundation): 25–45.

—— (2007), 'On Living with Negative Peace and a Half-Built State: Gender and Human Rights', *International Peacekeeping*, 14, 1: 127–42.

Azimi, Fakhreddin (2008), *The Quest for Democracy in Iran: A Century of Struggle Against Authoritarian Rule* (Cambridge: Harvard University Press).

Bacevich, Andrew J. (2008), *The Limits of Power: The End of American Exceptionalism* (New York: Metropolitan Books),

Baily, John (2001), *'Can you stop the birds singing?': The Censorship of Music in Afghanistan* (London: Freemuse).

Baitenmann, Helga (1990), 'NGOs and the Afghan War: The Politicisation of Humanitarian Aid', *Third World Quarterly,* 12, 1: 62–85.

Baldrauf, Scott (2006), 'A "Half Full" Afghan Army', *Christian Science Monitor*, 10 February.

Ball, Desmond (1989), *Soviet Signals Intelligence (SIGINT)* (Canberra: Canberra Papers on Strategy and Defence no. 47, Strategic and Defence Studies Centre, Research School of Pacific Studies, Australian National University).

Banerjee, Dipankar (1997), 'Use of Land Mines in War', Paper presented at the Regional Seminar for Asian Military and Strategic Studies Experts 'Anti-personnel Mines: What Future for Asia?', International Committee of the Red Cross, Government of the Republic of the Philippines, and Philippine National Red Cross Society, Manila, 20–23 July.

Barfield, Thomas J. (1984), 'Weak Links on a Rusty Chain: Structural Weaknesses in Afghanistan's Provincial Government Administration', in M. Nazif Shahrani and Robert L. Canfield (eds), *Revolutions and Rebellions in Afghanistan: Anthropological Perspectives* (Berkeley: Institute of International Studies, University of California, 1984): 170–84.

—— (1989), *The Perilous Frontier: Nomadic Empires and China, 221 BC to AD 1757* (Oxford: Blackwell).

—— (2005), 'An Islamic State Is a State Run by Good Muslims: Religion as a Way of Life and Not an Ideology in Afghanistan', in Robert W. Hefner (ed.), *Remaking Muslim Politics: Pluralism, Contestation, Democratization* (Princeton: Princeton University Press): 213–39.

Barry, Michael (1974), *Afghanistan* (Paris: Éditions du Seuil).

—— (1980), 'Répressions et guerre soviétiques', *Les Temps Modernes,* 408–9: 171–234.

—— (2002), *Massoud: De l'Islamisme à la Liberté* (Paris: Éditions Louis Audibert).

Barry, Michael, Johan Lagerfelt, and Marie-Odile Terrenoire (1986), 'International Humanitarian Enquiry Commission on Displaced Persons in Afghanistan', *Central Asian Survey,* 5, 1: 65–99.

Batkin, Leonid (1989), 'Two Worlds Meet at the Congress of Deputies', *Moscow News,* 11 June.

Beall, Jo, and Stefan Schütte (2006), *Urban Livelihoods in Afghanistan* (Kabul: Afghanistan Research and Evaluation Unit).

Bearak, Barry (2001), 'In Village Where Innocents Died, Anger Cannot Be Buried', *The New York Times*, 16 December.

Bearden, Milton (2001), 'Afghanistan, Graveyard of Empires', *Foreign Affairs*, 80, 6: 17–30.

Bell, Gavin (1987), 'Paradise Lost in Afghan Valley of Death', *The Times*, 21 July.

Bellamy, Alex J. (2006), *Just Wars: From Cicero to Iraq* (Cambridge: Polity Press).

Bender, Bryan, Kim Burger, and Andrew Koch (2001), 'Afghanistan: First Lessons', *Jane's Defence Weekly*, 36, 25: 18–21.

Bergen, Peter L. (2001a), *Holy War, Inc.: Inside the Secret World of Osama Bin Laden* (New York: The Free Press).

—— (2001b), 'The Bin Laden Trial: What Did We Learn?', *Studies in Conflict and Terrorism*, 24, 6: 429–34.

Bermudez, Joseph S., Jr. (1992), 'Ballistic Missiles in the Third World – Afghanistan 1979–1992', *Jane's Intelligence Review*, 4, 2: 51–8.

Beschloss, Michael R., and Strobe Talbott (1993), *At the Highest Levels: The Inside Story of the End of the Cold War* (Boston, MA: Little, Brown & Co.).

Bet-El, Ilana, and Rupert Smith (2008), 'The Bell Tolls for NATO', *The National Interest*, 93: 62–66.

Bhatia, Michael (2007), 'The Future of the Mujahideen: Legitimacy, Legacy and Demobilization in Post-Bonn Afghanistan', *International Peacekeeping*, 14, 1: 90–107.

Bhatia, Michael, and Mark Sedra (2008), *Afghanistan, Arms and Conflict: Armed groups, disarmament and security in a post-war society* (New York: Routledge).

Bialer, Seweryn (1980), *Stalin's Successors: Leadership, Stability, and Change in the Soviet Union* (Cambridge: Cambridge University Press).

Billington, James H. (1992), *Russia Transformed: Breakthrough to Hope* (New York: The Free Press).

Birgisson, Karl Th. (1993), 'United Nations Good Offices Mission in Afghanistan and Pakistan', in William J. Durch (ed.), *The Evolution of UN Peacekeeping: Case Studies and Comparative Analysis* (New York: St. Martin's Press).

Biró, Daniel (2007), 'The (Un)bearable Lightness of... Violence: Warlordism as an Alternative Form of Governance in the "Westphalian Periphery"?', in Tobias Debiel and Daniel Lambach (eds), *State Failure Revisited II: Actors of Violence and Alternative Forms of Governance* (Duisburg: Institute for Development and Peace: Universität Duisburg-Essen): 7–49.

Black, Jeremy (1998), *Why Wars Happen* (London: Reaktion Books).

Blainey, Geoffrey (1973), *The Causes of War* (Basingstoke: Macmillan).

Boesen, Inger W. (1988), 'What Happens to Honour in Exile? Continuity and Change among Afghan Refugees', in Bo Huldt and Erland Jansson (eds), *The Tragedy of Afghanistan: The Social, Cultural and Political Impact of the Soviet Invasion* (London: Croom Helm): 2 19–39.

—— (2004), *From Subjects to Citizens: Local Participation in the National Solidarity Programme* (Kabul: Afghanistan Research and Evaluation Unit).

Bogomolov, Oleg (1988), 'Kto zhe oshibalsia?', *Literaturnaia gazeta*, 16 March.

Bokhari, Imtiaz H. (1995), 'Internal Negotiations among Many Actors: Afghanistan', in I. William Zartman (ed.), *Elusive Peace: Negotiating an End to Civil Wars* (Washington DC: The Brookings Institution).

Bonner, Michael (2006), *Jihad in Islamic History: Doctrines and Practice* (Princeton: Princeton University Press).

Borchgrave, Arnaud de (2001), 'Analysis: Pakistan's Aid to Taliban', *United Press International*, 18 June.

Borer, Douglas A. (1999), *Superpowers Defeated: Vietnam and Afghanistan Compared* (London: Frank Cass).

Borovik, Artyom (1988), 'Afganistan – predvaritel'nye itogi', *Ogonek*, 30: 25–7.

—— (1990), *The Hidden War: A Russian Journalist's Account of the Soviet War in Afghanistan* (London: Faber & Faber).

Bose, Sumantra (2003), *Kashmir: Roots of Conflict, Paths to Peace* (Cambridge: Harvard University Press).

Boutros-Ghali, Boutros (1999), *Unvanquished: A U.S–U.N. Saga* (New York: Random House).

Bowler, Shaun, David M. Farrell and Robin T. Pettitt (2005), 'Expert Opinion on Electoral Systems: So Which Electoral System is "Best"?', *Journal of Elections, Public Opinion and Parties*, 15, 1: 3–19.

Bradsher, Henry S. (1985), *Afghanistan and the Soviet Union* (Durham, NC: Duke University Press).

—— (1987), 'Communism in Afghanistan', in Hafeez Malik (ed.), *Soviet-American Relations with Pakistan, Iran and Afghanistan* (London: Macmillan Press): 333–54.

—— (1999), *Afghan Communism and Soviet Intervention* (Karachi: Oxford University Press).

Brigot, André, and Olivier Roy (1988), *The War in Afghanistan* (London: Harvester Wheatsheaf).

Brodie, Bernard (1973), *War and Politics* (New York: Macmillan).

Brown, Archie (1996), *The Gorbachev Phenomenon* (Oxford: Oxford University Press).

—— (2007), *Seven Years that Changed the World: Perestroika in Perspective* (Oxford: Oxford University Press).

Brown, Douglas J. (1992), '*Dedovshchina*: Caste Tyranny in the Soviet armed forces', *Journal of Soviet Military Studies*, 5, 1: 53–79.

Brown, Vahid (2008), 'Foreign Fighters in Historical Perspective: The Case of Afghanistan', in Brian Fishman (ed.), *Bombers, Bank Accounts, and Bleedout: Al-Qa'ida's Road In and Out of Iraq* (West Point: Combating Terrorism Center at West Point): 16–31.

Broxup, Marie (1988), 'Afghanistan According to Soviet Sources, 1980–1985', *Central Asian Survey*, 7, 2/3: 197–204.

Brzezinski, Zbigniew (1998), 'Les Révélations d'un Ancien Conseiller de Carter: "Oui, la CIA est entrée en Afghanistan avant les Russes..."', *Le Nouvel Observateur*, 14 January.

Burke, Jason (2007), 'The new Taliban', *The Observer*, 14 October.

Burns, John F. (1989), 'In Afghanistan, Soviet Airlift Brings Bread and Guns', *The New York Times*, 24 May.

—— (1996), 'Stoning of Afghan Adulterers: Some Go to Take Part, Others Just to Watch', *The New York Times*, 3 November.

—— (1997), 'A Year of Harsh Islamic Rule Weighs Heavily for Afghans', *The New York Times*, 24 September.

—— (1998), 'Bhutto Clan Leaves Trail of Corruption in Pakistan', *The New York Times*, 9 January.

—— (2001), 'Pakistan Makes Last-Ditch Appeal to Taliban', *The New York Times*, 28 September.

Burns, Robert (2007), 'Mullen: Afghanistan Isn't Top Priority', *The Washington Post*, 11 December.

Burton, Michael, and John Higley (1987), 'Elite Settlements', *American Sociological Review,* 52, 3: 295–307.

Burton, Michael, Richard Gunther, and John Higley (1992), 'Introduction: Elite Transformations and Democratic Regimes', in John Higley and Richard Gunther (eds), *Elites and Democratic Consolidation in Latin America and Southern Europe* (Cambridge: Cambridge University Press): 1–37.

Bush, George, and Brent Scowcroft (1998), *A World Transformed* (New York: Alfred A. Knopf).

Byman, Daniel (2005), *Deadly Connections: States that Sponsor Terrorism* (Cambridge: Cambridge University Press).

Campbell, Matthew (2001), 'Taliban Forced Orphanage Girls to Become Married Sex Slaves', *The Sunday Times,* 23 December.

Carnahan, Michael (2004), 'Next Steps in Reforming the Ministry of Finance', in Michael Carnahan, Nick Manning, Richard Bontjer and Stéphane Guimbert (eds), *Reforming Fiscal and Economic Management in Afghanistan* (Washington DC: The World Bank): 123–49.

Centlivres, Pierre (1997), 'Violence légitime et violence illégitime: À propos des pratiques et des répresentations dans la crise afghane', *L'Homme,* 144: 51–67.

—— (2001), *Les Bouddhas d'Afghanistan* (Lausanne: Éditions Favre).

Centlivres, Pierre, and Micheline Centlivres-Demont (1988a), 'Hommes d'influence et hommes de partis: L'organisation politique dans les villages de réfugiés afghans au Pakistan', in Erwin Grötzbach (ed.), *Neue Beiträge zur Afghanistanforschung* (Liestal: Stiftung Bibliotheca Afghanica): 29–43.

Centlivres-Demont, Micheline (1994), 'Afghan Women in Peace, War, and Exile', in Myron Weiner and Ali Banuazizi (eds), *The Politics of Social Transformation in Afghanistan, Iran, and Pakistan* (Syracuse, NY: Syracuse University Press): 333–65.

Chandrasekaran, Rajiv (2001), 'Key Allies of Afghan Rebels Reject Future Taliban Role', *The Washington Post,* 21 October.

—— (2006), *Imperial Life in the Emerald City: Inside Iraq's Green Zone* (New York: Alfred A. Knopf).

Chayes, Sarah (2006), *The Punishment of Virtue: Inside Afghanistan after the Taliban* (New York: Penguin Press).

Chernyaev, Anatoly S. (2000), *My Six Years with Gorbachev* (University Park: The Pennsylvania State University Press).

Chevalerias, Alain (1985), 'Guerre et subversion dans le nord de l'Afghanistan', *Les Nouvelles d'Afghanistan,* 23: 6–7.

Chipaux, Françoise (2000), 'Le rôle ambigu des talibans dans l'affaire du détournement de l'Airbus', *Le Monde,* 7 January.

Choudhary, G. W. (1974), *The Last Days of United Pakistan* (Perth: University of Western Australia Press).

Churchill, Winston (1990), *The Story of the Malakand Field Force* (New York: W. W. Norton).

Cirincione, Joseph, with Jon B. Wolfsthal and Miriam Rajkumar (2002), *Deadly Arsenals: Tracking Weapons of Mass Destruction* (Washington DC: Carnegie Endowment for International Peace).

Clark, William A. (1993), *Crime and Punishment in Soviet Officialdom: Combating Corruption in the Political Elite, 1965–1990* (Armonk: M. E. Sharpe).

Clarke, Richard A. (2004), *Against All Enemies: Inside America's War on Terror* (New York: The Free Press).

Clausewitz, Carl von (1984), *On War* (Princeton, NJ: Princeton University Press).

Cloughley, Brian (1999), *A History of the Pakistan Army: Wars and Insurrections* (Karachi: Oxford University Press).

Cogan, Charles G. (1993), 'Partners in Time: The CIA and Afghanistan since 1979', *World Policy Journal,* 10, 2: 73–82.

Cohen, Craig (2007), *A Perilous Course: U.S. Strategy and Assistance to Pakistan* (Washington DC: Post-Conflict Reconciliation Project, Center for Strategic and International Studies).

Cohen, Craig, and Derek Chollet (2007), 'When $10 Billion Is Not Enough: Rethinking U.S. Strategy toward Pakistan', *The Washington Quarterly,* 30, 2: 7–19.

Cohen, Stephen P. (1985), *The Pakistan Army* (Berkeley and Los Angeles: University of California Press).

Coll, Steve (1989), 'U.S. and Pakistan Shift Afghan Tactics', *International Herald Tribune,* 4 September.

—— (1992a), 'New Ray of Hope for Afghans', *International Herald Tribune,* 17 February.

—— (1992b), 'Peace Plan offered for Afghanistan', *The Washington Post,* 11 April.

—— (2005), *Ghost Wars: The Secret History of the CIA, Afghanistan and Bin Laden, from the Soviet Invasion to September 10, 2001* (London: Penguin).

Colton, Timothy J. (1979), *Commissars, Commanders, and Civilian Authority: The Structure of Soviet Military Politics* (Cambridge, MA: Harvard University Press).

—— (1986), *The Dilemma of Reform in the Soviet Union* (New York: Council on Foreign Relations).

Colville, Rupert (1997), 'The Biggest Case Load in the World', *Refugees,* 108: 3–9.

—— (1999), 'One Massacre That Didn't Grab the World's Attention', *International Herald Tribune,* 7 August.

Communist Party of the Soviet Union (1986), *Materialy XXVII s"ezda Kommunisticheskoi partii Sovetskogo Soiuza* (Moscow: Izdatel'stvo politicheskoi literatury).

Connor, Kerry M. (1987), 'Rationales for the Movement of Afghan Refugees to Peshawar', in Grant M. Farr and John G. Merriam (eds), *Afghan Resistance: The Politics of Survival* (Boulder, CO: Westview Press): 151–90.

Constable, Pamela (2001), 'U.S. Hopes to Attract Moderates in Taliban', *The Washington Post,* 17 October.

Cook, David (2005), *Understanding Jihad* (Berkeley and Los Angeles: University of California Press).

Cooper, Helene (2008), 'As Ills Persist, Afghan Leader is Losing Luster', *The New York Times,* 7 June.

Cooper, Kenneth J. (1998), 'Taliban Massacre Based on Ethnicity', *The Washington Post,* 28 November.

Cooperation Centre for Afghanistan (1998), *Ethnic Cleansing in Mazar: Eye Witnesses Stories* (Peshawar: Department of Human Rights: Cooperation Centre for Afghanistan).

Cordesman, Anthony H. (2002), *The Lessons of Afghanistan: War Fighting, Intelligence, and Force Transformation* (Washington DC: Center for Strategic and International Studies).

Cordesman, Anthony H., and Abraham R. Wagner (1990), *The Lessons of Modern War. Volume III: The Afghan and Falklands Conflicts* (Boulder, CO: Westview Press).

Cordovez, Diego, and Selig S. Harrison (1995), *Out of Afghanistan: The Inside Story of the Soviet Withdrawal* (New York: Oxford University Press).

Corera, Gordon (2006), *Shopping for Bombs: Nuclear Proliferation, Global Insecurity, and the Rise and Fall of the A.Q. Khan Network* (New York: Oxford University Press).

Cornell, Svante E. (2006), 'Taliban Afghanistan: A True Islamic State?', in Brenda Shaffer (ed.), *The Limits of Culture: Islam and Foreign Policy* (Cambridge: The MIT Press): 263–89.

Corwin, Phillip (2003), *Doomed in Afghanistan: A UN Officer's Memoir of the Fall of Kabul and Najibullah's Failed Escape, 1992* (New Brunswick: Rutgers University Press).

Crews, Robert D., and Amin Tarzi (eds) (2008), *The Taliban and the Crisis of Afghanistan* (Cambridge: Harvard University Press).

Crossette, Barbara (2000), 'Gentle Negotiations Said to Soften Taliban's Rules for Women', *The New York Times,* 23 January.

Cryer, Robert (2002), 'The Fine Art of Friendship: *Jus in Bello* in Afghanistan', *Journal of Conflict and Security Law,* 7, 1: 37–83.

Cullison, Alan, and Andrew Higgins (2002), 'Computer in Kabul Holds Chilling Memos', *The Wall Street Journal,* 1 January.

D'Afghanistan, Ehsanullah (1994), 'L'Afghanistan enfin', *Les Nouvelles d'Afghanistan,* 66: 6–10.

Danspeckgruber, Wolfgang, and William Maley (2009), 'Taliban Toxin', *The World Today,* 65, 6: 7–9.

Daugherty, Leo J. (1995), 'The Bear and the Scimitar: Soviet Central Asians and the War in Afghanistan', *Journal of Slavic Military Studies,* 8, 1: 73–96.

Davis, Anthony (1993a), 'The Afghan Army', *Jane's Intelligence Review,* 5, 3: 134–9.

—— (1993b), 'Foreign Combatants in Afghanistan', *Jane's Intelligence Review,* 5, 7: 327–31.

—— (1998), 'How the Taliban Became a Military Force', in William Maley (ed.), *Fundamentalism Reborn?: Afghanistan and the Taliban* (London: Hurst & Co.): 43–71.

—— (2002), 'How the Afghan War Was Won', *Jane's Intelligence Review,* 14, 2: 6–13.

Dekmejian, R. Hrair (1994), 'The Rise of Political Islamism in Saudi Arabia', *The Middle East Journal,* 48, 4: 627–43.

Delpho, Marc (1989), 'Aperçus sur le Badakhchân', *Les Nouvelles d'Afghanistan,* 41–2: 8, 49.

Desai, Raj, and Harry Eckstein (1990), 'Insurgency: The Transformation of Peasant Rebellion', *World Politics,* 42, 4: 441–65.

Deutscher, Isaac (1954), *The Prophet Armed: Trotsky: 1879–1921* (Oxford: Oxford University Press).

DeYoung, Karen, and Walter Pincus (2001), 'In Bin Laden's Own Words', *The Washington Post,* 14 December.

Diamond. Larry (2005), *Squandered Victory: The American Occupation and the Bungled Effort to Bring Democracy to Iraq* (New York: Times Books).

Dibb, Paul (1986), *The Soviet Union: The Incomplete Superpower* (London: Macmillan Press).

Diehl, Paul (1994), *International Peacekeeping* (Baltimore, MD: The Johns Hopkins University Press).

DiGiovanni, Janine (2001), 'Radicals Abroad Urged Destruction of Bamiyan Buddhas', *The Times,* 24 November.

DiManno, Rosie (2008), 'When Afghan tempers explode', *The Toronto Star,* 7 June.

DiPalma, Giuseppe (1990), *To Craft Democracies: An Essay on Democratic Transitions* (Berkeley and Los Angeles: University of California Press).

Dixit, J. N. (2000), *An Afghan Diary: Zahir Shah to Taliban* (Delhi: Konark Publishers).

Dobbins, James (2006), 'Moral Clarity and the Middle East', Speech to the New America Foundation, 24 August.

—— (2007), 'How to Talk to Iran', *The Washington Post*, 22 July.

—— (2008), *After The Taliban: Nation-Building in Afghanistan* (Washington DC: Potomac Books).

Dobbs, Michael (1992), 'Dramatic Politburo Meeting Led to End of War', *The Washington Post*, 16 November.

—— (1996), *Down With Big Brother: The Fall of the Soviet Empire* (New York: Alfred A. Knopf).

—— (2001), 'A Moment of Candor from a Manipulator', *The Washington Post*, 14 December.

Dobrynin, Anatoly (1995), *In Confidence: Moscow's Ambassador to America's Six Cold War Presidents* (Seattle: University of Washington Press).

Dodge, Toby (2003), *Inventing Iraq: The Failure of Nation Building and a History Denied* (New York: Columbia University Press).

Donini, Antonio (1996), *The Policies of Mercy: UN Coordination in Afghanistan, Mozambique and Rwanda* (Providence, RI: Occasional Paper no. 22, Thomas J. Watson Jr. Institute for International Studies, Brown University).

—— (2004), 'Principles, Politics, and Pragmatism in the International Response to the Afghan Crisis', in Antonio Donini, Norah Niland and Karin Wermester (eds), *Nation-Building Unraveled? Aid, Peace and Justice in Afghanistan* (Bloomfield: Kumarian Press): 117–42.

—— (2007), 'Negotiating with the Taliban', in Larry Minear and Hazel Smith (eds), *Humanitarian Diplomacy: Practitioners and Their Craft* (Tokyo: United Nations University Press): 153–73.

Dorronsoro, Gilles (1993), 'Leaders et partis à Kandahar', *Les Nouvelles d'Afghanistan*, 61: 3–5.

—— (1993–1994), 'Le parti de Dostom: Le Jumbesh', *Afghanistan Info*, 34: 11–14.

—— (1994), 'L'assassinat d'un journaliste', *Les Nouvelles d'Afghanistan*, 66: 20.

—— (1995), 'Afghanistan's Civil War', *Current History*, 84, 588: 37–40.

—— (2005), *Revolution Unending: Afghanistan, 1979 to the Present* (New York: Columbia University Press).

—— (2008), 'The Security Council and the Afghan Conflict', in Vaughan Lowe, Adam Roberts, Jennifer Welsh and Dominik Zaum (eds), *The United Nations Security Council and War: The Evolution of Thought and Practice since 1945* (Oxford: Oxford University Press): 452–65.

Dorronsoro, Gilles, and Chantal Lobato (1989), 'The Militias in Afghanistan', *Central Asian Survey*, 8, 4: 95–108.

Doyle, Michael W. (1997), *Ways of War and Peace* (New York: W. W. Norton).

D'Souza, Frances (1984), *The Threat of Famine in Afghanistan* (London: Afghanaid).

Dugger, Celia W. (2001), 'Taliban Foe Saw "Blue, Thick Fire" of Assassin Bomb', *The New York Times*, 26 October.

Dupaigne, Bernard (1983), 'La trêve au Panjshir', *Les Nouvelles d'Afghanistan*, 14: 8.

—— (1993–1994), 'Herat, un modèle et une chance pour l'Afghanistan', *Afghanistan Info*, 34: 7–10.

—— (1995), 'L'émergence du mouvement des Tâlebân', *Les Nouvelles d'Afghanistan*, 68: 13–17.

Dupree, Louis (1961), 'The Durand Line of 1893: A Case Study in Artificial Political Boundaries and Culture Areas', in *Current Problems in Afghanistan* (Princeton: The Princeton University Conference): 77–93.

—— (1973), *Afghanistan* (Princeton, NJ: Princeton University Press).

Dupree, Louis (1979), 'Red Flag over the Hindu Kush: Part II: The Accidental Coup, or Taraki in Blunderland', *American Universities Field Staff Reports,* 45 (Asia).

—— (1980a), 'Red Flag over the Hindu Kush: Part V: Repressions, or Security Through Terror Purges I–IV', *American Universities Field Staff Reports,* 28 (Asia).

—— (1980b), 'Red Flag over the Hindu Kush: Part VI: Repressions, or Security Through Terror Purges IV–VI', *American Universities Field Staff Reports,* 29 (Asia).

—— (1989), 'Post-Withdrawal Afghanistan: Light at the End of the Tunnel', in Amin Saikal and William Maley (eds), *The Soviet Withdrawal from Afghanistan* (Cambridge: Cambridge University Press): 29–51.

Dupree, Nancy Hatch (1984), 'Revolutionary Rhetoric and Afghan Women', in M. Nazif Shahrani and Robert L. Canfield (eds), *Revolutions and Rebellions in Afghanistan: Anthropological Perspectives* (Berkeley: Institute of International Studies, University of California, 1984): 306–40.

—— (1987), 'The Demography of Afghan Refugees in Pakistan', in Hafeez Malik (ed.), *Soviet-American Relations with Pakistan, Iran and Afghanistan* (Basingstoke: Macmillan): 366–95.

—— (1988a), 'Demographic Reporting on Afghan Refugees in Pakistan', *Modern Asian Studies,* 22, 4: 845–65.

—— (1988b), 'The Role of the VOLAGS', in Bo Huldt and Erland Jansson (eds), *The Tragedy of Afghanistan: The Social, Cultural and Political Impact of the Soviet Invasion* (London: Croom Helm): 248–62.

—— (1992), 'Afghanistan: Women, Society and Development', in Joseph G. Jabbra and Nancy W. Jabbra (eds), *Women and Development in the Middle East and North Africa* (Leiden: E. J. Brill): 30–42.

—— (1996), 'Museum Under Siege', *Archaeology,* 49, 2: 42–51.

—— (1998), 'Afghan Women Under the Taliban', in William Maley (ed.), *Fundamentalism Reborn?: Afghanistan and the Taliban* (London: Hurst & Co.): 145–66.

Dziedzic, Michael J., and Michael K. Seidl (2005), *Provincial Reconstruction Teams and Military Relations with International and Nongovernmental Organizations in Afghanistan* (Washington DC: Special Report no.147, United States Institute of Peace).

Edwards, David B. (1993), 'Summoning Muslims: Print, Politics, and Religious Ideology in Afghanistan', *Journal of Asian Studies,* 52, 3: 609–28.

—— (1996), *Heroes of the Age: Moral Fault Lines on the Afghan Frontier* (Berkeley and Los Angeles: University of California Press).

—— (2002), *Before Taliban: Genealogies of the Afghan Jihad* (Berkeley and Los Angeles: University of California Press).

Eickelman, Dale F., and James Piscatori (2004), *Muslim Politics* (Princeton: Princeton University Press).

Eighmy, Thomas H. (1990), *Afghanistan's Population Inside and Out* (Islamabad: Office of the A.I.D. Representative for Afghanistan).

Elias, Barbara (2007), *Pakistan: 'The Taliban's Godfather?'* (Washington DC: National Security Archive Electronic Briefing Book No. 227, National Security Archive, George Washington University, 2007).

Ellis, Deborah (2000), *Women of the Afghan War* (Westport, CT: Praeger).

Evans, Anne, Nick Manning, Yasin Osmani, Anne Tully and Andrew Wilder (2004), *A Guide to Government in Afghanistan* (Kabul: Afghanistan Research and Evaluation Unit).

Ewens, Martin (2002), *Afghanistan: A Short History of Its People and Politics* (New York: HarperCollins).

—— (2005), *Conflict in Afghanistan: Studies in asymmetric warfare* (New York: Routledge).

Fänge, Anders (1995), 'Afghanistan after April 1992: A Struggle for State and Ethnicity', *Central Asian Survey*, 14, 1: 17–24.

FAO/WFP (1999), *FAO/WFP Crop and Food Supply Assessment Mission to Afghanistan: Special Report* (Rome: Food and Agriculture Organization and World Food Programme, 7 July).

Farber, David (2005), *Taken Hostage: The Iran Hostage Crisis and America's First Encounter with Radical Islam* (Princeton: Princeton University Press).

Farr, Grant M., and Azam Gul (1984), 'Afghan Agricultural Production: 1978–1982', *Journal of South Asian and Middle Eastern Studies*, 8, 1: 65–79.

Fein, Helen (1993), 'Discriminating Genocide from War Crimes: Vietnam and Afghanistan Reexamined', *Denver Journal of International Law and Policy*, 22, 1: 29–62.

Feith, Douglas J. (2008), *War and Decision: Inside the Pentagon at the Dawn of the War on Terror* (New York: Harper).

Felbab-Brown, Vanda (2005), 'Afghanistan: When Counternarcotics Undermines Counterterrorism', *The Washington Quarterly*, 28, 4: 55–72.

—— (2009), 'Peacekeepers Among Poppies: Afghanistan, Illicit Economies and Intervention', *International Peacekeeping*, 16, 1: 100–14.

Fergusson, James (1997), 'Afghanistan: The Peace Brought by the Taliban', *The Independent*, 19 February.

Ferrero, Guglielmo (1942), *The Principles of Power: The Great Political Crises of History* (New York: G. P. Putnam's Sons).

Fetherston, A. B. (1994), *Towards a Theory of United Nations Peacekeeping* (Basingstoke: Macmillan).

Fielden, Matthew, and Jonathan Goodhand (2001), 'Beyond the Taliban? The Afghan Conflict and United Nations Peacemaking', *Conflict, Security and Development*, 1, 3: 5–32.

Filkins, Dexter (2001a), 'Rebel Leader Rejects Role for Taliban in New Regime', *The New York Times*, 17 October.

—— (2001b), 'Mysteries in Kunduz after the Taliban Fled', *International Herald Tribune*, 28 November.

—— (2008), 'Right at the Edge', *The New York Times*, 7 September.

Fischer, Felix (2005), 'Financial Sector Development in Afghanistan: Seeking a Renaissance', in Adam Bennett (ed.), *Reconstructing Afghanistan* (Washington DC: International Monetary Fund): 72–83.

Fitchett, Joseph (2001), 'Did Bin Laden Kill Afghan Rebel?', *International Herald Tribune*, 17 September.

Fitzhardinge, Hope Verity (1968), 'The Establishment of the North-West Frontier of Afghanistan, 1884–1888', Ph.D. thesis, Australian National University.

Forsythe, David P. (2005), *The Humanitarians: The International Committee of the Red Cross* (Cambridge: Cambridge University Press).

Fox, Jonathan (1998), 'The Effects of Religion on Domestic Conflict', *Terrorism and Political Violence*, 10, 4: 43–63.

Franck, Thomas M., and Georg Nolte (1993), 'The Good Offices Function of the UN Secretary-General', in Adam Roberts and Benedict Kingsbury (eds), *United Nations, Divided World: The UN's Roles in International Relations* (Oxford: Oxford University Press): 143–82.

Frantz, Douglas (2001), 'Pakistan Ended Aid to Taliban Only Hesitantly', *The New York Times*, 8 December.

Fry, Maxwell J. (1974), *The Afghan Economy: Money, Finance and the Critical Constraints to Economic Development* (Leiden: E. J. Brill).

Fukuyama, Francis (2001), 'Social Capital, Civil Society, and Development', *Third World Quarterly*, 22, 1: 7–20.

—— (2004), *State-Building: Governance and World Order in the 21st Century* (Ithaca: Cornell University Press).

Galeotti, Mark (1995), *Afghanistan: The Soviet Union's Last War* (London: Frank Cass & Co.).

—— (1997), *Gorbachev and His Revolution* (Basingstoke: Macmillan).

Gall, Carlotta (2004), 'Afghan Talks Adjourn, Deeply Divided on Ethnic Lines', *The New York Times*, 2 January.

—— (2006), 'Pakistan Link Seen in Afghan Suicide Attacks', *The New York Times*, 13 November.

—— (2007a), 'At Border, Signs of Pakistani Role in Taliban Surge', *The New York Times*, 21 January.

—— (2007b), 'Rough Treatment for 2 Journalists in Pakistan', *The New York Times*, 21 January.

—— (2008a), '3 Western Aid Workers and an Afghan Driver Killed in Attack', *The New York Times*, 13 August.

—— (2008b), 'Afghans Want a Deal on Foreign Troops', *The New York Times*, 26 August.

—— (2008c), 'Taliban Gain New Foothold in Afghan City', *The New York Times*, 27 August.

—— (2008d), 'Bombing at Hotel in Pakistan Kills at Least 40', *The New York Times*, 21 September.

Gall, Carlotta, and Abdul Waheed Wafa (2008), 'Karzai Escapes Attack in Kabul By Gunmen', *The New York Times*, 28 April.

Gall, Carlotta, and Sangar Rahimi (2008), 'Taliban Escalate Afghan Fighting', *The New York Times*, 20 August.

Gall, Sandy (1988), *Afghanistan: Agony of a Nation* (London: The Bodley Head).

Ganguly, Rajat (1998), *Kin State Intervention in Ethnic Conflicts: Lessons from South Asia* (New Delhi: SAGE Publications).

Ganguly, Sumit (1997), *The Crisis in Kashmir: Portents of War, Hopes of Peace* (Cambridge: Cambridge University Press).

—— (2001), *Conflict Unending: India-Pakistan Tensions since 1947* (New York: Oxford University Press).

Gannon, Kathy (2008), 'Taliban factions unite to battle Pakistan', *The Boston Globe*, 27 January.

Gardiner, Beth (2006), 'World Pledges $10.5B for Afghanistan Aid'. *The Washington Post*, 1 February.

Gargan, Edward A. (1992a), 'Afghan President Agrees to Step Down', *The New York Times,* 19 March.

—— (1992b), 'Afghan President Ousted as Rebels Approach Capital', *The New York Times,* 17 April.

Garthoff, Raymond L. (1994), *Détente and Confrontation: American-Soviet Relations from Nixon to Reagan* (Washington, DC: The Brookings Institution).

Gauhari, Farooka (1996), *Searching for Saleem: An Afghan Woman's Odyssey* (Lincoln: University of Nebraska Press).

Gélinas, Sylvie (1997), *Afghanistan du communisme au fondamentalisme* (Paris: L'Harmattan).

General Accounting Office (2004), *Afghanistan Reconstruction: Deteriorating Security and Limited Resources Have Impeded Progress; Improvements in U.S. Strategy Needed* (Washington DC: United States General Accounting Office).

Gerecht, Reuel Marc (2001), 'Taking Sides in Afghanistan', *The New York Times,* 8 March.

Ghani, Ashraf (1985), 'Afghanistan: Administration', in Ehsan Yarshater (ed.), *Encyclopædia Iranica,* Vol. I (London: Routledge & Kegan Paul): 558–64.

Ghani, Ashraf, and Clare Lockhart (2008), *Fixing Failed States: A Framework for Rebuilding a Fractured World* (New York: Oxford University Press).

Ghani, Ashraf, Clare Lockhart, Nargis Nehan, and Baqer Massoud (2007), 'The Budget as the Linchpin of the State: Lessons from Afghanistan', in James K. Boyce and Madalene O'Donnell (eds), *Peace and the Public Purse: Economic Policies for Postwar Statebuilding* (Boulder: Lynne Rienner): 153–83.

Ghaus, Abdul Samad (1988), *The Fall of Afghanistan: An Insider's Account* (McLean: Pergamon-Brassey's).

Gill, Graeme (1994), *The Collapse of a Single-Party System: The Disintegration of the Communist Party of the Soviet Union* (Cambridge: Cambridge University Press).

Gille, Etienne (1980), 'Avec les manifestants d'avril à Kaboul', *Les Nouvelles d'Afghanistan,* 2: 10–11.

—— (1986), 'Les purges du Docteur Najibullah', *Les Nouvelles d'Afghanistan,* 29–30: 4.

—— (1993), 'Crimes à Afchâr', *Les Nouvelles d'Afghanistan,* 60: II–III.

—— (1994), 'Djallâlâbâd', *Les Nouvelles d'Afghanistan,* 65: 3–5.

—— (1996), 'Les combats à Kaboul depuis 1992', *Les Nouvelles d'Afghanistan,* 72: 4.

—— (1997), 'Le nom d'Afghanistan', *Les Nouvelles d'Afghanistan,* 79: 5.

Gille, Etienne, and Sylvie Heslot (eds) (1989), *Chronique d'un témoin privilégié: Lettres d'Afghanistan de Serge de Beaurecueil – I – 1979: la Terreur* (Paris: Centre de Recherches et d'Études Documentaires sur l'Afghanistan).

Girardet, Edward (1985), *Afghanistan: The Soviet War* (London: Croom Helm).

Giustozzi, Antonio (2000), *War, Politics and Society in Afghanistan 1978–1992* (London: Hurst & Co.).

—— (2007), *Koran, Kalashnikov and Laptop: The Neo-Taliban Insurgency in Afghanistan* (London: Hurst & Co.).

—— (2008), 'Bureaucratic façade and political realities of disarmament and demobilisation in Afghanistan', *Conflict, Security and Development,* 8, 2: 169–92.

—— (2009), *Empires of Mud: War and Warlordism in Afghanistan* (London: Hurst & Co.).

Glasser, Susan B., and Kamran Khan (2001), 'Pakistan Closes Taliban's Last Embassy', *The Washington Post,* 23 November.

Glatzer, Bernt (1977), *Nomaden von Gharjistan: Aspekte der wirtschaftlichen, sozialen und politischen Organisation nomadischer Durrani-Paschtunen in Nordwestafghanistan* (Wiesbaden: Franz Steiner Verlag).

—— (1997), 'Die Talibanbewegung: Einige religiöse, lokale und politische Faktoren', *Afghanistan Info,* 41: 10–14.

—— (1998), 'Is Afghanistan on the Brink of Ethnic and Tribal Disintegration?', in William Maley (ed.), *Fundamentalism Reborn? Afghanistan and the Taliban* (London: Hurst & Co.): 167–81.

Golden, Tim (2005), 'In U.S. Report, Brutal Details of 2 Afghan Inmates' Deaths', *The New York Times,* 20 May.

Goldman, Minton F. (1992), 'President Bush and Afghanistan: A Turning Point in American Policy', *Comparative Strategy*, 11, 2: 177–93.

Goldsmith, Ben R. (1997), 'A Victory to Fear or a Source of Hope?', *The World Today*, 53, 7: 182–4.

Goodhand, Jonathan (2008), 'Corrupting or Consolidating the Peace?: The Drugs Economy and Post-Conflict Peacebuilding in Afghanistan', *International Peacekeeping*, 15, 3: 405–423.

Goodhand, Jonathan, and Mark Sedra (2007), 'Bribes or Bargains? Peace Conditionalities and "Post-Conflict" Reconstruction in Afghanistan', *International Peacekeeping*, 14, 1: 41–61.

Goodson, Larry P. (1998), 'Periodicity and Intensity in the Afghan War', *Central Asian Survey*, 17, 3: 471–88.

—— (2001), *Afghanistan's Endless War: State Failure, Regional Politics, and the Rise of the Taliban* (Seattle: University of Washington Press).

Goodwin, Jan (1987), *Caught in the Crossfire* (London: Macdonald).

Gorbachev, Mikhail (1996), *Memoirs* (New York: Doubleday).

Gordon, Michael R. (2001), 'U.S. Hopes to Break the Taliban with Pounding from the Air', *The New York Times*, 17 October.

—— (2007), 'U.S. Says Iranian Arms Seized in Afghanistan', *The New York Times*, 18 April.

Gordon, Michael R., and David E. Sanger (2001), 'Bush Approves Covert Aid for Taliban Foes', *The New York Times*, 1 October.

Gordon, Michael R., and Thom Shanker (2001), 'Bush Says Aim Is to Ease Entry of Land Force', *The New York Times*, 18 October.

Government Accountability Office (2008), *Combating Terrorism: The United States Lacks Comprehensive Plans to Destroy the Terrorist Threat and Close the Safe Havens in Pakistan's Federally Administered Tribal Areas* (Washington DC: United States Government Accountability Office).

Government of Afghanistan (2004), *Securing Afghanistan's Future: Accomplishments and the Strategic Path Forward* (Kabul: Government of Afghanistan, Asian Development Bank, United Nations Assistance Mission to Afghanistan, United Nations Development Program and The World Bank Group).

Grare, Frédéric (2006), *Pakistan-Afghanistan Relations in the Post-9/11 Era* (Washington DC: Carnegie Endowment for International Peace).

—— (2007), *Rethinking Western Strategies toward Pakistan: An Action Agenda for the United States and Europe* (Washington DC: Carnegie Endowment for International Peace).

Grasselli, Gabriella (1996), *British and American Responses to the Soviet Invasion of Afghanistan* (Aldershot: Dartmouth).

Grau, Lester W. (1998), *The Bear Went Over the Mountain: Soviet Combat Tactics in Afghanistan* (London: Frank Cass & Co.).

Gray, Colin S. (1999), *Modern Strategy* (Oxford: Oxford University Press).

Greenhill, Kelly M., and Solomon Major (2006–2007), 'The Perils of Profiling: Civil War Spoilers and the Collapse of Intrastate Peace Accords', *International Security*, 31, 3: 7–40.

Gregory, Shaun (2007), 'The ISI and the War on Terrorism', *Studies in Conflict and Terrorism*, 30, 12: 1013–31.

Griffin, Michael (2004), *Reaping the Whirlwind: Afghanistan, Al Qa'ida and the Holy War* (London: Pluto Press).

Gromov, Boris V. (1994), *Ogranichennyi kontingent* (Moscow: Izdatel'skaia gruppa «Progress» – «Kul'tura»).

Gromyko, Anatolii, and Vladimir Lomeiko (1984), *Novoe myshlenie v iadernyi vek* (Moscow: «Mezhdunarodnye otnosheniia»).

Grossman, A. S. (1993), 'Sekretnye dokumenty iz osobykh papok: Afganistan', *Voprosy istorii*, 3: 3–33.

Gutman, Roy (2008), *How We Missed the Story: Osama Bin Laden, the Taliban, and the Hijacking of Afghanistan* (Washington DC: United States Institute of Peace Press).

Hafvenstein, Joel (2007), *Opium Season: A Year on the Afghan Frontier* (Guilford: The Lyons Press).

Haider, Ejaz (1998), 'Pakistan's Afghan Policy and its Fallout', *Central Asian Monitor*, 5: 1–6.

Hallaq, Wael B. (2005), *The Origins and Evolution of Islamic Law* (Cambridge: Cambridge University Press).

Halliday, Fred (1999), 'Soviet Foreign Policymaking and the Afghanistan War: From "Second Mongolia" to "Bleeding Wound"', *Review of International Studies*, 25, 4: 675–91.

Halliday, Fred, and Zahir Tanin (1998), 'The Communist Regime in Afghanistan 1978–1992: Institutions and Conflicts', *Europe-Asia Studies*, 50, 8: 1357–80.

Hamilton, Alexander, James Madison, and John Jay (1961), *The Federalist Papers* (New York: Mentor).

Hanifi, M. Jamil (2004), 'Editing the Past: Colonial Production of Hegemony Through the "*Loya Jerga*" in Afghanistan', *Iranian Studies*, 37, 2: 295–322.

Haqshenas, Sher Ahmad Nasri (1999), *Tawalat-e siasi jihad-e Afghanistan* (New Delhi: Jayyed Press) Vols. I–III.

Harasymiw, Bohdan (1969), '*Nomenklatura:* The Soviet Communist Party's Leadership Recruitment System', *Canadian Journal of Political Science*, 2, 4: 493–512.

Harel, Amos, and Avi Issacharoff (2008), *34 Days: Israel, Hezbollah, and the War in Lebanon* (New York: Palgrave Macmillan).

Haroon, Sana (2007), *Frontiers of Faith: Islam in the Indo-Afghan Borderland* (London: Hurst & Co.).

Harpviken, Kristian Berg (1996), *Political Mobilization among the Hazara of Afghanistan: 1978–1992* (Oslo: Report no. 9, Department of Sociology, University of Oslo).

—— (1997), 'Transcending Traditionalism: The Emergence of Non-State Military Formations in Afghanistan', *Journal of Peace Research*, 34, 3: 271–87.

Harrison, Mark (1993), 'Soviet Economic Growth since 1928: The Alternative Statistics of G. I. Khanin', *Europe-Asia Studies*, 45, 1: 141–67.

Harrison, Selig S. (1979), 'The Shah, Not Kremlin, Touched Off Afghan Coup', *The Washington Post*, 13 May.

Hartzell, Caroline A. (1999), 'Explaining the Stability of Negotiated Settlements to Intrastate Wars', *Journal of Conflict Resolution*, 43, 1: 3–22.

Hashim, Ahmed S. (2006), *Insurgency and Counter-Insurgency in Iraq* (Ithaca: Cornell University Press).

Hersh, Seymour M. (2004), *Chain of Command: The Road from 9/11 to Abu Ghraib* (London: Allen Lane).

Hershberg, James G. (ed.) (1996–1997), 'New Evidence on the Soviet Intervention in Afghanistan', *Cold War International History Bulletin*, 8–9: 128–84.

Herspring, Dale R. (1990), *The Soviet High Command 1967–1989: Personalities and Politics* (Princeton, NJ: Princeton University Press).

Higgins, Holly Barnes (2007), 'To Helmand and Back', *The American Interest*, 3, 2: 60–72.

Higley, John, and Michael G. Burton (1989), 'The Elite Variable in Democratic Transitions and Breakdowns', *American Sociological Review*, 54, 1: 17–32.

Hobsbawm, Eric, and Terence Ranger (eds) (1983), *The Invention of Tradition* (Cambridge: Cambridge University Press).

Hodes, Cyrus, and Mark Sedra (2007), *The Search for Security in Post-Taliban Afghanistan* (London: Adelphi Paper no.391, International Institute for Strategic Studies, Routledge).

Hoffman, Bruce, and Seth G. Jones (2008), 'Cellphones in the Hindu Kush', *The National Interest*, 96: 42–51.

Holloway, David (1989–1990), 'State, Society, and the Military under Gorbachev', *International Security*, 14, 3: 5–24.

Holmes, Leslie (1989), 'Afghanistan and Sino-Soviet Relations', in Amin Saikal and William Maley (eds), *The Soviet Withdrawal from Afghanistan* (Cambridge: Cambridge University Press): 122–41.

—— (1993), *The End of Communist Power: Anti-Corruption Campaigns and Legitimation Crisis* (New York: Oxford University Press).

Holsti, Kalevi J. (1996), *The State, War, and the State of War* (Cambridge: Cambridge University Press).

Hosking, Geoffrey (1990), *The Awakening of the Soviet Union* (London: Heinemann).

Hosseini, Khaled (2007), *A Thousand Splendid Suns* (London: Bloomsbury).

Hough, Jerry F. (1986), *The Struggle for the Third World: Soviet Debates and American Options* (Washington, DC: The Brookings Institution).

—— (1987), 'Moscow Deals from Strength in Afghanistan', *The Los Angeles Times*, 16 January.

—— (1997), *Democratization and Revolution in the USSR 1985–1991* (Washington, DC: Brookings Institution Press).

Human Rights Watch (1991), *Afghanistan: The Forgotten War. Human Rights Abuses and Violations of the Laws of War since the Soviet Withdrawal* (New York: Human Rights Watch).

—— (1998), *Afghanistan: The Massacre in Mazar-i Sharif* (New York: Human Rights Watch).

—— (2001a), *Afghanistan – Crisis of Impunity: The Role of Pakistan, Russia and Iran in Fuelling the Civil War* (New York: Human Rights Watch).

—— (2001b), *Massacres of Hazaras in Afghanistan* (New York: Human Rights Watch).

—— (2005), *Blood-Stained Hands: Past Atrocities in Kabul and Afghanistan's Legacy of Impunity* (New York: Human Rights Watch).

—— (2006), *Afghanistan: Conviction and Death Sentence of Former Intelligence Chief Flawed* (New York: Human Rights Watch).

—— (2008), *"Troops in Contact": Airstrikes and Civilian Deaths in Afghanistan* (New York: Human Rights Watch).

Hume, Cameron R. (1995), 'The Secretary-General's Representatives', *SAIS Review*, 15, 2: 75–90.

Hussain, Rizwan (2005), *Pakistan and the Emergence of Islamic Militancy in Afghanistan* (Aldershot: Ashgate).

Hussain, Shaiq, and Pamela Constable (2008), '21 Foreigners Among Dead in Islamabad Suicide Bomb Blast', *The Washington Post*, 22 September.

Hussain, Zahid (2001), 'US "allows Pakistani fighters to escape"', *The Times*, 24 November.

Hyman, Anthony (1990), 'Afghanistan's Uncertain Future', *Report on the USSR*, 3, 12: 15–16.

—— (1994), 'Arab Involvement in the Afghan War', *The Beirut Review*, 7: 73–89.

IISS (1979), *The Military Balance 1979–1980* (London: International Institute for Strategic Studies).

Iklé, Fred C. (1991), *Every War Must End* (New York: Columbia University Press).

International Commission on Intervention and State Sovereignty (2001), *The Responsibility to Protect: Report of the International Commission on Intervention and State Sovereignty* (Ottawa: International Development Research Centre).

International Crisis Group (2002), *Securing Afghanistan: The Need for More International Action* (Kabul and Brussels: International Crisis Group).

—— (2003a), *Afghanistan: The Problem of Pashtun Alienation* (Kabul and Brussels: International Crisis Group).

—— (2003b), *Disarmament and Reintegration in Afghanistan* (Kabul and Brussels: International Crisis Group).

—— (2006a), *Pakistan's Tribal Areas: Appeasing the Militants* (Islamabad and Brussels: International Crisis Group).

—— (2006b), *Countering Afghanistan's Insurgency: No Quick Fixes* (Kabul and Brussels: International Crisis Group).

—— (2007), *Reforming Afghanistan's Police* (Kabul and Brussels: International Crisis Group).

—— (2008a), *After Bhutto's Murder: A Way Forward for Pakistan* (Islamabad and Brussels: International Crisis Group).

—— (2008b), *Taliban Propaganda: Winning the War of Words?* (Kabul and Brussels: International Crisis Group).

—— (2008c), *Policing in Afghanistan: Still Searching for a Strategy* (Kabul and Brussels: International Crisis Group).

Isby, David C. (1989), *War in a Distant Country. Afghanistan: Invasion and Resistance* (London: Arms and Armour Press).

—— (1991), 'Soviet Arms Deliveries and Aid to Afghanistan 1989–91', *Jane's Intelligence Review*, 3, 8: 348–54.

Ispahani, Mahnaz Z. (1989), *Roads and Rivals: The Politics of Access in the Borderlands of Asia* (London: I. B. Tauris).

Jackson, Robert (1969), *A Study of the Capacity of the United Nations Development System* (Geneva: United Nations): Vols I–II.

Jalal, Ayesha (1995), *Democracy and Authoritarianism in South Asia: A Comparative and Historical Perspective* (Cambridge: Cambridge University Press).

Jalali, Ali Ahmad, and Lester W. Grau (n.d.), *The Other Side of the Mountain: Mujahideen Tactics in the Soviet-Afghan War* (Quantico: SCN: DM-980701, Marine Corps Combat Development Command).

James, Alan (1990), *Peacekeeping in International Politics* (Basingstoke: Macmillan).

Jawad, Nassim (1992), *Afghanistan: A Nation of Minorities* (London: Minority Rights Group).

Jenkins, Kate, and William Plowden (2006), *Governance and Nationbuilding: The Failure of International Intervention* (Cheltenham: Edward Elgar).

Jervis, Robert (1976), *Perception and Misperception in International Politics* (Princeton, NJ: Princeton University Press).

Johnson, Chris, and Jolyon Leslie (2008), *Afghanistan: The Mirage of Peace* (London: Zed Books).

Johnson, Thomas H. (2006), 'Afghanistan's post-Taliban transition: the state of state-building after war', *Central Asian Survey*, 25, 1–2: 1–26.

Johnson, Thomas H., and M. Chris Mason (2007), 'Understanding the Taliban and Insurgency in Afghanistan', *Orbis*, 51, 1: 71–89.

—— (2008), 'No Sign until the Burst of Fire: Understanding the Pakistan-Afghanistan Frontier', *International Security*, 32, 4: 41–77.

Johnston, Michael (2005), *Syndromes of Corruption: Wealth, Power and Democracy* (Cambridge: Cambridge University Press).

Jones, Ann (2006), *Kabul in Winter: Life without Peace in Afghanistan* (New York: Metropolitan Books).

Jones, Ellen (1985), *Red Army and Society: A Sociology of the Soviet Military* (Boston, MA: Allen & Unwin).

Jones, Robert A. (1990), *The Soviet Concept of 'Limited Sovereignty' from Lenin to Gorbachev: The Brezhnev Doctrine* (Basingstoke: Macmillan).

Jones, Seth G. (2007), 'Pakistan's Dangerous Game', *Survival*, 49, 1: 15–32.

—— (2008a), 'The Rise of Afghanistan's Insurgency: State Failure and Jihad', *International Security*, 32, 4: 7–40.

—— (2008b), *Counterinsurgency in Afghanistan* (Santa Monica: RAND National Defence Research Institute).

Jossinet, J. C. (1986), 'La Résistance autour d'Herat', *Les Nouvelles d'Afghanistan*, 28: 8–10.

Judah, Tim (2002), 'The Taliban Papers', *Survival*, 44, 1: 68–80.

Juergensmeyer, Mark (2000), *Terror in the Mind of God: The Global Rise of Religious Violence* (Berkeley and Los Angeles: University of California Press).

Jukes, Geoffrey (1989), 'The Soviet armed forces and the Afghan War', in Amin Saikal and William Maley (eds), *The Soviet Withdrawal from Afghanistan* (Cambridge: Cambridge University Press): 82–100.

Kakar, Hasan (1978), 'The Fall of the Afghan Monarchy in 1973', *International Journal of Middle East Studies*, 9: 195–214.

—— (1979), *Government and Society in Afghanistan: The Reign of Amir 'Abd al-Rahman Khan* (Austin: University of Texas Press).

—— (1995), *Afghanistan: The Soviet Invasion and the Afghan Response, 1979–1982* (Berkeley and Los Angeles: University of California Press).

—— (2006), *A Political and Diplomatic History of Afghanistan 1863–1901* (Leiden: Brill).

Kamm, Henry (1989), 'Pakistanis Report Ordering Attack by Afghan Rebels', *The New York Times,* 23 April.

Kaplan, Robert D. (1989), 'How Zia's Death Helped the U.S.', *The New York Times,* 23 August.

Karklins, Rasma (1987), 'The Dissent/Coercion Nexus in the USSR', *Studies in Comparative Communism,* 20, 3–4: 321–41.

—— (1994), 'Explaining Regime Change in the Soviet Union', *Europe-Asia Studies,* 46, 1: 29–45.

Karzai, Hamed (1988), 'Attitude of the Leadership of Afghan Tribes towards the Regime from 1953 to 1978', *Central Asian Survey*, 7, 2/3: 33–9.

Katzman, Kenneth (2005), *Afghanistan: Post-War Governance, Security, and U.S. Policy* (Washington DC: Congressional Research Service, The Library of Congress).

Keating, Michael (1997), 'Women's Rights and Wrongs', *The World Today*, 53, 1: 11–12.

Keep, John (1995), *Last of the Empires: A History of the Soviet Union 1945–1991* (Oxford: Oxford University Press).

Kelsay, John (2007), *Arguing the Just War in Islam* (Cambridge: Harvard University Press).

Kepel, Gilles (2000), *Jihad, expansion et déclin de l'islamise* (Paris: Gallimard).

Khalidi, Noor Ahmad (1991), 'Afghanistan: Demographic Consequences of War, 1978–1987', *Central Asian Survey,* 10, 3: 101–26.

Khalili, Khalilullah (1984), *'Ayari az Khorasan: Amir Habibullah, Khadim-e Din-e Rasulallah* (Peshawar: Tarikh-e Ramadan).

Khalilzad, Zalmay (1996), 'Afghanistan: Time to Re-Engage', *The Washington Post,* 7 October.

Khalilzad, Zalmay, and Daniel Byman (2000), 'Afghanistan: The Consolidation of a Rogue State', *The Washington Quarterly,* 23, 1: 65–78.

Khalilzad, Zalmay, Daniel Byman, Elie Krakowski, and Don Ritter (1999), *U.S. Policy in Afghanistan: Challenges and Solutions* (Washington DC: The Afghanistan Foundation).

Khan, Aimal (2000), 'Taliban Release a Rapist', *The Frontier Post,* 21 September.

Khan, Gohar Ayub (2007), *Glimpses into the Corridors of Power* (Karachi: Oxford University Press).

Khan, Riaz M. (1991), *Untying the Afghan Knot: Negotiating Soviet Withdrawal* (Durham, NC: Duke University Press).

Kifner, John, with Eric Schmitt (2001), 'U.S. Officials Say Al Qaeda Is Routed From Afghanistan', *The New York Times,* 17 December.

Kilcullen, David J. (2005), 'Countering Global Insurgency', *Journal of Strategic Studies,* 28, 4: 597–617.

—— (2006–2007), 'Counter-insurgency *redux*', *Survival,* 48, 4: 111–30.

—— (2009), *The Accidental Guerrilla: Fighting Small Wars in the Midst of a Big One* (New York: Oxford University Press).

Kimball, Charles (2002), *When Religion Become Evil* (San Francisco: HarperCollins).

King, Charles (1997), *Ending Civil Wars* (Oxford: Adelphi Paper no. 308, International Institute for Strategic Studies, Oxford University Press).

King, Laura (2006), 'Pakistani city serves as refuge for the Taliban', *The Los Angeles Times,* 21 December.

—— (2007), 'Taliban leader's powerful vanishing act', *The Los Angeles Times,* 5 January.

Kippen, Grant (2008), *Elections in 2009 and 2010: Technical and Contextual Challenges to Building Democracy in Afghanistan* (Kabul: Afghanistan Research and Evaluation Unit).

Kleiner, Juergen (2006), 'Diplomacy with Fundamentalists: The United States and the Taliban', *The Hague Journal of Diplomacy,* 1, 3: 209–34.

Klijn, Floortje, and Adam Pain (2007), *Finding the Money: Informal Credit Practices in Rural Afghanistan* (Kabul: Afghanistan Research and Evaluation Unit).

Knight, Amy (1993), *Beria: Stalin's First Lieutenant* (Princeton: Princeton University Press).

Kober, Stanley (2008), *Cracks in the Foundation: NATO's New Troubles* (Washington DC: Policy Analysis no. 608, Cato Institute).

Koelbl, Susanne (2009), 'Verrückt, aber nicht total', *Der Spiegel,* 5 January.

Kolakowski, Leszek (1978), *Main Currents of Marxism* (Oxford: Oxford University Press): Vols I–III.

Kolkowicz, Roman (1967), *The Soviet Military and the Communist Party* (Princeton, NJ: Princeton University Press).

Kornienko, G. M. (1993), 'Kak prinimalis' resheniia o vvode sovetskikh voisk v Afganistan i ikh vyvode', *Novaia i noveishaia istoriia,* 3: 107–18.

Kronenfeld, Daniel A. (2008), 'Afghan Refugees in Pakistan: Not All Refugees, Not Always in Pakistan, Not Necessarily Afghan?', *Journal of Refugee Studies,* 21, 1: 43–63.

Krygier, Martin (1986), 'Law as Tradition', *Law and Philosophy,* 5, 2: 237–62.

Kubálková, Vendulka, and A. A. Cruickshank (1980), *Marxism-Leninism and Theory of International Relations* (London: Routledge & Kegan Paul).

—— (1989), *Thinking New about Soviet "New Thinking"* (Berkeley: Institute of International Studies, University of California).

Kunz, E. F. (1973), 'The Refugee in Flight: Kinetic Models and Forms of Displacement', *International Migration Review,* 7, 2: 125–46.

Kuperman, Alan J. (1999), 'The Stinger Missile and U.S. Intervention in Afghanistan', *Political Science Quarterly,* 114, 2: 2 19–63.

Kuran, Timur (1995), *Private Truths, Public Lies: The Social Consequences of Preference Falsification* (Cambridge: Harvard University Press).

Kux, Dennis (2001), *The United States and Pakistan 1947–2000: Disenchanted Allies* (Washington, DC: Woodrow Wilson Center Press).

Laber, Jeri (1986), 'Afghanistan's Other War', *New York Review of Books,* 33, 20: 3, 6–7.

Laber, Jeri, and Barnett R. Rubin (1988), *'A Nation is Dying': Afghanistan under the Soviets 1979–87* (Evanston, IL: Northwestern University Press).

Lafraie, Najibullah (2006), 'The way out is to get out', *International Herald Tribune,* 5 September.

—— (2009), *Revolutionary Ideology and Islamic Militancy: The Iranian Revolution and Interpretations of the Quran* (London: I.B. Tauris).

Lamb, Christina (2008), 'War on Taliban cannot be won, says army chief', *The Sunday Times,* 5 October.

Lander, Mark (2002), 'Afghan Plan a New Army of 70,000', *The New York Times,* 3 December.

Lane, Jan-Erik (1996), *Constitutions and political theory* (Manchester: Manchester University Press).

Lapidus, Ira M. (1988), *A History of Islamic Societies* (Cambridge: Cambridge University Press).

Lauterpacht, Hersch (1948), *Recognition in International Law* (Cambridge: Cambridge University Press).

Lee, Jonathan L. (1996), *The 'Ancient Supremacy': Bukhara, Afghanistan and the Battle for Balkh, 1731–1901* (Leiden: E. J. Brill).

Leggett, George (1981), *The Cheka: Lenin's Political Police* (Oxford: Oxford University Press).

Lemercier-Quelquejay, Chantal, and Alexandre Bennigsen (1984), 'Soviet Experience of Muslim Guerilla Warfare and the War in Afghanistan', in Yaacov Ro'i (ed.), *The USSR and the Muslim World* (London: George Allen & Unwin): 206–14.

Lepingwell, John W. R. (1992), 'Soviet Civil-Military Relations and the August Coup', *World Politics,* 44, 4: 539–72.

Leslie, J. (1995), 'Towards Rehabilitation: Building Trust in Afghanistan', *Disaster Prevention and Management,* 4, 1: 27–31.

LeVine, Steve (1997), 'Helping Hand', *Newsweek,* 14 October.

Lewis, Bernard (1988), *The Political Language of Islam* (Chicago: University of Chicago Press).

Lezhnev, Sasha (2005), *Crafting Peace: Strategies to Deal with Warlords in Collapsing States* (Lanham: Lexington Books).

Liakhovskii, A. A. (2004), *Tragediia i doblest' Afgana* (Iaroslavl': NORD).

Liakhovskii, A. A., and V. M. Zabrodin (1991), *Tainy afganskoi voiny* (Moscow: Izdatel'stvo «Planeta»).

Lieven, Anatol (1998), *Chechnya: Tombstone of Russian Power* (New Haven: Yale University Press).

Lifschultz, Lawrence (1987), 'Soviet Intervention a Tragedy', *The Times of India*, 26 May.

Light, Margot (1987), *The Soviet Theory of International Relations* (Brighton: Wheatsheaf Books).

Lischer, Sarah Kenyon (2005), *Dangerous Sanctuaries? Refugee Camps, Civil War, and the Dilemmas of Humanitarian Aid* (Ithaca: Cornell University Press).

Lobato, Chantal (1985), 'Islam in Kabul: The Religious Politics of Babrak Karmal', *Central Asian Survey*, 4, 4: 111–20.

Lorentz, John H. (1987), 'Afghan Aid: The Role of Private Voluntary Organizations', *Journal of South Asian and Middle Eastern Studies*, 11, 1–2: 102–11.

Lundberg, Kirsten (1999), *Politics of a Covert Action: The US, the Mujahideen, and the Stinger Missile* (Cambridge: Kennedy School of Government Case Program C15-99-1546.0, Harvard University).

Lutz, Donald S. (2006), *Principles of Constitutional Design* (Cambridge: Cambridge University Press).

Maass, Peter (2002), 'Gul Agha Gets His Province Back' *The New York Times Magazine*, 6 January.

Macdonald, David (2007), *Drugs in Afghanistan: Opium, Outlaws and Scorpion Tales* (London: Pluto Press).

Mack, Andrew J. R. (1983), 'Why Big Nations Lose Small Wars: The Politics of Asymmetric Conflict', in Klaus Knorr (ed.), *Power, Strategy, and Security* (Princeton, NJ: Princeton University Press): 126–51.

Mackenzie, Richard (1998), 'The United States and the Taliban', in William Maley (ed.), *Fundamentalism Reborn?: Afghanistan and the Taliban* (London: Hurst & Co.): 90–103.

Mackinlay, John (2000), 'Defining Warlords', *International Peacekeeping*, 7, 1: 48–62.

Magnus, Ralph H., (1986), 'The Military and Politics in Afghanistan: Before and After the Revolution', in Edward A. Olsen and Stephen Jurika, Jr. (eds), *The Armed Forces in Contemporary Asian Societies* (Boulder, CO: Westview Press): 325–44.

Magnus, Ralph H., and Eden Naby (1998), *Afghanistan: Mullah, Marx, and Mujahid* (Boulder, CO: Westview Press).

Maimbo, Samuel Munzele (2003), *The Money Exchange Dealers of Kabul: A Study of the Hawala System in Afghanistan* (Washington DC: World Bank Working Paper no. 13, The World Bank).

Makinda, Samuel (2003), 'Disarmament and reintegration of combatants', in William Maley, Charles Sampford and Ramesh Thakur (eds), *From Civil Strife to Civil Society: Civil and Military Responsibilities in Disrupted States* (Tokyo: United Nations University Press): 309–26.

Maley, William (1985), 'Prospects for Afghanistan', *Australian Outlook*, 39, 3: 157–64.

—— (1986), 'L'Afghanistan vu d'Australie', *Les Nouvelles d'Afghanistan*, 27: 19–20.

—— (1987a), 'Political Legitimation in Contemporary Afghanistan', *Asian Survey*, 27, 6: 705–25.

—— (1987b), 'Images of Afghanistan', *Review of International Studies*, 13, 4: 311–19.

Maley, William (1989a), 'Afghan Refugees: From Diaspora to Repatriation', in Amin Saikal (ed.), *Refugees in the Modern World* (Canberra: Canberra Studies in World Affairs no. 25, Department of International Relations, Research School of Pacific Studies, Australian National University): 17–44.

—— (1989b), 'The Geneva Accords of April 1988', in Amin Saikal and William Maley (eds), *The Soviet Withdrawal from Afghanistan* (Cambridge: Cambridge University Press): 12–28.

—— (1991a), 'Ethnonationalism and Civil Society in the USSR', in Chandran Kukathas, David W. Lovell and William Maley (eds), *The Transition from Socialism: State and Civil Society in the USSR* (Melbourne: Longman Cheshire): 177–97.

—— (1991b), 'Social Dynamics and the Disutility of Terror: Afghanistan, 1978–1989', in P. Timothy Bushnell, Vladimir Shlapentokh, Christopher K. Vanderpool, and Jeyaratnam Sundram (eds), *State Organized Terror: The Case of Violent Internal Repression* (Boulder, CO: Westview Press): 113–31.

—— (1991c), 'Soviet-Afghan Relations after the Coup', *Report on the USSR*, 3, 38: 11–15.

—— (1993a), 'Regional Conflicts: Afghanistan and Cambodia', in Ramesh Thakur and Carlyle A. Thayer (eds), *Reshaping Regional Relations: Asia-Pacific and the Former Soviet Union* (Boulder, CO: Westview Press): 183–200.

—— (1993b), 'The Future of Islamic Afghanistan', *Security Dialogue*, 24, 4: 383–96.

—— (1995a), 'The Shape of the Russian Macroeconomy', in Amin Saikal and William Maley (eds), *Russia in Search of its Future* (Cambridge: Cambridge University Press): 48–65.

—— (1995b), 'Peacekeeping and Peacemaking', in Ramesh Thakur and Carlyle A. Thayer (eds), *A Crisis of Expectations: UN Peacekeeping in the 1990s* (Boulder, CO: Westview Press): 237–50.

—— (1996), 'Women and Public Policy in Afghanistan: A Comment', *World Development*, 24, 1: 203–6.

—— (1997a), 'The Dynamics of Regime Transition in Afghanistan', *Central Asian Survey*, 16, 2: 167–84.

—— (1997b), 'Afghanistan Observed', *Australian Journal of International Affairs*, 51, 2: 265–71.

—— (1998a), 'Mine Action in Afghanistan', *Refuge*, 17, 4: 12–16.

—— (1998b), 'Afghanistan', in Janie Hampton (ed.), *Internally Displaced People: A Global Survey* (London: Earthscan Publications): 155–8.

—— (1998c), 'Introduction: Interpreting the Taliban', in William Maley (ed.), *Fundamentalism Reborn?: Afghanistan and the Taliban* (London: Hurst & Co.): 1–28.

—— (1998d), 'The UN and Afghanistan: "Doing its Best" or "Failure of a Mission"?', in William Maley (ed.), *Fundamentalism Reborn?: Afghanistan and the Taliban* (London: Hurst & Co.): 182–98.

—— (1998e), 'The Perils of Pipelines', *The World Today*, 54, 8–9: 231–2.

—— (1999a), 'Review of Sarah E. Mendelson, *Changing Course: Ideas, Politics, and the Soviet Withdrawal from Afghanistan*', *American Political Science Review*, 93, 1: 241–2.

—— (1999b), 'Reconstructing Afghanistan: Opportunities and Challenges', in Geoff Harris (ed.), *Recovery from Armed Conflict in Developing Countries: An Economic and Political Analysis* (New York: Routledge): 225–57.

—— (2000a), *The Foreign Policy of the Taliban* (New York: Council on Foreign Relations).

—— (2000b), 'The UN and East Timor', *Pacifica Review*, 12, 1: 63–76.

——— (2001a), 'Talibanisation and Pakistan', in Denise Groves (ed.), *Talibanisation: Extremism and Regional Instability in South and Central Asia* (Berlin: Conflict Prevention Network: Stiftung Wissenschaft und Politik): 53–74.

——— (2001b), 'Moving Forward in Afghanistan', in Stuart Harris, William Maley, Richard Price, Christian Reus-Smit, and Amin Saikal, *The Day the World Changed? Terrorism and World Order* (Canberra: 'Keynotes' no. 1, Department of International Relations, Research School of Pacific and Asian Studies, Australian National University): 18–24.

——— (2002a), 'Confronting Creeping Invasions: Afghanistan, the UN and the World Community', in K. Warikoo (ed.), *The Afghanistan Crisis: Issues and Perspectives* (New Delhi: Bhavana Books): 256–74.

——— (2002b), 'The Reconstruction of Afghanistan', in Ken Booth and Tim Dunne (eds), *Worlds in Collision: Terror and the Future of Global Order* (London: Palgrave Macmillan): 184–93.

——— (2003a), 'Institutional Design and the Rebuilding of Trust', in William Maley, Charles Sampford, and Ramesh Thakur (eds), *From Civil Strife to Civil Society: Civil and Military Responsibilities in Disrupted States* (New York and Tokyo: United Nations University Press): 163–79.

——— (2003b), 'Executive, Legislative, and Electoral Options for Afghanistan', in *Afghanistan: Towards a New Constitution* (New York: Center on International Cooperation, New York University): 107–11.

——— (2003c), 'The "War Against Terrorism" in South Asia', *Contemporary South Asia*, 12, 2: 203–17.

——— (2003–2004), 'Afghanistan on the Brink', *The Diplomat*, 2, 5: 10–11.

——— (2004), 'State-Building and Political Development in Afghanistan', in Masako Ishii and Jacqueline A. Siapno (eds), *Between Knowledge and Commitment: Post-conflict Peace-building and Reconstruction in Regional Contexts* (Osaka: JCAS Symposium Series no. 21, Japan Center for Area Studies, National Museum of Ethnology): 165–83.

——— (2005), 'International force and political reconstruction: Cambodia, East Timor and Afghanistan', in Albrecht Schnabel and Hans-Georg Ehrhart (eds), *Security Sector Reform and Post-Conflict Peacebuilding* (New York and Tokyo: United Nations University Press): 297–312.

——— (2006a), *Rescuing Afghanistan* (London: Hurst & Co.).

——— (2006b), 'Democratic Governance and Post-Conflict Transitions', *Chicago Journal of International Law*, 6, 2: 683–701.

——— (2007a), 'Order and Justice in Afghanistan: Some Reflections on the Problem of Amnesty', *Afghanistan Info*, 60: 9–10.

——— (2007b), 'Talking to the Taliban, *The World Today*, 63, 11: 4–6.

——— (2008a), 'Human Rights in Afghanistan', in Shahram Akbarzadeh and Benjamin MacQueen (eds), *Islam and Human Rights in Practice: Perspectives Across the Ummah* (New York: Routledge): 89–107.

——— (2008b), 'In Defense of Hamid Karzai', *The Washington Post*, 17 February (Letter to the Editor).

——— (2008c), 'NATO and Afghanistan: Made for Each Other?', *Foreign Service Journal*, 85, 7: 36–40.

——— (2008d), 'Corruption, Nepotism and Trust: Problems of Governance in Afghanistan', in *State, Security and Economy in Afghanistan: Current Challenges, Possible Solutions* (Princeton: Liechtenstein Colloquium Report Volume III, Liechtenstein Institute on Self-Determination, Princeton University): 38–41.

Maley, William (2008e), 'Looking Back at the Bonn Process', in Geoffrey Hayes and Mark Sedra (eds), *Afghanistan: Transition Under Threat* (Waterloo: Wilfrid Laurier University Press): 3–24.

—— (2008f), 'La politique afghane du Pakistan', *Les Nouvelles d'Afghanistan*, 122: 10–11.

—— (2008g), *Stabilizing Afghanistan: Threats and Challenges* (Washington DC: Policy Brief no.68, Carnegie Endowment for International Peace).

—— (2008h), 'Building Legitimacy in post-Taliban Afghanistan', in Ruth Rennie (ed.), *State Building, Security, and Social Change in Afghanistan: Reflections on a Survey of the Afghan People* (Kabul and San Francisco: The Asia Foundation): 11–26.

—— (2009a), 'Afghanistan and Its Region', in J. Alexander Thier (ed.), *The Future of Afghanistan* (Washington DC: United States Institute of Peace): 81–91.

—— (2009b), 'Democracy and legitimation: challenges in the reconstruction of political processes in Afghanistan', in Brett Bowden, Hilary Charlesworth and Jeremy Farrall (eds), *The Role of International Law in Rebuilding Societies after Conflict: Great Expectations* (Cambridge: Cambridge University Press): 111–33.

Maley, William, and Fazel Haq Saikal (1992), *Political Order in Post-Communist Afghanistan* (Boulder, CO: Lynne Rienner).

Malia, Martin (1994), *The Soviet Tragedy: A History of Socialism in Russia, 1917–1991* (New York: The Free Press).

Mani, Rama (2003), *Ending Impunity and Building Justice in Afghanistan* (Kabul: Afghanistan Research and Evaluation Unit).

Mann, Judy (1999), 'The Grinding Terror of the Taliban', *The Washington Post*, 9 July.

Mansfield, David (2007), ' "Economical with the truth": the limits of price and profitability in both explaining opium poppy cultivation in Afghanistan and in designing effective responses', in Adam Pain and Jacky Sutton (eds), *Reconstructing Agriculture in Afghanistan* (Rugby: FAO and Practical Action Publishing): 213–34.

Marigo, Véra (1988), 'Hypothèse sur l'origine du mot "afghan" ', *Les Nouvelles d'Afghanistan*, 38: 21.

—— (2001), 'Bamyan: Naissance et destruction de deux géants', *Les Nouvelles d'Afghanistan*, 93: 16–21.

Markey, Daniel (2008), *Securing Pakistan's Tribal Belt* (New York: Council Special Report no.36, Council on Foreign Relations).

Marlowe, Ann (2008), 'Two Myths About Afghanistan', *The Washington Post*, 11 February.

Marsden, Peter (1998), *The Taliban: War, Religion and the New Order in Afghanistan* (Karachi: Oxford University Press).

Marsden, Peter, and Emma Samman (2001), 'Afghanistan: The Economic and Social Impact of Conflict', in Frances Stewart, Valpy Fitzgerald, and Associates, *War and Underdevelopment: Volume 2: Country Experiences* (Oxford: Oxford University Press): 21–55.

Martel, William C. (2007), *Victory in War: Foundations of Modern Military Policy* (Cambridge: Cambridge University Press).

Marten, Kimberly (2006–2007), 'Warlordism in Comparative Perspective', *International Security*, 31, 3: 41–73.

Matlock, Jack F. (2004), *Reagan and Gorbachev: How the Cold War Ended* (New York: Random House).

Matthews, Mervyn (1986), *Poverty in the Soviet Union* (Cambridge: Cambridge University Press).

Maurice, Frédéric, and Jean de Courten (1991), 'ICRC Activities for Refugees and Displaced Civilians', *International Review of the Red Cross,* 280: 9–21.

Mawdsley, Evan, and Stephen White (2000), *The Soviet Elite from Lenin to Gorbachev: The Central Committee and its Members, 1917–1991* (Oxford: Oxford University Press).

Mayer, Arno J. (2000), *The Furies: Violence and Terror in the French and Russian Revolutions* (Princeton, NJ: Princeton University Press).

Mayotte, Judy A. (1992), *Disposable People? The Plight of Refugees* (Maryknoll: Orbis Books).

Mazzetti, Mark (2007), 'U.S. defense secretary says arms flow into Afghanistan from Iran', *International Herald Tribune,* 4 June.

Mazzetti, Mark, and Eric Schmitt (2008a), 'C.I.A. Outlines Pakistan Links With Militants', *The Washington Post,* 30 July.

—— (2008b), 'Pakistanis Aided Attack in Kabul, U.S. Officials Say', *The Washington Post,* 1 August.

MccGwire, Michael (1987), *Military Objectives in Soviet Foreign Policy* (Washington, DC: The Brookings Institution).

McChesney, Robert D. (1999), *Kabul Under Siege: Fayz Muhammad's Account of the 1929 Uprising* (Princeton, NJ: Markus Wiener Publishers).

McFarlane, John, and William Maley (2001), 'Civilian Police in UN Peace Operations: Some Lessons from Recent Australian Experience', in Ramesh Thakur and Albrecht Schnabel (eds), *United Nations Peacekeeping Operations: Ad Hoc Missions, Permanent Engagement* (New York and Tokyo: United Nations University Press): 182–211.

McGrath, Rae (2000), *Landmines and Unexploded Ordnance: A Resource Book* (London: Pluto Press).

McGrory, Daniel, and Dalya Alberge (2001), 'Taleban Ministers Led Art Raid', *The Times,* 23 November.

McKechnie, Alistair J. (2007), 'Rebuilding a Robust Afghan Economy', in Robert I. Rotberg (ed.), *Building a New Afghanistan* (Washington DC: Brookings Institution Press): 98–133.

McMichael, Scott R. (1991), *Stumbling Bear: Soviet Military Performance in Afghanistan* (London: Brassey's).

MCPA (1993), *Report of the National Survey of Mines Situation: Afghanistan* (Islamabad: Mine Clearance Planning Agency): Vols I–II.

Mearsheimer, John J. (1988), *Liddell Hart and the Weight of History* (Ithaca: Cornell University Press).

Meier, Andrew (1997), 'Afghanistan's Drug Trade', *Muslim Politics Report,* 11: 3–4.

Mendelson, Sarah E. (1998), *Changing Course: Ideas, Politics, and the Soviet Withdrawal from Afghanistan* (Princeton, NJ: Princeton University Press).

Meray, Tibor (1959), *Thirteen Days that Shook the Kremlin: Imre Nagy and the Hungarian Revolution* (New York: Praeger).

Metcalf, Barbara D. (1982), *Islamic Revival in British India: Deoband, 1860–1900* (Princeton, NJ: Princeton University Press).

Migdal, Joel S. (1988), *Strong Societies and Weak States: State-Society Relations and State Capabilities in the Third World* (Princeton, NJ: Princeton University Press).

—— (1994), 'The State in Society: An Approach to Struggles for Domination', in Joel S. Migdal, Atul Kohli, and Vivienne Shue (eds), *State Power and Social Forces: Domination and Transformation in the Third World* (Cambridge: Cambridge University Press): 7–34.

Milani, Mohsen M. (2006), 'Iran's Policy Toward Afghanistan', *Middle East Journal*, 60, 2: 235–56.

Miles, M. (1990), 'Disability and Afghan Reconstruction: Some Policy Issues', *Disability, Handicap and Society*, 5, 3: 257–67.

Miller, John H. (1987), 'How Much of a New Elite?', in R. F. Miller, J. H. Miller, and T. H. Rigby (eds), *Gorbachev at the Helm: A New Era in Soviet Politics?* (London: Croom Helm): 61–89.

—— (1988), 'The Geographical Disposition of the Soviet armed forces', *Soviet Studies*, 40, 3: 406–33.

—— (1993), *Mikhail Gorbachev and the End of Soviet Power* (Basingstoke: Macmillan).

Miller, Robert F. (1991), *Soviet Foreign Policy Today: Gorbachev and the New Political Thinking* (Sydney: Allen & Unwin).

Miller, William H. (2000), 'Insurgency Theory and the Conflict in Algeria: A Theoretical Analysis', *Terrorism and Political Violence*, 12, 1: 60–78.

Mills, Nick B. (2007), *Karzai: The Failing American Intervention and the Struggle for Afghanistan* (New York: John Wiley & Sons).

Misdaq, Nabi (2006), *Afghanistan: political frailty and external interference* (New York: Routledge).

Misra, Amalendu (2004), *Afghanistan: The Labyrinth of Violence* (Cambridge: Polity Press).

Misra, Neelesh (2000), *173 Hours in Captivity: The Hijacking of IC814* (New Delhi: HarperCollins).

Misztal, Barbara A. (1996), *Trust in Modern Societies* (Oxford: Polity Press).

Moghadam, Valentine M. (1994), 'Building Human Resources and Women's Capabilities in Afghanistan: A Retrospect and Prospects', *World Development*, 22, 6: 859–75.

Momen, Moojan (1985), *An Introduction to Shi'i Islam* (New Haven, CT: Yale University Press).

Monbiot, George (2008), 'The US missile defence system is the magic pudding that will never run out', *The Guardian*, 19 August.

Moore, Molly (2001), 'Turmoil in Home of Taliban', *The Washington Post*, 2 October.

Moshref, Rameen (1997), *The Taliban* (New York: Occasional Paper no. 35, The Afghanistan Forum).

Mousavi, Sayed Askar (1997), *The Hazaras of Afghanistan: An Historical, Cultural, Economic and Political Study* (New York: St. Martin's Press).

Muggeridge, Malcolm (ed.) (1947), *Ciano's Diary 1939–1943* (London: William Heinemann).

Murray, Tonita (2007), 'Police-Building in Afghanistan: A Case Study of Civil Security Reform', *International Peacekeeping*, 14, 1: 108–26.

Murshed, S. Iftikhar (2006), *Afghanistan: The Taliban Years* (London: Bennett & Bloom).

Musharraf, Pervez (2006), *In the Line of Fire: A Memoir* (New York: The Free Press).

Nägler, Horst (1971), *Privatinitiative beim Industrieaufbau in Afghanistan* (Düsseldorf: Bertelsmann Universitätsverlag).

Naji, Kasra (2008), *Ahmadinejad: The Secret History of Iran's Radical Leader* (London: I.B. Tauris).

Najimi, A. W. (1997), *Report on a Survey on SCA Supported Girls' Education and SCA Built School Buildings in Afghanistan in Regions under Southern and Eastern SCA Regional Management* (Peshawar: Education Technical Support Unit, Swedish Committee for Afghanistan).

Naqvi, Zareen F. (1999), *Afghanistan-Pakistan Trade Relations* (Islamabad: The World Bank).

Nasr, S. V. R. (2000a), 'The Rise of Sunni Militancy in Pakistan: The Changing Role of Islamism and the Ulama in Society and Politics', *Modern Asian Studies, 34*, 1: 139–80.

—— (2000b), 'International Politics, Domestic Imperatives, and Identity Mobilization: Sectarianism in Pakistan, 1979–1998', *Comparative Politics, 32*, 2: 171–90.

—— (2008), 'Pakistan after Islamization: Mainstream and Militant Islam in a Changing State', in John L. Esposito, John O. Voll, and Osman Bakar (eds), *Asian Islam in the 21st Century* (New York: Oxford University Press): 31–48.

Nassery, Fahima (1986), 'Une femme torturée', in Bernard Dupaigne (ed.), *Femmes en Afghanistan* (Paris: AFRANE): 10–11.

National Intelligence Council (2007), *National Intelligence Estimate: Iran: Nuclear Intentions and Capabilities* (Washington DC: National Intelligence Council).

Nawa, Fariba (2006), *Afghanistan, Inc.: A CorpWatch Investigative Report* (Oakland: CorpWatch).

Nawaz, Shuja (2008), *Crossed Swords: Pakistan, its Army and the Wars Within* (Karachi: Oxford University Press).

Nawid, Senzil K. (1999), *Religious Response to Social Change in Afghanistan 1919–1929: King Aman-Allah and the Afghan Ulama* (Costa Mesa: Mazda Publishers).

Negroponte, John D. (2007), *Annual Threat Assessment of the Director of National Intelligence* (Washington DC: Office of the Director of National Intelligence, 11 January).

Neilan, Terence (2001), 'Thousand Flee Kandahar in Wake of U.S. Airstrikes', *The New York Times*, 11 October.

Newman, Edward (1998), *The UN Secretary-General from the Cold War to the New Era: A Global Peace and Security Mandate?* (Basingstoke: Macmillan).

Niland, Norah (2004), 'Justice Postponed: The Marginalization of Human Rights in Afghanistan', in Antonio Donini, Norah Niland and Karin Wermester (eds), *Nation-Building Unraveled? Aid, Peace and Justice in Afghanistan* (Bloomfield: Kumarian Press): 61–82.

9/11 Commission (2004), *The 9/11 Commission Report: Final Report of the National Commission on Terrorist Attacks Upon the United States* (New York: W.W. Norton).

Noelle, Christine (1995), 'The Anti-Wahhabi Reaction in Nineteenth-Century Afghanistan', *The Muslim World, 85*, 1–2: 23–48.

—— (1998), *State and Tribe in Nineteenth-Century Afghanistan: The Reign of Amir Dost Muhammad Khan (1826–1863)* (Richmond: Curzon Press).

Noetzel, Timo, and Sibylle Scheipers (2007), *Coalition Warfare in Afghanistan: Burden-Sharing or Disunity?* (London: Briefing Paper ASP/IP BP 07/01, Chatham House).

Nojumi, Neamatollah (2002), *The Rise of the Taliban in Afghanistan: Civil War, Mass Mobilization, and the Future of the Region* (New York: Palgrave Macmillan).

Noorzoy, M. S. (1985), 'Long-Term Economic Relations between Afghanistan and the Soviet Union: An Interpretive Study', *International Journal of Middle East Studies, 17*: 151–73.

Norell, Magnus (2007), 'The Taliban and the Muttahida Majlis-e-Amal (MMA)', *China and Eurasia Forum Quarterly, 5*, 3: 61–82.

Norris, Pippa (2004), *Electoral Engineering: Voting Rules and Political Behavior* (Cambridge: Cambridge University Press).

Norton, Augustus Richard (2007), *Hezbollah: A Short History* (Princeton: Princeton University Press).

Nossal, Kim Richard (1989), 'Knowing When to Fold: Western Sanctions Against the USSR 1980–1983', *International Journal*, 44, 3: 698–724.

Novichkova, I. (1956), *N. A. Bulganin i N. S. Khrushchev v Afganistane* (Moscow: Gosudarstvennoe izdatel'stvo izobrazitel'nogo iskusstva).

O'Connor, Ronald W. (1994), *Health Care in Muslim Asia: Development and Disorder in Wartime Afghanistan* (Lanham, MD: University Press of America).

Odom, William E. (1998), *The Collapse of the Soviet Military* (New Haven, CT: Yale University Press).

O'Donnell, Guillermo, and Philippe C. Schmitter (1986), *Transitions from Authoritarian Rule: Tentative Conclusions about Uncertain Democracies* (Baltimore, MD: The Johns Hopkins University Press).

Okulov, V. (1987), 'Afganistan: Dialektika primireniia', *Pravda*, 17 August: 6.

Olesen, Asta (1995), *Islam and Politics in Afghanistan* (Richmond: Curzon Press).

Olson, Elizabeth (2002), 'UN Official Calls for Larger International Force in Afghanistan', *The New York Times*, 28 March.

Orywal, Erwin (ed.) (1986), *Die ethnischen Gruppen Afghanistans: Fallstudien zu Gruppenidentität und Intergruppenbeziehungen* (Wiesbaden: Dr. Ludwig Reichert Verlag).

Ostermann, Christian Friedrich (ed.) (2003–2004), 'New Evidence on the War in Afghanistan', *Cold War International History Bulletin*, 14–15: 139–271.

Packer, George (2005), *The Assassins' Gate: America in Iraq* (New York: Farrar, Straus and Giroux).

Pakistan Policy Working Group (2008), *The Next Chapter: The United States and Pakistan* (Washington DC: Pakistan Policy Working Group).

Pakulski, Jan (1986), 'Legitimacy and Mass Compliance: Reflections on Max Weber and Soviet-Type Societies', *British Journal of Political Science*, 16, 1: 35–56.

Papp, Daniel S. (1985), *Soviet Perceptions of the Developing World in the 1980s: The Ideological Basis* (Lexington, MA: D. C. Heath).

Parsi, Trita (2007), *Treacherous Alliance: The Secret Dealings of Israel, Iran, and the U.S.* (New Haven: Yale University Press).

Pérez de Cuéllar, Javier (1991), *Statement by Secretary-General Javier Pérez de Cuéllar* (New York: United Nations Department of Public Information, 21 May).

—— (1997), *Pilgrimage for Peace: A Secretary-General's Memoir* (New York: St. Martins Press).

Perlez, Jane, and Somini Sengupta (2008), 'Mumbai Attack Is Test for Pakistan on Curbing Militants', *The New York Times*, 4 December.

Perlez, Jane, and Waqar Gillani (2009), '20 Are Detained After Cricket Attack', *The New York Times*, 5 March.

Peters, Gretchen (2009), *Seeds of Terror: How Heroin is Bankrolling the Taliban and al Qaeda* (New York: Thomas Dunne Books).

Phillips, David L. (2005), *Losing Iraq: Inside the Postwar Reconstruction Fiasco* (Boulder, CO: Westview Press).

Physicians for Human Rights (1998a), *The Taliban's War on Women: A Health and Human Rights Crisis in Afghanistan* (Boston, MA: Physicians for Human Rights).

—— (1998b), *Medical Group Condemns UN Agreement with Taliban* (Boston, MA: Physicians for Human Rights).

—— (2001), *Women's Health and Human Rights in Afghanistan: A Population-Based Assessment* (Boston, MA: Physicians for Human Rights).

Picco, Giandomenico (1999), *Man Without a Gun: One Diplomat's Secret Struggle to Free the Hostages, Fight Terrorism, and End a War* (New York: Random House).

Pickering, Thomas W. (1999), 'Afghanistan Land Mine', *The Washington Post,* 23 December.

Piiparinen, Touko (2007) 'A Clash of Mindsets? An Insider's Account of Provincial Reconstruction Teams', *International Peacekeeping,* 14, 1: 143–57.

Pipes, Richard (1980), 'Militarism and the Soviet State', *Dædalus,* 109, 4: 1–12.

—— (1999), *Property and Freedom* (London: The Harvill Press).

Poggi, Gianfranco (1978), *The Development of the Modern State: A Sociological Introduction* (London: Hutchinson).

Popper, Karl R. (1977), *The Open Society and its Enemies* (London: Routledge and Kegan Paul): Vols I–II.

Poullada, Leon B. (1973), *Reform and Rebellion in Afghanistan: King Amanullah's Failure to Modernize a Tribal Society* (Ithaca, NY: Cornell University Press).

—— (1981), 'Afghanistan and the United States: The Crucial Years', *The Middle East Journal,* 35, 1: 178–90.

Powell, G. Bingham, Jr. (2000), *Elections as Instruments of Democracy: Majoritarian and Proportional Visions* (New Haven, CT: Yale University Press).

Qassem, Ahmad Shayeq (2007), 'Afghanistan-Pakistan Relations: border controversies as counter-terrorist impediments', *Australian Journal of International Affairs,* 61, 1: 65–80.

Rabinovich, Abraham (2007), 'Khatami "from material that makes for great leaders"', *The Australian,* 29 January.

Rae, Douglas W. (1967), *The Political Consequences of Electoral Laws* (New Haven, CT: Yale University Press).

Rahimi, Fahima (1986), *Women in Afghanistan* (Liestal: Stiftung Bibliotheca Afghanica).

Rais, Rasul Bakhsh (1994), *War without Winners: Afghanistan's Uncertain Transition after the Cold War* (Karachi: Oxford University Press).

—— (2008), *Recovering the Frontier State: War, Ethnicity, and State in Afghanistan* (Lanham: Lexington Books).

Rakowska-Harmstone, Teresa (1990), 'Nationalities and the Soviet Military', in Lubomyr Hajda and Mark Beissinger (eds), *The Nationalities Factor in Soviet Politics and Society* (Boulder, CO: Westview Press): 72–94.

Randal, Jonathan (2004), *Osama: The Making of a Terrorist* (New York: Alfred A. Knopf).

Randle, Robert F. (1973), *The Origins of Peace: A Study of Peacemaking and the Structure of Peace Settlements* (New York: The Free Press).

Rapoport, David C. (1988), 'Messianic Sanctions for Terror', *Comparative Politics,* 20, 2: 195–213.

Rashid, Ahmed (1996), 'A New Proxy War: Foreign Powers Again Feeding Arms to Factions', *Far Eastern Economic Review,* 1 February.

—— (1997a), 'Playing Dirty: Taliban Try to Starve Hazaras into Submission', *Far Eastern Economic Review,* 27 November.

—— (1997b), *The Turkmenistan-Afghanistan-Pakistan Pipeline: Company-Government Relations and Regional Politics* (Washington, DC: Focus on Current Issues, The Petroleum Finance Company).

—— (1999), 'The Taliban: Exporting Extremism', *Foreign Affairs,* 78, 6: 22–35.

—— (2000), *Taliban: Militant Islam, Oil and Fundamentalism in Central Asia* (New Haven, CT: Yale University Press).

—— (2001a), 'Inside the Taliban', *Far Eastern Economic Review,* 10 October.

—— (2001b), 'Intelligence Team Defied Musharraf to Help Taliban', *The Daily Telegraph,* 10 October.

—— (2002), 'Still Waiting To Be Rescued', *Far Eastern Economic Review,* 21 March.

Rashid, Ahmed (2008), *Descent into Chaos: The United States and the Failure of Nation Building in Pakistan, Afghanistan, and Central Asia* (New York: Viking Press).

Read, Anthony (2004), *The Devil's Disciples: The Lives and Times of Hitler's Inner Circle* (London: Pimlico).

Record, Jeffrey (2004), *Dark Victory: America's Second War against Iraq* (Annapolis: Naval Institute Press).

Reeves, Phil (2003), 'Afghan Elite Seizes Land for Mansions as Poor Lose Homes', *The Independent*, 19 September.

Reilly, Benjamin (2001), *Democracy in Divided Societies: Electoral Engineering for Conflict Management* (Cambridge: Cambridge University Press).

—— (2006), *Democracy and Diversity: Political Engineering in the Asia-Pacific* (Oxford: Oxford University Press).

Reisman, W. Michael, and James Silk (1988), 'Which Law Applies to the Afghan Conflict?', *American Journal of International Law*, 82, 3: 459–86.

Reporters sans Frontières (2000), *The Taliban and the Media: A Country with No News or Pictures* (Paris: Reporters sans Frontières).

Reshtia, Said Qassem (1997), *Khaterat-e siasi 1311 (1932) ta 1371 (1992)* (Virginia: American Speedy Press).

Reuveney, Rafael, and Aseem Prakash (1999), 'The Afghanistan War and the Breakdown of the Soviet Union', *Review of International Studies*, 25, 4: 693–708.

Reynolds, Andrew (2006), 'The Curious Case of Afghanistan', *Journal of Democracy*, 17, 2: 104–17.

RFE/RL (1985), *The Soviet Public and the War in Afghanistan: Perceptions, Prognoses, Information Sources* (Munich: Radio Free Europe/Radio Liberty, Soviet Area Audience and Opinion Research, AR 4-85).

Richardson, J. L. (1989), 'Conclusions: Management of the Afghan Crisis', in Amin Saikal and William Maley (eds), *The Soviet Withdrawal from Afghanistan* (Cambridge: Cambridge University Press): 161–70.

—— (1994), *Crisis Diplomacy: The Great Powers since the Mid-Nineteenth Century* (Cambridge: Cambridge University Press).

Richburg, Keith B. (2001), 'In Kabul, a Wide Wake of Destruction: Looting and Vandalism Mark Taliban's Retreat', *The Washington Post*, 15 November.

Richelson, Jeffrey T. (1986), *Sword and Shield: Soviet Intelligence and Security Apparatus* (Cambridge, MA: Ballinger Publishing).

Ricks, Thomas E. (2006), *Fiasco: The American Military Adventure in Iraq* (New York: The Penguin Press).

Ricks, Thomas E., and Vernon Loeb (2001), 'Initial Aim Is Hitting Taliban's Defenses', *The Washington Post*, 8 October.

Riedel, Bruce (2008), *The Search for Al Qaeda: Its Leadership, Ideology, and Future* (Washington DC: Brookings Institution Press).

Rigby, T. H. (1970), 'The Soviet Leadership: Towards a Self-Stabilizing Oligarchy', *Soviet Studies*, 22, 2: 167–91.

—— (1976), 'Politics in the Mono-Organizational Society', in Andrew C. Janos (ed.), *Authoritarian Politics in Communist Europe: Uniformity and Diversity in One-Party States* (Berkeley: Research Series no. 28, Institute of International Studies, University of California): 31–80.

—— (1989), 'The Afghan Conflict and Soviet Domestic Politics', in Amin Saikal and William Maley (eds), *The Soviet Withdrawal from Afghanistan* (Cambridge: Cambridge University Press): 67–81.

—— (1990), *The Changing Soviet System: Mono-Organisational Socialism from its Origins to Gorbachev's Restructuring* (Aldershot: Edward Elgar).

Rikhye, Indar Jit (1984), *The Theory and Practice of Peacekeeping* (London: Hurst & Co).

Rizvi, Hasan-Askari (2000), *Military, State and Society in Pakistan* (London: Macmillan Press).

Roberts, Adam, (2009), 'Doctrine and Reality in Afghanistan', *Survival*, 51, 1: 29–60.

Roddy, Dennis (2002), 'Homefront: Taliban Spokeswoman Keeps Low Profile in N.J.', *Pittsburgh Post-Gazette,* 13 January.

Rohde, David (2001a), 'U.S. Tactics Thwart Afghan Rebels', *The New York Times,* 18 October.

—— (2001b), 'Afghan Leader is Sworn In, Asking for Help to Rebuild', *The New York Times,* 23 December.

Rohde, David, and David E. Sanger (2007), 'How a "Good War" in Afghanistan Went Bad', *The New York Times*, 12 August.

Rohde, David, with Eric Schmitt (2001), 'Taliban Give Way in Final Province Where They Ruled', *The New York Times,* 10 December.

Rondeaux, Candace, and Karen DeYoung (2008), 'U.N. Finds Airstrike Killed 90 Afghans', *The Washington Post*, 27 August.

Rose, Richard (1992), 'Toward a Civil Economy', *Journal of Democracy,* 3, 2: 13–26.

Roy, Olivier (1990), *Islam and Resistance in Afghanistan* (Cambridge: Cambridge University Press).

—— (1991), *The Lessons of the Soviet/Afghan War* (London: Adelphi Paper no. 259, International Institute for Strategic Studies, Brassey's).

—— (1994), *The Failure of Political Islam* (Cambridge, MA: Harvard University Press).

—— (1995), *Afghanistan: From Holy War to Civil War* (Princeton, NJ: The Darwin Press).

—— (2008), *The Politics of Chaos in the Middle East* (New York: Columbia University Press).

Rubin, Barnett R. (1988), 'Soviet Lessons of Afghanistan Assure Pullout Will Go On', *Los Angeles Times,* 14 November.

—— (1989), 'Afghanistan: The Next Round', *Orbis,* 33, 1: 57–72.

—— (1989–1990), 'The Fragmentation of Afghanistan', *Foreign Affairs,* 68, 5: 150–68.

—— (1991), 'Afghanistan: Political Exiles in Search of a State', in Yossi Shain (ed.), *Governments-in-Exile in Contemporary World Politics* (New York: Routledge): 69–91.

—— (1995a), *The Fragmentation of Afghanistan: State Formation and Collapse in the International System* (New Haven, CT: Yale University Press).

—— (1995b), *The Search for Peace in Afghanistan: From Buffer State to Failed State* (New Haven, CT: Yale University Press).

—— (1995c), 'The Failure of an Internationally Sponsored Interim Government in Afghanistan', in Yossi Shain and Juan J. Linz (eds), *Between States: Interim Governments and Democratic Transitions* (Cambridge: Cambridge University Press): 211–36.

—— (1997a), 'Arab Islamists in Afghanistan', in John L. Esposito (ed.), *Political Islam: Revolution, Radicalism, or Reform?* (Boulder, CO: Lynne Rienner): 179–206.

—— (1997b), 'Women and Pipelines: Afghanistan's Proxy Wars', *International Affairs,* 73, 2: 283–96.

—— (2004), 'Crafting a Constitution for Afghanistan', *Journal of Democracy,* 15, 3: 5–19.

Rubin, Barnett R. (2005), 'Constructing Sovereignty for Security', *Survival*, 47, 4: 93–106.
—— (2006a), *Afghanistan's Uncertain Transition From Turmoil to Normalcy* (New York: Council Special Report no. 12, Council on Foreign Relations).
—— (2006b), 'The Death of an Afghan Optimist', *The Washington Post*, 17 September.
Rubin, Barnett R., and Ahmed Rashid (2008), 'From Great Game to Grand Bargain: Ending Chaos in Afghanistan and Pakistan', *Foreign Affairs*, 87, 6: 30–44.
Rubin, Barnett R., Ashraf Ghani, William Maley, Ahmed Rashid, and Olivier Roy (2001), *Afghanistan: Reconstruction and Peacebuilding in a Regional Framework* (Bern: KOFF Peacebuilding Reports 1/2001, Swiss Peace Foundation).
Rubin, Barnett R., Hamid Hamidzada, and Abby Stoddard (2003), *Through the Fog of Peace Building: Evaluating the Reconstruction of Afghanistan* (New York: Center on International Cooperation, New York University).
Rubin, Barnett R., and Jake Sherman (2008), *Counter-Narcotics to Stabilize Afghanistan: The False Promise of Crop Eradication* (New York: Center on International Cooperation, New York University).
Ruiz, Hiram A. (1992), *Left Out in the Cold: The Perilous Homecoming of Afghan Refugees* (Washington, DC: US Committee for Refugees).
Ruttig, Thomas (2006), *Islamists, Leftists – and a Void in the Center: Afghanistan's Political Parties and where they come from (1902–2006)* (Kabul: Konrad Adenauer Stiftung).
—— (2008), *Afghanistan: Institutionen ohne Demokratie: Strukturelle Schwächen des Staatsaufbaus und Ansätze für eine politische Stabilisierung* (Berlin: Stiftung Wissenschaft und Politik).
Sadjadpour, Karim (2008a), *Reading Khamanei: The World View of Iran's Most Powerful Leader* (Washington DC: Carnegie Endowment for International Peace).
—— (2008b), *Iran: Is Productive Engagement Possible?* (Washington DC: Policy Brief no.65, Carnegie Endowment for International Peace).
Sadruddin Aga Khan (1990), *Extemporaneous Remarks of Prince Sadruddin Aga Khan* (Washington, DC: Center for Strategic and International Studies, 16 May).
Saikal, Amin (1980), *The Rise and Fall of the Shah* (Princeton, NJ: Princeton University Press).
—— (1984a), 'The Afghanistan Crisis: A Negotiated Settlement?', *The World Today*, 40, 11: 48 1–9.
—— (1984b), 'The Method of Soviet Intervention: The Cases of Poland and Afghanistan', in Robert F. Miller (ed.), *Poland in the Eighties: Social Revolution Against 'Real Socialism'* (Canberra: Occasional Paper no. 18, Department of Political Science, Research School of Social Science, Australian National University): 171–83.
—— (1989), 'The Regional Politics of the Afghan Crisis', in Amin Saikal and William Maley (eds), *The Soviet Withdrawal from Afghanistan* (Cambridge: Cambridge University Press): 52–66.
—— (1996), 'The UN and Afghanistan: A Case of Failed Peacemaking Intervention?', *International Peacekeeping*, 3, 1: 19–34.
—— (1998a), 'The Rabbani Government, 1992–1996', in William Maley (ed.), *Fundamentalism Reborn?: Afghanistan and the Taliban* (London: Hurst & Co.): 29–42.
—— (1998b), 'Afghanistan's Ethnic Conflict', *Survival*, 40, 2: 114–26.
—— (2004), *Modern Afghanistan: A History of Struggle and Survival* (London: I.B. Tauris).
—— (2006a), 'Afghanistan's Transition: ISAF's stabilisation role?', *Third World Quarterly*, 27, 3: 525–34.

—— (2006b), 'Securing Afghanistan's Border', *Survival*, 48, 1: 129–42.

—— (2007), 'Don't cave in to the Taliban', *International Herald Tribune*, 18 October.

Saikal, Amin, and William Maley (1991), *Regime Change in Afghanistan: Foreign Intervention and the Politics of Legitimacy* (Boulder, CO: Westview Press).

—— (2008), 'The President Who Would Be King', *The New York Times*, 6 February.

Saikal, Fazel Haq, and William Maley (1986), *Afghan Refugee Relief in Pakistan: Political Context and Practical Problems* (Canberra: Department of Politics, University College, University of New South Wales).

Sakharov, Andrei (1988), 'Neizbezhnost' perestroiki', in Iu. N. Afanas'ev (ed.), *Inogo ne dano* (Moscow: Progress): 122–34.

Sampson, Anthony (2001), 'Military Reprisals Play into Bin Laden's Strategy', *International Herald Tribune,* 24 September.

Sanger, David E. (2009), *The Inheritance: The World Obama Confronts and the Challenges to American Power* (New York: Harmony Books).

Sanger, David E., with Michael R. Gordon (2001), 'U.S. and Britain Male Late Push to Forge Coalition for Combat', *The New York Times,* 6 October 2001.

Sarin, Oleg, and Lev Dvoretsky (1993), *The Afghan Syndrome: The Soviet Union's Vietnam* (San Francisco: Presidio Press).

SCA (1988), *The Agricultural Survey of Afghanistan: First Report* (Peshawar: Swedish Committee for Afghanistan).

Schaffer, Teresita C. (2008), 'Pakistan: Transition to What?', *Survival*, 50, 1: 9–14.

Scheffer, Jaap de Hoop (2009), 'Afghanistan: We Can Do Better', *The Washington Post*, 18 January.

Schetter, Conrad (2001), 'Die Schimäre der Ethnie in Afghanistan: Volkszugehörigkeit keine Basis für eine neue Regierung', *Neue Zürcher Zeitung,* 26 October.

—— (2003), *Ethnizität und ethnische Konflikte in Afghanistan* (Berlin: Dietrich Reimer Verlag).

—— (2005), 'Ethnoscapes, National Territorialisation, and the Afghan War', *Geopolitics*, 10: 50–75.

Schetter, Conrad, Rainer Glassner, and Masood Karokhail (2007), 'Beyond Warlordism: The Local Security Architecture in Afghanistan' *Internationale Polilitk und Gesellschaft*, 2: 136–52.

Schiewek, Eckart (2007), 'Keeping the Peace without Peacekeepers', in Wolfgang Danspeckgruber and Robert P. Finn (eds), *Building State and Security in Afghanistan* (Princeton: Liechtenstein Institute on Self-Determination, Princeton University): 167–211.

Schmeidl, Susanne (2002), '(Human) Security Dilemmas: Long-term Implications of the Afghan Refugee Crisis', *Third World Quarterly*, 23, 1: 7–29.

—— (2007), 'The Emperor's New Clothes: The Unravelling of Peacebuilding in Afghanistan', *Die Friedens-Warte*, 82, 1: 69–86.

Schmeidl, Susanne, and William Maley (2008), 'The Case of the Afghan Refugee Population: Finding Durable Solutions in Contested Transitions', in Howard Adelman (ed.), *Protracted Displacement in Asia: No Place to Call Home* (Aldershot: Ashgate): 131–79.

Schmitt, Eric, and James Dao (2001), 'Use of Pinpoint Air Power Comes of Age in New War', *The New York Times,* 24 December.

Schöch, Rüdiger (2008), 'UNHCR and the Afghan Refugees in the early 1980s: Between Humanitarian Action and Cold War Politics', *Refugee Survey Quarterly*, 27, 1: 45–57.

Schofield, Carey (1993), *The Russian Elite: Inside Spetsnaz and the Airborne Forces* (London: Greenhill Books).

Schweich, Thomas A. (2008), 'Is Afghanistan a Narco-State?', *The New York Times Magazine*, 27 July.

Sciolino, Elaine (1996), 'U.S. to Distance Itself From New Kabul Regime', *The New York Times,* 23 October.

—— (2008), 'Afghan "Dictator" Proposed in Leaked Cable', *The New York Times*, 4 October.

Scott, James M. (1996), *Deciding to Intervene: The Reagan Doctrine and American Foreign Policy* (Durham, NC: Duke University Press).

Sedra, Mark (2006), 'Security Sector Reform in Afghanistan: The Slide Towards Expediency', *International Peacekeeping*, 13, 1: 94–110.

Sen, Amartya (1999), *Development as Freedom* (New York: Alfred A. Knopf).

Serchuk, Vance (2006), 'Don't Undercut the Afghan Army', *The Washington Post*, 2 June.

Shah, Taimoor, and Carlotta Gall (2007), 'Afghan Rebels Find Aid in Pakistan, Musharraf Admits', *The New York Times*, 13 August.

Shahrani, M. Nazif (1998), 'The Future of the State and the Structure of Community Governance in Afghanistan', in William Maley (ed.), *Fundamentalism Reborn? Afghanistan and the Taliban* (London: Hurst & Co.): 212–42.

Shahrani, M. Nazif, and Robert L. Canfield (eds) (1984), *Revolutions and Rebellions in Afghanistan: Anthropological Perspectives* (Berkeley: Institute of International Studies, University of California).

Shalinsky, Audrey C. (1994), *Long Years of Exile: Central Asian Refugees in Afghanistan and Pakistan* (Lanham, MD: University Press of America).

Shanker, Thom (2008a), 'Gates Says Anger Over Iraq Hurts Afghan Effort', *The New York Times*, 9 February.

—— (2008b), 'U.S. Defense Department to back $20 billion plan to increase Afghan Army', *International Herald Tribune*, 8 August.

Sharifian, Farzad (2007), 'Politics and/of Translation: Case Studies between Persian and English', *Journal of Intercultural Studies*, 28, 4: 413–24.

Sharp, Paul (2008), *Sustainable Diplomacy and the US-Iranian Conflict: The Value of Talk and a Predisposition to Appease* (The Hague: Clingendael Diplomacy Papers no. 17, Netherlands Institute of International Relations).

Shevardnadze, Eduard (1990), 'Afganistan – trudnaia doroga k miru', *Izvestiia,* 14 February.

—— (1991), *The Future Belongs to Freedom* (London: Sinclair-Stevenson).

Shils, Edward (1997), *The Virtue of Civility: Selected Essays on Liberalism, Tradition, and Civil Society* (Indianapolis, IN: Liberty Fund).

Shultz, George P. (1993), *Turmoil and Triumph: My Years as Secretary of State* (New York: Scribner's).

Shurygin, Veniamin (1986), 'Kabul'skie vstrechi: Rasskaz o zhizni afganskoi stolitsy', *Pravda*, 21 July.

Simon, Steven, and Daniel Benjamin (2001–2002), 'The Terror', *Survival,* 43, 4: 5–18.

Sinno, Abdulkader H. (2008a), *Organizations at War in Afghanistan and Beyond* (Ithaca: Cornell University Press).

—— (2008b), 'Explaining the Taliban's Ability to Mobilize the Pashtuns', in Robert D. Crews and Amin Tarzi (eds), *The Taliban and the Crisis of Afghanistan* (Cambridge: Harvard University Press): 59–89.

Sipress, Alan (2002), 'Peacekeepers Won't Go Beyond Kabul, Cheney Says', *The Washington Post,* 20 March.

Sipress, Alan, and Thomas E. Ricks (2001), 'Military Strike Not Imminent, Officials Say', *The Washington Post,* 27 September.

Sirrs, Julie (2001a), 'The Taliban's International Ambitions', *Middle East Quarterly,* 8, 3: 61–71.

—— (2001b), 'Lifting the Veil on Afghanistan', *The National Interest,* 65-S: 43–8.

Sixsmith, Martin (1991), *Moscow Coup: The Death of the Soviet System* (London: Simon & Schuster).

Skaine, Rosemarie (2002), *The Women of Afghanistan Under the Taliban* (Jefferson, MO: McFarland & Company, Inc.).

Skjelsæk, Kjell (1991), 'The UN Secretary-General and the Mediation of International Disputes', *Journal of Peace Research,* 28, 1: 99–115.

Sliwinski, Marek (1989a), 'Afghanistan: The Decimation of a People', *Orbis,* 33, 1: 39–56.

—— (1989b), 'On the Routes of "Hijrat"', *Central Asian Survey,* 8, 4: 63–93.

Smith, Anthony D. (1986), *The Ethnic Origins of Nations* (Oxford: Basil Blackwell).

Smith, Graeme (2008a), 'Inside the Taliban jailbreak', *The Globe and Mail* (Toronto), 2 July.

—— (2008b), 'UN envoy backs Karzai against Pakistan', *The Globe and Mail* (Toronto), 28 July.

Smith, Hugh (2005), *On Clausewitz: A Study of Military and Political Ideas* (New York: Palgrave Macmillan).

Smith, Nancy DeWolf (1995), 'These Rebels Aren't So Scary', *The Wall Street Journal,* 22 February.

Snegirev, Vladimir (1991), 'On byl zalozhnikom kremlia: Babrak Karmal' rasskazyvaet', *Trud,* 24 October.

Solnick, Steven L. (1998), *Stealing the State: Control and Collapse in Soviet Institutions* (Cambridge, MA: Harvard University Press).

Spillmann, Markus (2001), 'Die Taliban und die Macht der «Ausländer»', *Neue Zürcher Zeitung,* 7 May.

Springborg, Patricia (1992), *Western Republicanism and the Oriental Prince* (Cambridge: Polity Press).

Stapleton, Barbara J. (2007), 'The Failure to Bridge the Security Gap: The PRT Plan, 2002–2004', in Wolfgang Danspeckgruber and Robert P. Finn (eds), *Building State and Security in Afghanistan* (Princeton: Liechtenstein Institute on Self-Determination, Princeton University): 147–66.

—— (2008), 'Security and PRTs' in *State, Security and Economy in Afghanistan: Current Challenges, Possible Solutions* (Princeton: Liechtenstein Colloquium Report Volume III, Liechtenstein Institute on Self-Determination, Princeton University): 29–32.

Starr, S. Frederick (1999), 'Afghanistan Land Mine', *The Washington Post,* 19 December.

—— (2001), 'Afghan Northern Alliance Makes a Dangerous Friend', *The Baltimore Sun,* 17 October.

—— (2006), 'Sovereignty and Legitimacy in Afghan Nation-Building', in Francis Fukuyama (ed.), *Nation-Building: Beyond Afghanistan and Iraq* (Baltimore: The Johns Hopkins University Press): 107–24.

Stedman, Stephen John (1997), 'Spoiler Problems in Peace Processes', *International Security,* 22, 2: 5–53.

Steele, Jonathan (1986), 'Karmal Not to Seek More Soviet Troops', *Guardian Weekly,* 134, 9: 7.

Stephens, Joe, and David B. Ottaway (2005), 'A Rebuilding Plan Full of Cracks', *The Washington Post,* 20 November.

Stolee, Margaret K. (1988), 'Homeless Children in the USSR 1917–1967', *Soviet Studies*, 40, 1: 64–83.

Suhrke, Astri (2006), *When More is Less: Aiding Statebuilding in Afghanistan* (Madrid: Fundación para las Relaciones Internacionales y el Diálogo Exterior).

—— (2007), 'Reconstruction as Modernisation: the "post-conflict" project in Afghanistan', *Third World Quarterly*, 28, 7: 1291–308.

—— (2008a), 'Democratizing a Dependent State: The Case of Afghanistan', *Democratization*, 15, 3: 630–48.

—— (2008b), 'A Contradictory Mission? NATO from Stabilization to Combat in Afghanistan', *International Peacekeeping*, 15, 2: 214–36.

Suhrke, Astri, and Arne Strand (2005), 'The Logic of Conflictual Peacebuilding' in Sultan Barakat (ed.), *After the Conflict: Reconstruction and Development in the Aftermath of War* (London: I.B. Tauris): 141–54.

Sullivan, Kevin (2002), 'A Body and Spirit Broken by the Taliban', *The Washington Post*, 5 January 2002.

Tadjbakhsh, Shahrbanou, and Michael Schoiswohl (2008), 'Playing with Fire? The International Community's Democratization Experiment in Afghanistan', *International Peacekeeping*, 15, 2: 252–67.

Talmon, Stefan (1998), *Recognition of Governments in International Law: With Particular Reference to Governments in Exile* (Oxford: Oxford University Press).

Tapper, Nancy (1983), 'Abd Al-Rahman's North-West Frontier: The Pashtun Colonisation of Afghan Turkistan', in Richard Tapper (ed.), *The Conflict of Tribe and State in Iran and Afghanistan* (London: Croom Helm): 233–61.

—— (1991), *Bartered Brides: Politics, Gender and Marriage in an Afghan Tribal Society* (Cambridge: Cambridge University Press).

Tarzi, Amin (2008), 'The Neo-Taliban', in Robert D. Crews and Amin Tarzai (eds), *The Taliban and the Crisis of Afghanistan* (Cambridge: Harvard University Press): 274–310.

Taylor, Telford (1979), *Munich: The Price of Peace* (New York: Doubleday).

Teimourian, Hazhir (1989), 'Drug Baron in the Border Hills', *The Times*, 25 September.

Tellis, Ashley J. (2008), *Pakistan and the War on Terror: Conflicted Goals, Compromised Performance* (Washington DC: Carnegie Endowment for International Peace).

Tellis, Ashley J. (2009), *Reconciling with the Taliban? Toward An Alternative Grand Strategy in Afghanistan* (Washington DC: Carnegie Endowment for International Peace).

Terry, Fiona (2002), *Condemned to Repeat?: The Paradox of Humanitarian Action* (Ithaca, NY: Cornell University Press).

Thakur, Ramesh (2000), 'Human Security Regimes', in William T. Tow, Ramesh Thakur and In-Taek Hyun (eds), *Asia's Emerging Regional Order: Reconciling Traditional and Human Security* (New York and Tokyo: United Nations University Press): 229–55.

Thier, J. Alexander (2006), 'Afghanistan', in William J. Durch (ed.), *Twenty-First-Century Peace Operations* (Washington DC: United States Institute of Peace Press): 467–572.

Thier, J. Alexander, and Azita Ranjbar (2008), *Killing Friends, Making Enemies: The Impact and Avoidance of Civilian Casualties in Afghanistan* (Washington DC: United States Institute of Peace Press).

Thomas, Christopher (1991), 'Kabul Radiates Confidence in Soviet Support', *The Times*, 31 August.

—— (1997), 'Buddhists Condemn Taleban over Threat to Blow Up Statue', *The Times*, 25 April.

Thornton, Thomas Perry (1999), 'Pakistan: Fifty Years of Insecurity', in Selig S. Harrison, Paul H. Kreisberg, and Dennis Kux (eds), *India and Pakistan: The First Fifty Years* (Cambridge: Cambridge University Press): 170–88.

Tilly, Charles (2005), *Trust and Rule* (Cambridge: Cambridge University Press).

Townsend, Frances F. (2007), *Press Briefing by White House Homeland Security Advisor Fran Townsend* (Washington DC: Office of the Press Secretary, The White House, 17 July).

Tsagolov, Kim M., and Selig S. Harrison (1991), 'Afganskaia voina: Vzgliad iz segodniashnego dnia', *Vostok,* 3: 42–57.

Turton, David, and Peter Marsden (2002), *Taking Refugees for a Ride? The Politics of Refugee Return in Afghanistan* (Kabul: Afghanistan Research and Evaluation Unit).

Tyler, Patrick E. (2001), 'Bush Warns "Taliban Will Pay a Price"', *The New York Times,* 8 October.

Tyson, Ann Scott (2007), 'General Warns of Perils in Afghanistan', *The Washington Post,* 14 February.

Ullmann-Margalit, Edna (1977), *The Emergence of Norms* (Oxford: Oxford University Press).

United Nations (1985a), *Rapport sur la situation des droits de l'homme en Afghanistan* (New York: United Nations, E/CN.4/1985/21, Human Rights Commission, Economic and Social Council, 19 February).

—— (1985b), *Situation of Human Rights in Afghanistan* (New York: United Nations, A/40/843, General Assembly, 5 November).

—— (1988), *Agreements on Settlement of Situation Relating to Afghanistan* (Geneva: United Nations Information Service, Press Release Afghanistan/9, 14 April).

—— (1992), *Situation of Human Rights in Afghanistan* (New York: United Nations, A/47/656, General Assembly, 17 November).

—— (1993a), *Afghan Peace Accord* (New York: United Nations S/25435, 19 March).

—— (1993b), *Situation of Human Rights in Afghanistan* (New York: United Nations, A/48/584, General Assembly, 16 November).

—— (1994a), *Situation of Human Rights in Afghanistan* (New York: United Nations, A/49/650, General Assembly, 8 November).

—— (1994b), *Report of the Secretary General on the Situation in Afghanistan* (New York: United Nations A/49/688, 22 November).

—— (1997), *Final Report on the Situation of Human Rights in Afghanistan Submitted by Mr. Choong-Hyun Paik, Special Rapporteur, in accordance with Commission on Human Rights resolution 1996/75* (New York: United Nations, E/CN.4/1997/59, Human Rights Commission, Economic and Social Council, 20 February).

—— (1998), *UN Peacekeeping: 50 Years 1948–1998* (New York: Department of Public Information DPI/2004).

—— (1999), *The Situation in Afghanistan and its Implications for International Peace and Security: Report of the Secretary-General* (New York: United Nations, S/1999/994, 21 September).

—— (2000), *Report of the Secretary-General on the Situation of Women and Girls in Afghanistan Submitted in Accordance with Sub-Commission Resolution 1999/14* (New York: United Nations, E/CN.4/Sub.2/2000/18, 21 July).

—— (2001a), *Global Illicit Drug Trends 2001* (Vienna: United Nations Office for Drug Control and Crime Prevention).

—— (2001b), *Report of the Secretary-General on the Humanitarian Implications of the Measures Imposed by Security Council Resolutions 1267 (1999) and 1333 (2000) on Afghanistan* (New York: United Nations, S/2001/695, 13 July).

—— (2001c), *Report of the Committee of Experts Appointed Pursuant to Security Council Resolution 1333 (2000), Paragraph 15 (a), Regarding Monitoring of the Arms Embargo*

Against the Taliban and the Closure of Terrorist Training Camps in the Taliban-Held Areas of Afghanistan (New York: United Nations, S/2001/511, 21 May).

United Nations (2001d), *The Situation in Afghanistan and its Implications for International Peace and Security: Report of the Secretary-General* (New York: United Nations, A/56/681, S/2001/1157, 6 December).

—— (2002), *The Situation in Afghanistan and its Implications for International Peace and Security: Report of the Secretary-General* (New York: United Nations, A/56/875, S/2002/278, 18 March).

—— (2007), *Suicide Attacks in Afghanistan (2001–2007)* (Kabul: United Nations Assistance Mission in Afghanistan).

—— (2008), *Special Report of the Secretary-General pursuant to Security Council resolution 1806 (2008) on the United Nations Assistance Mission in Afghanistan* (New York: United Nations, S/2008/434, 3 July).

United Nations Development Program (2004), *Afghanistan: National Human Development Report 2004. Security with a Human Face: Challenges and Responsibilities* (Kabul: United Nations Development Program).

—— (2007), *Afghanistan Human Development Report 2007. Bridging Modernity and Tradition: Rule of Law and the Search for Justice* (Kabul: United Nations Development Program).

United Nations Office on Drugs and Crime (2007), *Afghanistan: Opium Survey 2007* (Vienna: United Nations Office on Drugs and Crime).

—— (2008), *Afghanistan: Opium Survey 2008: Executive Summary* (Vienna: United Nations Office on Drugs and Crime).

United Nations Security Council (1994), *Statement by the President of the Security Council* (New York: United Nations, S/PRST/1994/77, 30 November).

United Nations Special Mission (1994), *Progress Report of the Special Mission to Afghanistan* (New York: United Nations, A/49/208, S/1994/766, 1 July).

United States Institute of Peace (1998), *The Taliban and Afghanistan: Implications for Regional Security and Options for International Action* (Washington, DC: United States Institute of Peace).

UNO (1994), *The Status of Education in Afghanistan* (Peshawar: University of Nebraska at Omaha and ESSP Research and Planning): Vols I–II.

UNOCA (1988), *First Consolidated Report* (Geneva: Office of the United Nations Coordinator for Humanitarian and Economic Assistance Programmes Relating to Afghanistan, UNOCA/1988/1, September).

Urban, Mark (1990), *War in Afghanistan* (London: Macmillan Press).

US Army and Marine Corps (2007), *The U.S. Army/Marine Corps Counterinsurgency Field Manual* (Chicago: University of Chicago Press).

US Department of State (1985), 'USSR: Unofficial Poll on Popular Opposition to Afghan War', *Current Analyses* (Washington, DC: Bureau of Intelligence and Research, Report 1107-CA, 18 June).

—— (1998), *International Narcotics Control Strategy Report, 1997* (Washington, DC: Bureau for International Narcotics and Law Enforcement Affairs, March 1998).

Uslaner, Eric M. (2008), *Corruption, Inequality, and the Rule of Law* (Cambridge: Cambridge University Press).

USSR Supreme Soviet (1989), 'Postanovlenie Verkhovnogo Soveta SSSR Ob Amnistii Sovershivshikh Prestupleniia Byvshikh Voennosluzhashchikh Kontingenta Sovetskikh Voisk v Afganistane', *Pravda*, 30 November: 1.

Van Creveld, Martin (2004), *Defending Israel: A Controversial Plan Toward Peace* (New York: St. Martin's Press).

Van Dyke, Carl (1996), 'Kabul to Grozny: A Critique of Soviet (Russian) Counter-Insurgency Doctrine', *Journal of Slavic Military Studies*, 9, 4: 689–705.

Vasil'ev, A. (1991), 'Pochemu my ne ukhodim iz Afganistan', *Komsomol'skaia pravda*, 29 June.

Vertzberger, Yaacov Y. I. (1990), *The World in Their Minds: Information Processing, Cognition, and Perception in Foreign Policy Decisionmaking* (Stanford, CA: Stanford University Press).

Vogelsang, Willem (2002), *The Afghans* (Oxford: Blackwell).

VTsIOM (1991), *Chelovek i legenda: Obraz A.D. Sakharova v obshchestvennom mnenii. Vsesoiuznyi opros VTsIOM* (Moscow: Vsesoiuznyi tsentr izucheniia obshchestvennogo mneniia).

Wafa, Abdul Waheed (2008), 'Blast at Kabul Hotel Kills 6', *The New York Times*, 15 January.

Wafa, Abdul Waheed, and Alan Cowell (2008), 'Suicide Car Blast Kills 41 in Afghan Capital', *The New York Times*, 8 July.

Waldman, Amy (2002), 'A Fertile Valley Left Barren by the Taliban', *The New York Times*, 7 January.

Walicki, Andrzej (1995), *Marxism and the Leap to the Kingdom of Freedom: The Rise and Fall of the Communist Utopia* (Stanford, CA: Stanford University Press).

Walter, Barbara F. (1997), 'The Critical Barrier to Civil War Settlement', *International Organization*, 51, 3: 335–64.

—— (2002), *Committing to Peace: The Successful Settlement of Civil Wars* (Princeton: Princeton University Press).

Waltz, Kenneth N. (1959), *Man, the State and War: A Theoretical Analysis* (New York: Columbia University Press).

Wardak, Ali (2004), 'Building a post-war justice system in Afghanistan', *Crime, Law and Social Change*, 41: 319–341.

Wardak, Ghulam Dastagir (1989), *The Voroshilov Lectures: Materials from the Soviet General Staff Academy: Volume I: Issues of Soviet Military Strategy* (Washington, DC: National Defense University Press).

Watson, Paul (2006), 'In Afghanistan, money tips the scales of justice', *The Los Angeles Times*, 18 December.

Waxman, Sharon (1999), 'A Cause Unveiled: Hollywood Women Have Made the Plight of Afghan Women Their Own – Sight Unseen', *The Washington Post*, 30 March.

Waziri, Rafiq (1973), 'Symptomatology of depressive illness in Afghanistan', *American Journal of Psychiatry*, 130, 2: 213–17.

Weber, Max (1948), 'Politics as a Vocation', in H. H. Gerth and C. Wright Mills (eds), *From Max Weber: Essays in Sociology* (London: Routledge & Kegan Paul): 77–128.

Weinbaum, Marvin G. (1994), *Pakistan and Afghanistan: Resistance and Reconstruction* (Boulder, CO: Westview Press).

Weinbaum, Marvin G., and Jonathan B. Harder (2008), 'Pakistan's Afghan policies and their consequences', *Contemporary South Asia*, 16, 1: 25–38.

Weinberg, Gerhard L. (1994), *A World at Arms: A Global History of World War II* (Cambridge: Cambridge University Press).

Weiner, Tim (2007), *Legacy of Ashes: The History of the CIA* (New York: Penguin).

Weintraub, Craig (1989), 'Ferkhar Massacre of Jami'at Commanders Gives a Sad Air to Eid Celebrations', *AFGHANews*, 1 August.

Weitz, Richard (1992), 'Moscow's Endgame in Afghanistan', *Conflict Quarterly*, 12, 1: 25–46.

314 REFERENCES

Westad, Odd Arne (1994), 'Prelude to Invasion: The Soviet Union and the Afghan Communists, 1978–1979', *International History Review*, 16, 1: 49–69.

Westad, Odd Arne (2005), *The Global Cold War: Third World Interventions and the Making of our Times* (Cambridge: Cambridge University Press).

White, Josh (2008), 'A Shortage of Troops in Afghanistan: Ira War Limits U.S. Options, Says Chairman of Joint Chiefs', *The Washington Post*, 3 July.

White, Stephen (1983), 'What is a Communist System?', *Studies in Comparative Communism*, 16, 4: 247–63.

WHO (1995), *Brief Note on Health Sector of Afghanistan: From Emergency to Recovery and Building from Below* (Stockholm: Donors' Meeting on Assistance for Afghanistan's Long-Term Rehabilitation and its Relationship with Humanitarian Programmes, 1–2 June).

Wilder, Andrew (2005), *A House Divided? Analysing the 2005 Afghan Elections* (Kabul: Afghanistan Research and Evaluation Unit).

—— (2007), *Cops or Robbers?: The Struggle to Reform the Afghan National Police* (Kabul: Afghanistan Research and Evaluation Unit).

Wiles, Peter (1985), 'Irreversibility: Theory and Practice', *The Washington Quarterly*, 8, 1: 29–40.

Willerton, John P. (1992), *Patronage and Politics in the USSR* (Cambridge: Cambridge University Press).

Williams, Brian Glyn (2008), 'Talibanisation: History of a Transnational Terrorist Sanctuary', *Civil Wars*, 10, 1: 40–59.

Wily, Liz Alden (2003), *Land Rights in Crisis: Restoring Tenure Security in Afghanistan* (Kabul: Afghanistan Research and Evaluation Unit).

—— (2004), *Looking for Peace on the Pastures: Rural Land Relations in Afghanistan* (Kabul: Afghanistan Research and Evaluation Unit).

Wimbush, S. Enders (1985), 'Nationalities in the Soviet armed forces', in S. Enders Wimbush (ed.), *Soviet Nationalities in Strategic Perspective* (London: Croom Helm): 227–48.

Winchester, Michael (1998), 'Ethnic Cleansing', *Asiaweek*, 6 November.

Woodward, Bob (2001), 'Bin Laden Said to "Own" The Taliban', *The Washington Post*, 11 October.

—— (2002), *Bush at War* (New York: Simon & Schuster).

World Bank (2005), *Afghanistan–State Building, Sustaining Growth, and Reducing Poverty* (Washington DC: The World Bank).

—— (2008a), *Afghanistan: Building an Effective State. Priorities for Public Administration Reform* (Washington DC: Report no.42166-AF, The World Bank).

—— (2008b), *Afghanistan: Public Financial Management Performance Assessment* (Washington DC: The World Bank).

Wright, Robin (2007), 'Iranian Arms Destined for Taliban Seized in Afghanistan, Officials Say', *The Washington Post*, 16 September.

Yaqub, Daoud, and William Maley (2008), 'NATO and Afghanistan: Saving the State-Building Enterprise', in Robin Shepherd (ed.), *The Bucharest Papers* (Washington, DC: German Marshall Fund of the United States, and London: Chatham House): 5–17.

Yassari, Nadjma (ed.) (2005), *The Shari'a in the Constitutions of Afghanistan, Iran and Egypt – Implications for Private Law* (Tübingen: Mohr Siebeck).

Yousaf, Mohammad, and Mark Adkin (1992), *The Bear Trap: Afghanistan's Untold Story* (London: Leo Cooper).

Zaman, Muhammad Qasim (1998), 'Sectarianism in Pakistan: The Radicalization of Shi'i and Sunni Identities', *Modern Asian Studies,* 32, 3: 689–716.

—— (1999), 'Religious Education and the Rhetoric of Reform: The Madrasa in British India and Pakistan', *Comparative Studies in Society and History,* 41, 2: 294–323.

—— (2002), *The Ulama in Contemporary Islam: Custodians of Change* (Princeton: Princeton University Press).

Index